Developing Countries and Technology Inclusion in the 21st Century Information Society

Alice S. Etim
Winston Salem State University, USA

A volume in the Advances in IT Standards and
Standardization Research (AITSSR) Book Series

Published in the United States of America by
IGI Global
Information Science Reference (an imprint of IGI Global)
701 E. Chocolate Avenue
Hershey PA, USA 17033
Tel: 717-533-8845
Fax: 717-533-8661
E-mail: cust@igi-global.com
Web site: http://www.igi-global.com

Library of Congress Cataloging-in-Publication Data

Names: Etim, Alice S., DATE- editor.
Title: Developing countries and technology inclusion in the 21st century
  information society / Alice S. Etim, editor.
Description: Hershey, PA : Information Science Reference, 2020. | Includes
  bibliographical references and index. | Summary: "This book explores the
  adoption, diffusion, use, and impact of information and communication
  technology (ICT) tools and services"-- Provided by publisher.
Identifiers: LCCN 2019053029 (print) | LCCN 2019053030 (ebook) | ISBN
  9781799834687 (h/c) | ISBN 9781799834694 (s/c) | ISBN 9781799834700
  (eISBN)
Subjects: LCSH: Internet--Economic aspects--Developing countries. |
  Internet--Social aspects--Developing countries. | Information
  technology--Developing countries. | Information society--Developing
  countries.
Classification: LCC HC59.72.I55 D475 2020 (print) | LCC HC59.72.I55
  (ebook) | DDC 303.48/33091724--dc23
LC record available at https://lccn.loc.gov/2019053029
LC ebook record available at https://lccn.loc.gov/2019053030

This book is published in the IGI Global book series Advances in IT Standards and Standardization Research (AITSSR) (ISSN: 1935-3391; eISSN: 1935-3405)

Advances in IT Standards and Standardization Research (AITSSR) Book Series

Kai Jakobs
RWTH Aachen University, Germany

ISSN:1935-3391
EISSN:1935-3405

MISSION

IT standards and standardization are a necessary part of effectively delivering IT and IT services to organizations and individuals, as well as streamlining IT processes and minimizing organizational cost. In implementing IT standards, it is necessary to take into account not only the technical aspects, but also the characteristics of the specific environment where these standards will have to function.

The **Advances in IT Standards and Standardization Research (AITSSR) Book Series** seeks to advance the available literature on the use and value of IT standards and standardization. This research provides insight into the use of standards for the improvement of organizational processes and development in both private and public sectors.

COVERAGE

- Standardization and Public Policy Formation
- Descriptive Theory of Standardization
- Standardization and economic development
- Management of Standards
- Emerging roles of formal standards Organizations and consortia
- Prescriptive Theory of Standardization
- Tools and Services Supporting Improved Standardization
- Standardization and regulation
- Future of Standardization
- Impacts of Market-Driven Standardization and Emerging Players

IGI Global is currently accepting manuscripts for publication within this series. To submit a proposal for a volume in this series, please contact our Acquisition Editors at Acquisitions@igi-global.com or visit: http://www.igi-global.com/publish/.

Titles in this Series

701 East Chocolate Avenue, Hershey, PA 17033, USA
Tel: 717-533-8845 x100 • Fax: 717-533-8661
E-Mail: cust@igi-global.com • www.igi-global.com

Table of Contents

Detailed Table of Contents

Section 1

Chapter 1

Alice S. Etim, Winston Salem State University, USA

Information and communication technology (ICT) adoption is cardinal to the sustainability of all societies, and it is the engine that can transform developing countries. This first chapter for the book uses the theories of poverty, human needs, and information poverty as the lenses to examine the framework for ICT adoption and inclusion. A world pyramid of needs that embodies information needs is developed. Information poverty is discussed along with the case of Coronavirus (COVID-19), the global pandemic that brought to a halt many communities in 2020. A mobile phone technology adoption model (MOPTAM) is presented as the framework to understanding ICT adoption and inclusion in developing countries.

Chapter 2

Jurgita Bruneckiene, Kaunas University of Technology, Lithuania
Robertas Jucevicius, Kaunas University of Technology, Lithuania
Ineta Zykiene, Kaunas University of Technology, Lithuania
Jonas Rapsikevicius, Kaunas University of Technology, Lithuania
Mantas Lukauskas, Kaunas University of Technology, Lithuania

The chapter is designed to stimulate a discussion on a new approach that combines quantum theory with artificial intelligence in the analysis of the economic development of socio-economic systems. The chapter introduces the specifics of the modern socio-economic system and the challenges to economic development. After that, the chapter discusses the possibility and compatibility of approaches (quantum theory) and tools (artificial intelligence) for analysing economic development. The chapter contributes to a new approach in economic development theory by integrating quantum theory and artificial intelligence possibilities. Additionally, the competences needed to use artificial intelligence in the analysis of economic development are presented. The value of the chapter is in its contribution to the original methodological justification of the use of quantum theory and artificial intelligence in the analysis of economic development.

Chapter 3

Ernest Etim, Cape Peninsula University of Technology, South Africa

This chapter presents a descriptive and critical overview of IT/IS adoption theories/models in developed economies. The theories examined include task technology fit (TTF), technology readiness index (TRI), technology acceptance model (TAM and TAM2), self-efficacy theory (SET), and unified theory of acceptance and use of technology (UTAUT) together with their appropriateness to developed countries/ economies. Furthermore, an extensive look at limitations of both TAM and UTAUT (widely utilized) models as applicable to digital/mobile technologies is emphasized. The critical analysis provided thus far did reveal that none of these (IT/IS) models/theories individually are powerful enough to appropriately assess all the complex constructs embedded in the study of mobile technology adoption in developing countries. The contextual nature of individual differences in developing countries together with all cultural and country indicators (ICT infrastructure, internet penetration) would have to be integrated into any developed theory for meaningful analysis to be achieved.

Section 2

Chapter 4

Nana Yaw Asabere, Accra Technical University, Ghana
Amevi Acakpovi, Accra Technical University, Ghana
Ezer Osei Yeboah-Boateng, Ghana Communication Technology University, Ghana
Wisdom Kwawu Torgby, Accra Technical University, Ghana
Eric Amoako, Accra Technical University, Ghana

Globally, choosing the right tertiary programme for university (higher) education is quite a difficult task for students. A wide range of programmes are offered by the individual universities which differ in terms of delivery modes and entry requirements. Technology inclusion in the 21st century has paved the way for the proliferation of electronic/computing systems such as electronic counseling (e-counseling) and electronic learning (e-learning). By employing a quantitative research instrument (questionnaire) to ascertain technology acceptance of Senior High School (SHS) in Ghana, this chapter proposes a web-based (e-counseling) expert system which will match students' backgrounds with the right tertiary programme towards career development. Evaluation of our proposed approach suggests that majority of the selected students (80%) out of 100 who used the system accepted and embraced it. Such a system will therefore solve and improve career guidance, counseling, and development problems of SHS students in Ghana.

Chapter 5

Sherwin E. Ona, De La Salle University, Philippines
Emmanuel C. Lallana, Ideacorp, Philippines

The need to improve local disaster risk reduction (DRR) capacities in the Philippines is crucial in mitigating and responding to future disaster events. Despite being one the most disaster-prone countries in the world, national protocols remain inefficient, marred by corruption and poor inter-agency coordination. In addition, the current top-down and reactive practices have proven to be inadequate in responding to the needs of various stakeholders. The chapter examined these disaster preparation practices through a qualitative-descriptive research design and by using disaster information management (DIM) as the framework. In particular, the authors focused on the disaster preparedness practices of selected parishes of the Diocese of Legazpi and their partner organizations. The study also examined their information management practices and the current information and communications technology (ICT) tools in disaster preparedness.

Chapter 6

Ahmed Mokhtar Abdelaziz, Saudi Aramco, Saudi Arabia

This chapter focuses on the role of mobile learning in developing employability and job-related skills in vocational and technical education and training (VTET) contexts. It is hoped that this chapter will contribute to the academic discussion on this topic by identifying a list of skills and discussing how mobile technologies can play a role in developing them. This chapter will also provide some insights and practical examples for instructors and program designers on effective utilization of mobile technologies for developing both the technical and soft skills. Finally, this chapter will provide some insights on the future direction of research in this area of study.

Chapter 7

Alice S. Etim, Winston Salem State University, USA
Chandra Prakash Jaiswal, Winston Salem State University, USA
Marsheilla Subroto, Winston Salem State University, USA
Vivian E. Collins Ortega, Winston Salem State University, USA

The management of information technology (IT) projects has experienced a shift from predictive and traditional project management methodology to more adaptive practices like Agile. Agile method and its developmental stages are a response to current business-changing trends and computing needs of society. The process assists in accelerating product delivery with rapid feedback and cost-conscious, consecutive iteration, distinguishing it from other traditional practices like the waterfall method. This chapter contributes to the existing literature by discussing agile project management for IT projects, with a specific case of the Africa IT project – the Books for Africa Project (hereafter called, Book Project). The first part of the chapter is used to review the literature on Agile IT projects. The Book Project as a case is an IT project, and it is discussed in detail in the chapter. The chapter concludes with transferable lessons for projects in developing countries, specifically those located in Sub-Saharan Africa.

Chapter 8

Toluwase Victor Asubiaro, University of Ibadan, Nigeria & Western University, Canada
Ebelechukwu Gloria Igwe, University of Ibadan, Nigeria

African languages, including those that are natives to Nigeria, are low-resource languages because they lack basic computing resources such as language-dependent hardware keyboard. Speakers of these low-resource languages are therefore unfairly deprived of information access on the internet. There is no information about the level of progress that has been made on the computation of Nigerian languages. Hence, this chapter presents a state-of-the-art review of Nigerian languages natural language processing. The review reveals that only four Nigerian languages; Hausa, Ibibio, Igbo, and Yoruba have been significantly studied in published NLP papers. Creating alternatives to hardware keyboard is one of the most popular research areas, and means such as automatic diacritics restoration, virtual keyboard, and optical character recognition have been explored. There was also an inclination towards speech and computational morphological analysis. Resource development and knowledge representation modeling of the languages using rapid resource development and cross-lingual methods are recommended.

Chapter 9

Abdulsalami Ibrahim, Millersville University of Pennsylvania, USA
Crystal Machado, Indiana University of Pennsylvania, USA

While teacher educators in Sub-Saharan Africa have increased access to information and communication technology (ICT), there is a lack of empirical research that describes the detail of educators' use of technology. This chapter addresses the gap in the literature with an exploratory mixed method study in a region of Nigeria. Researchers developed a survey to collect quantitative data from 190 teacher educators and added data from 10 interviewees to verify and the survey findings. The survey assessed the types of technologies in use and the demographics of teachers who use them. As expected, use is dependent on access, and overall access was high. Demographic differences in use were not great, but women were slightly more accepting than men, and more recent graduates more accepting than older ones. Teachers overall were moderately comfortable with technology. Researchers did not collect data about enabling factors like technical support or professional development. This suggests that next steps would be to define instructional software and assess technical support needs.

Chapter 10

Prakash Bhagwan Dongardive, University of Mekelle, Ethiopia

Progress in information communication technology (ICT) has become the backbone for every branch of knowledge in academic arena and library, and information centers are not apart from it. Social networking is playing a significant role in serving to the library users. The chapter examines libraries and their importance in accepting the Web 2.0 phenomenon of social networking sites like Facebook Twitter, YouTube, and a number of social networking tools to enable libraries to engage with students in the virtual environment to promote library event and services, teaching and learning, and humanizing the concept of library and librarians. This chapter also focuses on the importance of social networking sites, which improve the professional relationships within the library profession and across the boundaries of particular national library education systems across the world, which is increasingly sharing information that ensures libraries are the head of changes in demands and needs of their users.

Chapter 11

Okanlade Adesokan Lawal-Adebowale, Federal University of Agriculture, Abeokuta, Nigeria
Olalekan Oyekunle, Federal University of Agriculture, Abeokuta, Nigeria

Emergence and integration of information and communication technology (ICT) in the global education system has significantly enhanced intelligible teaching and learning, particularly in the developing countries. Among the developing countries, Nigeria has equally integrated ICT in its educational system. While the information driven technology has little or no integration in the lower level of education, it is intensively integrated in the higher education system. Although the Nigerian education system lacks integration of robust ICT tools to support virtual and in learning, the installed basic ICT tools such as computers, multimedia projectors, process, and internet have greatly changed the face of the country's educational administration and teaching and learning from the traditional practice. Effective and efficient use of ICT are however affected by extrinsic and intrinsic barriers. The need to strengthen the ICT framework and deployment for a more robust teaching and learning process in the country's education system is emphasized.

Chapter 12

Adwaita Maiti, Prabhat Kumar College, Contai, India
Sebak Kumar Jana, Vidyasagar University, India

Information and communication technology (ICT) cannot be separated from our daily needs. ICT helps in reducing the disparity in wealth of educational resources. The uses of ICT in education add value in teaching and learning by enhancing the effectiveness of learning or by adding a dimension to learning. ICT may also be a significant motivational factor in students' learning. Uses of ICT in eastern states in India are lagging behind all other regions of India. In this background, the authors review the use of ICT by higher education students of four states in eastern India. They have attempted to find the factors responsible for use of ICT by the students. As the findings suggest, region, gender, education levels of households, type of courses, possession of computer and internet facility, consumption levels of households, and whether students stay in institutional hostel or not are the influencing factors to use of ICT.

Chapter 13

Consolata Kemirembe Angello, Sokoine University of Agriculture, Tanzania

Information and communication technologies (ICTs) are very important tools for economic development and poverty reduction when used effectively by individuals in all economic sectors including agriculture. Urban livestock keepers need ICTs in their activities so that they can make informed decisions that can lead to improvement of the livestock industry. Despite its importance, ICT use is hindered by several factors including unawareness of the radio and television programmes and lack of computer skills. This chapter reveals the extent of use of ICTs by urban and peri-urban livestock keepers whereby different types of ICTs are used by urban livestock keepers to access livestock information, though some ICTs, for example, mobile phones are used more than other ICTs (radio and television). Internet is used by very few livestock keepers due computer illiteracy. Policy implications include improvement of the telecommunications services by the government through relevant bodies in order to facilitate more access to information through mobile phones, radio, television, and the internet.

Foreword

It is a great honor for me to be asked to compose the Foreword for this book *Developing Countries and Technology Inclusion in the 21st Century Information Society*. The book is the work of established professors, researchers and scholars in Information and Communication Technology (ICT), Computer Science and other areas that support the use of ICT for service delivery. There are thirteen chapters in the book.

I have known the editor, Dr. Alice S. Etim as a profound academician and a colleague for more than a decade. She has not only crafted a clever theoretical framework for the book but has also been able to assemble a great line of scholars who have done research that will be helpful for policy makers, researchers, students, organizers and different partners who utilize ICT strategies in their research, field of study and line of work.

The United Nations (UN) regularly provides economic predictions for countries in its *World Economic Situation and Prospects (WESP)* briefings/reports. As countries of the world battle a unique and unprecedented COVID-19 global pandemic in 2020 that has infected over 19 million people and claimed more than 710 thousand lives globally as at the beginning of August 2020, the burning questions are: What shall we do at this moment? What are the relevant lessons that are being learned by the emerging and developing economies? The WESP 2020 predictions are (i) a sluggish economic growth that will threaten or hurt the global effort on sustainable development (ii) per capita income in most countries will stagnate or decline sharply. In addition to these UN economic predictions, this book is a timely and an excellent contribution to capturing this moment for sharing lessons on ICT that will lead developing countries foreword in this 21st Century. I am honored to be called upon to write the Foreword for this book.

Beginning with Chapter 1, Dr. Alice S. Etim, the chapter author and the editor of the book lays a strong foundation by using many theories of poverty, human needs and information poverty to present a framework for Information and Communication Technology (ICT) adoption and inclusion in developing countries. In the chapter, she develops the World Pyramid of Needs and examines information poverty from the lens of COVID-19 global pandemic. Dr. Etim concludes by laying out a MOPTAM (Mobile Technology Adoption Model) for developing countries. As the editor of the book, Dr. Etim has leaned on her extended scholarship, knowledge and editorial work on ICT adoption or the lack of it (Digital Divide). Dr. Etim is currently the Editor-in-Chief of the *International Journal of ICT Research in Africa and the Middle East (IJICTRAME)*. Her research aims at supporting both experienced and early career researchers from developing countries to succeed in their research endeavors. These experienced and vibrant researchers have helped her in editing this book. Some of the ICT research that she led recently (2019 and 2020) that resulted in peer-reviewed journal articles were on gender differences on ICT use in Ghana, ICT convergence and impact on women in Nigeria; economically disadvantaged communities and ICT for schools, and mobile health and telemedicine for the underserved groups and these publications are in reputable peer-reviewed journal articles.

In Chapter 2, Professor Jurgita Bruneckiene and the colleagues at Kaunas University of Technology, Lithuania provide a stimulating discussion on a new approach or methodology for economic development theory and analysis using quantum theory and Artificial Intelligence (AI). An analysis of economic development theory using quantum theory or AI will be attractive to economists in developing countries and beyond to understand better how to move their economic development research foreword in the age of information and knowledge transfer among different economies. In Chapter 3, Ernest Etim, a PhD Scholar from Cape Peninsula University of Technology, Cape Town, South Africa, completes the Part 1 of the book by connecting the dots on ICT adoption theories that are relevant for transitioning economies. Some of the theories that he examines in the chapter include: Task Technology Fit (TTF), Technology Readiness Index (TRI), Technology Acceptance Model (TAM and TAM2), Self-Efficacy Theory (SET), and Unified Theory of Acceptance and Use of Technology (UTAUT). He concludes with an analysis on the appropriateness of these theories to developing countries and transitioning economies.

In Section 2 of the book, Dr. Etim sought out many scholars from different emerging and developing economies and they have written the chapters to help readers from different backgrounds to understand the use of ICT and application of the same to support development in many developing countries of Africa, the Middle East, Asia and Eastern Europe. Each chapter highlights a specific type of application or use of ICT to support specific initiatives or for service delivery. Dr. Nana Asabere and colleagues from Ghana examine a web-based expert system for counseling in order to help match students' backgrounds with appropriate higher education programs as well as better predict career choices. Chapter 5 is on the challenges and opportunities of using ICT for disaster preparedness in the Legazpi City, Albay Province of the Philippines; the chapter author, Dr. Sherwin Ona provides an analysis that includes information management practices and current ICT tools for disaster preparedness. The role of mobile learning in vocational and technical education & training (VTET) programs in Saudi Arabia is discussed in Chapter 6. Dr. Ahmed Mokhtar Abdelaziz, the Head of English Unit at one of Saudi Aramco's Industrial Training Centers writes as a practitioner and focuses the chapter on how VTET programs can be enhanced using mobile learning including ease of identifying employable skills.

In Chapter 7, the editor of the book, Dr. Alice S. Etim and three of her graduate students discuss managing information technology (IT) projects using agile project methodology. Using an IT project called *Books for Africa*, the authors discuss transferrable lessons to the developing countries, specifically those that are located in Sub-Saharan Africa (SSA). Two doctoral students, Mr. Toluwase Victor Asubiaro, University of Western Ontario, Canada and Miss Ebelechukwu Gloria Igwe, University of Ibadan, Nigeria are the authors of Chapter 8. They provide a state-of-the-art review of Nigerian Languages using natural language processing (NLP) research by addressing a key problem that many languages that are native to developing world regions face – not being known and lacking computing resources to support them. The analysis reveals that only four Nigerian languages have so far been studied in NLP published papers. Chapter 9 is on the subject of increasing teacher educators' access and use of instructional web-based technologies in SSA. Using a mixed method study, Dr. Abdulsalami Ibrahim, Millersville University of Pennsylvania and Dr. Crystal Machado, Indiana University of Pennsylvania (chapter authors) surveyed 190 teacher educators on the types of technologies that they use, access and demographic differences. In a related area of education (Chapter 10), Dr. Prakash Bhagwan Dongardive, Mekelle University, Ethiopia discusses Web 2.0 technologies in libraries in Mekelle University – a case of post graduate (PG) students' preferences. Acceptance and adoption of Web 2.0 technologies and use of social networking sites like Facebook, Twitter, YouTube are enabling libraries to engage with students in virtual environments.

The Nigerian educational system and ICT integration is the subject matter of Chapter 11. The authors, Dr. Okanlade Adesokan Lawal-Adebowale and Dr. Olalekan Oyekunle, both from the University of Agriculture, Abeokuta, Nigeria, examine issues by integrating ICT into the Nigerian educational system by raising an important problem of the lack of robust ICT tools to support virtual learning. Thinking immensely as the writer of this Foreword, having robust ICT tools to support virtual learning in this unprecedented Coronavirus pandemic can help learning to go on even when students cannot meet face-to-face with their instructors and teachers. In Chapter 12, Professor Adwaita Maiti of Prabhat Kumar College, Contai, West Bengal, India, and Dr. Sebak Kumar Jana, Vidyasagar University, Midnapore, West Bengal, India examine ICT use in higher education in Eastern States of India. They present the strengths of having access to ICT as enhancing effective learning and as motivating the learner, however, the Eastern States of India are lagging behind when compared to all other regions of the country in the use of ICT by higher education students. The final chapter in Section 2 of the book looks at ICT in the field of Agriculture. Lecturer Consolata Kemirembe Angello, Sokoine University of Agriculture, Tanzania, writes on the adoption and use of ICTs by livestock keepers for improved access to livestock information in selected urban areas of Tanzania. The study discussed in the chapter informs the reader that various ICTs are being used by the urban farmers, but mobile phones are used more than radio and television (TV). Internet is used by very few livestock keepers due to computer illiteracy.

Overall, I strongly recommend the book to its target audience. I am pleased with the editorial work that the book editor, Dr. Alice S. Etim has done. The authors of the 13 chapters have provided high-level scholarship with rich literature and analyses that will help inform the target audience of this book on ICT adoption and use in emerging and developing economies. They have given developing countries and beyond a rich resource on ICT and inclusion in the 21st century. Indeed, I am pleased to be called upon to review and write this Foreword to support an excellent work.

Ravinder Rena
North-West University Business School, North-West University, Mahikeng Campus, South Africa
6 August 2020

Preface

The idea to write or edit a book on developing countries and technology inclusion has been with me for about a decade. The foundation was laid when I completed a PhD dissertation in 2010 that examined the Base of the Pyramid (BoP) populations and their adoption of information and communication technology (ICT). In the course of the decade since after my PhD work, I have conducted many field studies in developing countries and most of the studies have been published as peer-reviewed journal articles and book chapters. There is also the angle of the rich experiences and lessons learned through interactions with research participants, colleagues in academia, students, practitioners, and entrepreneurs. For example, the field research experiences and attendance/presentation at conferences outside the USA between 2009 and 2014 were very relevant and meaningful to my work in developing world regions. I had multiple opportunities through funded research to present at conferences and spend several weeks in the summer to conduct ICT research in Ghana, Nigeria and Benin (formerly, Dahomey). These published works were investigations into ICT for bottom-up development, mobile phone adoption & use for services delivery such as with mobile money and payment systems as well as ICT impact (Etim, 2010, 2011, 2012a, 2012b, 2013, 2014). At an AITEC World Conference in Accra in the summer of 2012, the mobile technology revolution in the region was very evident - developing countries, particularly those in Sub Saharan Africa (SSA) were leapfrogging computer technology and fixed-line telephony to adopt cell/mobile phone technologies. There were many trade shows which I observed that there was a concerted effort by mobile network operators (MNOs) to expose potential subscribers to new mobile technologies and/or migrate existing users from second generation (2G) mobile devices and services to data-capable third generation (3G) mobile phones. In recent times the MNOs are doing the same for fourth generation (4G) mobile devices, products and services. According to Etim (2014), the MNOs and bankers have been forging partnerships to provide subscribers with banking and payment applications (apps). Information and communication technology policy discussions and actions have been moving rapidly in order to help facilitate the dynamics for widespread ICT adoption and technology inclusion.

This edited book *Developing Countries and Technology Inclusion in the 21st Century Information Society* is written in this era of modern global networks where developed countries are migrating speedily to fifth generation (5G) technologies. In order to discuss research accomplishments and major transformations in ICT adoption and inclusion in many developing countries, it is worth noting here that the governments of many developing countries helped by crafting ICT policies. These policies, though in most cases are not well implemented, have yielded minimal returns such as allowing privatization of the telecommunication sectors in order to increase local as well as offshore investments. The MNOs like MTN, Airtel, Vodafone, 9Mobile and many others that operate in developing countries are competing very hard for market share in their target markets. Several MNOs are working hard in their various market segments to attempt to secure a spot in the top 100 list of MNOs (see Appendix A). At Accra and other big cities, for example, it is very easy to see young entrepreneurs/vendors in busy markets or in outdoor tents registering new mobile phone subscribers or selling contracts in exchange for daily wages from the MNOs.

Despite these great strides, ICT investments as well as impact in developing countries is still very low. There are many reasons for the low ICT impact but an obvious one is that investment in infrastructure like broadband is still lacking or at very low level in developing countries (Bankole et al, 2011). The World Economic Forum, a non-governmental organization (NGO) that is based in Geneva, Switzerland, publishes a yearly Network Readiness Index (NRI, also called Technology Readiness) since 2002. The NRI is an important indicator that assesses how countries are performing with technology and ICT impact on the economic outlook. Dutta & Lanvin (2019) have revised the 2019 NRI Report to use some common variables for assessing the multi-faceted impact of ICT in developed, developing and less developed countries in order to rank the countries on their network readiness. Some of the indices are (1) the environment for ICT (includes infrastructure, political, regulatory and market), (2) the ICT readiness of each country (government, individuals/consumers and the private sector), and (3) the adoption/use of ICT by all demographics and stakeholders. The 2019 NRI ranked 121 countries and the first ten countries were Sweden, Singapore, Netherlands, Norway, Switzerland, Denmark, Finland, United States, Germany and United Kingdom. The few developing countries that made the 2019 NRI list of the 121 countries as their regional performers were United Arab Emirates (#29), Qatar (#33), Bahrain (#40), Mauritius (#53), Kazakhstan (#60), South Africa (#72), and Rwanda (#89).

Manuel Castells, a Spanish Sociologist and author of many resources on ICT and globalization posits that information technology has combined with capitalistic market structures to create an Information Society. The paradox is that the transition to the new paradigm of the Information Society has created a "Fourth World" (Castells, 1996, 1997, 1998). The "Fourth World", according to Donner (2008) is a world of marginalized peoples and regions that have been bypassed by information technologies. The people and the regions are not integrated nor are they able to participate effectively in information networks and exchanges, as well as the advanced production and consumption of the Information Age. For the countries to be integrated into the 21st Information Society, every constituent has much work to do. Reading this book is a good place to start and it will help inform many target audiences.

TARGET AUDIENCE FOR THE BOOK

The target audience for this book includes researchers in the field of ICT, development economics, engineering and computing, business, information science, sociology, political science and other social sciences. The book can be used as a resource for courses taught in these fields and those in developing societies and ICT for development. University libraries in every country and world region need this resource to serve as a roadmap for ICT and inclusion discussions for their patrons. Business organizations that seek to go global will be helped by reviewing information in chapters that affect the countries that they want to do business. PhD students will gain much understanding in the Part One of the book as the authors have discussed theoretical frameworks on poverty, ICT, Artificial Intelligence (AI), Quantum Theory (QT) and many models of ICT acceptance/adoption.

HIGHLIGHT AND IMPORTANCE OF CHAPTERS IN THE BOOK

There are two parts to the book, Section 1 and Section 2. Section 1 covers the theoretical framework and relevant ICT models; and these are discussed in the first three chapters. Section 2 of the book covers ICT adoption, application, use, and impact for service delivery in both private and public sectors of different developing countries. Section 2 has 10 chapters.

Before laying out a Mobile Technology Adoption Model (MOPTAM) for developing countries, Dr. Alice S. Etim, the author of Chapter 1 and the editor of the book reviews theories of poverty, human needs and information poverty to present a framework for ICT adoption and inclusion in developing countries. In the Chapter, she creates the World Pyramid of Needs and examines information poverty from the lens of COVID-19 global pandemic. Her extended research in developing countries, underserved and economically disadvantaged populations and ICT adoption, use and impact for service delivery along with other important research in the fields of business, information science and technology were cited and integrated into the Chapter in order to build MOPTAM.

Economic development theory and analysis using quantum theory (QT) or artificial intelligence (AI) is the subject of Chapter 2. The authors are Professors Jurgita Bruneckiene and Robertas Jucevicius from Kaunas University of Technology, Lithuania. They have laid out a proposition for development economists especially those in developing countries that deserve attention; approaching economic development research in the age of information and knowledge transfer among different economies using QT and AI.

Mr. Ernest Etim, a PhD Candidate at Cape Peninsula University of Technology, Cape Town, South Africa is the author of Chapter 3. He uses foundation IS theories like Technology Acceptance Model (TAM) to discuss relevance and application in transitioning economies. The Chapter is relevant from the theory angle especially for graduate students in IS and related that can find a good review of Task Technology Fit (TTF), Technology Readiness Index (TRI), and TAM2, Self-Efficacy Theory (SET), Unified Theory of Acceptance and Use of Technology (UTAUT) in one place to read and compare. He concludes with an analysis on the appropriateness of these theories to developing countries and transitioning economies.

Section 2 of the book has 10 chapters. Beginning with Chapter 4, five colleagues from Accra Technical University, Ghana—Dr. Nana Asabere, Professor Amevi Acakpovi, Dr. Ezer Osei Yeboah-Boateng, Mr. Wisdom Kwawu Torgby and Mr. Eric Amoako—examine a web-based expert system for counseling and career decision making. The authors use a quantitative research instrument (questionnaires) to determine technology acceptance of seniors in high schools in Ghana, and then propose a web-based (e-counseling) expert system to help match students' backgrounds with the right tertiary educational programs and career choices. A test evaluation of the proposed system with the high school students led to the finding that the students (80%) accepted it; leading to a conclusion that such an expert system can help to support a nation-wide (Ghana) career guidance and counseling.

Chapter 5 is on the challenges and opportunities of using ICT for disaster preparedness. Dr. Sherwin E. Ona, the current chairperson of the Political Science Department at De La Salle University, the Philippines taps on his consultancy experiences with the Department of Information and Communication Technology for the National Government Portal-Government Interoperability Initiative (2018) and UN-Asia Pacific Center for ICT Development (APCICT, 2019) to provide an analysis that includes information management practices and current ICT tools for disaster preparedness. The co-author is Dr. Emmanuel C. Lallana, the Chief Executive Officer (CEO) of Ideacorp, an independent, not-for-profit organization in the Philippines. The Chapter authors discuss a common problem that disaster-prone countries like the Philippines have protocols that are inefficient and lack inter-agency coordination. Using a qualitative-descriptive research design with disaster management information (DIM) as the framework, they examine the disaster preparedness of selected parishes of the Diocese of Legazpi, the Philippines.

In Chapter 6, a practitioner, Dr. Ahmed Mokhtar Abdelaziz, the head of an English Unit at one of Saudi Arabia's Aramco's Industrial Training Centers writes on the role of mobile learning in vocational and technical education and training (VTET) programs. The focus of the chapter is on how VTET programs can be enhanced using mobile learning, including ease of identifying employable skills. The chapter has practical examples for instructors and program designers on how to effectively use mobile technologies to develop both technical and soft job skills.

Chapter 7 is my collaborative work with three of my MBA students at Winston Salem State University, North Carolina, USA—Mr. Chandra Prakash Jaiswal, Ms. Marsheilla Subroto and Mrs. Vivian E. Collins Ortega. The first part of the chapter is used to discuss Agile project management methodology for Information Technology (IT) Projects. The second part focuses on the Case of Books for Africa Project, which was a project that was initiated out of a need to support a disaster relief effort - collecting books for a large University library in Africa that was damaged by fire. The Case covers how the Project was managed as an IT Project using Agile method as well as transferrable lessons for projects in developing countries, specifically those that are located in Sub-Saharan Africa (SSA).

Chapter 8 is a review of literature on Nigerian languages using Natural Language Processing (NLP). It is important to inform the reader that Nigeria has more than 250 native languages with English as the official language. Written by two doctoral students, Mr. Toluwase Victor Asubiaro, University of Western Ontario, Canada and Miss Ebelechukwu Gloria Igwe, University of Ibadan, Nigeria, provide a state-of-the-art review that identifies only four Nigerian languages namely Hausa, Ibibio, Igbo and Yoruba as having been studied in NLP published papers. The NLP studies for the four languages cover mostly alternatives for the keyboard like virtual keyboard, auto diacritics restoration and optical character recognition. The authors recommend growth in NLP for Nigerian languages using resource development, knowledge representation modeling and cross-lingual techniques.

Chapter 9 covers the topic of increasing teacher educators' access and use of instructional web-based technologies in SSA. Using a mixed method study, Dr. Abdulsalami Ibrahim, Millersville University of Pennsylvania and Dr. Crystal Machado, Indiana University of Pennsylvania (Chapter authors) surveyed 190 teacher educators on the types of technologies that they have access to or use and demographic differences. The findings were that actual use of the various technologies was dependent on having access; women and recent schools' graduates were more accepting of the technologies than men or older graduates.

In Chapter 10, Dr. Prakash Bhagwan Dongardive, Mekelle University, Ethiopia discusses Web 2.0 technologies in libraries. Examining the cases of Mekelle University's post graduate (PG) students' preferences of the technologies, the findings were that acceptance and adoption of web 2.0 technologies and the use of social networking sites like Facebook, Twitter, YouTube by the PG students have enabled libraries to engage better with students in virtual environments.

Chapter 11 centers on the Nigerian educational system and ICT integration into learning. The authors, Dr. Okanlade Adesokan Lawal-Adebowale and Dr. Olalekan Oyekunle, both from the University of Agriculture, Abeokuta, Nigeria, discuss issues with integrating ICT into the Nigerian educational system by raising an important problem of the lack of robust ICT tools to support virtual learning. This issue has become very important to Nigeria and other countries especially as students and their instructors/teachers transition to online or virtual learning in recent times due to COVID-19 global pandemic.

There is a need to have robust ICT tools instruction and learning virtually especially when and where face-to-face meetings are not possible.

Similar to Chapter 11, the authors of Chapter 12 discuss issues of ICT in education. Professor Adwaita Maiti of Prabhat Kumar College, Contai, West Bengal, India, and Dr. Sebak Kumar Jana, Vidyasagar University, Midnapore, West Bengal, India, examine ICT use in higher education in the Eastern States of India. The authors present the strengths of having access to ICT as enhancing effective learning as well as motivating the learner, however, the Eastern States of India are lagging behind other parts of India in ICT use to support students in higher educational level.

Chapter 13, the final chapter in Section 2 of the book deals with ICT adoption in agricultural sector of Tanzania. Lecturer Consolata Kemirembe Angello, Sokoine from the University of Agriculture, Tanzania writes on the adoption and use of ICTs by livestock keepers for improved access to livestock information in selected urban areas of Tanzania. The study that is discussed in the Chapter informs the reader that various ICTs are being used by the urban farmers but mobile phones are used more than radio and television (TV). Internet is used by very few livestock keepers due to computer illiteracy.

IMPACT OF THE BOOK

Finally, the book is written to have a wide range impact on developing countries as they navigate their path to using ICT for sustainable development, inclusion and strengthening their 21st Century global connections to the Information Society. The editor and chapter contributors are scholars and subject matter experts from the fields of Agriculture, Business, Computer Science, Developmental Studies, Economics, Education, Humanities, ICT, Information Science, Information Systems and Technology, Natural Sciences, Social Sciences, and Telecommunication. They have contributed content and studies to the book to support how ICT acceptance, adoption and use can effect service delivery in their specialized fields of research and practice. They have written their chapters to include rich literature and studies in the adoption/use and impact of ICT. Each chapter also highlights a specific type of application or use of ICT to support development initiatives and sustainability of developing countries.

REFERENCES

Bankole, F. O., Shirazi, F., & Brown, I. (2011). Investigating the impact of ICT investments on human development. *The Electronic Journal on Information Systems in Developing Countries*, *48*(8), 1–19. doi:10.1002/j.1681-4835.2011.tb00344.x

Castells, M. (1996). The information age: Economy, society and culture: Vol. 1. *The rise of the network society*. Blackwell Publishing.

Castells, M. (1997). The information age: Economy, society and culture: Vol. 2. *The power of identity*. Blackwell Publishing.

Castells, M. (1998). The information age: Economy, society and culture: Vol. 3. *The end of millennium*. Blackwell Publishing.

Donner, J. (2008). Shrinking fourth world? Mobiles, development, and inclusion. In *Handbook of mobile communication studies*. The MIT Press. doi:10.7551/mitpress/9780262113120.003.0003

Dutta, S., & Lanvin, B. (2019). *NRI 2019 Analysis*. World Economic Forum & Portulans Institute. Available at https://networkreadinessindex.org/nri-2019-analysis/#analysis-and-results

Etim, A. S. (2010). *The adoption and diffusion of information and communication technology in the Base of the Pyramid populations of Sub-Saharan Africa: A study of Nigerian students* (Thesis). University of North Carolina - Dissertations & Theses. doi:10.17615/ngh7-8v35

Etim, A. S. (2011). Bottom-up business development: Empowering low income societies through microfinance and mobile technologies. *International Journal of Humanities and Social Science, 1*(13), 1–11.

Etim, A. S. (2012). The emerging market of Sub-Saharan Africa and technology adoption: Features users desire in mobile phones. *International Journal of ICT Research and Development in Africa, 3*(1), 14–26. doi:10.4018/jictrda.2012010102

Etim, A. S. (2013). Mobile technology adoption for microfinance delivery in Sub-Saharan Africa. *Research in Business and Economics Journal, 7*. http://www.aabri.com/rbej.html

Etim, A. S. (2014). Mobile banking and mobile money adoption for financial inclusion. *Research in Business and Economics Journal, 9*. http://www.aabri.com/rbej.html

Acknowledgment

To my husband and children, James, David, and Christiana, for their encouragement, patience, and support throughout this Book Project.

To my late mom and dad, Akon and Sunday Etim, for their love for education and sacrificial service to help build a school for me and other children in my childhood community in Africa to attend.

To my 4th grade teacher, Mrs. Arit Ekanem, and all other teachers in my learning pathways that inspired and mentored me to become a scholar.

Section 1

Chapter 1
A Theoretical Framework and Model of ICT Adoption and Inclusion in Developing Countries

Alice S. Etim

Winston Salem State University, USA

ABSTRACT

Information and communication technology (ICT) adoption is cardinal to the sustainability of all societies, and it is the engine that can transform developing countries. This first chapter for the book uses the theories of poverty, human needs, and information poverty as the lenses to examine the framework for ICT adoption and inclusion. A world pyramid of needs that embodies information needs is developed. Information poverty is discussed along with the case of Coronavirus (COVID-19), the global pandemic that brought to a halt many communities in 2020. A mobile phone technology adoption model (MOPTAM) is presented as the framework to understanding ICT adoption and inclusion in developing countries.

INTRODUCTION

Information and communication technology (ICT) is a term that is used to consolidate an array of technologies into one group of information technology ecosystem. A standard definition of ICT by Kling et al (2005) states:

Artifacts and practices for recording, organizing, storing, manipulating, and communicating information. Today, many people's attention is focused on new ICTs, such as those developed with computers and telecommunication equipment. But ICTs include a wider array of artifacts, such as telephones, faxes, photocopiers, movies, books and journal articles. They also include practices such as software testing methods, and approaches to cataloging and indexing documents in the library (p.11).

DOI: 10.4018/978-1-7998-3468-7.ch001

One important factor in the different roles of ICT tools and services is that they are interpreted and used in different ways by different people. Social informatics researchers have found that people frequently interpret and interact with ICT tools and services in more complex and different ways (Kling et al, 2005; Etim 2020; Grant & Meadows, 2021). The ICT tools are used in unpredictable ways, such as providing a mobile phone or land line telephone calling service, creating a computer-based search service via a desktop or a laptop or a browser client to access the internet or a Cloud-based service for any type of information including commerce; the use of an e-mail tool, accessing information in a digital library, an indexed database or the use of a smartphone to access and post information at a social media site.

This first chapter of the book discusses the poverty framework as a foundation for ICT inclusion in developing countries. It includes *information need* and *information poverty* as part of the *World Pyramid of Needs*. Information need and the type of poverty that results from the lack of ICT tools and services, *information poverty* are examined as a new category of poverty. Before information poverty is introduced and discussed, the poverty framework (based mostly on economic poverty) is examined and a review of literature on information poverty is written. The case of the 2020 Coronavirus (COVID-19) global pandemic is used in the chapter to support information poverty and to show implications for health information poverty. The second part of the chapter examines an ICT adoption framework and guide for developing countries using the Mobile Phone Technology Adoption Model (MOPTAM). Overall, the book is written to help the reader grasps very quickly the great work of various scholars on ICT adoption, use, applications and impact in different developing countries.

This chapter and the other chapters in the book are written in a format that is easy to read and there are hundreds of resources that have been cited and referenced by the various contributors. There are adequate data, figures, cases, examples, models and tables to support the text. The book is an important and relevant resource for undergraduate and graduate course work in ICT and related, developing countries, sustainable development and inclusion of underserved communities. Librarians and researchers in the fields of computing, business, economics, health, the social sciences and related will find the book a valuable resource.

THE FRAMEWORK FOR THE BOOK

The Poverty Framework

Developing countries in general are challenged by economic and extreme poverty (Ayittey, 1992, 1998 & 2005; Collier, 2007; Easterly, 2006; Sachs, 2005; World Bank, 2015 & 2019). The writers, however, lack consensus on the definition and causes of poverty, particularly extreme poverty. In this sections, several definitions of poverty is provided in order to establish a poverty framework that will link to the lack of access or affordability of ICT tools and services.

Saunders (2004), *Towards a credible poverty framework: From income poverty to deprivation*, summarizes several definitions of income or extreme poverty as part of his effort to develop a credible poverty framework. Some of the definitions from Saunders (2004) are provided (italics added).

Seebohm Rowntree (1899):

A family is counted as poor if their total earnings are insufficient to obtain the minimum necessities of merely physical efficiency.

Peter Townsend (1979):

Individuals' families and groups in the population can be said to be in poverty when they lack the resources to obtain the types of diet, participate in the activities and have the living conditions and amenities which are customary, or at least widely encouraged or approved, in the societies to which they belong.

Joanna Mack and Stewart Lansley (1985):

Poverty is an enforced lack of socially perceived necessities.

Amartya Sen (1992):

Poverty is the failure of basic capabilities to reach certain minimally acceptable levels. The functioning relevant to this … can vary from such elementary physical ones as being well-nourished, being adequately clothed and sheltered, avoiding preventable morbidity, etc., to more complex social achievements such as taking part in the life of the community, being able to appear in public without shame, and so on.

Sachs (2005) defines extreme poverty as a situation that "… households cannot meet basic needs for survival. They are chronically hungry, unable to access health care, lack the amenities of safe drinking water and sanitation, cannot afford education for some or all of the children, and perhaps lack rudimentary shelter – a roof to keep the rain out of the hut, a chimney to remove the smoke from the cook stove – and basic articles of clothing, such as shoes," (p. 20). Sachs adds that unlike moderate and relative poverty, extreme poverty occurs mostly in developing countries. In his book, *The end of poverty: Economic possibilities of our time,* Sachs (2005) identifies the causes of extreme poverty as primarily hunger and diseases; he puts more than a billion people with most of them in Sub-Saharan Africa in the epicenter of the crisis. Sachs cites many examples from his visits to the African countries of Malawi, Nigeria and Zambia to argue that prolonged destitution might put people at risk of not being able to recover from extreme poverty. According to Sachs, breaking the poverty trap will require foreign aid and investment to improve state planning, agriculture, technology, infrastructure, and health care, such as providing anti-Malaria bed nets to combat Malaria.

Another viewpoint on extreme poverty is presented by Paul Collier (2007). He discusses an undisclosed list of 58 countries that fall into the extreme poverty definition and some are "trapped" and heading toward a "black hole." The list of the 58 countries is not published, but some of them mentioned in his book, *The Bottom billion: Why the poorest countries are failing and what can be done about it,* are Zimbabwe, Malawi, Ethiopia, Sierra Leone, Haiti, Laos, Burma, Central African Republic, Bolivia, Cambodia, Kenya, Nigeria, Yemen, and the Central Asian countries. The per capita income of these countries is very low and they are not the countries that companies are eager to invest in. According to Collier, many of the countries are not only falling behind in development but they are falling apart. They coexist with the societies of the 21st century but their reality is the 14th century because they are battling civil wars, diseases, plague, and ignorance. While the rest of the world is developing, these extremely poor countries are trapped. Collier identifies four traps: the conflict trap, natural resource trap, landlocked trap (the trap of bad neighbors), and the bad governance trap.

The countries in Collier's list are distinctive not only in being the poorest, but having also failed to grow. These countries are not following the development pathways of many nations that passed through development (now called developed countries). Collier agrees with Sachs on the issue of traps, but disagrees with him on how to solve extreme poverty. Unlike Sachs who recommends foreign aid and investments, Collier sees foreign aid as a "headless heart syndrome". According to him, a headless heart syndrome with respect to aid is regarded as some sort of reparation for colonialism. It is a statement that shows that western society is giving to developing countries because of the guilt feeling that these countries are victims of past colonial practices. Collier states that the key to ending extreme poverty rests in the countries themselves. He advocates the use of tools that have worked in other places in the past for these extremely poor countries. In discussing the range of solutions for the landlocked trap, Collier pleads with the trapped countries to not be electronic locked (e-locked) but to encourage investments in technologies, electronic services (e-services) and telecommunication infrastructure investments because they have potential for economic growth.

E-services now have the potential to deliver rapid economic growth. This is the story of recent economic development in India. Because India is a coastal economy, it has many options for global integration. The landlocked [countries] do not have such a range of options. E-services are attractive because distance is irrelevant. The twin pillars of being competitive in e-services are having good telecommunications infrastructure and having workers with post-primary education. Good telecommunications depend upon getting regulatory and competition policies right. It is a relatively simple matter to tell when they are wrong: prices are too high relative to global benchmarks and coverage is inadequate (p.60).

Easterly (2006), a one-time colleague of Collier at the World Bank, agrees with him on the headless heart syndrome analogy, and criticizes Sachs' aid and investments fix to developing countries. Why has development failed for the most part for countries in Africa, South East Asia and some others in the Caribbean and Central/South America? According to Easterly, failed development can be attributed to issues of lack of accountability; emphasis are placed on large plans instead of small measurable goals; corrupt governments, and the mindset of donor government and organizations. Taking the last item, for example, Easterly puts out an argument that development has failed largely because of the mind-set of donor governments, the World Bank, International Monetary Fund (IMF) and other donor/lending organizations. The donors, who in their home countries' economies no longer believe in central planning, continue to impose central planning on the recipient countries. Easterly contrasts the activities of "Planners" and "Searchers". Planners are those who believe in command and control economics while Searchers are those who look for ways to make something work. In foreign aid, Easterly sees Planners as announcing good intentions but do not motivate the people on the ground to follow through while Searchers find ways to get things to work. Planners apply global blueprints while Searchers adapt to the local environment. Planners lack knowledge of the clients in the developing countries while Searchers find out if the clients in these countries are satisfied. In sum, Easterly's position is that the present day western philanthropists are more likely to fail in developing countries because they are mostly Planners who lack knowledge about the countries' disposition.

Unlike most of the other development economists, Ayittey (1998), a Ghanaian economist uses a rich historical perspective to trace the problems from the era of African colonization. He argues that countries in Africa are rich in many natural resources such as oil, gold, manganese, and copper. However, the African Continent, despite its abundant natural endowment, is in chaos, poverty and endless cycles of conflicts. In *Africa in Chaos* (1998), Ayittey writes:

By the beginning of the 1990s, it was clear something had gone terribly wrong in Africa. The continent was wracked by a never-ending cycle of civil wars, carnage, chaos, and instability. Economies have collapsed. Poverty, in both absolute and relative terms, had increased. Malnutrition was rife. In addition, censorship, persecution, detention, arbitrary seizure of property, corruption, capital flight, and tyranny continually plagued the continent...Infrastructure had decayed and crumbled in much of Africa [p. 8].

In *Africa Unchained* (2005), Ayittey takes a less pessimistic approach to argue for solutions to a troubled continent (Africa). He proposes as part of the solution an indigenous development effort and entrepreneurship and calls for the rise of the *Cheetah* generation who would take power from their parents, the Hippos.

Karnani (2007) emphasizes that the way out for developing and poor nations is for the global society to help them to become producers and not consumers so that people can improve their own income and earning potential.

The United Nations (UN, 2015) uses a perspective of goal settings and projects to attempt to tackle poverty. After the 2000 – 2015 United Nations (UN) Millennium Development Goals (MDGs), the UN Sustainable Development Goals (UN SDGs, 2015) were developed in 2015 with a target end date of 2030. There are 17 SDGs and in Report, some of the SDGs directly address issues of poverty:

- Goal #1 "End poverty in all its form everywhere" (UN, 2015, p. 18).
- Goal #8 "Promote sustained, inclusive and sustainable economic growth, full and productive employment and decent work for all" (UN, 2015, p. 18).
- Goal #9: "Build resilient infrastructure, promote inclusive and sustainable industrialization and foster innovation" (UN, 2015, p. 18).

In addition to extreme poverty, the writers views on poverty can be categorized into: *income poverty* (lack of sufficient income to meet needs) and *capability poverty* (the lack of needed goods and services). The World Bank explains mostly extreme poverty as an embodiment of both categories but weighs more towards the economic lens with the following key statistics (World Bank, 2018 & 2020):

- In 2015, 10 percent of the world's population lived on less than $1.90 (US dollars) per day; a slight improvement from 11 percent in 2013.
- In 2019, less than 1.1 billion people lived in extreme poverty than in 1990.
- In 2019, the international poverty line was redrawn from $2.00 to $1.90 (U.S. dollar) per day.

The World Bank (2020) is concerned that the progress of several years could be eroded by COVID-19 global pandemic as more people get sick, not employed and lose income; causing a severe fall back into extreme poverty.

Information Poverty and the World Pyramid of Need: A Framework for Inclusion

My position in discussing the poverty framework in the previous section is not to take sides but rather, to bring to focus information poverty as a third and very important category of poverty. In this section, information poverty is discussed and information need is integrated into a newly developed *World Pyramid of Need*. The human needs theories of Abraham Maslow (1943), Alderfer (1969), Reiss (1998) and

Wilson (1981, 1997) is revised to include information needs. It is an important revision that is used to examine ICT adoption and inclusion framework in developing countries.

Abraham Maslow (Hierarchy of Needs, 1943) tiers human needs from the very basic needs of food, clothing, shelter and safety at the bottom and self-actualization at the top of his Pyramid of Needs. His theory was embellished by Alderfer (ERG theory, 1969) and extended by Reiss (16 Basic Needs, 1998) but the revisions/extensions did not include information needs. Wilson (1981, 1997), in his research on human information-seeking behavior, discussed information seeking and human needs together stating that people seek information to tackle different human needs. He illustrated his point by broadening health needs to include health information needs, thereby raising an argument that when information that one seeks, if it is not found or gets distorted, the need or value of that information increases and could result in the person becoming *information poor*.

In this book, I propose that information poverty should be considered as a third category of poverty and also should be integrated into the Pyramid of Human Needs with a new framework, the *World Pyramid of Need*, Figure 1.

Figure 1. The world pyramid of need with information as a need

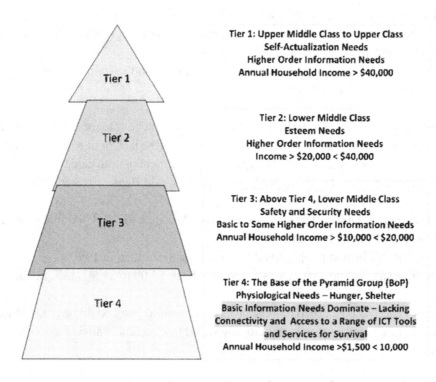

Tier 1: Upper Middle Class to Upper Class
Self-Actualization Needs
Higher Order Information Needs
Annual Household Income > $40,000

Tier 2: Lower Middle Class
Esteem Needs
Higher Order Information Needs
Income > $20,000 < $40,000

Tier 3: Above Tier 4, Lower Middle Class
Safety and Security Needs
Basic to Some Higher Order Information Needs
Annual Household Income > $10,000 < $20,000

Tier 4: The Base of the Pyramid Group (BoP)
Physiological Needs – Hunger, Shelter
Basic Information Needs Dominate – Lacking
Connectivity and Access to a Range of ICT Tools
and Services for Survival
Annual Household Income >$1,500 < 10,000

Explaining the World Pyramid of Need With Information Needs Framework

Both information poverty and the human needs framework apply to many developing countries. A large population of people in these countries are faced with the issue of information supply in a two worlds' phenomenon – *the world of the haves* and *those who are looking for a chance to have.* With reference to information needs, it can be described as the *outsider's world* and the in*sider's world.* The *haves* live in a cosmopolitan or outsider's world with amenities and information access. They live on a lot more than $1.90 US dollars per day and can easily access information through the internet, libraries, mobile and fixed line telephones, social media sites, videos, and other ICT tools or services. The *insider's world* describes *those who are looking for a chance to have;* they are impoverished and live on $1.90 US dollars or less per day. The good news is that many of them seek for opportunities to raise their net worth; Karnani (2007) agrees that they are producers but highly constrained. They lack the financial resources to purchase ICT tools such as smartphones and computers, or lack access to the internet with their 2nd generation mobile devices and broadband/Wi-Fi services are not available where they live. Moreover, since 80 percent of the developing countries' regions are predominantly rural, they lack basic infrastructure like stable electricity supply, making the location of amenities such as libraries or information center kiosks very difficult.

Figure 1, the *World's Pyramid of Needs with Information Needs* (thereafter called, the World's Pyramid) is a framework that includes both human needs, information needs and an estimated economic power of the different tier groups. The poorest group, those shown in the framework as the Base of the Pyramid (BoP) population is located on Tier 4 when compared to other people in the world who are in the other tier groups. The World's Pyramid also shows the overlap between the tiers with regards to both their needs and economic potential. The number of people at the base of each tier is larger than at the top of that tier. In the World's Pyramid framework, I have combined Maslow's Hierarchy of Needs (1943) with Prahalad and Hart's Economic Pyramid (1999) model to create and revise forward the World's Pyramid that illustrates human needs, including their information needs and economic power. I have also revised the data forward based on a combination of factors such as inflation and earning potential. The framework shows that *information needs* in the lowest or BoP tier competes with human *basic and survival needs.* The people in Tier 4, the BoP are not only constrained with basic needs such as clean air, nutritive food, drinking water, healthcare and shelter, but they are also challenged by access to information that helps with daily survival, healthcare and sustainability of lives. Higher order information needs are found in Tiers 3 and 4 (sometimes can be found in Tier 2). When information needs is resolved, it can bring about better economic empowerment and self-expression. With this understanding, the World's Pyramid provides information that differs from Maslow's framework that needs do not tier cleanly. One important reason for this is that people at different tiers share a common need for information that can help to pave the way to upward mobility when their information and other needs are met.

Information access and sharing for learning, research, and business strategic management become the *higher order information needs.* The ability to own and to use modern information and communication technology such as smart phones, computers, smart cards, or to access the library, and internet databases to search for and retrieve information for various e-learning needs fit into the higher order information needs (Etim, 2012, 2016).

Additionally, Maslow's Hierarchy of Needs theory is often grouped with theories of workplace motivation and personality. There is a need for the global society to motivate the BoP communities in developing countries and even pockets of BoP in developed societies to join the knowledge workforce for better productivity and work life achievements. As was discussed in the previous section, Easterly (2006) cited an important group in the BOP, the *Searchers* whom the world can motivate and support with necessary ICT tools and services so that they can work with their local populations more effectively to reduce both extreme and information poverty.

As people move up the World Pyramid relative to higher order needs, information needs can also change. This implies that at each tier, information needs can be differentiated. At the physiological needs level for example, there is critical need for information for gathering food, finding shelter, getting healthcare and medical help or staying safe from getting sick or infected as in the case of *COVID-19* (Coronavirus) global pandemic in 2020. People need to alleviate the information poverty by having access to on-demand and quality information sources that they can access via their medical & hospital networks, mobile phones, computers, the internet, television, radio, libraries and other reliable databases/Cloud-based systems. The ability for governments and organizations both private and public to use different information tools/services to reach citizens, customers (in the case of businesses) and families becomes very critical to survival and sustaining of lives in the COVID-19 global pandemic.

LITERATURE

Information Poverty as a Category of Poverty and Covid-19 Case: Implications for Health Information Poverty

Although information poverty has been studied since the 1970s, it has not been explicitly discussed as a category of poverty. Childers and Post (1975) define information poverty as *information void*. Chatman (1996) examines information poverty from the social angle and agrees with Childers and Post (1975). Some writers that discuss information poverty link it to economic poverty. The association has been about the lack of resources to acquire or access modern ICT tools and services to meet different needs (Bishop et al, 1999; ADB, 2003; Fisher, et al, 2004; Elijah & Ogunlade, 2006; Ssewanyana, 2007, Etim 2010, 2012 & 2020). My research focus lies in this area and I am therefore motivated to define information poverty as "the scarcity of information and communication technology tools and services that can enable an individual, community or country to have access at any point in time to needed information." The ICT tools include computers, smartphones, land lines, mobile phones, radios, televisions; and services such as having access to reliable news source in the era of fake news, the internet & its many databases, social media sites like Facebook, YouTube, Instagram, Twitter and other telecommunication services and libraries.

Information poverty is linked to human needs. Wilson (1981) is one of the few researchers that extends the human needs theory to the field of Information Science by identifying three types of information needs: (1) need for new information; (2) need to elucidate the information held; and (3) need to confirm information held. He argues that needs are subjective and various types of needs have been defined through deduction. For example, he cites Morgan and King (1971) who propose that what motivates people to perform or behave in a certain way could be linked to three kinds of motives – physiological motives (hunger, thirst, shelter); unlearned motives (curiosity and sensory stimulation); and social motives (desires for affiliation, approval, and status). The concept of motive, though not the focus of this chapter or book, is very much linked to human needs and it is implicit in the information need and information poverty concept.

The 17 United Nations' Sustainable Development Goals (SDGs, UN 2015) bring to the forefront many aspects of poverty: Goal 1 "No Poverty", Goal 2 "Zero Hunger", Goal 3 "Good Health & Wellbeing" and Goal 9 "Industry, Innovation and Infrastructure," have direct links to information poverty. Chatman (1996) examines information poverty using two key phrases "risk taking" and "situational relevance".

Risk taking, according to Chatman, is defined as "an attribute affecting the acceptance of an innovation based on our perception of whether it is worthwhile or not. It does not seem to merit consideration if, weighed against personal cost, the result would be negative" (Chatman, 1996, p.196). Situational relevance, on the hand is seen by Chatman as being consistent with the "utility" of a specific information (Chatman 1996, p. 201).

Information poverty is evident across the different World Pyramid Tier groups (Figure 1). The COVID-19 global pandemic is used here as a case to discuss information poverty and implications for health information needs. In early 2020 when the COVID-19 global pandemic arrived at the shores of many developing countries and even the developed ones like the United States of America (USA), the risks of it deepening the information poverty that already existed in these countries or the implications that it had on health information needs were not fully known or understood. Information poverty was very quickly evident as people could not easily get information about where and how COVID-19 testing was being done in their communities in order to isolate positive cases and protect the most vulnerable members of the population (Roser, et al, 2020). According to Hasell et al (2020), actual testing was a "window" to the disease and the lack of such testing constituted information poverty. Table 1 shows the statistics from Our World in Data (May 10, 2020) for different countries, including developed ones on testing per 1,000 people. The developing countries like Senegal, South Africa, Ecuador, Indonesia and India had very limited number of testing per 1,000 people. Many developing countries had no data to show for COVID-19 testing as at the date this statistics was pulled. Developed countries were also challenged as countries like Norway, Switzerland and the USA had 36.14, 35.77 and 26.32 testing per 1,000 people respectively (Our World in Data, May 10, 2020).

The COVID-19 global pandemic is a case that makes information poverty very relevant not only in developing countries but globally. New safety measures such as physical or social distancing (6ft apart in many countries following the Center for Disease Control, CDC guidelines), effective use of personal protective equipment (PPE), contact tracing & testing, travel restrictions were quickly put in place to save lives when the pandemic started in early 2020. These were new information concepts that people first had a need to learn, understand and embrace quickly in order to stay safe. If people lack access to quality information sources or if the information that they receive daily are distorted or incorrect, it would result in people experiencing information poverty. One way that information poverty is experienced is by not believing the information source or not using the information (even if it is accurate) to meet the information need because it is not from the "insider" source that a person values (Chatman 1996, 1999; Childers & Post, 1975; Etim, 2010, 2020). With COVID-19 pandemic, people may resort to believing inaccurate information because it comes from the source that they value "insider information" and not necessarily because the information is accurate. The consequences of this type of health information poverty (relying on inaccurate or distorted health-related information) in a global pandemic like COVID-19 are enormous; the prominent one is that communities in many countries risk having unmanageable cases daily as hospitals reach maximum capacity and even some people losing their lives.

Craven et al (2020) in their May 13 briefing note informed that the official counts of all known cases of COVID-19 global pandemic was surging over four million cases globally and the disease had also claimed more than 280,000 lives globally as at the date of the report (May 13, 2020). One month later (June 14, 2020), the country with the highest infections and deaths from COVID-19, the USA had 2.13 million cases and 117 thousand deaths (Table 2). The data in Table 2 also shows the number of COVID-19 infections (used for the ranking), deaths and recoveries for 40 countries as at June 14, 2020. The statistics presented in Table 2 is also a strong evidence of a case of information poverty. Without

Table 1. Total COVID-19 tests per 1,000 people, May 10, 2020 –an evidence of information poverty across the world pyramid tier groups

Country	COVID-19 Tests
Iceland	155.95
Estonia	47.77
Italy	41.58
Norway	36.14
Switzerland	35.77
United States	26.31
Singapore	21.11
United Kingdom	18.71
Turkey	15.82
South Korea	12.95
South Africa	5.46
Taiwan	2.82
Ecuador	2.3
Senegal	1.21
India	1.17
Indonesia	0.41

Source: Our World in Data, https://ourworldindata.org/coronavirus

a unified and scientific approach to managing COVID-19, people and communities across the globe are more likely to ignore the warnings of social distancing or the wearing of PPE (face coverings/ masks, face shields, gloves, etc.) when in public and it will cause the number of cases per day to keep rising. As at July 6, 2020, the total confirmed COVID-19 cases, deaths and recoveries worldwide were 11,517,076,087, 535,112, 5,104,282 respectively (Our World in Data, 2020). The USA still peaked; the number of confirmed cases as at July 6, 2020 exceeded 2.9 million and the number of confirmed deaths exceeded 130,000; daily average cases in the country during the first week of July hit and exceed 50,000 (Beachum et al, 2020).

The information poverty and lack are greater in underserved and economically disadvantaged populations. Florant et al (2020) examine the implication of COVID-19 for black lives and their livelihoods in the USA for example, and caution that with the rising infections and deaths mostly affecting blacks and other disadvantaged groups, there is a crisis at hand that could lead to the disruption of major social and economic systems. According to Florant et al (2020), black people in the USA are among the groups at the highest risk of health and economic disruption as caused by the COVID-19 global pandemic; referencing both economic and information poverty. As healthcare companies, academic institutions, not-for-profit organizations and governments across the world collaborate or race for a cure for COVID-19 through vaccines and medication, there is a greater need to disseminate accurate health information to all constituents. Etim et al (2020) encourage the need to raise awareness and encourage adoption of telemedicine. Faezipour & Faezipour (2020) discuss a model for sustainable smartphone-based breathing monitoring system. The studies cited in this section point to the need to use easily accessible tools like

Table 2. COVID-19 statistics for 40 countries (ranked by the number of cases), June 14, 2020

Ranked by Highest Cases	Location		Cases	Deaths	Recovery
	Worldwide		7,873,221	432,173	3,755,576
1		United States[e]	2,132,468	117,400	653,952
2		Brazil[f]	867,882	43,389	437,512
3		Russia[g]	528,964	6,948	280,050
4		India	320,922	9,195	162,379
5		United Kingdom[h]	295,889	41,698	No data
6		Spain[i]	243,928	27,136	150,376
7		Italy	236,989	34,345	176,370
8		Peru	229,736	6,688	115,579
9		Iran	187,427	8,837	148,674
10		Germany[j]	187,423	8,867	172,199
11		Turkey	178,239	4,807	151,417
12		Chile[k]	174,293	3,323	No data
13		France[l]	157,220	29,407	72,859
14		Mexico	146,837	17,141	108,110
15		Pakistan	139,230	2,632	51,735
16		Saudi Arabia	127,541	972	84,720
17		Canada	98,787	8,146	60,272
18		Bangladesh	87,520	1,171	18,730
19		China[m]	83,181	4,634	78,370
20		Qatar	79,602	73	56,898
21		South Africa	70,038	1,480	38,531
22		Belgium[n]	60,029	9,655	16,589
23		Belarus	53,973	308	30,103
24		Sweden	51,614	4,874	No data
25		Netherlands[o]	48,783	6,059	No data
26		Colombia	48,746	1,592	19,426
27		Ecuador	46,751	3,896	4,725
28		Egypt[p]	44,598	1,575	11,931
29		United Arab Emirates	42,294	289	27,462
30		Singapore	40,604	26	29,589
31		Indonesia	38,277	2,134	14,531
32		Portugal	36,463	1,512	22,438
33		Kuwait	35,920	296	26,759
34		Ukraine[q]	31,154	889	14,082
35		Switzerland	31,094	1,677	28,800
36		Argentina[r]	30,282	815	9,070
37		Poland	29,017	1,237	14,104
38		Philippines	25,930	1,088	5,954
39		Ireland	25,303	1,706	23,213
40		Afghanistan	24,766	471	4,725

Adapted from: https://en.wikipedia.org/wiki/Template:COVID-19_pandemic_data

smartphones and mobile apps to effectively information people as well as test/monitor the breathing to detect lung related problems that are linked to COVID-19 global pandemic.

In remote villages and rural communities, hospitals are inaccessible to people because such facilities are located many miles away in cities. People are carried on bicycles and motorcycles on non-motorable roads to the hospitals. In critical and emergency situations, mobile phones can become an important tool to save lives because healthcare providers can be contacted quickly and a clinic on wheels can reach the individual much sooner than he or she can get to a hospital. The need for safety may arise during a hurricane, storm or tornado. During such critical moments, information tools such as smartphones can help track data and provide location information as well as help the dissemination of information to save lives.

ICT ADOPTION PATTERNS IN DEVELOPING COUNTRIES AND THE MOBILE PHONE TECHNOLOGY ADOPTION MODEL (MOPTAM)

The ICT adoption literature in developing countries has established that most of the countries have faced challenging factors with technology adoption. However, mobile phones have been adopted (Fisher et al, 2004; Elijah & Ogunlade, 2006; Ssewanyana, 2007; Donner, 2008 & Etim 2010, 2012 & 2020). Figure 2 shows the International Telecommunication Union (ITU) data on mobile-cellular telephone subscriptions per 100 inhabitants (2010 – 2019) for developed, developing and less-developing countries. The developing countries show a better adoption pattern compared to less developing countries (LDCs) but a lower pattern of adoption than the developed countries.

Figure 2. Mobile-cellular telephone subscription per 100 inhabitants (2010 – 2019)

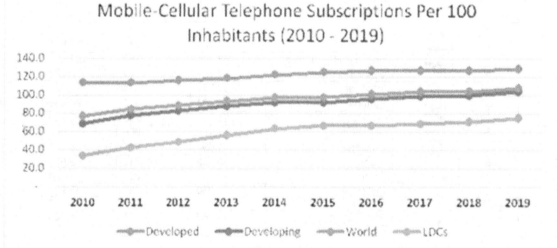

Some of the factors that hinder the adoption of ICT tools and services like computers, the internet and related infrastructure are linked to broadband/Wi-Fi connectivity and lack of computer technology. The personal factors are technology advancement & skills of the users, technology orientation; and illiteracy. Facilitating factors such as access to the ICT tools & services, features users want, cost & affordability and quality of service influence adoption and attitude toward use (Donner, 2008; van Biljon & Kotze, 2007; Ssewanyana, 2007; Elijah & Ogunlade, 2006, Etim, 2010, 2012 & 2020). The ITU data for active mobile-broadband subscriptions per 1000 inhabitants for 2010 – 2019 for developed, developing countries, the world and less developing countries (LDCs) is shown in Figure 3. Developing countries' subscription as at 2019 was still lagging behind the World subscription and far behind that of developed countries.

Figure 3. Active mobile-broadband subscriptions per 100 inhabitants (2010 – 2019)

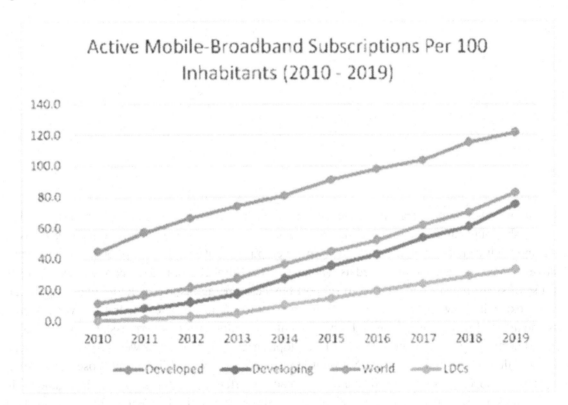

Figure 4 shows the percentage of households with internet in different world regions and Africa as a whole, with more than 50 developing countries fared the worst with 17.8 percent.

ICT Convergence and Economic Impact

The ICT convergence means that a person can use one device like a smartphone to complete multiple ICT tasks that address information needs and economic activities/impact (Annan, 2015; Etim, 2020). Any successful ICT convergence has great economic impact. In developed countries like the USA, access to information on Cloud-based systems is growing rapidly. Yang et al (2017) inform that in the era of Big Data, there is no limit to our use of integrated smart and peripheral devices to access Cloud datasets

Figure 4. Percentage of household with internet by developed and developing world regions, 2019

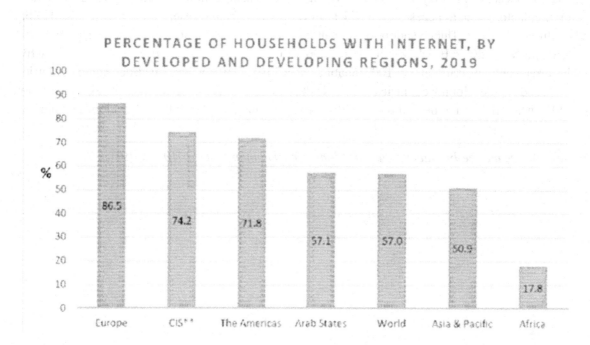

or build ubiquitous networks and smart data centers that provide us with array of information services like online shopping capabilities, knowledge management, business strategic development & decision making and healthcare/telemedicine solutions. In developing countries, ICT adoption and convergence is relatively a new concept and in limited use (Annan, 2015; Etim, 2020). In a study of women entrepreneurs' use of smart phones and internet to support business operations, it was found that a significant difference exists in the women interest to use the internet to support business operations versus actual access and affordability for it; adding to both economic and information poverty issues (Etim, 2020).

An earlier study by Ssewanyana (2007) on ICT adoption and convergence as well as economic impact used data collected through a Uganda National Household Survey (NHS). The purpose of the study was to measure poverty reduction and economic impact of different ICT tools/services in Uganda. The ICT tools and services range from radio, telephones and the internet in the Central, Eastern, Northern to the Western regions of Uganda. The results showed that ICT helped to alleviate economic poverty by providing employment directly and indirectly to many citizens of Uganda. Some of the ICT projects in Uganda that helped to lower unemployment and alleviate information poverty included the *Acacia* project; it extended the internet to schools in rural areas, allowed the MTN village phone sub-project that benefitted women to set up micro enterprises - built around the purchasing and selling of mobile phones and accessories in order to help them to earn income. This is an example of convergence to overcome systemic risks of economic and information poverty. As part of the MTN village phone project for example, the women sold communication time to people in their communities, used their mobile phones to conduct small business operations, communicate with family and friends, participated in phone-in radio shows, check prices of agricultural goods, and transfer money through MTN built-in text messaging and financial software.

THE MODEL: MOPTAM

Mobile Phone Technology Adoption Model (MOPTAM) and Inclusion

This section focuses on a model and guide for the adoption of mobile phones in developing countries as a framework for inclusion. The Mobile Phone Technology Adoption Model (MOPTAM, Figure 5) is based on studies by van Biljon & Kotze (2007) and Etim (2010). Mobile phones are the most been widely adopted ICT in developing countries and much needed for service delivery & inclusion (Fisher et al, 2004; Elijah & Ogunlade, 2006; Ssewanyana, 2007; Donner, 2008 & Etim 2010, 2012 & 2020). In the studies by van Biljon & Kotze (2007) and Etim (2010), MOPTAM was developed based on studies from two developing countries, South Africa and Nigeria. Both studies reference the technology acceptance model (TAM). The TAM model is well known in literature; it was developed by Fred Davis in the late 1980s to explain some of the reasons behind why people accept or reject computers. Among the many variables that might influence technology use, according to Davis (1989) are that people who are in a position to use an ICT such as computers are influenced by *perceived usefulness* and *ease of use*. Perceived usefulness is the degree to which a person believes that using a particular system or technology will enhance his or her job performance. Ease of use is the degree to which a person believes that using a particular system or technology will be free of effort (Davis, 1989). One of the theoretical foundations of TAM is the diffusion of technology innovation work of Everett Rogers (Rogers and Shoemaker, 1971). Adoption of innovation research suggests that ease of use takes prominence in the adoption of an innovation. The TAM model developed for the acceptance & adoption of computers by Fred Davis (1989 is also drawn from the theory of reasoned action, which has its base in the field of social psychology (Fishbein & Ajzen, 1975). Both TAM and the theory of reasoned action attempt to identify relationships between beliefs, attitudes, intentions and behavior. The focus for this chapter and book is on technology adoption.

There are six variables in TAM: external variables (EV), perceived usefulness (PU), perceived ease of use (PEU), attitude toward use (A), behavioral intention to use (BI) and the actual or system use. Figure 5 shows these six variables in TAM and their dependencies. The EV comprise of demographic variables and prior experience; these influence both PU and PEU. Attitude toward use (A) is determined by PU and PEU variables. Behavioral intention (BI) to use is influenced by attitude (A) and PU. The actual use of the technology innovation is influenced by BI. These relationships can be expressed in simple algebraic terms.

A = PU + PEU

BI = A + PU or BI = 2(PU) + PEU

In Van Biljon and Kotze (2007) variation, TAM is criticized as assuming "free" infrastructure or that the infrastructure is already there, but this is a risky assumption in their country of South Africa or even in many developing countries. In addition, TAM does not account for a user's prior usage experience.

Another variation of the technology acceptance model that is worth mentioning as it is very closely linked to TAM is the Unified Theory of Acceptance and Use of Technology (UTAUT) model by Venkatesh et al (2003). The UTAUT model is drawn from several theories and models – the theory of reasoned action, TAM, the theory of planned behavior, diffusion of innovation, and motivational models such as

Figure 5. Technology adoption model (TAM)

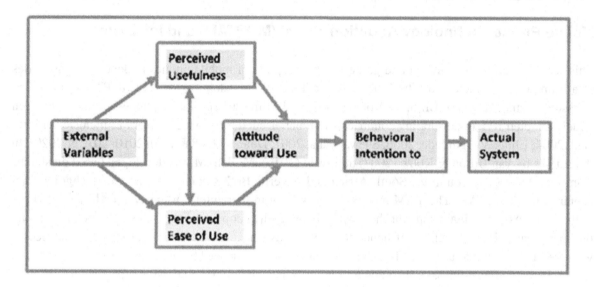

Vroom's expectancy theory. The major addition from UTAUT model is the separation of mediating factors such as expectancy, effort, social influence from determining factors (age, gender, experience, and voluntariness of use). Effort have been made to apply both TAM and UTAUT model to other technologies beside computers in developed countries. In Teo and Pok (2003),the adoption of WAP (Wireless Application Protocol) enabled mobile phones among internet users was studied and they reported that attitude was an important factor in the adoption of WAP-enabled mobile phones.

The studies by van Biljon and Kotze (2007) and Etim (2010) gave rise to MOPTAM, a model for mobile phone adoption in developing countries. The MOPTAM is derived from TAM and UTAUT models and it has both determining and mediating variables, which are grouped and linked in the model to show that both influence the actual system use (Figure 6).

In MOPTAM, the determining variables are the same as TAM, but external variables (EV) have been replaced with social influence (SI) and facilitating conditions (FC) have been added. The SI is the set of cultural factors that influence PU and PEU while FC is the infrastructure, which could include the cost of the mobile phone, the cost of service, and the quality of service that the service providers set, based on their business models.

CONCLUSION: THE RELEVANCE OF MOPTAM FOR DEVELOPING COUNTRIES

The MOPTAM is particularly relevant as it applies to mobile phones, the most widely adopted ICT in developing countries. It can be used as a better guide to evaluating ICT adoption & inclusion in developing countries as the mediating factors, which were not in the original TAM (Figure 5), have been included (Figure 6). The mediating factors include demographic factors (DF), personal factors (PF) and socio-economic factors (SF) are very important in economically disadvantaged communities of developing countries. Demographic factors (DF) include age, gender, education, and prior technology experience or advancement. Personal factors (PF) consist of the user's perception of technology

Figure 6. Mobile phone technology adoption model (MOPTAM)

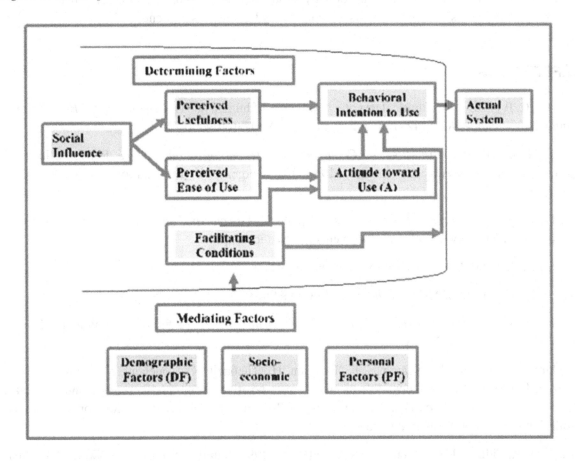

(technology orientation) - derived from the five characteristics put forth by Rogers (2003) – relative advantage, complexity, compatibility, trialability and observability. The socioeconomic factors (SF) are income and job-related status.

In both van Biljon and Kotze (2007) and Etim (2010), some DF, PF and SF were tested and these are still very relevant factors. The Correlation (Pearson R) for the data in both studies showed significant positive correlations between technology advancement (DF) and the perceived ease of use (PEU) as well as with technology orientation (a personal factor, PF) with PEU. Socioeconomic factors (SF) were not tested because an assumption was made in both studies that the study participants were homogenous (from the same socioeconomic groups). The demographic factors (DF) like age and gender on users' perceptions of mobile phone innovation were omitted but in a developed society (USA) study, Kwon and Chidambaram (2000) finding was that gender and age had no significant impact on users' perceptions about mobile phones use (2000).

Organizations that design various ICT tools continue to make great strides with providing user-friendly systems and software that allow PEU. What this chapter has attempted to do is provide MOPTAM to developing countries so that many factors, particularly the personal factors (PF) become very inclusive in the design. There is also a growing need for more research on how to develop technologies that emphasize not only PEU but PU for the educationally disadvantaged and those not familiar with technology in developing countries and MOPTAM is a recommended guide for researchers.

REFERENCES

Alderfer, C. P. (1969). An empirical test of a new theory of human needs. *Organizational Behavior and Human Performance, 4*(2), 142–175. doi:10.1016/0030-5073(69)90004-X

Annan, N. K. (2015). *Information and Communication Technology Convergence*. Retrieved June 14, 2018, from https://www.academia.edu/11195363/Convergence_in_Information_and_Communication_Technology

Asia Development Bank. (2003). *Toward e-Development in Asia and the Pacific, ADB*. Retrieved October 14, 2007, from https://www.adb.org/documents/policies/ict/ict.pdf

Ayittey, G. B. N. (1992). *Africa betrayed*. St. Martin's Press.

Ayittey, G. B. N. (1998). *Africa in chaos*. St. Martin's Press.

Ayittey, G. B. N. (2005). *African unchained: The blueprint for Africa's future*. Macmillan Publishers. doi:10.1007/978-1-137-12278-0

Beachum, L., Bellware, K., Shammas, B., Denham, H., Thebault, R., Copeland, K., Knowles, H., & Sonmez, F. (2020). Live updates: Atlanta mayor tests positive for covid-19; states mandate masks, shut down again. *Washington Post*. Retrieved July 6, 2020, from https://www.washingtonpost.com/nation/2020/07/06/coronavirus-live-updates-us/

Bishop, A. P., Tidline, T. J., Shoemaker, S., & Salela, P. (1999). Public libraries and networked information services in low-income communities. *Library & Information Science Research, 21*(3), 361–390. doi:10.1016/S0740-8188(99)00017-1

Chatman, E. A. (1996). The Impoverished life-world of outsiders. *Journal of the American Society for Information Science, 47*(3), 193–206. doi:10.1002/(SICI)1097-4571(199603)47:3<193::AID-ASI3>3.0.CO;2-T

Chatman, E. A. (1999). A Theory of life in the round. *Journal of the American Society for Information Science, 50*(3), 207–217. doi:10.1002/(SICI)1097-4571(1999)50:3<207::AID-ASI3>3.0.CO;2-8

Childers, T., & Post, J. (1975). *The information poor in America*. Scarecrow Press.

Collier, P. (2007). *The Bottom billion: Why the poorest countries are failing and what can be done about it*. Oxford University Press.

Craven, M., Mysore, M., & Wilson, M. (2020). *COVID-19: Briefing note, May 13, 2020*. Retrieved May 23, 2020, from https://www.mckinsey.com/business-functions/risk/our-insights/covid-19-implications-for-business

Davis, F. D. (1989). Perceived usefulness, perceived ease of use, and user acceptance of information technology. *Management Information Systems Quarterly, 13*(3), 319–340. doi:10.2307/249008

Donner, J. (2008). Research approaches to mobile use in developing world: A review of the literature. *The Information Society, 24*(3), 140–159. doi:10.1080/01972240802019970

Easterly, W. (2006). *The White Man's Burden: Why the West's efforts to aid the rest have done so much ill and so little good.* Penguin Press.

Elijah, O., & Ogunlade, I. (2006). Analysis of the uses of information and communication technology for gender empowment and sustainable poverty alleviation in Nigeria. *International Journal of Education and Development Using Information and Communication Technology, 2*(3), 45–69.

Etim, A., Etim, J., Robinson, A., & Smith, P. (2016). Mobile learning apps to support students learning goals. *Int'l Journal of Computing, Communications & Instrumentation Eng., 3*(2).

Etim, A. S. (2010). *The adoption and diffusion of information and communication technology in the Base of the Pyramid populations of Sub-Saharan Africa: A study of Nigerian students* (Thesis). University of North Carolina - Dissertations & Theses. doi:10.17615/ngh7-8v35

Etim, A. S. (2012). The emerging market of Sub-Saharan Africa and technology adoption: Features users desire in mobile phones. *International Journal of ICT Research and Development in Africa, 3*(1), 14–26. doi:10.4018/jictrda.2012010102

Etim, A. S. (2020). The ICT convergence and impact on women-owned micro and small business enterprises: An analysis based on information poverty. *International Journal of Gender Studies in Developing Societies, 3*(3), 271–292. doi:10.1504/IJGSDS.2020.104607

Etim, A. S., Etim, D. N., & Scott, J. (2020). Mobile health and telemedicine: Awareness, adoption and importance of health study. *International Journal of Healthcare Information Systems and Informatics.* https://www.igi-global.com/journal/international-journal-healthcare-information-systems/1094

Fisher, K. E., Durance, J. C., & Hinton, M. B. (2004). Information grounds and the use of need-based services by immigrants in Queens, New York: A context-based, outcome evaluation approach. *Journal of the American Society for Information Science and Technology, 55*(8), 754–766. doi:10.1002/asi.20019

Florant, A., Noel, N., Stewart, S., III, & Wright, J. (2020). *COVID-19: Investing in black lives and livelihoods.* Retrieved May 17, 2020, from https://www.mckinsey.com/industries/public-sector/our-insights/covid-19-investing-in-black-lives-and-livelihoods

Grant, A. E., & Meadows, J. H. (2021). *Communication Technology Update and Fundamentals* (17th ed.). Routledge.

Hasell, J., Ortiz-Ospina, E., Mathieu, E., Ritchie, H., Beltekian, D., Macdonald, B., & Roser, M. (2020). *Statistics & Research: Coronavirus (COVID-19) testing.* Retrieved May 20, 2020, from https://ourworldindata.org/coronavirus-testing

Karnani, A. (2007). Fortune at the bottom of the pyramid: A mirage. *Social Science Research Network.* Retrieved August 12, 2007, from http://ssrn.com/abstract=914518

Kling, R., Rosembaum, H., & Sawyer, S. (2005). *Understanding and communicating social informatics: A framework for studying and teaching the human contexts of information and communication technologies*. Information Today.

Maslow, A. H. (1943). A theory of human motivation. *Psychological Review*, *50*(40), 370–396. doi:10.1037/h0054346

Morgan, C. T., & King, R. A. (1971). *Introduction to psychology* (4th ed.). McGraw-Hill.

Our World in Data. (2020). Daily confirmed COVID-19 cases, rolling 3-day average. *OurWorldinData*. Retrieved July 6, 2020, from https://ourworldindata.org/grapher/daily-covid-cases-3-day-average

Reiss, S. (1998). Who am I? *The 16 basic desires that motivate our actons and define our personality*. Retrieved February 2, 2017, from http://www.personalityplusinbusiness.com/mbti-and-other-assessments/other-assessments/reiss-profile

Rogers, E. M. (2003). *Diffusion of innovations* (5th ed.). Free Press.

Roser, M., Ritchie, H., Ortiz-Ospina, E., & Hasell, J. (2020). *Coronavirus Pandemic (COVID-19)*. Retrieved May 20, from https://ourworldindata.org/coronavirus

Sachs, J. (2005). *The End of poverty: Economic possibilities for our time*. Penguin Press.

Saunders, P. (2004). *Towards a credible poverty framework: From income poverty to deprivation*. Social Policy Research Centre, University of New South Wales, Sydney, Australia. Retrieved July 7, 2015, from http://www.sprc.unsw.edu.au/dp/DP131.pdf

Ssewanyana, J. (2007). ICT access and poverty in Uganda. *International Journal of Computing and ICT Research*, *1*(2), 10–19.

Teo, T. S. H., & Pok, S. H. (2003). Adoption of WAP-enabled mobile phones among internet users. *Omega*, *31*(6), 483–498. doi:10.1016/j.omega.2003.08.005

United Nations. (2015). About the Sustainable Development Goals. *United Nations*. Retrieved March 5, 2020, from https://www.un.org/sustainabledevelopment/sustainable-development-goals/

van Biljon, J. & Kotze, P. (2007, Oct.). Modeling the factors that influence mobile phone adoption. *South African Institute of Computer Scientist & Information Technologists*, 152-160.

Venkatesh, V., Morris, Davis, & Davis. (2003). User acceptance of information technology: Towards a unified view. *Management Information Systems Quarterly*, *27*(3), 425–478. doi:10.2307/30036540

Wilson, T. D. (1981). On user studies and information needs. *The Journal of Documentation*, *37*(1), 3–15. doi:10.1108/eb026702

Wilson, T. D. (1997). Information behavior: An interdisciplinary perspective. *Information Processing & Management*, *33*(4), 551–572. doi:10.1016/S0306-4573(97)00028-9

World Bank. (2018). Decline of global extreme poverty continues but has slowed. *World Bank*. Retrieved June 2, 2020, from https://www.worldbank.org/en/news/press-release/2018/09/19/decline-of-global-extreme-poverty-continues-but-has-slowed-world-bank

World Bank. (2020). Poverty – Overview. *World Bank*. Retrieved May 28, 2020, from https://www.worldbank.org/en/topic/poverty/overview

Yang, C., Huang, Q., Li, Z., Liu, K. L., & Hu, F. (2017). Big Data and Cloud computing: Innovation opportunities and challenges. *International Journal of Digital Earth*, *10*(1), 13–53. doi:10.1080/1753 8947.2016.1239771

Chapter 2
Quantum Theory and Artificial Intelligence in the Analysis of the Development of Socio-Economic Systems:
Theoretical Insights

Jurgita Bruneckiene
Kaunas University of Technology, Lithuania

Robertas Jucevicius
Kaunas University of Technology, Lithuania

Ineta Zykiene
Kaunas University of Technology, Lithuania

Jonas Rapsikevicius
Kaunas University of Technology, Lithuania

Mantas Lukauskas
Kaunas University of Technology, Lithuania

ABSTRACT

The chapter is designed to stimulate a discussion on a new approach that combines quantum theory with artificial intelligence in the analysis of the economic development of socio-economic systems. The chapter introduces the specifics of the modern socio-economic system and the challenges to economic development. After that, the chapter discusses the possibility and compatibility of approaches (quantum theory) and tools (artificial intelligence) for analysing economic development. The chapter contributes to a new approach in economic development theory by integrating quantum theory and artificial intel-

DOI: 10.4018/978-1-7998-3468-7.ch002

ligence possibilities. Additionally, the competences needed to use artificial intelligence in the analysis of economic development are presented. The value of the chapter is in its contribution to the original methodological justification of the use of quantum theory and artificial intelligence in the analysis of economic development.

INTRODUCTION

Politicians, investors, businessmen, economists, and residents have always been interested in the peculiarities, tendencies, and trajectories of the economic development of nations. Indicators of country development directly affect the strategic decisions of investors and businessmen, as well as the welfare of residents and economic subjects, economic competitiveness, resilience to economic shocks, and the attractiveness of living, working, and investing. Since ancient times scholars have been trying to understand, explain, and find the answers to why countries develop differently and why some reach a higher level of development than others.

The economic development of countries is still a popular and attractive topic for researchers, who try intensively to formulate means and ways of analysing development, to explain the causes of underdevelopment, to classify countries according to their development levels, and to contribute to the construction of economies according to ideological bias (Dulupçu & Okçu, 2000). While this topic has for a decade given up its predominant position in the face of opposition from studies on globalisation, integration, competitiveness, resistance, and other social phenomena, it has recently been rediscovered and is attracting ever-increasing attention. This was prompted by the fact that today's top-level strategies for decision-making are no longer sufficient to characterise the global economy as a binary category consisting of developed and less developed; "primary," "secondary," and "tertiary" sector models; or as an element of the linear conception of economic history. Disappointment in traditional approaches has stimulated policy makers to reconsider the old instruments to suggest the kinds of interventions that are expected to enhance economic development more successfully (Varga, 2017).

In most cases, researchers use the features of economic development as a tool for analysing or classifying, structuring, or ranking economies. The traditional concept of economic development explains the difference in development amongst countries in close reference to income distribution equality and economic growth connections. The use of advanced technologies has enabled the expansion of the field of economic research and has helped in attempts to predict the future and to answer the questions how and why. Sachs (2000) analysed countries' economic by asking why globalisation seems to help some places much more than others; Kim (2014, 2017) sought an answer to how a country's economic growth affects the quality of life. Escosura (2005) asked why there is a divergence between early starters and latecomers in modern Europe. Chen et al (2014) examined the relationship between urbanisation and economic development. Leimbach (2017) forecast how the regions of the world will develop in the 21st century. The analysis of scientific literature has supported a broad spectrum of research on the analysis of economic development, ranging from comparing one or several countries to a very large number of countries (e. g., 149 or 222), or one or more economic growth determinants with the impact of structural reforms on overall economic development; urban or regional analysis; and past to future development bias.

Globalisation, the 4th industrial revolution, and the transition to low carbon economies have created a new challenge for researchers: to answer the question "which," i.e., which economic development path is the most successful under certain defined conditions. What are the features of today's economic development in countries that achieve higher long-term (rather than short-term) competitiveness, sustainability, economic progress or other multi-criteria dimensions (i.e., goal seeking)? Only when it knows the key to success can a country achieve its development objectives, at the right time and using the least amount of resources.

The challenges and requirements of scholars are to broaden the boundaries of economic research and encourage the use of more data. At the same time, the abundance of information makes it difficult to interpret results, to see bias, and to draw conclusions. Researchers agree that the models and methods used in the analysis of economic development often have limitations because of the abundance of data, the complexity of economic systems, and the use of multi-criteria concepts. Therefore, it is recognised that the accuracy of the analysis depends not only on economic assumptions, methodological frameworks, and mathematical formulas, but also on human error and inadequate conclusions as a result of this wealth of data. However, examples of the use of artificial intelligence (further – AI) in economic research show that some of these problems can be partially resolved. AI allows researchers to use much larger amounts of data and find hidden connections; this improves the speed and accuracy of research (Zieba et al, 2016), and allows us to find the answer to the question "which." Although AI, or more specifically machine learning, is already applied in various economic areas, for example marketing, production, finance, and bankruptcy, it has been applied only episodically in the context of the analysis of economic development.

Sophisticated economic analysis requires innovative insights and theories. There is much need for a new economic compass, providing information about the economic development of countries in the context of the 4th industrial revolution (World Economic Forum, 2019). Taking the above into consideration, the purpose of this chapter is to investigate theoretically the issues and challenges of using quantum theory and AI in the analysis of economic development and goal seeking, thereby closing the gap in analysis of the connection of these concepts in the literature.

The main means of answering the question "which is the best" in the discipline of political economy is to formulate a methodological approach that would align with modern global challenges and issues in contemporary economic development against a theoretical background and undertaking empirical analysis.

The method of the research involves systematic, comparative, and logical analysis of the scientific literature based on comparison, classification, systematisation, and generalisation.

LITERATURE REVIEW

Economic development theories are applied to various socio-economic systems: countries, groups of countries, regions, and cities. The socio-economic system is defined as a complex system that consists of social, economic, environmental, cultural, political, and technological elements, and the relationships between them and other systems. Due to their intricacy and complexity, modern socio-economic systems are dynamic, in continual development (Ginevicius et al, 2018), vital, sensitive, and responsive to various shocks. They have creative and constructive structures. More socio-economic systems are engaged in industrial and commercial development. They are not homogenous, and nor do they display similar features; each system is unique. Dulupçu and Okçu (2000) stressed that developing countries act in a dynamic, chaotic, and unstable environment; economic and other myriad determinants affect them, and processes, relationships, and interactions are important. Economic development is a form of performance improvement, which is facilitated by reliance on process rather than economic structure and economic goals (Dulupçu & Okçu, 2000). An advanced society is an economically highly developed informational society (Akulich & Kaźmierczyk, 2018).

Another distinctive feature of socio-economic systems is that subjects as never before learn not only individually but also from each other. They monitor the behaviour of others, and this promotes the availability and transmission of the necessary information through technology, highlighting the importance of information and communication technologies (ICT), innovation and technological progress, networking, and network learning. The 4th industrial revolution is changing the economic development paths of countries. The modernisation of economic development is characterised also by social responsibility, environmental friendliness, and climate change (de Jong et al, 2015; Gazzola et al, 2019; Martin et al, 2018, 2019). The transition to low carbon economies is now a reality. Davies and Mullin (2011) recognised that economic development might encourage the reduction of carbon dioxide emissions in industry, and they suggested investing in clean economies.

The other feature of modern economic development is connected with the growing divergence in living standards, income, and economic welfare of various countries. The 20th century was characterised broadly by a divergence between high-income countries and the developing world, with only a limited number (less than 10% of economies) managing to progress from lower or middle-income to high-income status. The global economy is dominated by a few industrialised economies, and most of these had become industrialised either as leaders or earlier followers of the 19th century industrial revolution (Lin & Rosenblatt, 2012). Their main features and conditions might be treated as challenges for many countries, so improvement in strategies of economic development is needed.

The various theories of economic development are used to explain how socio-economic systems develop. These theories are dynamic, constantly changing over time. Economic development was initially analysed using Keynesian and neo-Keynesian economic growth theories (using, e.g., the Keynesian, Domar, and Harod economic growth models) and neoclassical economic growth theory (using, e.g., the Solow economic growth model). The main works on economic growth were written in the 20th century by Schumpeter, Lewis, Kuznets, Rostow, Romer, Lucas, and others, and comprised the endogenous or new growth theories.

Various theories identify and explain different determinants of economic development. The new growth theories stressed that it was not isolated but combined determinants that encouraged economic development. In a changing environment, the success of economic development is increasingly determined not by static determinants and resources, but by dynamic capacities. These imply the ability to cope with a rapidly changing environment. They show an economy's capacity to achieve new and innovative forms of development and competitive advantage (Harmaakorpi, 2006; Pihkala et al, 2007). Technological progress; Industry 4.0; ICT; innovations (Galperina et al, 2016; Martin, 2019, 2018); human capital and entrepreneurship (Caseiro & Coelho, 2018; Korez-Vide & Tominc, 2016); learning (Edwards et al, 2014; Florida 2013); networking (Bakici et al, 2013; Kickbusch & Gleicher, 2014); smartness (Kumar, 2017); social responsibility and sustainability (Gazzola et al, 2019); and agility and intelligence (Jucevicius & Juceviciene, 2015) came to be regarded as modern determinants in economic development. Recently, researchers have re-emphasised the importance of the economic environment (Athukorala, 2014; Escosura, 2005) and governance efficiency (Anttiroiko et al, 2013; Bakici et al, 2013). Ten years after the 2008 financial crisis, monetary policies began to run out of steam, and so now it is crucial that economies rely on fiscal policy, structural reforms, and public incentives to allocate more resources to the full range of determinants of productivity to leverage fully the new opportunities presented by the 4th industrial revolution (WEF, 2019). The fiscal elements in a development context tend to show a significant correlation with public debt and inflation in less developed countries (Da Veiga et al, 2016). This implies that government intervention in the economic environment has a close relationship with development. Sachs (2000), quoting Smith (1776), identified national policies, geopolitics, and physical geography as the three determinants that would lead to divergent outcomes. Varga (2017) argued that properly designed place-based policies are an appropriate means of economic development, and recognised the importance of geographic determinants. Resource endowments, industry structure, spatial concentration of firms and centripetal forces, population growth, and other determinants also cause countries to experience very different levels of economic development (Gries et al, 2018; Sachs, 2000; Ström & Wahlqvist, 2009; Varga 2017).

Success in economic development cannot be seen just in terms of growth (Soejoto et al., 2016). A holistic approach is needed (Capello & Perucca, 2015; Dell'Anno & Amendola, 2015) to analyse more deeply the development process in combination with conditions and their extensive connections and to explain the causality of different determinants (i.e., human capital, research and development, knowledge, and so on). As economies face modern development challenges, determination and evaluation of the causality effect becomes progressively problematic (Artelaris et al, 2011; Dotti & Spithoven, 2017; Kim, 2017, 2014). Various theories and approaches for the analysis of economic development are employed by researchers (see Table 1).

The theoretical framework of the economic development changes over the years. The classical approach is built on the bases of Keynesian, Neo-Keynesian Economic Growth Theories (Keynesian, Domar and Harod Economic Growth Models) and Neoclassical Economic Growth Theory (Solow Economic Growth Model), which use several determinants such as income, growth, fiscal elements, etc. The main works of modern economic development approach are from the twentieth century: Schumpeter, Lewis, Kuznets, Rostow, Romer, Lucas and others (the endogenous or new growth theory). The modern economic development approach stress that not isolated but combined determinants encourage economic development. In a changing environment, the success of economic development is increasingly determined not by static determinants and resources, but by dynamic capacities (Pihkala et al, 2007; Harmaakorpi, 2006). The modern economic development approach covers the set of indicators, such as knowledge-based, social, urbanization, technological, innovative determinants, which cause more sophisticated analysis of economic development by explanation of the diverse effect comparing development among the countries. Despite the variety of determinants of modern economic development, the technological progress and innovations (Martin, 2019, 2018, Galperina et al, 2016) are set as the key elements, because the differences in causal effects of economic development depend on the technological development (Gries et al, 2017). The determinants of modern economic development stress also geographical aspects. The geographical determinants allow us not only to identify differences in geographical areas but also to identify space-neutral and place-based areas (Varga, 2017).

Economic development is not replicated from country to country. It requires not only certain determinants and indicators, flows (economic, information, traffic, financial, social, and so on) and network analysis, but also methodological approaches and theories, allowing the socio-economic system to be viewed as a unique, but complex entity. The philosophical focus of research should combine universal rules, specific cases, practical advice, and more pluralistic microeconomic approaches.

Table 1. Economic development theories and approaches, methodologies, research fields, and researchers

Theories and approaches	Methodology of economic development	Research field	Researchers
The spatial distribution of framework programmes	Research and development – driven by economic development and growth, the competitiveness effect is being reached through regional specialisation effects	Specialisation and spatial determinants	Dotti & Spithoven, 2017
Patterns of economic development	Economic growth variables and quality of life variables – the structure of economic development is being evaluated from a various set of socio-economic indicators	Knowledge-, free trade-, savings-, and ethnic-based, and religiously-influenced patterns	Kim, 2017
The role of human capital on economic development	Human capital – regional human capital difference in different economic phases and its collinearity effects with GDP and physical capital	Divergent growth and trade	Li et al, 2016
Regional growth model	Economic growth – defined by a model constructed from: a set of dummies representing the taxonomy of regions defined on their degree of openness to globalisation; high education; patents; share of urban population; social capital; GDP per capita	Knowledge and economy accumulation	Capello & Perucca, 2015
The relationship between the index of social exclusion and economic growth	Economic growth – defined by model constructed from: lagged economic growth; social exclusion index; economic recession dummy; trade openness index	Social integration	Dell'Anno & Amendola, 2015
Trends of intra-regional foreign direct investment	Foreign direct investment – as a result of economic development and integration is evaluated with criterial analysis by exchange indicators, import restriction indicators; logistics performance index and doing business index	Production, trade, intra-regional foreign direct investment	Athukorala, 2014
The inverse domino effect	Subsidies and taxes – effects of competition and labour mobility; economic reforms – causality domestic effect or international competition and related countries	Comparative advantage and interaction	Gassebner et al, 2011
Convergence	Economic dynamism indicators (EDI) – a valuation tool based on various economic development elements	Economic performance growth	Artelaris et al, 2011

RESEARCH METHODOLOGY

For the identification of methodological insights which might have been taken into account when analysing modern economic development, the meta analysis was used. The sources include high ranked peer-reviewed papers in the economic development area and more noticeably publishing papers on the practical use of AI in economic researches. A systematic search of the following electronic databases was done: Scopus, Ebsco, ISI Web of Science, Sage, Emerald, Elsevier, Wiley Online Library and Science Direct. The Global Competitiveness Report of World Economic Forum was also included to the reference list. The books related to issues were also included. No specific time period has been mentioned, but the main focus was on the period from 2010 till 2019. The issues of interest cover keywords: economic development patterns, artificial intelligence, quantum theory, socio-economic system, modern, smartness, economic development approaches and theories, technological progress, fourth industrial revolution, competences. For the analysis of economic development area, many terms like 'determinants', 'factors', 'enablers', 'critical success factors' and 'focus areas' are synonymously used. For the analysis of the use of artificial intelligence in economic development area, terms like 'artificial intelligence', 'machine learning', 'neuron networks' are combined to the one term 'artificial intelligence'.

The meta analysis of scientific literature was done on the basis of these approaches:

1. Holistic approach, representing the interaction among various inside and outside determinants of development.
2. Uniqueness approach, representing the socio-economic system as a unique unit with a self-development process.
3. Sustainable approach, representing continuance, harmony with external environments and general (generally agreed) approaches, and social responsibility in economic development.
4. Spatial approach, representing the relationship of development determinants in spatial context.
5. Dynamic approach, representing the time impact and infiniteness of economic development.

The features of modern economic development justify the selection of the identified approaches:

1. Economic development meets the effects of various economic, social, environmental, political, and technological shocks, the challenges of the 4th Industrial Revolution, the transition to low carbon economies, and so on. Modern economic development has a relationship with common economic trends and approaches (such as holistic and sustainable approaches).
2. Economic development is not identical. Countries behave on the one hand independently (self-developmental and unique), and on the other hand interconnected. The economies of countries under globalisation and digitalisation are very open and they are more transparent and interconnected, so the relationships between countries are starting to have a very important effect on theirs development. So, the relationship between development determinants is gaining in importance, that is, the relationship between the inside development determinants and outside determinants (uniqueness, holistic approach).
3. The determinants of current economic development are affected by those of earlier periods, and they have an impact on future change. Thus, the effects at different periods are gaining increasing importance (dynamic approach) in future development.
4. The use of quantitative indicators narrows the features of economic development, eliminating qualitative aspects. Thus, the combination of quantitative and qualitative determinants in the spatial context is gaining increasing importance (the spatial approach).

For the identification of methodological insights, the meta analysis was additionally supplemented by heterodox theories, namely institutional and ecological. The focus on institutional aspects, fiscal policy, structural reforms, and public incentives has increased, and monetary policies decreased. Despite the fact that there are no inherent trade-offs between building competitiveness, creating more equitable societies, and transitioning to environmentally sustainable systems (World Economic Forum, 2019), the need to move to low carbon economies requires the analysis of economic development in the context of environmentally friendly and sustainable approaches.

Not every article addressed the issue of interest. Thus, the authors independently evaluated the 143 articles and a restricted sample of the 88 more relevant articles was obtained and subjected to full analysis.

Table 2. Quantum theory compatibility with approaches towards the analysis of economic development

Approaches	Basics of quantum theory
Holistic approach	Quantum theory analyses responsiveness motion
Uniqueness approach	Quantum theory analyses emerging fluctuations and adaptation to them (self-development) The subjects of the quantum universe have self-creating capacities
Sustainable approach	The quantum universe is a participatory universe
Spatial approach	Whole parts are interrelated in very fundamental ways. Quantum theory analyses connections between things that count, not things themselves
Holistic approach	Quantum theory analyses responsiveness motion

63 articles have been selected after the search and consideration of relevance. The systematic, comparative and logical analysis of the scientific literature based on the methods of comparison, classification, systematization and generalization were used.

FINDINGS

The specifics of modern economic development requires the new methodological insights into its analysis. The meta analysis of scientific literature showed that the combination of quantum theory and AI is a novel approach for a profound analysis of socio-economic systems' development.

For an analysis of the philosophy of quantum theory we refer to David (2018), Haven et al (2017), Wendt (2017), Dulupçu and Okçu (2000). The idea is to view the process of economic development from a physical point of view and to treat socio-economic systems like electrons, which routinely jump from one orbit to another and spontaneously disappear from one reality and appear in another. This mean that socio-economic systems affect and are affected by others, and they can make various political, economic, or geographic unions. Quantum theory does not describe the world as one of certainty. The changes and transformations of socio-economic systems of and among themselves are important, and no one cannot know exactly all their properties. Energy is transferred or transformed (at an atomic scale) discontinuously in an indeterministic way. Quantum theory suggests the analysis of the economic development of socio-economic systems only through their interactions. This mean that various type of cooperation among socio-economic systems are increasingly important and continuous. Quantum theory stresses that all socio-economic systems have unique features and self-organising and self-developing capacities. This means that they have the ability to learn, adapt, and create, and that this ability is nourished by information.

Table 2 presents the basic concepts of quantum theory, which are shown to be compatible with ideas regarding modern economic development.

The limitation of using quantum theory in the analysis of economic development might be identified in the fact that quantum theory relies on informal processes. The priorities of socio-economic systems, which are less identified by numerical values or indicators, are neglected.

Quantum theory is a new subject in economics and even social science, and it is still at a high level of abstraction, offering little in the way of contributing to current development practices or methodological insights (see table 3). However, it is compatible with the analysis of economic development. Theoretical insights undoubtedly require empirical affirmations, and this could be an area for future research. There are only few economics-related articles that refer to quantum theory (Sobey, 2012; Svirina et al, 2014). Svirina et al (2014) used quantum principles for the analysis of economic development through the stages of the business cycle; Sobey (2012) used them to create a quantum economic development model. These researchers concluded that these principles should be implemented to evaluate socio-economic performance. Although papers on quantum theory applications in the analysis of economic development have not been discovered, the aforementioned articles confirm the possible use of this theory in economic analysis.

Despite the fact that the complex algorithms of AI (or more specifically one of its branches – machine learning) mean that it is applied less frequently than various linear regression models, it is easy to imagine that the situation will soon change, and its use in economic modelling will no longer be the "future" but the present. This methodological change in economic analysis will be due to its increasing use in a range of disciplines and its practical deployment (Cockburn et al, 2018; Makridakis, 2018; Vafeiadis et al, 2015; Van Gerven & Bohte, 2017). There follows a list of benefits it provides:

1. Faster and more accurate answers compared with the methods currently used.
2. A solution to more sophisticated challenges, because it can handle very large quantities of indicators. This makes it directly compatible with a holistic approach.
3. Modelling of dynamic indicators, because algorithms can adapt to newly submitted data and can be retrained. This makes it directly compatible with a dynamic approach.
4. Possibilities of prediction and modelling values of indicators. This makes it directly compatible with a sustainable approach.
5. Possibilities for the analysis of individual countries and comparison with others. This makes it directly compatible with a uniqueness approach.

Potential limitations of the use of AI in economic analysis include the following:

1. Lack of data. Any AI methods are dependent on data; therefore, the accessibility of data, especially the latest data, is a crucial factor.
2. Some methods of AI, such as machine learning with a teacher, require the prior dissemination of training data to classes, and expert judgement is required (i.e., the expert must determine which class includes the observed observations). Incorrect expert judgements can lead to faulty model development, improper use of the models, and dubious conclusions.
3. Not all AI algorithms, such as in artificial neural networks, provide the results of variable interactions. Artificial neural networks use various combinations of indicators that are not known to the user when economic development is being analysed. For this reason, the possibility of interpreting interactions between indicators is forfeited.
4. AI methods use a considerable amount of computer resources and are time consuming, and thus they are not always useable.

Table 3 presents the compatibility of AI, namely machine learning, with economic analysis.

Limitations of the use of AI in the analysis of economic development might be identified principally as indeterminism and uncertainty. Indeterminism refers to the fact that in machine learning results are obtained through learning rather than knowing. Machine learning eliminates prior knowledge and values

Table 3. Compatibility of AI with approaches to the analysis of economic development

Approaches	Features of the use of AI
Holistic approach	Machine learning can explore many different indicators and build models using them.
Uniqueness approach	Machine learning algorithms learn from previous periods and look for rules that could create a model that describes relationships between variables. In one study, if the relationship is not found using other data, the algorithms are usually re-trained.
Sustainable approach	In machine learning, data is viewed as a set of operations that run for several periods.
Spatial approach	Machine learning algorithms make it possible to assess the impact of different determinants (through coefficients of heterogeneous weight) on different determinants at different times.
Dynamic approach	Machine learning can analyse a plurality of indicators of different times and create models using them.

(as does quantum theory) and, without pre-defined rules, searches them for model development and the characterisation of relationships between variables. Although indeterminism in the analysis of economic development might be treated as an advantage, the incorporation of qualitative understanding into a quantitative body of knowledge will be a challenge for future researchers. The other limitation regards the uncertainty principle. One of the methods of machine learning, in the case of neural networks, in the "black box," in which many different kinds of calculations, assessments of interactions, and so on, are performed, but after obtaining final results it can still be unclear how the model uses the data and how it performed inside the algorithm. Despite the fact that uncertainty principle limits exact knowledge, it is compatible with the economic development modelling principle: no one can know exactly all the properties of a system.

SOLUTIONS AND RECOMMENDATIONS

The meta analysis of scientific literature proved that the integration of quantum theory and AI is compatible with the analysis of modern economic development. However, the competences of the researcher play the crucial role for the application of this new approach in the economic analysis and interpretation of research results (Bruneckiene et al, 2019).

Thus, working in the context of rationality, self-control, and well-defined preferences, AI seeks and finds a solution that is very likely to be rational. But we should not forget the values, social connections, emotions, and other emotional intelligence competences of the user of the results and the interpreter of the findings. Research (Goleman, 2009) has shown that that emotional intelligence helps to solve complex problems effectively that can barely be solved even by robots; it also allows particular issues to be examined from different viewpoints and for multicultural teams to interact and co-operate. It enables people to think independently and critically, and to persuasively communicate and represent. Empirical research (Bruneckiene et al, 2019) enables the identification of the soft competences that are required for work with AI (see Table 4).

Table 4. Competences needed for working with AI in the analysis of economic development

Approaches	Competences	Features of the Competence
For all approaches	Innovativeness	This competence helps to identify and use new and effective approaches and techniques in the process of economic development analysis.
	Learning	This competence helps to ensure continuous improvement of the process and results of economic development analysis by accumulating information, knowledge, and experience, and by being able to use them.
	Curiosity and knowledge-driven	This competence helps to ground economic development analysis in scientific knowledge and re-thinking best practices.
Holistic approach	Intelligence	This competence helps to assess adequately processes and trends in the external environment of the object/concept analysed.
	Networked	This competence helps to create co-operative community culture by obtaining information and various resources, maintaining relations with other participants in the process, and sharing research results.
	Digital	This competence helps to make the economic development analysis process effective, more accurate, and faster.
Uniqueness and spatial approaches	Creativity	This competence helps the researcher to see the socio-economic system differently, and at the same time accurately, to create unique strategies for achieving ambitious developmental goals and for socio-economic systems to be effective.
Sustainable approach	Sustainability	This competence helps to reconcile environmental, economic, and socio-cultural determinants without posing a threat to the future.
	Social responsibility	This competence helps to identify and expand the connections between societal and economic progress, employing the philosophy of shared value creation.
Dynamic approach	Agility	This competence helps to foresee new changes or needs quickly, and make decisions and respond to new opportunities and threats in a timely manner.

CONCLUSION

The features of modern economic development and the challenges these present require new ways of thinking, theories, approaches, and methodological tools in their analysis. These features are learning, digitality, innovation, the desire for knowledge, sustainability, social responsibility, and networking, and they combine in different ways to make every socio-economic system unique. The process of development is continual and self-developmental. Socio-economic systems develop in a dynamic, unstable, open, and influencing environment. Modern economic development presents more complex, dynamic, self- and interrelated processes that require deeper explanations of causal effects and interactions, and these will vary between countries.

The analysis of economic development can involve a number of approaches: holistic, uniqueness, sustainable, spatial, and dynamic. The features of modern socio-economic systems, their development and the concomitant challenges, quantum theory, and the possibilities of AI are mutually compatible, and could be combined for the purpose of analysis. The use of AI requires professional and technological knowledge and emotional intelligence, and empirical analysis allows the identification of the required soft competences: creativity, intelligence, agility, networking, sustainability, social responsibility, innovativeness, digitality, learning, curiosity, and being knowledge-driven.

FUTURE RESEARCH DIRECTIONS

The insights from empirical research will clarify and supplement the theoretical discussions and methodological approaches presented in this article. There are a number of future research opportunities in this novel area of economic development analysis. It would be worthwhile carrying out further in-depth empirical analyses of features economic development using large samples from the most competitive (according to the WEF index) countries. Furthermore, detailed case studies could be undertaken using content analyses of strategic competitive policies and their interactions with economic development to gather a broader range of insight. Another possibility could be the integration of the smartness concept with economic development analysis.

ACKNOWLEDGMENT

This research was supported by the Research, Development and Innovation Fund of Kaunas University of Technology (project grant No. PP-91R/19).

REFERENCES

Akulich, M., & Kaźmierczyk, J. (2018). The socio-economic approach to the study of modern economic systems. Post-capitalism. Part 2. *Management, 22*(2), 299–310. doi:10.2478/manment-2018-0038

Anttiroiko, A. V., Valkama, P., & Bailey, S. J. (2013). Smart Cities in the New Service Economy: Building Platforms for Smart Services. *AI & Society, 29*(3), 323–334. doi:10.100700146-013-0464-0

Artelaris, P., Arvanitidis, P. A., & Petrakos, G. (2011). Convergence patterns in the world economy: Exploring the nonlinearity hypothesis. *Journal of Economic Studies (Glasgow, Scotland), 38*(3), 236–252. doi:10.1108/01443581111152373

Athukorala, P. (2014). Intra-regional FDI and Economic Integration in South Asia: Trends, Patterns and Prospects. *South Asia Economic Journal, 15*(1), 1–35. doi:10.1177/1391561414525710

Bakici, T., Almirall, E., & Wareham, J. (2013). A Smart City Initiative: The Case of Barcelona. *Journal of the Knowledge Economy, 4*(2), 135–148. doi:10.100713132-012-0084-9

Bruneckienė, J., Jucevicius, R., Zykienė, I., Rapsikevičius, J., & Lukauskas, M. (2019). Assessment of investment attractiveness in European countries by artificial neural networks: What competences are needed to make a decision on collective well-being? *Sustainability, 11*(24), 1–23. doi:10.3390u11246892

Capello, R., & Perucca, G. (2014). Openness to Globalization and Regional Growth Patterns in CEE Countries: From the EU Accession to the Economic Crisis. *Journal of Common Market Studies, 53*(2), 218–236. doi:10.1111/jcms.12157

Caseiro, N., & Coelho, A. (2018). Business intelligence and competitiveness: The mediating role of entrepreneurial orientation. *Competitiveness Review*, *28*(2), 213–226. doi:10.1108/CR-09-2016-0054

Chen, M., Zhang, H., Weidong, L., & Zhang, W. (2014). The Global Pattern of Urbanization and Economic Growth: Evidence from the Last Three Decades. *PLoS One*, *9*(8), e103799. doi:10.1371/journal.pone.0103799 PMID:25099392

Cockburn, I. M., Henderson, R., & Stern, S. (2018). *The impact of artificial intelligence on innovation* (NBER Working paper No. w24449). Retrieved from National Bureau of Economic Research website: https://www.nber.org/chapters/c14006

Da Veiga, J. A. L., Ferreira-Lopes, A., & Sequeira, T. N. (2015). Public Debt, Economic Growth and Inflation in African Economies. *The South African Journal of Economics*, *84*(2), 294–322. doi:10.1111aje.12104

Davies, A. R., & Mullin, S. J. (2011). Greening the economy: Interrogating sustainability innovations beyond the mainstream. *Journal of Economic Geography*, *11*(5), 793–816. doi:10.1093/jeg/lbq050

De Jong, M., Joss, S., Schraven, D., Zhan, C., & Weijnen, M. (2015). Sustainable-smart-resilient-low carbon-eco-knowledge cities; making sense of a multitude of concepts promoting sustainable urbanisation. *Journal of Cleaner Production*, *109*, 25–38. doi:10.1016/j.jclepro.2015.02.004

Dell'Anno, R., & Amendola, A. (2015). Social Exclusion and Economic Growth: An Empirical Investigation in European Economies. *Review of Income and Wealth*, *61*(2), 274–301. doi:10.1111/roiw.12096

Dotti, N. F., & Spithoven, A. (2017). Economic drivers and specialization patterns in the spatial distribution of Framework Programme's participation. *Journal of Regional Science*, *97*(4), 863–882. doi:10.1111/pirs.12299

Dulupçu, M. A., & Okçu, M. (2000). Towards quantum economic development: transcending boundaries. *Ankara Üniversitesi SBF Dergisi*. Retrieved from http://dergiler.ankara.edu.tr/dergiler/42/475/5477.pdf

Edwards, R., Raggatt, P., & Small, N. (Eds.). (2014). *The Learning Society: Trends and Issues*. Routledge.

Escosura, L. P. (2005). *Gerschenkron revisited. European patterns of development in historical perspective* (Working Paper 05-79 (10) Dpto de Historia Económica e Instituciones, Economic History and Institutions Series 10, Universidad Carlos III de Madrid, December 2005). Retrieved from https://econpapers.repec.org/paper/ctewhrepe/wh057910.htm

Florida, R. (2013). The learning region. In Z. J. Acs (Ed.), *Regional innovation, knowledge, and global change* (2nd ed.). Routledge.

Galperina, L. P., Girenko, A. T., & Mazurenko, V. P. (2016). The Concept of Smart Economy as the Basis for Sustainable Development of Ukraine. *International Journal of Economics and Financial Issues*, *6*, 307–314.

Gassebner, M., Gaston, N., & Lamla, M. J. (2011). The inverse domino effect: Are economic reforms contagious? *International Economic Review*, *52*(1), 183–200. doi:10.1111/j.1468-2354.2010.00624.x

Gazzola, P., Gonzalez Del Campo, A., & Onyango, V. (2019). Going green vs going smart for sustainable development: Quo vadis? *Journal of Cleaner Production*, *214*, 881–892. doi:10.1016/j.jclepro.2018.12.234

Ginevicius, R., Gedvilaite, D., Stasiukynas, A., & Sliogeriene, J. (2018). Quantitative Assessment of the Dynamics of the Economic Development of Socioeconomic Systems Based on the MDD Method. *The Engineering Economist*, *29*(3), 264–271. doi:10.5755/j01.ee.29.3.20444

Goleman, D. (2007). *Emotional Intelligence:Why It Can Matter More Than IQ*. Bantam Book.

Gries, T., Grundmann, R., Palnau, I., & Redlin, M. (2018). Technology diffusion, international integration and participation in developing economies - a review of major concepts and findings. *International Economics and Economic Policy*, *15*(1), 215–253. doi:10.100710368-017-0373-7

Harmaakorpi, V. (2006). Regional Development Platform Method (RDPM) as a Tool for Regional Innovation Policy. *European Planning Studies*, *14*(8), 1085–1114. doi:10.1080/09654310600852399

Haven, E., Khrennikov, A., & Robinson, T. (2017). *Quantum Methods in Social Science: A First Course*. World Scientific Publishing Co. Pte. Ltd. Retrieved from: https://EconPapers.repec.org/RePEc:wsi:wsbook:q0080

Jucevicius, R., & Juceviciene, P. (2015). Smart social system. In International practices of smart development (pp. 24-36). Frankfurt am Main: Peter Lang.

Kickbusch, I., & Gleicher, D. (2014). Smart Governance for Health. In I. Kickbusch & D. Gleicher (Eds.), *Smart Governance for Health and Well-being: The Evidence*. World Health Organizations.

Kim, H. S. (2014). Patterns of Economic Development in the World. *Journal of Global Economics*, *2*(2), 113. doi:10.4172/2375-4389.1000113

Kim, H. S. (2017). Patterns of Economic Development: Correlations Affecting Economic Growth and Quality of Life in 222 Countries. *Politics & Policy*, *45*(1), 83–104. doi:10.1111/polp.12190

Korez-Vide, R., & Tominc, P. (2016). Competitiveness, Entrepreneurship and Economic Growth. In *Competitiveness of CEE Economies and Businesses*. Springer. doi:10.1007/978-3-319-39654-5_2

Kumar, T. M. (Ed.). (2017). Smart Economy in Smart Cities. International Collaborative Research. doi:10.1007/978-981-10-1610-3

Leimbach, M., Kriegler, E., Roming, N., & Schwanitz, J. (2017). Future growth patterns of world regions – A GDP scenario approach. *Global Environmental Change*, *42*, 215–225. doi:10.1016/j.gloenvcha.2015.02.005

Li, H., He, J., Liu, Q., Fraumeni, B. M., & Zheng, X. (2016). *Regional Distribution and Dynamics of Human Capital in China 1985-2014: Education, Urbanization, and Aging of the Population* (NBER Working Paper No. 22906). Retrieved from https://www.nber.org/papers/w22906

Lin, J., & Rosenblatt, D. (2012). Shifting patterns of economic growth and rethinking development. *Journal of Economic Policy Reform*, *15*(3), 1–24. doi:10.1080/17487870.2012.700565

Makridakis, S. (2018). Forecasting the Impact of Artificial Intelligence, Part 3 of 4: The Potential Effects of AI on Businesses, Manufacturing, and Commerce. Foresight. *The International Journal of Applied Forecasting*, *49*, 18–27.

Martin, C., Evans, J., & Karvonen, A. (2018). Smart and sustainable? Five tensions in the visions and practices of the smart-sustainable city in Europe and North America. *Technological Forecasting and Social Change, 133*, 269–278. doi:10.1016/j.techfore.2018.01.005

Martin, C., Evans, J., Karvonenm, A., Paskaleva, K., Yang, D., & Linjordet, D. (2019). Smart-sustainability: A new urban fix? *Sustainable Cities and Society, 45*, 640–648. doi:10.1016/j.scs.2018.11.028

Orrel, D. (2018). *Quantum Economics: The New Science of Money*. Icon Books Ltd.

Pihkala, T., Harmaakorpi, V., & Pekkarinen, A. (2007). The role of Dynamic Capabilities and Social Capital in Breaking Socio – Institutional Inertia in Regional Development. *International Journal of Urban and Regional Research, 31*(4), 836–852. doi:10.1111/j.1468-2427.2007.00757.x

Sachs, J. D. (2000). Globalization and patterns of economic development. *Weltwirtschaftliches Archiv, 136*(4), 579–600. doi:10.1007/BF02707644

Sobey, C. (2012). *A Model of Quantum Economic Development* (MPRA Paper No. 36422). Retrieved from: https://mpra.ub.uni-muenchen.de/36422/

Soejoto, A., Fitrayati, D., Rachmawati, L., & Sholikhah, N. (2016). Typology of regional economic development pattern. *International Journal of Applied Business and Economic Research, 14*(13).

Ström, P., & Wahlqvist, E. (2010). Regional and Firm Competitiveness in the Service-Based Economy: Combining Economic Geography and International Business Theory. *Tijdschrift voor Economische en Sociale Geografie, 101*(3), 287–304. doi:10.1111/j.1467-9663.2009.00586.x

Svirina, A., Parfenova, E., & Shurkina, E. (2014). Evaluation of Uncertainty on the Stages of Business Cycle: Implementation of Quantum Principles. *Journal of Systemics, Cybernetics and Informatics, 12*(4), 79–85.

Vafeiadis, T., Diamantaras, K. I., Sarigiannidis, G., & Chatzisavvas, K. Ch. (2015). A comparison of machine learning techniques for customer churn prediction. *Simulation Modelling Practice and Theory, 55*, 1–9. doi:10.1016/j.simpat.2015.03.003

Van Gerven, M., & Bohte, S. (2017). Artificial Neural Networks as Models of Neural Information Processing Frontiers Research Topic. *Frontiers in Computational Neuroscience, 11*. Advance online publication. doi:10.3389/fncom.2017.00114 PMID:29311884

Varga, A. (2015). Place-based, Spatially Blind, or Both? Challenges in Estimating the Impacts of Modern Development Policies: The Case of the GMR Policy Impact Modeling Approach. *International Regional Science Review, 40*(1), 12–37. doi:10.1177/0160017615571587

WEF (World Economic Forum). (2019). *Global Competitiveness Report 2019: How to end a lost decade of productivity growth?* Retrieved from: https://www.weforum.org/reports/how-to-end-a-decade-of-lost-productivity-growth

Wendt, A. (2015). *Quantum Mind and Social Science: Unifying Physical and Social Ontology*. Cambridge University Press. doi:10.1017/CBO9781316005163

Zieba, M., Tomczak, S. K., & Tomczak, J. M. (2016). Ensemble boosted trees with synthetic features generation in application to bankruptcy prediction. *Expert Systems with Applications*, *58*, 93–101. doi:10.1016/j.eswa.2016.04.001

ADDITIONAL READING

Agrawal, A., Gans, J., & Goldfarb, A. (2018). Economic Policy for Artificial Intelligence. NBER Chapters. *Innovation Policy and the Economy*, *19*, 139–159. doi:10.1086/699935

Allam, Z., & Dhunny, Z. A. (2019). On big data, artificial intelligence and smart cities. *Cities (London, England)*, *89*, 80–91. doi:10.1016/j.cities.2019.01.032

Deloitte, A. G. (2017). *What key competencies are needed in the digital age? The impact of automation on employees, companies and education.* Retrieved from: https://www2.deloitte.com/content/dam/Deloitte/ch/Documents/innovation/ch-en-innovation-automation-competencies.pdf

Dwivedi, Y. K., Hughes, L., Ismagilova, E., Aarts, G., Coombs, C. R., Crick, T., Duan, Y., Dwivedi, R., Edwards, J. S., Eirug, A., Galanos, V., Ilavarasan, P. V., Janssen, M., Jones, P., Kar, A. K., Kizgin, H., Kronemann, B., Lal, B., Lucini, B., ... Williams, M. D. (2019). Artificial Intelligence (AI): Multidisciplinary Perspectives on Emerging Challenges, Opportunities, and Agenda for Research, Practice and Policy. [Available online]. *International Journal of Information Management*, 101994. Advance online publication. doi:10.1016/j.ijinfomgt.2019.08.002

Filippov, V., Chursin, A., Ragulina, J. V., & Popkova, E. G. (Eds.). (2019). *The Cyber Economy: Opportunities and Challenges for Artificial Intelligence in the Digital Workplace.* Springer International Publishing., doi:10.1007/978-3-030-31566-5

Karsten, S. G. (1990). Quantum Theory and Social Economics: The Holistic Approach of Modem Physics Serves Better Than Newton's Mechanics in Approaching Reality. *American Journal of Economics and Sociology*, *49*(4), 385–502. doi:10.1111/j.1536-7150.1990.tb02461.x

OECD. (2018). *Future of Education and Skills 2030: Conceptual Learning Framework Education and AI: preparing for the future & AI, Attitudes and Values.* Retrieved from: http://www.oecd.org/education/2030/Education-and-AI-preparing-for-the-future-AI-Attitudes-and-Values.pdf

Taylor, R. D. (2020). Quantum Artificial Intelligence: A "precautionary" U.S. approach? *Telecommunications Policy*, 101909. Advance online publication. doi:10.1016/j.telpol.2020.101909

KEY TERMS AND DEFINITIONS

Competence: The ability to do something well.

Dynamic Approach: An approach which represent the permanent process of economic development.

Economic Development: A process by which the economic well-being and quality of life of a socio-economic system is improved.

Holistic Approach: An approach which concern the socio-economic system as a whole rather than separate parts of it and the interactions among various socio-economic systems.

Modern Socio-Economic System: Dynamic and in a continual development, vital, sensitive and responsive to various shocks, having creative and constructive structures and acting in a dynamic, chaotic and unstable environment.

Quantum Theory: The theoretical basis of modern physics that explains the nature and behavior of matter and energy on the atomic and subatomic level.

Socio-Economic System: A complex system that consists of social, economic, environmental, cultural, political, technological elements and relationship among them and with other systems.

Spatial Approach: An approach which represent the interaction of economic development determinants with spatial context.

Sustainable Approach: An approach which represent the compatibility among environmental, economic, and sociocultural determinants without posing a threat to the future.

Uniqueness Approach: An approach which represent the socio-economic system as a unique unit with self-development process.

Chapter 3
Information Technology/ Information Systems Adoption in Developing and Transitioning Economies

Ernest Etim

Cape Peninsula University of Technology, South Africa

ABSTRACT

This chapter presents a descriptive and critical overview of IT/IS adoption theories/models in developed economies. The theories examined include task technology fit (TTF), technology readiness index (TRI), technology acceptance model (TAM and TAM2), self-efficacy theory (SET), and unified theory of acceptance and use of technology (UTAUT) together with their appropriateness to developed countries/ economies. Furthermore, an extensive look at limitations of both TAM and UTAUT (widely utilized) models as applicable to digital/mobile technologies is emphasized. The critical analysis provided thus far did reveal that none of these (IT/IS) models/theories individually are powerful enough to appropriately assess all the complex constructs embedded in the study of mobile technology adoption in developing countries. The contextual nature of individual differences in developing countries together with all cultural and country indicators (ICT infrastructure, internet penetration) would have to be integrated into any developed theory for meaningful analysis to be achieved.

INTRODUCTION

Over the years, technology adoption has evolved both at the macro and micro levels which has enabled it to feature prominently in business activities. These days it would be unthinkable for businesses to thrive without adoption and integration of intelligently managed business processes which help drive their efficiencies and competitiveness. The dynamism seen in business environments are solely driven by the rapid innovations and technologies as well as a greater demand from customers. They are becoming more interconnected in the decision-making of what to purchase and where or from whom to

DOI: 10.4018/978-1-7998-3468-7.ch003

buy. Broadly, technology adoption represents acceptance, integration, and use of new technology. Carr (1999) posits that technology adoption signifies stages of selecting a technology for use by an individual or organization. Thus, technology adoption is a process where the user initially is aware of technology, then embraces it, and finally decides to utilize it for a number of activities. An individual who has embraced technology is likely to innovatively use it and cannot envisage life without it. On the other hand, technology acceptance (comparatively to technology adoption) has more to do with attitude towards a technology influenced by competing factors. One can purchase a technology and not adopt it. This is where acceptance plays a crucial role. It is antecedent to adoption.

Technically, technology adoption theoretically signifies the acceptance, integration and utilization of new technology/innovation. Technology adoption lifecycle is a model in sociology used to descriptively explain adoption/ acceptance of new products or innovations as a function of demographic and psychological characteristics of defined adopter groups. The relevance of demographic, psychological, and sociological variables per the user group is responsible for the disparity in adoption behaviour. This is more pertinent when one considers that mobile services have become an integral part of human activities. In developing economies, mobile banking, e-commerce, e-government, e-learning, and m-healthcare form part of daily phenomena (Connor & Reilly, 2018; Kapoor et al., 2015). Roger's Diffusion of Innovation Theory (1962), uses a classical normal distribution or "bell curve" to indicate the adopter groups as: innovators; early adopters; early majority; late majority; and laggards. Innovators (2.5%) the first to be innovative generally adopt innovation despite the higher risk (Figure 1). They are younger in age with higher social class, highly educated/skilled, have greater financial resources which provides the cushioning when newer technologies fail (Rogers, 1962:282). Early Adopters (13.5%) are the second largest adopters of technology, have highest opinion among adopter groups. These individuals are younger in age, with higher social class, advanced education, more acceptable to technology than late adopters. However, are more discrete in innovation choice than innovators, as well as being judicious in the adoption process (Rogers 1962:283). The early majority (34%) acquire technology after some considerable lapses in time. These individuals take longer to adopt technology than either innovators or early adopters, have above average social status, establish contacts with early adopters and are seldom opinionated leaders in systems (Rogers, 1962:283). Late majority (34%) are average adopters to the rest in the society, are sceptical to technology, have below average social status, limited financial resources, always in contact with early and late majority, also with limited opinion leadership. Laggards (16%) are the very last in innovation adoption. They exhibit little to none of opinionated leadership, are averse to change agents and are oldest in population. Are more traditionally centric, have lowest social status, lowest financial resources as well as tending to let social influences of close friends and family drive their decisions. They have little or no leadership opinion.

It is important to emphasis here that not all individuals are 'innovators' in all areas of their decision-making. On might be a technology innovator in the home (with Internet of Things [IoT]), but might not own a smartphone or belong to a social network. The social status of any individual to technology adoption runs through the bell shaped curved. The determining factor is the pain tolerance we are willing to absorb in the solution of problems which involves the use of technology.

Several authors have indicated that adoption of technology is not predicated solely by technology, but rather on highly complexed phenomena involving users' attitudes and personality (Venkatesh et al., 2012); social influence (Ajzen & Fishbein, 1975); trust (Gefen, et al., 2003); facilitating condition (Thompson, et al., 1991); optimism, innovativeness, discomfort and insecurity (Parasuraman & Colby, 2001). Thus, it is important to understand IT/IS models in relationship to past and future direction of innovation adoption research. Advantageously, these models have been applied to digital technology (adoption of cell/smart phones, the internet). These models can assess impact of digital technology on its industry, or for businesses tailored to software/digital technology development. The models can assist businesses discover customers' readiness or willingness to use this type technology.

This chapter uses a descriptive literature review to examine the evolution of research in technology adoption from two perspectives. The first objective is to provide a critical overview of existing models to enhance the research capabilities of future researchers or practitioners. The emphasis is placed because of the adaptability of these models to advanced economies where computerization has permeated every aspect of human endeavour. These models might not be applicable in transitioning/developing economies where the use of digital technology (cell or smart phones) have leapfrogged computers in business, work and life activities. The second objective is to suggest other research models which can play a pivotal role in research targeted at emerging economies. Thus:

- Provide a synthetic literature analysis of research on IT models for technology adoption
- Categorise theoretical adoption models of TTF, TAM, UTAUT, TAM2, TPB, DOI, TOE etc; and
- Suggest other research conceptual frameworks which might best be suitable to developing economies

ISSUES, CONTROVERSIES, PROBLEMS.

Researchers in information systems have been perplexed as to why certain individuals prefer one technological innovation over another (Davis, 1989; Venkatesh, Morris, Davis & Davis, 2003). In cognizance of the cost implications in the purchase of newer innovations for organizational and individuals' usage, understanding the rationale for technology adoption and continued use is paramount to the success of innovations created for the market. The fact that users do not accept technology translates into abandonment (McCarroll, 1981; Gillooly, 1998). Concerns about technology utilization range from Information Systems (DeLone & McLean, 1992) to HCI [human-computer-interaction] research (Nickerson, 1981; Mun, 2003; Carroll & Rosson, 1987). The continued reliance on technology for management of businesses which ultimately makes them more efficient and competitive together with the rapid pace of innovation, understanding factors which enhance or limit IS utilization continues to plague both researchers and practitioners. Several authors over the decades have advanced theoretical models such as technology acceptance model (TAM) (Davis, 1989; Davis et al., 1989); Theory of Planned Behaviour (TPB) (Ajzen, 1985; 1991), the expectation confirmation model, or Task Technology Fit (TTF) (Goodhue & Thompson, 1995). [See Lucas & Spitler, 1999 for an extensive review]. The TAM model despite its parsimonious nature is a more powerful tool for predicting and elucidating users' intentions and behaviour acceptance. Accordingly, users' behaviour and intentions fall under two important perspectives (1) conscious control uniquely portrayed in the TAM model; and (2) automated/controlled habitualized fashion which turns out to be a daily function performed by the user (Mun, 2003) as is the case in the continued utilization of digital technologies applicable in developing/transitioning economies. The theory of interpersonal behaviour [TIB] (Triandis, 1980) detailing behaviour in social psychology opines that affect and perceived consequences (as social constructs) moderate user intentions which indirectly impacts user's behaviour. Moreover, it details that habit and facilitating conditions impact behaviour. Mun (2003) is of the opinion that studies from Chang and Cheung (2001); Gagnon et al., (2003); Thompson et al., (1991;1994) using

(TIB) model on computer and internet usage, did not cover extensively the continued usage of information systems. This is important when one considers the usage of mobile technology in developing economies.

DIGITAL TELEPHONY IN DEVELOPING COUNTRIES

The argument is always valid for the use of complex technologies in assisting developing countries solve myriad problems of economic, human capital development and slowing down urbanization due to rapid migration from rural communities. But recent trend in technology has shown that simple innovations (e.g. mobile telephones) can be part of the mix (iThink, 2013). World Bank (2012) posits that "about three quarters of the world's population are privileged to the possession of a mobile phone in their lifetime." iThink (2013) emphases targeted sectors of health [covering service and quality; administration and management, and prevention—the thrust being local knowledge/content integrated into available tools as well as determination by governments to use mobile technologies to drive down costs and healthcare campaigns]. This became the M-Health policy programs for governments and NGOs, leading to institutionalized/ grass roots healthcare systems in rural communities, distanced from urban centres; (2) M-entrepreneurship [connectivity has impacted market access; transaction costs; and job creation/ opportunities]. Mobile technology allows micro-enterprises to become information rich overcoming information asymmetries, and in the process enhance their customer base as well as new markets. The increasing social networks and mobile based innovations have created employments and income for entrepreneurs who rely on their enterprises for livelihood (iThink, 2013). Additionally, increased know-how and reliance on technology adoption and use, enhances sustainability of the ecosystem (mobile phones) and ultimately freedom, together with empowerment; (3) M-Finance leading to more financial inclusion for all genders and insurance. This is achievable through M-banking and insurance coverage for the very poor in society such as in sub-Saharan Africa [SSA] (pp. i - ii).

Interestingly a knowledge-based economy, is data-driven in which intellectual property [IP] happens to be the new capital and firms fortunate to have enough manpower/human capital in the areas of computerization, coding specialists/programmers and data analytical skills tend to get ahead of their peers (Organisation for Economic Cooperation and Development-[OECD], 2016). Unfortunately, developing countries are disadvantaged in this respect due to the following:

- Lower internet access and connectivity,
- Mobile services usage being driven by voice instead of data consumption,
- Millennials' limited access to and contact with technology, and
- Less access to banking and electronic payment services (Arthur D Little, 2017)
- Limited Direct Foreign Investments (DFI).
- Non-prioritizing technology acquisition by governments in developing countries,
- Non-prioritizing the development of digitally-enabled micro-, small and medium-scale enterprises, and
- Developing countries trying to find a niche for themselves in the marketplace (Centre for International Governance Innovation, 2019:3)

According to CIGI (2019), size of any nation is not a hindrance to finding a niche in the marketplace: Estonia (aggressively uses e-government for all citizens), Singapore (smart city design and its functionality), Rwanda's emphasizing technology in its development strategy [the development of its telecommunications infrastructure, technological adoption and education strategy (Science and Technology 2018). Apart from the above, developing countries could also leapfrog advanced economies in adopting solar-electric, internet urban systems, fibre directly (instead of analogue; copper to fibre-optics) (OECD, 2016). According to Muhleisen (2018), "it is striking that less developed countries are at the forefront of leading technologies –mobile payments (Kenya); digital-oriented registration of lands/property (India), and e-commerce (China). This process adaptations were possible due to lower limitations imposed by existing antiquated infrastructure.

TECHNOLOGY ADOPTION THEORIES AND MODELS

Task Technology Fit (TTF)

The (TTF) posits that Information Technology (IT) must have a positive impact on the performance of any individual, which then results in continued utilization if the capabilities of IT matches intended tasks to be performed (Goodhue & Thompson, 1995). The impact on the individual represents improved efficiency, effectiveness and higher quality delivery. The assumption introduced by Goodhue et al., (1995) portray that a good fit between tasks to be executed and technology is for increased utilization and also increased performance recognizing that the technology must meet the wants and needs of the user precisely. A measure of task technology fit by Goodhue and Thompson (1995) has a composition of 8 important factors (quality, locatability, authorization, and compatibility, ease of use/training, production timelines, systems reliability, and user relationships). Each of these constructs could be assessed with the help of Likert type questions ranching from strongly disagree (SD), disagree (D) to neutral (N), agree (A) and strongly agree (SA). The suitability and applicability of TTF is for testing of newer innovations introduced into the market and assessing customers' reactions and feedbacks.

Technology Readiness Index (TRI)

TRI model or Readiness for the Use of Technology (Parasuraman, 2000; Parasuraman & Colby, 2001) is an assessment tool for readiness of consumers for technology. It was developed for an advanced economy (typically the USA) and involved a qualitative analysis of focused groups (financial services, online services, ecommerce and telecommunications). The technology readiness index for the use of any technology or innovation has several constructs (four dimensions and 36 variables). Some are characterized as enhancers or inhibitors for technology adoption represented by optimism, innovativeness, discomfort and insecurity.

Optimism: Signifies a positive view of technology and the perception that it gives people more control, flexibility and efficiency in their work and lives.

Innovativeness: The tendency one has in being an innovator/pioneer in the use of technology, a leader or opinion former

Discomfort: The perception of lack of control over technology and the feeling of being overwhelmed/ oppressed by it

Insecurity: Tendency to distrust technology and scepticism of one's own ability to use it properly.

According to Parasuraman and Colby (2001), two constructs (optimism and innovativeness) can be accepted as drivers or positive inducers to using technology, while discomfort and insecurity are inhibitors or factors which has the potential in delaying technology adoption and utilization. In an attempt at characterization, Parasuraman and Colby (2001) classified customers into high, medium and low consumption potential as a function of the TRI score. Thus individuals differ remarkably in their use of technology, for technology use differs across applications and scenarios. The classification of consumers of technology, resulted in five technology readiness groups (explorers, pioneers, skeptics, paranoids, and laggards) which is in consonance with Rogers (1995) S--curve (represented as innovators, early adopters, early majority, late majority and laggards).

Technology Acceptance Model (TAM)

The technology acceptance model (TAM) introduced by Davis (1989; Davis et al., 1989) is adapted from the Theory of Reasoned Action (TRA) (Fishbein & Ajzen, 1975) specifically tailored to users of computers or information systems. This model then deals with the rationale for use of computers/IT generally, thus inherently trying to predict and explain why one system can be accepted or rejected. The essential premise of TAM model is the provision for the mapping of how external factors impact internal factors that an individual is exposed to such as beliefs, attitudes and behavioural intentions. This is achievable only by emphasizing fundamental variables as part of cognition and acceptance of computers. The TAM model is predicated on two main constructs embedded in belief, perceived usefulness and perceived ease of use (Davis, 1989; Davis et al., 1989; Gefen, 2003). Thus, it is worth emphasizing that actual system use by an individual is determined by behavioural intention driven jointly by perceived usefulness (PU) and perceived ease of use (PEOU)

Despite the parsimony of the TAM model, it has evolved to becoming a powerful model for predicting usage intentions and acceptance behaviour. Here perceived usefulness (PU) is defined as the potential of user's subjective likelihood that the use of a certain system (for example mobile telephony) will improve his/her action leading to increased performance relative to the object in use. Thus, the consumers of technology in developing systems/economies must rationalize between how the adoption of mobile telephony (innovative technology) be perceived to be more superior comparatively to traditional methods of productivity. The second important construct perceived ease of use (PEOU) signifying an individual's expectations that the use of innovation/technology would entail minimum mental and physical effort. Bandura's Theory of Self Efficacy (1982) gave rise to this construct (PEOU) defined as "the judgement of how well one can execute series of actions required to deal with prospective situation" and from Rogers and Shoemaker (1971) defining of complexity (interpreted as ease of use) as the "degree to which an innovation is perceived as relatively difficult to understand and use". Behavioural intention is defined as the degree to which an individual is desirous in performing a specific behaviour (Davis et al., 1989). Furthermore, TAM posits that external variable can impact behavioural intention mediated fully by these two beliefs of ease of use (Mun, 2003)

Technology Acceptance Model (TAM2).

An extension to TAM was made by Venkatesh and Davis (2000) to explain reasons users found systems to be appropriate at three (3) stages in time: pre implementation, one-month post implementation and three months' post implementation. The theory underlying TAM 2 is based on the preposition that users' mental assessment of important goals to be accomplished at work and the consequences of job task performance employing the system becomes the determinant driver to the usefulness of the system (Venkatseh & Davis, 2000). The ensuing results showed that TAM2 could be applied under voluntary and mandatory environments. Thus, the modified theory (TAM 2) included. key determinants of TAM's perceived usefulness and another construct of user intention. Other additional constructs -- social influence processes (subjective norm, voluntariness and image) together with cognitive instrumental processes (job relevance, output quality, result demonstrability and perceived ease of use)

Self-Efficacy Theory (SET)

Self-efficacy beliefs drive human motivation and behaviour together with influencing the actions which ultimately affect one's life. According to Bandura (1995:2), self-efficacy refers to "beliefs in one's capabilities to organize and execute the courses of action required to manage prospective situations". Simplistically, self-efficacy is the belief an individual entertains toward his/her ability to accomplish tasks with inert skills under different circumstances or scenarios (Synder & Lopez, 2007). Self-efficacy can be perceived as a task specific version of self-esteem (Lunenburg, 2011). Hence the underlying principle of Self Efficacy Theory can be stated thus: "that individuals are more driven to undertake activities/actions for which they have high self-efficacy and less inclined to engage in activities where lower self-efficacy applies" (Van der Biji & Shortridge-Bagett, 2002). In the views of Gecas (2004), peoples' behaviour is in accordance with their initial beliefs, hence self-efficacy can be interpreted as a self-fulfilling prophesy. Additionally, self-efficacy influences people's learning ability, motivation and ultimately their performance, as people attempt to learn and perform tasks only from the overall perception of their ability to succeed in the exercise (Lunenburg, 2011).

Measurements of self-efficacy is achieved from three basic scales: magnitude, strength and generalizability.

Self-Efficacy Magnitude: Determines the level of difficulty (easy, moderate, and hard) any individual thinks is required in the performance of a certain task (Van de Bajl & Shortridge-Baggett, 2002). How difficult is the use of technology with business application? More importantly how would the use of mobile technology enhance daily business activities for consumers in developing economies?

Self-Efficacy Strength: Signifies the amount of conviction an individual has about successful performance of activities with diverse levels of difficulty (Van der Bijl & Shortridge-Baggett, 2002). Would the adoption of mobile technology sufficiently meet the requirements for the intended activities?

Generality of Self-Efficacy: Represents the "degree to which the expectation is generalized across situations" (Lunenburg, 2011).

Bandura (1982) cited in Redmond (2010) states that the basic tenets of self-efficacy can be understood appropriately when one views performance and motivation to be determined partly by how effective people believe they can be.

Unified Theory of Acceptance and use of Technology (UTAUT)

UTAUT (Venkatesh et al., 2003) tries to justify user intention to use information system and continued user behaviour. The theory originated through the systematic review and consolidation of eight models (TRA, TAM, MM, TPB, TAM2, DOI, SCT and personal computer use model). Generally, it is envisaged a multipurpose model suitable across many applications. The theory posits that four key constructs (performance expectancy, effort expectancy, social influence and facilitating conditions) directly determine usage intention and behaviour (Venkatesh et al., 2003). Pertinent moderators (age, gender, experience and voluntariness of use) act on the four key constructs affecting usage intention and behaviour Similarly, five constructs. (perceived usefulness, intrinsic/extrinsic motivation, job fit, relative advantage and outcome expectations) relate to performance expectancy in UAUT model). Notably, effort expectancy is concerned with notions of perceived ease of use and complexity (Lai, 2017). UTAUT is supposedly more superior as it is able to provide for 70% of the variance while earlier theories accomplished this only by 30% to 40% variance in adoption behaviour (Venkatesh et al., 2003). Unfortunately, most research view it as being too complex, not being parsimonious in approaches as well as deficient in explanations of individual differences in behaviour (Casey & Wilson-Evered, 2012; Van Raaij & Schapers, 2008).

The introduction of UTAUT model made possible the prediction of system usage, technology adoption and technology usage related decisions in numerous fields including interactive whiteboards (Sumak & Sorgo, 2016; Sumak et al., 2017); near field communication technology (Khalilzadeh et al., 2017); mobile health (Hoque & Sorwar, 2017); home tele-health services (Cimperman et al., 2016) and acceptance of Enterprise Resource Planning (ERP), software (Chauhan & Jaiswal, 2016) possible. Several applied research that have integrated UTAUT models has been extensive (Chao, 2019), for it encompasses several TAMs--for example (TAM, TAM2, TAM3) and UTAUT models.

RESEARCH INTO MOBILE TECHNOLOGY ADOPTION IN DEVELOPING/TRANSITIONING ECONOMIES

The TAM Model

There are several studies using the TAM model that have been authored by several researchers. Hoque, Bao and Sorwar (2016) utilized a quantitative method on 350 respondents in Bangladesh. The research instrument (structured questionnaire) allowed the collation of data from the sample in trying to ascertain factors influencing the adoption of e-Health in developing countries. Partial Least Square on constructs including PEOU, PU, and trust (p<0.05) were statistically significant factors relative to the intention to adopt eHealth. However, privacy (p<0.05) happen to be a less important significant determinant on eHealth adoption. Importantly gender was strongly correlated with both adoption and eHealth services. Equally under the same contextual framework, Hoque (2016), exploring gender concerns as moderating effect (with TAM model) on an empirical studies of eHealth adoption in Bangladesh, performed partial least square (SEM) on 250 participants. He discovered that effects of personal innovativeness in IT (p>0.05) to be insignificant on eHealth adoption.

Also, Pavithran et al., (2016) developed a model to determine constructs impeding mobile money adoption in developing countries typified by India. The factors included in the model consisted of: - PU, PEOU, self-efficacy, perceived risks, perceived enjoyment, relative advantage, compatibility, trust, social influence and personal innovativeness. They discovered relative advantage to be correlated strongly on intention to use mobile money. Alotaibi, Houghton and Sandhu (2017) employed TAM (on 1152 participants together with SPSS AMOS for SEM analysis) to assist in the investigation of pertinent factors influencing users' intention to utilize mobile government applications in Saudi Arabia. Inter-relationships between behavioural intention to use [BIU] and six independent factors: 3 TAM constructs (PU, attitude to use [ATU], and PEOU, together with 3 external factors: perceived trustworthiness [TRU]; perceived security [SEC]; and awareness [AWAR]) formed the basis of the analyses. This study highlighted that constructs of PU, ATU and TRU significantly influenced BIU relative to e-government applications.

Technically, TAM as a model has been explored in SME research mainly, to help explain use, behaviour and attitude to e-commerce adoption (McCloskey, 2004; Johar & Awalludin, 2011; Nezakari et al., 2012). However, despite its wide applicability in IT/Information Systems research, generally the model has some limitations. These limitations are predicated on the parsimony nature of the model per two constructs PU and PEOU. According to Nistor et al., (2014) TAM is totally reliant on perceived usefulness (PU) as the most important and acceptable indicator without putting emphasis on actual systems/ technology use. This is systematically flawed because Nistor et al. (2012) posit that there was insignificant inter-relationship between a person's intent and actual use behaviour. Hence, it becomes incumbent upon the researcher, to study actual systems/ technology use rather than just perceived use, which TAM presupposes at the moment. Equally, Parker & Castleman (2009) opine that TAM is not suitably adapted to enabling the researcher have a more accurate understanding toward e-commerce adoption in SMEs, as TAM model directly or indirectly is devoid of contextual factors which characterize SMEs. This narrative is particularly important when one considers Parker & Castleman (2009) assertion. On the whole, characterization of SMEs in developing countries must include "complex issues such as infrastructural and social issues rather than just their behavioural intentions." (Idris et al., 2017).

UTAUT Model

Several authors have utilized UTAUT model to study mobile technology adoption. Bhatiasevi (2015) adapted an extended UTAUT model to explain mobile banking adoption in Thailand. He introduced important constructs (perceived credibility, perceived costs, perceived convenience). Using SEM on conducting discriminant and convergence validities, PE, EE, SI, perceived credibility, perceived convenience, and BI to use mobile banking were all positively related. Sarfaraz (n.d) using UTAUT model on participant from India, carried out analysis with SPSS AMOS via SEM to understand drivers to mobile banking adoption. The quantitative study indicated that constructs [PE, EE, and risk perception] had a significant influence on users' intention to adopt mobile services. Alwahaishi and Snasel (2013) using a combination of UTAUT and Flow Theory (as a new theoretical framework) in ascertaining factors that affect acceptance and use of mobile internet (as ICT app in a consumer context) incorporated 8 constructs [PE, EE, FC, SI, perceived value, perceived playfulness, attention focus, and BI] in the study. The survey population came from Saudi Arabia (20-30s age groups and college graduates). Analysis of data (with AMOS for SEM), indicated that (PE, perceived playfulness, SI, and FC) has a significant effect on behavioural intention. Similarly, Thomas et al., (2013) on the utility of UTAUT model to mobile learning adoption in higher education in Guyana, observed [after SEM on web-based data collection from University students] that some UTAUT relationships were confirmed while contradicting other. Therefore, they concluded that cultural and country-level differences moderated UTAUT affects. Likewise employing an extended UTAUT model [in factors determining the behavioural intention to use mobile learning], Chao (2019) carried out a cross-sectional survey on 1,562 university students in Taiwan using SEM. Partial least squares [PLS] regression assisted in hypotheses testing and concluded that (a) BI significantly and positively influenced by satisfaction, trust, PE and EE., (b) perceived enjoyment, PE, and EE positively associated with BI, (c) mobile self-efficacy affected perceived enjoyment positively and significantly, (d) perceived risks significantly moderated negatively the relationship between PE and BI.

In South Africa, Ndayizigamiye (2012) targeted 180 micro- small and medium scale enterprises to assess e-commerce adoption in developing countries with UTAUT model. The study's findings indicated that SI, PE, EE as constructs were important determinants per e-commerce adoption, while FC played minor role in e-commerce adoption within the study population (MSMEs in SA) The importance and relevance of UTAUT model has been stressed by Waehama et al., 2014, in cognizance of its capability in explaining 70% of acceptance behaviour of technology as against 40% acceptance rate in comparison to other IT developed model.

Technically, despite UTAUT's wider applicability in IT/IS research (comparatively to its antecedent model—TAM), there are a number of limitations experienced in the use of the model (Idris et al., 2017). Firstly, according to Vankatesh et al., 2008) Behavioural Intention (BI) as a construct is laden with weak predictive and explanatory power in an attempt at dealing with uncertainties and unanticipated events that may arise between time the intention has been arrived at and the actual performance of the behaviour. Second limitation (involving UTAUT model) is that behavioural intention [BI] might not be a true reflection of a person's internal belief. This might not represent the external factors that may affect the performance of behaviour (Idris et al., 2019). As a result, the UTAUT model does not capture the various external and internal stimuli that alter intentions overtime (Venkatesh et al. 2008). Theoretically, UTAUT happens to be an extension of TAM model, consequently both models maybe impacted with similar phenomena revolving around behavioural intention [BI] when it comes to technology adoption, including e-commerce. More so, it not clear whether UTAUT independently captures the contextual factors associated with SMEs in developing countries. This includes the complex interplay between the owners and size of SMEs, families, customers, employees and operational environments (Idris et al., 2019).

CONCEPTUAL FRAMEWORK FOR MOBILE TECHNOLOGY RESEARCH IN DEVELOPING COUNTRIES

A careful analysis of the above models adopted for explaining users' intention and behaviour were developed for advance economies. Unfortunately, these models may not feature prominently in the acceptance, adoption, and continued use of newer innovations in developing economies. This argument is predicated by the fact that computerization in developing/transitioning economies depend not on sophisticated processes but mainly on mobile/digital technology.

The recent advancement in mobile telecommunication technologies, means that mobile phone applications has brought about considerable differences in how we work, live and transact businesses across societies. Mobile devices are an integral part of e-commerce, e-banking, e-health, e-learning and entertainment. Effective implementation of IS/IT is dependent on user acceptance (Davis, 1989). From disciplines covering social psychology, the TAM and UTAUT models have contributed enormously to IT/IS research (Chauhan & Jaiswal, 2016; Cimperman et al., 2016; Sumak and Sorgo, 2016; Sumak et al., 2017). Unfortunately, other researchers (Tsai et al., 2018; Sumak et al., 2017) apart from emphasizing the parsimony of TAM, detailed other limitations of this model in terms of individual's perspectives to acceptance, adoption and utilization of IS tools. These limitations may be (a) not being able to justify individual's use of novel technologies, (b) ignoring indicators and emphasizing external variables linked to perceived ease of use (PEOU) construct, and (c) overlooking the relationships between usage attitude and intention (Chao, 2019).

TAM to date can be used in assessing the antecedents driving the adoption of several technologies in developed economies (Gbongli et al., 2019), but in studies tailored to mobile money adoption in Togo a developing West African country, self-efficacy, new technology anxiety, and personal innovativeness of IT as constructs were adopted. These constructs affected core TAM variables (perceived ease-of-use and perceived usefulness). The results after a structural equation modelling [SEM], proved conclusively that perceived ease-of-use was the most significant factor on consumers' attitude to mobile-based money (Gbongli et al., 2019).

Technology Readiness Index and TAM

The constructs within technology readiness index model can be integrated into TAM as facilitating conditions for ascertaining how the adoption and use of new technologies (e.g. mobile) in developing economies can be enhanced or inhibited. The four constructs: optimism, innovativeness (acting as enhancers/drivers) to technology adoption and discomfort, and insecurity (as inhibitors/impediments) can with TAM model form part of the model for the studies.

Hypothesis can be:

H01: Optimism offering people control, flexibility, and efficiency in use of mobile technology for daily life activities is statistically significant, and differentiates between adopters and non-adopters of mobile technology

H02: Innovativeness enabling leadership positions or opinion formers to mobile technology is significant statistically, and is a differentiating element between adopters and non-adopters in the use of mobile technology

H03: Discomfort defined as being overwhelmed by technology, or as lack of control over mobile technology is significant statistically, and differentiates between adopters and non-adopters.

H04: Insecurity as distrust of mobile technology for task accomplishments is significant statistically and differentiates between adopters and non-adopters.

CONCLUSION

A number of theories and models have been developed for ascertaining the acceptance, adoption and continued use of newer innovations or technologies by customers in developed countries. As previously stated above these models might not be applicable to developing economies who depend more on mobile technologies for business, work and life activities. Because of the parsimony of the TAM model, and Davis advising inclusion of external facilitating conditions for increased performance, a number of synthesized conceptual framework covering the original TAM and UTAUT models to study technology adoption in developing economies can be developed. Pertinent models could include (1) SET and TAM; (2) TRI and TAM; (3) SET and UTAUT; (4) TRI and UTAUT.

REFERENCES

Ajzen, I. (1985). From intentions to actions: a theory of planned behaviour. In J. Kuhl & J. Beckman (Eds.), *Action-Control: From cognition to behaviour* (pp. 11–39). Springer, Verlag. doi:10.1007/978-3-642-69746-3_2

Ajzen, I. (1991). The Theory of Planned Behaviour. *Organizational Behavior and Human Decision Processes, 50*(2), 179–211. doi:10.1016/0749-5978(91)90020-T

Ajzen, I., & Fishbein, M. (1975). *Belief, attitude, intention and behaviour: An introduction to Theory of Research.* Addison-Wesley.

Alotaibi, R., Houghton, L., & Sandhu, K. (2017). Factors influencing users' intention to use mobile government applications in Saudi Arabia. *International Journal of Advanced Computer Science and Applications, 8*(7), 200–211. doi:10.14569/IJACSA.2017.080727

Alwahaishi, A., & Snasel, V. (2013). Consumers' acceptance and use of information and communications technology: A UTAUT and Flow Based Theoretical Model. *Journal of Technology Management & Innovation, 89*(2), 61–73. doi:10.4067/S0718-27242013000200005

Bandura, A. (1977). *Self-efficacy: Toward a unifying theory of behavioural change.* Academic Press.

Bandura, A. (1982). Self-Efficacy: Mechanism in human agency. *The American Psychologist, 37*(2), 122–147. doi:10.1037/0003-066X.37.2.122

Bandura, A. (1995). Exercise of personal and collective efficacy in changing societies. In A. Bandura (Ed.), *Self-efficacy in changing societies* (pp. 1–45). Cambridge University Press. doi:10.1017/CBO9780511527692.003

Bhatiasevi, V. (2015). *An extended UTAUT model to explain the adoption of mobile banking in Thailand. Information Development.* Sage Publications. doi:10.1177/0266666915570764

Carr, V. H. Jr. (1999). *Technology adoption and diffusion.* The Learning Centre for Interactive Technology.

Carroll, J. M., & Rosson, M. B. (1987). Paradox of the active user. In J. M. Carroll (Ed.), *Interfacing Thought: Cognitive Aspect of Human-Computer Interaction* (pp. 80–111). MIT Press.

Casey, T., & Wilson-Evered, E. (2012). Predicting uptake of technology innovation in online family dispute resolution services: An application and extension of the UTAUT. *Computers in Human Behavior, 28*(6), 2034–2045. doi:10.1016/j.chb.2012.05.022

Centre for International Governance Innovation (CIGI). (2019). *Leveraging the digital transformation for development: A global South strategy for the data-driven economy.* Policy Brief No 148, 2019.

Chao, C. M. (2019). Factors determining the behavioral intention to use mobile learning. An application and extension of the UTAUT model. *Frontiers in Psychology, 10*, 1–52. doi:10.3389/fpsyg.2019.01652 PMID:31379679

Chauhan, S., & Jaiswal, M. (2016). Determination of acceptance of ERP software training in business schools: Empirical investigation using UTAUT model. *International Journal of Management Education, 14*(3), 248–262. doi:10.1016/j.ijme.2016.05.005

Cimperman, M., Brenic, M. M., & Trkman, P. (2016). Analyzing older users' home tele-health services acceptance behavior applying an extension of UTAUT model. *International Journal of Medical Informatics, 90*, 22–31. doi:10.1016/j.ijmedinf.2016.03.002 PMID:27103194

Compeau, D. R., & Higgins, C. A. (1995). Computer self-efficacy: Development of a measure and initial test. *Management Information Systems Quarterly, 19*(2), 189–211. doi:10.2307/249688

Connor, Y. O., & Reilly, P. O. (2018). Examining the infusion of mobile technology by healthcare practitioners in a hospital setting. *Information Systems Frontiers, 20*(6), 1297–1317. doi:10.100710796-016-9728-9

Davis, F. D. (1989). Perceived usefulness; perceived ease of use, and user acceptance of Information Technology. *Management Information Systems Quarterly, 13*(3), 319–341. doi:10.2307/249008

Davis, F. D., Bagozzi, R. P., & Warshaw, P. R. (1989). User acceptance of computer technology: A comparison of two theoretical models. *Management Science, 35*(8), 982–1004. doi:10.1287/mnsc.35.8.982

Fishbein, M., & Ajzen, I. (1975). *Beliefs, attitudes, intention and behaviour: An introduction to Theory and Research.* Addison-Wesley Publishing Company.

Gbongli, K., Dumar, K., & Mireku, K. K. (2016). MCDM technique to evaluating mobile banking adoption in the Togolese banking industry based on the perceived value; Perceived benefit and perceived sacrifice factors. *International Journal of Data Mining Knowledge Management Process, 6*(3), 37–56. doi:10.5121/ijdkp.2016.6304

Gbongli, K., Dumor, K., & Mireku, K. K. (2016). MCDM technique to evaluating mobile banking adoption in the Togolese banking industry based on the perceived value: Perceived benefit and perceived sacrifice factors. *International Journal of Data Mining Knowledge Management Process, 6*, 37–56.

Gefen, D. (2003). TAM or just plain habit: A look at experience online shoppers. *Journal of End User Computing, 15*(3), 1–13. doi:10.4018/joeuc.2003070101

Gillooly, C. (1998). Disillusionment. *Information Week, 669*, 46–51.

Goodhue, D., & Thompson, R. L. (1995). Task technology fit and individual performance. *Management Information Systems Quarterly, 19*(2), 213–236. doi:10.2307/249689

Hoggue, R., & Sorwar, G. (2017). Understanding factors influencing the adoption of m-Health by the elderly: An extension of the UTAUT model. *International Journal of Medical Informatics, 101*, 75–84. doi:10.1016/j.ijmedinf.2017.02.002 PMID:28347450

Hoque, M. R. (2016). An empirical study of mHealth adoption in a developing country: The moderating effect of gender concern. *BMC Medical Informatics and Decision Making, 16*(1), 51. doi:10.118612911-016-0289-0 PMID:27142844

Hoque, M. R., Bao, Y., & Sorwar, G. (2016). Investigating factors influencing the adoption of e-Health in developing countries: A patient's perspective. *Informatics for Health & Social Care*, *42*(1), 1–17. doi:10.3109/17538157.2015.1075541 PMID:26865037

Idris, A., Edwards, H., & McDonald, S. (2017). E-*commerce adoption in Developing Countries SMEs: What Do the Prevailing Theoretical Models Offer Us?* International Conference on E-Commerce, Putrajaya, Malaysia.

iThink. (2013). *Mobile telephony in developing countries: A global perspective*. The Innovation Knowledge Foundation. Think! Report No 4. Retrieved from www.thinkinnovation.org

Johar, G., & Awalluddin, J. (2011). The Role of Technology Acceptance Model in Explaining Effect on E-Commerce Application System. *International Journal of Managing Information Technology*, *3*(3), 1–14. doi:10.5121/ijmit.2011.3301

Kapoor, K. K., Dwivedi, Y. K., & William, M. D. (2015). Examining the role of three sets of innovation attributes for determining adoption of the interbank mobile payment service. *Information Systems Frontiers*, *17*(5), 1039–1056. doi:10.100710796-014-9484-7

Khalilzadeh, J., Ozturk, A. B., & Bilgihan, A. (2017). A security-related factors in extended UTAUT model for NFC based mobile payment in the restaurant industry. *Computers in Human Behavior*, *70*, 460–474. doi:10.1016/j.chb.2017.01.001

Lai, P. C. (2014). *Cashless. Cardless, contactless and convenience of MySIM*. GlobalCLAS Technology.

Lai, P. C. (2017). The literature review of technology adoption models and theories for the novelty technology. *Journal of Information Systems and Technology Management*, *14*(1), 21–38. doi:10.4301/S1807-17752017000100002

Lai, P. C., & Zainal, A. A. (2015). Perceived Risk as an Extension to TAM Model: Consumers' Intention to Use A Single Platform E-Payment. *Australian Journal of Basic and Applied Sciences*, *9*(2), 323–330.

Little. (2017). *Digital transformation in developing countries*. Retrieved from www.adl_digital-in_emerging_markets.

Lucas, H. C., & Spitler, V. K. (1999). Technology use and performance: A field study of broker workstation. *Decision Sciences*, *30*(2), 291–311. doi:10.1111/j.1540-5915.1999.tb01611.x

Lunenburg, F. (2011). *Self-efficacy in the workplace: Implications for motivation and performance*. Academic Press.

McCarroll, T. (1991). What new ages? *Time*, *138*, 44–46.

McCloskey, D. (2004). Evaluating Electronic Commerce Acceptance with The Technology Acceptance Model. *Journal of Computer Information Systems*, *44*(2), 49–57.

Moore, G. C., & Benbasat, I. (1991). Development of an instrument to measure the perceptions of adopting an information technology innovation. *Information Systems Research*, *2*(3), 192–222. doi:10.1287/isre.2.3.192

Muhleisen, M. (2018, June). The long and short of the digital revolution. *Finance & Development*, *55*(2).

Mum, Y. Y., & Hwang, Y. (2003). Predicting the use of web-based information systems: Self-efficacy, enjoyment, learning goal orientation, and the technology acceptance model. *International Journal of Human-Computer Studies, 59*(4), 431–449. doi:10.1016/S1071-5819(03)00114-9

Ndayizigamiye, P. (2012). A Unified Approach Towards E-Commerce Adoption by SMMEs In South Africa. *International Journal of Information Technology and Business Management, 16*(1), 92–101.

Nezakati, H., Jofreh, M., Liong, G., & Asgari, O. (2012). Assessing E-Commerce Adoption by Small and Medium Enterprises in Malaysia, Singapore and Thailand. *World Applied Sciences Journal, 19*(10), 1406–1411.

Nickerson, R. S. (1981). Why interactive computer systems are sometimes not used by people who might benefit from them. *International Journal of Man-Machine Studies, 15*(4), 469–481. doi:10.1016/S0020-7373(81)80054-5

Nistor, N., & Murillo Montes de Oca, A. (2014). Nonsignificant intention–behaviour effects in educational technology acceptance: A case of competing cognitive scripts? *Computers in Human Behavior, 34*, 333–338. doi:10.1016/j.chb.2014.01.026

OECD. (2016). *Harnessing the digital economy for developing countries*. Working Paper No. 334.

Parasuraman, A. (2000). Technology Readiness Index (TRI): A multiple item scale to measure readiness for embrace of new technologies. *Journal of Service Research, 2*(4), 307–320. doi:10.1177/109467050024001

Parasuraman, A., & Colby, C. (2001). *Techno ready marketing: how and why your customers adopt technology*. The Free Press.

Parker, C. M. & Castleman, T. (2009). Small firm e-business adoption: a critical analysis of theory. *Journal of Enterprise Information Management, 22*(1, 2), 167-182.

Pavithran. (2016). *Empirical investigation of mobile banking adoption in developing countries. International J or Enterprise Information Systems, 10(1)*.

Redmond, B. F. (2010). *7 Self-efficacy and Social Cognitive Theories*. Retrieved from http://wikispace.psu.edu/display/PSYCH484/7.Self-EfficacyandSocialCognitiveTheories/

Roger, E. M., & Shoemaker, F. F. (1971). *Communication of Innovation: A cross cultural approach*. Free Press.

Sarfaraz, J. (n.d.). Unified theory of acceptance and use of technology (UTAUT) model-mobile banking. *Journal of Internet Banking and Commerce*. Retrieved from icommercecentral.com/open-access/unified-thoery-of-acceptance-and-use-of-technology-utaut=modelmobile-banking.php?aid-865

Science and Technology. (2018). How Rwanda is Becoming an African Tech Powerhouse. *Science and Technology*. Retrieved from https://wgi.world/rwandaafrican-tech-powerhouse

Sharma, R. & Mishra, R. (2014). *A review of theories and models of technology adoption*. Academic Press.

Sumak, B., Pusnik, M., Herieko, M., & Sorgo, A. (2017). Differences between prospective, existing, and former users of interactive whiteboards on external factors affecting their adoption, usage and abandonment. *Computers in Human Behavior, 72*, 733–756. doi:10.1016/j.chb.2016.09.006

Šumak, B., & Šorgo, A. (2016). The acceptance and use of interactive whiteboards among teachers: differences in UTAUT determinants between pre- and post-adopters. *Computer Human Behaviour, 64,* 602–620. doi:.07.037 doi:10.1016/j.chb.2016

Thomas, T. D., Singh, L., & Gaffar, K. (2013). The utility of the UTAUT model in explaining mobile learning adoption in higher education in Guyana. *International Journal of Education and Development Using Information and Communication Technology, 9*(3), 71–85.

Thompson, R. L., Higgins, C. A., & Howell, J. M. (1991). Personal computing: Toward a conceptual model of utilization. *Management Information Systems Quarterly, 15*(1), 125–143. doi:10.2307/249443

Van der Bijl, J. J., & Shortridge-Baggett, L. M. (2002). The theory and measurement of the self-efficacy construct. In E. A. Lentz & L. M. Shortridge-Baggett (Eds.), Self-efficacy in Nursing. Research and Measurement Perspectives (pp. 9-28). New York: Springer.

Van Raaji, E. M., & Schepears, I. J. (2008). The acceptance and use of virtual learning environments in China. *Computers & Education, 50*(3), 838–852. doi:10.1016/j.compedu.2006.09.001

Venkatesh, V., Brown, S. A., Maruping, L. M., & Bala, H. (2008). Predicting Different Conceptualizations of System Use: The Competing Roles of Behavioural Intention, Facilitating Conditions, And Behavioural Expectation. *Management Information Systems Quarterly, 32*(3), 483–502. doi:10.2307/25148853

Venkatesh, V., & Davis, F. (2000). A theoretical extension of the technology acceptance model: Four longitudinal field studies. *Management Science, 46*(2), 186–204. doi:10.1287/mnsc.46.2.186.11926

Venkatesh, V., & Davis, F. D. College, S. M. W. (. (2000). Theoretical acceptance extension model: Field four studies of the technology longitudinal. *Management Science, 46,* 186–204. doi:10.1287/mnsc.46.2.186.11926

Venkatesh, V., Morris, M. G., Davis, G. B., & Davis, F. D. (2003). User acceptance of information technology: Towards a unified view. *Management Information Systems Quarterly, 27*(3), 425–478. doi:10.2307/30036540

Venkatesh, V., Thong, J. Y. L., & Xu, X. (2012). Consumer acceptance and use of information technology: Extending the unified theory of acceptance and use of technology. *Management Information Systems Quarterly, 36*(1), 157–178. doi:10.2307/41410412

Waehama, W., McGrath, M., Korthaus, A., & Fong, M. (2014). *ICT Adoption and the UTAUT Model.* Paper presented at the International Conference on Educational Technology with Information Technology, Bangkok, Thailand.

World Bank. (2012). Information and Communications for Development (2012) Maximizing Mobile. Washington, DC: World Bank.

Zigurs, I., & Buckland, B. K. (1998). A theory of technology fit and group support system effectiveness. *Management Information Systems Quarterly, 22*(3), 313–334. doi:10.2307/249668

Section 2

Chapter 4
Towards Career Development for High School Students:
A Case Study of a Web–Based Expert System in Ghana

Nana Yaw Asabere
https://orcid.org/0000-0003-4908-8528
Accra Technical University, Ghana

Amevi Acakpovi
https://orcid.org/0000-0003-1838-0155
Accra Technical University, Ghana

Ezer Osei Yeboah-Boateng
https://orcid.org/0000-0002-1355-8586
Ghana Communication Technology University, Ghana

Wisdom Kwawu Torgby
Accra Technical University, Ghana

Eric Amoako
Accra Technical University, Ghana

ABSTRACT

Globally, choosing the right tertiary programme for university (higher) education is quite a difficult task for students. A wide range of programmes are offered by the individual universities which differ in terms of delivery modes and entry requirements. Technology inclusion in the 21st century has paved the way for the proliferation of electronic/computing systems such as electronic counseling (e-counseling) and electronic learning (e-learning). By employing a quantitative research instrument (questionnaire) to ascertain technology acceptance of Senior High School (SHS) in Ghana, this chapter proposes a web-based

DOI: 10.4018/978-1-7998-3468-7.ch004

(e-counseling) expert system which will match students' backgrounds with the right tertiary programme towards career development. Evaluation of our proposed approach suggests that majority of the selected students (80%) out of 100 who used the system accepted and embraced it. Such a system will therefore solve and improve career guidance, counseling, and development problems of SHS students in Ghana.

INTRODUCTION

The Oxford English Dictionary defines the term "Discipline" as "a branch of learning or scholarly instruction." As defined by fields of study, academic discipline provides the framework for a student's programme in a college or university, and consequently defines the academic world inhabited by scholars. Globally, tertiary education training in an academic discipline results in a system of orderliness, which is recognized as a characteristic of that particular academic discipline. Such characteristics are demonstrated in an academic scholar's approach to understanding and investigating new knowledge, ways of working, and viewpoints on the world around them (The Gale Group Inc., 2002; Bordons, Zulueta, Romero, & Barrigón, 1996; Dogan, 1996; Klein, 1996).

An academic discipline which is chosen well will ensure that individuals in a country are equipped with the necessary skills that are relevant to their career objectives. The summation of each individual's career driven skills is the summation of national development (Wondoh, 2012; The Gale Group Inc., 2002; Bordons et al., 1996; Dogan, 1996; Klein, 1996). During a person's lifetime, career-related choices are among the most important decisions people make. These career choices have substantial long-term consequences for individuals' lifestyles, emotional welfare, economic and social status, as well as their sense of personal productivity and contribution to society (Gati and Tal, 2008; Gati, Saka, & Krausz, 2001; Gata & Ram, 2000). Consequently, it is only natural that individuals at different stages of their lives are preoccupied with career choices. Therefore, career guidance into the selection of an academic discipline must be carefully and systematically performed in order to achieve national development.

Career guidance involves a guidance and counseling process for students and can be described as a process of information exchange that empowers students to realize their maximum educational potential (Seng and Zeki, 2014; Covner, 1963; Gati and Tal, 2008; Gati, Saka, & Krausz, 2001; Gata & Ram, 2000). The guidance process is student-centred and will result in the student gaining a clearer view of himself/ herself, and the experience of higher education (Srivathsan, Garg, Bharambe, Varshney, & Bhaskaran, 2017; Gati & Gutentag; 2015). In career guidance, an academic advisor/counselor provides guidance, advice and help for students in recognizing their academic strengths and to select an academic discipline for higher education which will impact them throughout their lives. Taking into consideration factors such as financial status and so on, the academic (advisor) recommends an academic discipline (university programme) for the student. This system ensures high school students are able to identify their career objectives and pursue higher education towards it. In effect, the academic advisor in the guidance process should be able to identify the right career objective for the student. The advisor in question here refers to an expert with knowledge in assisting decision making (Al Ahmar, 2011; Nambair and Dutta, 2010; Pokrajac and Rasamny, 2006; Razak, Hashim, Noor, Halim, & Shamsul, 2014; Gati & Gutentag; 2015).

The identification of a student's ability and capabilities through career guidance is the greatest key to national development (Wondoh, 2012; Gati and Tal, 2008; Gati, Saka, & Krausz, 2001; Gata & Ram,

2000). Suitable development is measured based on individual development; that is, the development of each individual in a nation sums up to determine the total development of the whole nation (Wondoh, 2012; Gati and Tal, 2008; Gati, Saka, & Krausz, 2001; Gata & Ram, 2000; Bordons et al., 1996; Dogan, 1996; Klein, 1996). Additionally, the summation of each individual's input to productivity is a reflection of the productivity of that nation.

Kesson (2013) identified a common attitude of Senior High School (SHS) students in Ghana refraining from guidance and counseling. Aside the unavailability of counselors especially in the rural areas, one noteworthy reason was that guidance and counseling was geared at enforcing attitudinal discipline rather than assisting the student in identifying an academic discipline. Kesson (2013) recommended further research into methods of improving students' participation in guidance and counseling. The identification of an academic discipline is part of the guidance process. However, Ghanaian SHS students are not partaking in the guidance process and as a result are not able to make the right career choices to foster national development.

The research objectives involved in this study include: (i) To verify whether students in the selected SHSs in Accra have heard about web-based expert systems and are willing to adopt it as a career advicing (e-counseling) methodology, (ii) To find out whether counselors in the selected SHSs in Accra have heard about web-based expert systems and are willing to adopt it as a career advicing (e-counseling) methodology for students, and (iii) To identify the most appropriate methods and frameworks that can be used to integrate a web-based expert (e-counseling) system for career advicing in SHSs.

This study seeks utilized quantitative research instrument and software development methodologies to propose a web-based expert (e-counseling) system that would recommend tertiary courses for SHS students in Accra, Ghana. However, despite the effort by large private organizations and the government towards investing heavily in information systems and computing research, less study has been carried out to ascertain the behavioral intentions of students to adopt and use ICT in Ghana (Kolog et al., 2015). In spite of the need to integrate ICT into counseling, the factors that encourage students to adopt and use e-counseling cannot be disregarded. Consequently, we were motivated to take up this study. This chapter therefore focuses on investigating students' behavioral intention towards adoption and use of e-counseling through the Technology Acceptance Model (Venkatesh & Davis, 2000).

The proposed expert system in this chapter can conveniently emulate the task of the academic counselor. This system will provide decision support to primarily assist Senior High School (SHS) students in selecting an academic discipline for higher education. Secondary usage of the system could be support to various academic advisors (parents, teachers etc.) and/or educational bodies in the student's academic discipline decision making. Being an expert system, it is expected to serve the same purpose as an academic advisor/counselor and even better through the World Wide Web. This will make guidance counselling in relation to academic discipline identification readily available to SHS students all over the country and as a result improve national development.

BACKGROUND

With reference to Internet World Stats in Africa (IWA, 2019), as at December 2017, there were 10,110,000 Internet users in Ghana, representing 34.3% of the population (29,463,643 as at 2018). Access to internet services is of great significance to a developing country such as Ghana (Yebowaah, 2018). Additionally, current and updated information is well organized on the internet for easy search, and has contributed significantly to students' academic laurels (Sahin, Balta, & Ercan, 2018; Yesilyurt, Basturk, Yesilyurt, & Kara, 2014). Advancements in technology has come so far that even the youth of today consisting of many SHS students are able to educate themselves through video tutorials available on the internet and also prefer to search for information on the internet instead of seeking an expert advice. The student's inability to make the right choice of academic discipline in effect affects national development. On the basis of internet usage, there is therefore the need for an internet system that will easily assist SHS students in decision making in relation to the selection of an academic discipline (Gati and Tal, 2008; Gati, Saka, & Krausz, 2001; Gata & Ram, 2000; Bordons et al., 1996; Dogan, 1996; Klein, 1996).

In the computing world, Expert Systems have proven to be effective in a number of problem-solving domains which normally requires human expertise (Duan, Edwards, & Xu, 2005; Zimmermann, 2012). Expert systems are software that use symbolic knowledge representation in terms of rules, networks or frames to draw conclusions. For example, in education, the modern era of teaching requires more knowledge of complex relationships and multiple concepts, enhanced interaction with students where they can explore more with different course materials. Nevertheless, computer-based training already has a relatively long history and has been shown to positively influence the amount of material learned, the time taken to learn it, and the enjoyment of the learning experience (Khanna, Kaushik, & Barnela, 2010).

The swift accessibility of high-tech graphics, animation, video and sound capabilities and the proliferation of multimedia authoring software have made it very easy to quickly produce impressive presentations and interactive modules. The introduction of Expert Systems in the field of education can provide deeper levels of interaction of students with course materials. Expert System techniques have found wide applications in the field of education, where knowledge is always evolving and characterized by uncertainty (Khanna et al., 2010). Furthermore, in relation to career development, expert systems have played a key role. Researchers such as (Srivathsan et al., 2017; Sridharan & Goel, 2010; Razak et al., 2014; Nambair and Dutta, 2010; Pokrajac and Rasamny, 2006) have all developed expert systems towards career development of students.

MAIN FOCUS OF THE CHAPTER

Issues, Controversies, Problems

The process of finding information regarding higher education from a large number of websites is time-consuming and challenging. Helping students to make the right choice from a myriad of available tertiary programmes in order to meet their individual needs is a real challenge. A wide range of programmes in higher education are offered by the individual universities who have different delivery modes and entry requirements. Such abundant information means that prospective university (tertiary) students need to search, organize and use the resources that can enable them to match their individual goals, interests and current levels of knowledge. This can be a time-consuming process as it involves students with the help of counselors accessing each platform, searching for available courses/programmes, carefully reading every course syllabus and then choosing the one that is most appropriate for the student (Apaza & Cervantes, 2014). Furthermore, even though some course titles are similar, they can lead to different career paths. Studies have shown that, naturally, choices of students are influenced by their background, personal interests and career interests (Ibrahim, Yang, Ndzi, Yang, & Al-Maliki, 2019). According to

Cuseo (2003), three out of every four students were uncertain or tentative about their career choice at the time of college entry.

Most high school students in Ghana especially SHS students are not able to identify a tertiary programme that suits their intended future career. This is because they do not engage in guidance and counseling sessions with their school counselors. As explained by Kesson (2013), in Ghanaian SHSs, the aim of guidance and counseling towards students is disciplinary rather than assisting them in academically related concerns such as the selecting an academic or a career course. The students also indicated the lack of counselors in most SHSs as part of their indecisiveness on relevant tertiary programmes.

LITERATURE REVIEW

Traditional and Technological Concepts of Counseling in Ghanaian SHSs

The creation of counseling department/units in schools has a tremendous benefit towards students' holistic life development. In Ghana, counseling gained importance through its implementation in the health sector to help patients towards life decisions, anxieties and trauma (Essuman, 2001). However, in 1975, realizing the importance and prominence of counseling, the Ghana Education Service (GES) saw the need to establish counseling centers in all the schools in Ghana (Essuman, 2001). GES's idea was to administer counseling to students in a bid to help them develop rapidly. Since this inception by GES, although counseling is recognized as one of the key elements of the guidance programme in Ghana, less attention has been given to it in terms of resourcing the sector to meet students' demand for counseling.

In Ghana, SHS education consists of both resident (boarding) and non-resident (day) students, for which all students are entitled to counseling services. In spite of school counselors having the prerogative to administer counseling to students, the school staff also forms part of the school counseling team. Meanwhile, traditional face-to-face (F2F) counseling was, and is still the sole method on which most educational counsellors rely for counseling delivery (Kolog, Sutinen, & Vanhalakka-Ruoho, 2014; Kolog, Sutinen, Vanhalakka-Ruoho, Suhonen, & Anohah, 2015). Consequently, geographically isolated and physically challenged students are disadvantaged in accessing counseling services due to the limited scope of the face-to-face counseling. This situation is worrying considering the demand for counseling in the 21st Century (Kolog et al., 2014; Kolog et al., 2015).

Kolog et al. (2015) described counseling in a school system as a tool for eliminating ignorance of young people towards making career choices for academic development. In the broader viewpoint, school counseling should help students to develop holistically (Athanasou & Esbroeck, 2008). Holistic model of counseling is "an incorporative counseling approach which combines a wide range of counseling techniques that focus on the whole being or well-being of individuals" (Kolog et al., 2014; Kolog et al., 2015). In this regard, the responsibility rests on the school counselors to bring out the latent capabilities of students by helping them to contain unavoidable life challenges.

In the 21st century, rapid technological inclusion coupled with the advancements and use of ICT in education and other related disciplines is gradually gaining roots in the African context although with less focus on its integration into counseling (Aker & Mbiti, 2010; Kolog et al., 2015). Despite the challenges associated with the implementation of ICT-mediated counseling, Kolog et al. (2015) observed that changes due to the growing pace of ICT would influence an individual's development. This intention highlights the relevance to integrate ICT into counseling in order to meet the increasing diverse demand for counseling (Aker & Mbiti, 2010; Kolog et al., 2014; Kolog et al., 2015). Stakeholders have come under harsh criticisms for their inability to adequately resource SHSs with ICT to meet the current pace of technology. This brings to the fore the challenges that impede digital revolution. In line with this, Kessy, Kaemba & Gachoka (2006); Buabeng-Andoh (2012) carried out a study to unravel the possible challenges of ICT implementation in the developing countries. Key findings in these studies discovered challenges were lack of skilled human resources and perceived difficulty in ICT integration in developing countries.

In relation to national development, there is the need for the government to invest or to research into ICT and e-counseling pertaining to the issue of how to efficiently assist SHS graduates in making career course choices. When a psychologist, counselor or an academic advisor dies valuable knowledge and experience perishes (Jabbar and Khan, 2016). An expert system can retain the knowledge of such experts which will guide SHS students in Ghana to identify their right career course choices without imposition or ethical misconduct. There is therefore the need for a web-based expert (e-counseling) system to be used by SHS graduates in Ghana which will assist them to make the right career course choices.

Web-Based Expert Systems

Convergence of technologies in the Internet and the field of expert systems have paved the way for new ways of sharing and distributing knowledge. Expert systems (ES) developed as a division of Artificial Intelligence (AI), from the effort of AI researchers to develop computer programs that could reason as humans (Zimmermann, 2012). Many organizations have leveraged this technology to increase productivity and profits through better ES business decisions (Zimmermann, 2012).

Globally, Internet-centered Information and Communication Technologies (ICTs) are changing applications. Duan et al. (2005) argued that rapid advances in Internet technologies have opened new opportunities for enhancing traditional Decision Support Systems (DSS) and ES. Consequently, the way that an ES is developed and distributed can be changed through Internet technology. According to Duan et al. (2005), for the first time, knowledge on any subject can directly be delivered to users through a web-based ES. Since its main function is to mimic expertise and distribute expert knowledge to non-experts, such benefits can be greatly enhanced by using the Internet.

Dagger, O'Connor, Lawless, Walsh, & Wade (2007) pointed out that rapid advances in Internet technologies have opened new opportunities for enhancing traditional Standalone Expert Systems (Duan et al., 2005; Li, Fu, & Duan, 2002; Thomson & Willoughby, 2004; Zetian, Feng, Yun, & XiaoShuan; 2005). Furthermore, web-based expert systems have benefits such as: online knowledge acquisition, sharing of online knowledge representation tools, testing cases submitted by users via, user validation process with online feedback form, sharing of online inference tools, possibility for teleconsulting with real experts through video conferencing, chat rooms, message boards and email facilities, and online user evaluation.

Additionally, some challenges relating to web-based expert systems include: offline user support when the user base grows in size and in geographical location, Internet speed bottlenecks for teleconsulting, development of common inference engines, keeping up with the rapid changes in web technologies, development of generic online debugging tools, Development of web-based expert system shells, information overload, knowledge mining on Internet locations, and verifying online "experts" (Duan et al., 2005; Li, et al., 2002).

Related Work

In this section of the chapter, we discuss related work. We structure our related work as follows: (i) Stand-Alone Expert Systems for E-Counseling and (ii) Web-Based Expert Systems for E-Counseling.

Stand-Alone Expert Systems for E-Counseling

ICT-mediated counseling is often referred to as e-counseling or online counseling (Tate, Jackvony, & Wing, 2003; Kolog et al., 2014; Kolog et al., 2015). E-counseling in Ghana is viewed as a digital form of receiving supportive counseling either through an exchange of emails or a live webcam session over the internet. The basic concept of e-counseling is to expand the sector to allow people with varied interests to access counseling services irrespective of the location and time (Kolog et al., 2015). Therefore remote (day) students, especially those who are geographically isolated and physically challenged could access counseling services efficiently. In Ghana, e-counseling gained prominence in 2007's educational reform in which ICT was introduced as a core subject of study in schools (Kevor, 2013). The aim was to propel students to acquire knowledge in ICT, which of course would motivate students to use e-counseling.

In relation to stand alone expert systems for e-counseling, Srivathsan et al. (2011) proposed and implemented a Question and Answer based AI application to provide students with career counseling services. Through the utilization of an Intelligent Expert System, the software is equipped with all the necessary domain specific information about various vocations and also the capability to draw appropriate inferences based on heuristic and judgmental knowledge, while providing the human psychologist touch.

Similar to Srivathsan et al. (2011), Deorah, Sridharan, & Goel (2010) proposed an expert system-SAES which aims to provide intelligent advice to students regarding which major he/she should choose/select. SAES acquires knowledge of academic performances as well as explicit and implicit interests of the candidate. Knowledge representation in SAES is done by the use of a combination of case-based and rule-based reasoning. SAES draws inferences on the basis of acquired knowledge and also takes into account the degree of dilemma faced by the candidate and the time he/she takes to decide his/her interest areas. SAES then recommends the most suitable majors for each candidate, which are further classified as strong, mild and weak on the basis of calculated relative probabilities of success.

Furthermore, Career Path Selection Recommendation System (CPSRS) was proposed and developed by Razak et al. (2014). This system was developed using fuzzy logic technique. CPSRS was designed for providing direction and guidance to final year students for Faculty of Computer and Mathematical Science, University Teknologi students in Malaysia for choosing suitable career.

Similar to Razak et al. (2014), Nambair and Dutta (2010) developed an expert system using JESS (a Java based rule engine and scripting environment) that allows students to seek quick responses to their queries regarding their plan of study and progress in the program. This expert system separates the rules from the execution thus enabling users to customize or extend the system by changing or updating the XML file that stores the rules.

Similar to Nambiar and Dutta (2010), Pokrajac and Rasamny (2006) proposed and developed In-VEStA—Interactive Virtual Expert System for Advising—to assist undergraduate students and their advisors in providing timely, accurate and conflict-free schedules. Their proposed system was based on Java and object-relational database technologies, which was made up of the Database Layer, Transaction Layer, Scheduler and the Front End.

Web-Based Expert (E-Counseling) Systems

Although, the advent of ICT has made it possible for clients to vary counseling methods (Kolog et al., 2014; Kolog et al., 2015) based on choice and convenience, yet few technologies have been developed contextually to meet counseling demands. Meanwhile, a substantial number of Information Technology tools have been adopted in counseling delivery. Popular among these technologies are video conferencing, e-mail, Skype, and telephone (Kolog et al., 2015, Kevor, 2013). The aforementioned technologies have existed for a long time but rarely used in the context of the Ghanaian SHS counseling sector (Kolog et al., 2015).

As stated above, institutions of higher learning in Ghana have set up special counseling units to cater for the psychological needs of students. There is physical access to the units but preliminary investigations indicate that, most students are not comfortable having physical interaction with counselors or being seen visiting the unit for fear of stigmatization (Kevor, 2013). It is therefore significant to find a way of maintaining high confidentiality, privacy and even allow students to receive counseling services on anonymity. Kevor (2013) therefore verified the requirements that could be used to develop an e-counseling system for institutions of higher learning in Ghana.

Conversely, Khandelwal, Joshi, Singhania & Dutta (2013) developed a semantic web-based e-counseling system to assist students to surf for relevant information from the web, especially career and academic exploration. The study identified a problem of large volumes of irrelevant information retrieval by students from the web upon a specific query. The system was built through a Natural Language Processing (NLP) approach using semantic web algorithm (Khandelwal et al., 2013). The key functionality of the system, according to the researchers aims at helping students to organize and sort substantial but relevant web information. In a related study, Wang, Chen, Xin & Yi (2010) developed a global web peer counseling system for clients. The system was designed to provide students with the opportunity to address each other's (peer) concerns. Also, the researchers recommended the peer counseling system to be used to offer mental healthcare services by peer counselors.

In relation to web-based expert systems for career counseling/development, Harris-Bowlsbey & Sampson (2005) reviewed the trends in the use of computers for delivering support of career guidance and counseling. Their review revealed that 20th-century computer-based systems continue to be used and are mainly delivered via the World Wide Web. These systems are enhanced through audio, video, graphics, strategies to provide needs assessment, and support by cyber counselors or expert system design.

Cao and Zhang (2011) practically combined AI expert system technology and college students' career-counseling work to provide a web-based career counseling expert system for college students. Their proposed system consists of the basic intelligence career counseling, career counseling solutions management, auxiliary decision-making, information management, and evaluation management etc.

Similar to Cao and Zhang (2011), Grupe (2002) proposed a web-based expert system, which provides advice to high school students and college freshmen that are seeking to select a potential major or discipline. The proposed system in Gruppe (2002) gathers information about a student's grades, interests, test scores, interests and aptitudes. It assesses student qualifications for a variety of majors or disciplines. The expert system recommends six majors for them to consider and provides further information sources about the major or discipline.

The above reviewed literature has shows that one of the major factors that has led to a student's inability to choose a relevant tertiary programme is the lack of career counselors in most SHSs in Ghana. A reflection of the above related work shows that the presence of web-based expert (e-counseling) systems for career counseling/development is rare. To the best of our knowledge, there is currently no web-based expert (e-counseling) system in Ghana that can support SHS students to make the right decisions in terms of their career development and improvising the current counseling system has become very vital and necessary.

Theoretical Framework

In order to successfully implement our proposed web-based expert system for e-counseling, the stakeholders involved i.e. high school counselors/teachers, SHS students as well as other relevant administrators should be conversant and familiar with technology usage. As a consequence, it is very important to select an appropriate framework which involves the concepts and ideologies regarding technology acceptance. Examples of such theoretical frameworks include: (i) Technology Acceptance Model (TAM) and (ii) Technology Acceptance Model 2 (TAM-2). A brief description of our selected theoretical framework (TAM) is presented below (Davis, 1989; Venkatesh & Davis, 2000).

TAM

The adoption and use of ICT in workplaces and organizations remains a central concern of information systems research and practice. Considerable progress has been made over the last decade in explaining and predicting user acceptance of ICT at work. In particular, significant theoretical and empirical support has accumulated in favour of the Technology Acceptance Model (TAM) (Davis, 1989; Davis, Bagozzir, & Warshaw, 1989). Many empirical studies have found that TAM consistently explains a considerable proportion of the variance (typically about 40%) in usage intentions and behavior, and that TAM compares favourably with alternative models such as the Theory of Planned Behavior (TPB) and the Theory of Reasoned Action (TRA) (Venkatesh & Davis, 2000; Davis, 1989; Davis et al., 1989).

TAM hypothesizes that an individual's behavioural intention to use a system is determined by two beliefs: *Perceived Usefulness* (*PU*), defined as the extent to which a person believes that using the system will enhance his or her job performance, and *Perceived Ease Of Use* (*PEOU*), defined as the extent to which a person believes that using the system will be free of effort. TAM has been applied into many contexts and fields investigating user acceptance of Information Technology, including the World Wide Web (Lederer, Maupin, Sena, & Zhuang, 2000), mobile banking (Lule, Omwansa, & Waema, 2012) and healthcare (Chau and Hu, 2002). However, along with the relationships suggested by TAM, many researchers have also examined the antecedents of both *PEOU* and *PU* (Porter & Donthu, 2006; Yu, Liu, & Yao, 2003). Most importantly, the majority of technology acceptance models have been developed and modified in Western countries, particularly in Europe and South America and (Al-Adwan, Al-Adwan, & Smedley, 2013).

Figure 1 shows the relationship between the components of TAM. This indicates that *PU* and *PEOU* jointly predict the attitudes towards using technology. *PU* also influences the user's *Behavioural Intention* (*BI*) or *Usage Behaviour* in using technology. *Intention to Use* (*ITU*) also determines the actual use of technology.

In relation to the relationship between *PU* and *Usage Behaviour*, "within organizational settings, people form intentions toward behaviours they believe will increase their job performance, over and above whatever positive or negative feelings may be evoked towards the behaviour per se". Additionally, the model posits that *PEOU* is likely to influence *PU*, where the increase of *PEOU* leads to improved performance. Consequently, *PEOU* has a direct influence on *PU* (Davis, 1989; Venkatesh & Davis, 2000; Davis et al., 1989).

Figure 1. TAM framework

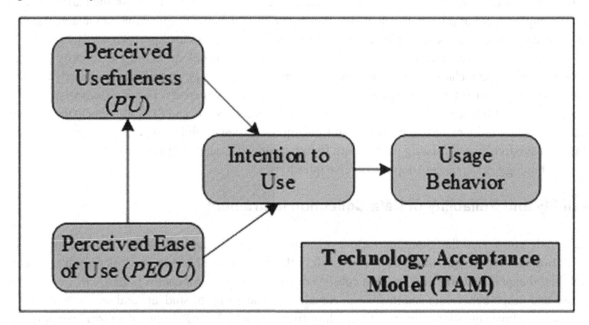

RESEARCH PROCESS AND METHODOLOGY

This section of the chapter discusses the research process and methodology we adopted to collect/acquire relevant and necessary data for effective analysis. Figure 2 depicts our research process.

Figure 2. Research process

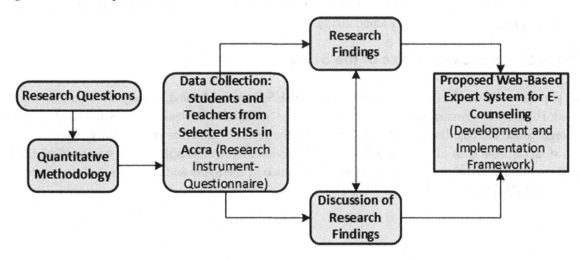

Data Collection Instrument

The research in this study employed a quantitative approach using a questionnaire. The questions which constituted the questionnaire were made up of both closed-ended and open-ended questions. We considered ethical issues strictly in the questionnaire. Therefore, the questionnaires did not ask the participants to answer any personal or private questions. In order to achieve the benefit of reaching out a large number of research participants and obtaining more information, the questionnaire approach was selected.

The questionnaire targeted both SHS students and teachers (counselors) in order to identify the possibility of adopting technology for a web-based expert (e-counseling) system which expertly advises students on appropriate tertiary programmes towards their respective careers. The questions were distributed by means of printed paper material (hard copy) to both counselors and SHS students in the defined sample. Each questionnaire for counselors and students consisted of eighteen (18) main questions with three (3) subdivisions consisting of Bio Data (two questions), Counseling Information (six questions) and Technology Acceptance/Adoption (twelve questions).

Validity and Reliability of Data Collection Instrument

This study considered the important factors regarding the validity and reliability of the adopted data collection instrument (questionnaire). As a result of the fact that the TAM framework for our proposed web-based expert (e-counseling) system consists of four (4) main components (*PEOU, PU,* intentions to use and usage behaviour) and involves a sample size consisting of students and teachers (counselors), we employed questionnaires as a research instrument for gathering enough data that is required to guarantee validity and reliability.

Construct validity was authenticated by verifying the extent to which our questionnaire precisely represents a construct such as students and counselors belief or attitude in relation to using web-based technology for academic counselling activities (Litwin & Fink, 1995; Liu, 2010; Lamar, 2012). We also utilized content validity to verify the extent to which items in our questionnaire represents the content we wish to measure (Litwin & Fink, 1995; Liu, 2010; Lamar, 2012).

We substantiated internal consistency reliability by verifying how consistent the score of individual items are with scores of a set of items in our questionnaire. Additionally, we employed the test-retest reliability to substantiate the correlation of scores from one administration of our questionnaire to another (Litwin & Fink, 1995; Liu, 2010; Lamar, 2012).

Population and Sample Size of the Study

The population chosen for the study involved four (4) SHSs in Accra, Ghana, namely: St. John's Grammar Senior High School, Amasaman Senior High/Technical School, Kinbu Senior High School and Victoria College. Since the population is too large to study, the research aimed at purposefully sampling fifty (50) students from each of the four SHSs, which constituted a total sample size of two hundred (200) students and ten (10) counselors (a set of three from two of the SHSs and another set of two from the other two SHSs) for the study.

DATA ANALYSIS AND STUDY RESULTS

This section of the chapter discusses our procedure for analyzing data received as well as interpretation of results through tables and figures. Table 1 summarizes the socio-demographic profile of the respondents (students and counselors). As stated above, this study employed two hundred (200) students and ten (10) counselors. In relation to the dataset of sampled students, out of the total of 200, 114 (57%) were males, while 86 (43%) were females.

Furthermore, Table 1 depicts that 124 (62%) of the students are aged 11-15 years, 75 (37.5%) are aged 16-20 years and the remaining 1 (0.5%) is aged between 21-26 years. The analysis also revealed that 58 (29%) of the students are in first year of their programme, 70 (35%) are in their second year while 72 (36%) are in their final year of their programme. Students were asked whether they are been counseled by their teachers and the result shows that, 119 (59.5%) indicated that, they are been counseled by their teachers while 81 (40.5%) indicated otherwise. The result obtained further shows that 94 (47%) of the students indicated that counseling session in their SHS involves career guidance and tertiary programme selection. Students who indicated that, their counseling sessions with counselors does not involve career guidance and tertiary programme selection represent 106 (53%).

The study utilized ten (10) counselors selected from the schools used for the study. The distribution of the sex of the counselors shows that, 6 (60%) were males and 4 (40%) were females. Out of this number, 4 (40%) of the teachers are aged between 21-26 years while 2 (20%) each of the teachers are aged between 27-32 years, 33-38 years and 39-44 years respectively. Seven counselors (70%) indicated that they had taught at the senior high school (SHS) level for 1-5 years.

Normality Analysis and Descriptive Statistics

We employed two (2) main constructs (*PU* and *PEOU*) for the study. Six (6) questions under each of the constructs were asked. In each instance there were no missing responses resulting in zero percent (0%) in each case. The descriptive statistics used are the mean, standard deviation (SD), minimum and maximum as well as skewness and kurtosis. The estimated mean value of each construct item for each category (students and counselors) ranged from 2.24 to 2.53 and 1.6 to 2.9 and the deviation from the mean took values from 1.11 to 1.20 and 1.10 to 1.60 for students and counselors respectively. The estimated mean values for each of the category (students and counselors) shows that, respondents agreed to the items. George and Mallery (2016) indicated that items must have skewness value below ±2 to be considered normal. This is also applicable to the kurtosis value estimated for each item. From the result in Figures 3 and 4, all items were within acceptable values.

The internal consistency of constructs was assessed using the Cronbach's alpha (α). Nunnally (1978) indicated that, to ensure consistency in the responses provided by respondents, each construct must at least have a reliability coefficient of 0.70. In this study, the student's data had a reliability value of 0.73 which is within the acceptable value while, in the counselor data there were high levels of internal consistency of a value of 0.90. The descriptive statistics, test results for normality, and reliabilities for each category of respondents (students and teachers) are shown in Figures 3 and 4 respectively.

In Figure 3, the following items are represented as follows: (1) Using a web-based expert (e-counseling) system for career development in my learning activities would enable me to accomplish tasks more quickly (*represented as A*), (2) Using a web-based expert (e-counseling) system for career development would improve my career prospects (*represented as B*), (3) Using a web-based expert (e-counseling) system for

Table 1. Demographic profile of respondents (students and counselors)

Student			Counselors		
Variable	**N**	**%**	**Variable**	**N**	**%**
Age			**Age group**		
11-15 years	124	62	21-26 years	4	40
16-20 years	75	37.5	27-32 years	2	20
21-26 years	1	0.5	33-38 years	2	20
Gender			39-44 years	2	20
Male	114	57	**Gender**		
Female	86	43	Male	6	60
What is your current SHS Level?			Female	4	40
SHS year 1	58	29	**How long have you been teaching in SHS**		
SHS year 2	70	35	1-5 years	7	70
SHS year 3	72	36	6-10 years	1	10
Do your teachers in you school counsel you?			11-15 years	1	10
Yes	119	59.5	16-20 years	1	10
No	81	40.5	**Do you counsel students**		
Does their counselling activities involve career advice/tertiary programme selection?			Yes	9	
			No	1	
Yes	94	47	**How many students do you counsel**		
No	106	53	1-5	5	50
If No to 3, what's the reason why?			6-10	1	10
No counseling activities in my SHS	66	33	>10	4	40
Counseling in my SHS is optional	58	29	**Do your counseling activities involve career advice/tertiary programme selection**		
I don't know	76	38			
			Yes	4	40
			No	6	60

Note: N=Frequency, %=Percentage

career development in my learning and studying activities would increase my productivity (*represented as C*), (4) Using a web-based expert (e-counseling) system for career development would enhance my effectiveness on choosing a career path (*represented as D*), (5) Using a web-based expert (e-counseling) system for career development would make it easier to select a tertiary programme (*represented as E*), (6) I would find a web-based expert (e-counseling) system for career development useful (*represented as F*), (7) Learning to operate a web-based expert (e-counseling) system for career development would be easy for me (*represented as G*), (8) I would find it easy to get a web-based expert (e-counseling) system for career development to do what I want it to do (*represented as H*), (9) My interaction with a web-based expert system (e-counseling) for career development would be clear and understandable (*represented as I*), (10) I would find a web-based expert (e-counseling) system for career development to be flexible to interact with (*represented as J*), (11) It would be easy for me to become skillful at using a web-based expert (e-counseling) system for career development (*represented as K*) and (12) It

Figure 3. Mean, standard deviation, normality and reliability of items for students

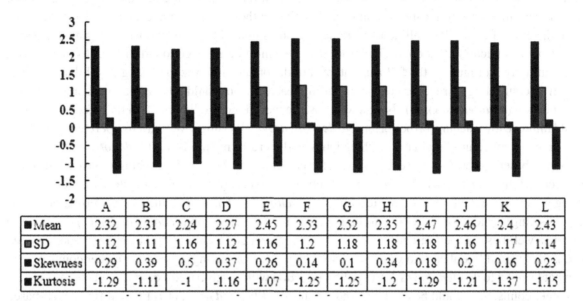

	A	B	C	D	E	F	G	H	I	J	K	L
■Mean	2.32	2.31	2.24	2.27	2.45	2.53	2.52	2.35	2.47	2.46	2.4	2.43
■SD	1.12	1.11	1.16	1.12	1.16	1.2	1.18	1.18	1.18	1.16	1.17	1.14
■Skewness	0.29	0.39	0.5	0.37	0.26	0.14	0.1	0.34	0.18	0.2	0.16	0.23
■Kurtosis	-1.29	-1.11	-1	-1.16	-1.07	-1.25	-1.25	-1.2	-1.29	-1.21	-1.37	-1.15

would be easy for me to become skillful at using a web-based expert (e-counseling) system for career development (**represented as L**).

To further discuss these results, it can further be observed from Figure 3 that, students are in support of using a web-based expert (e-counseling) system for their learning activities and career development. The estimated mean value for the item 1 is ($\bar{x} = 2.32, SD = 1.12$). In Figure 3, Item 2 (**represented a B**) recorded an estimated mean value of 2.31 and a deviation of 1.11 indicating agreement. Items 3-12

Figure 4. Mean, standard deviation, normality and reliability of items for counselors

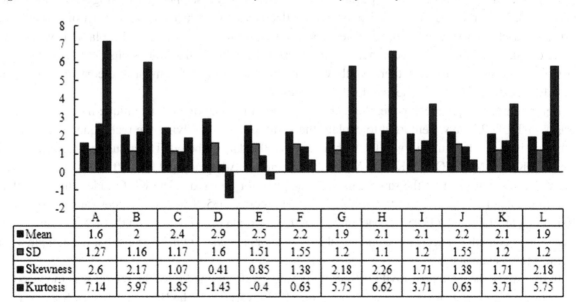

	A	B	C	D	E	F	G	H	I	J	K	L
■Mean	1.6	2	2.4	2.9	2.5	2.2	1.9	2.1	2.1	2.2	2.1	1.9
■SD	1.27	1.16	1.17	1.6	1.51	1.55	1.2	1.1	1.2	1.55	1.2	1.2
■Skewness	2.6	2.17	1.07	0.41	0.85	1.38	2.18	2.26	1.71	1.38	1.71	2.18
■Kurtosis	7.14	5.97	1.85	-1.43	-0.4	0.63	5.75	6.62	3.71	0.63	3.71	5.75

all have mean values of less than 3, indicating agreement that students are in support or in agreement that e-counseling systems must be put in place to enhance their learning and career development.

In the case of counselors, all items were having an estimated mean value below 3, which is a sign of agreement indicating that counselors want this system to be in place to aid them deliver their task well. Similarly, in Figure 4, the following items are denoted as follows: (1) Using a web-based expert system (e-counseling) for career counseling in my teaching job would enable me to accomplish tasks more quickly (*denoted as A*), (2) Using a web-based expert (e-counseling) system for career counseling would improve my teaching job performance (*denoted as B*), (3) Using a web-based expert (e-counseling) system for career counseling in my teaching job would increase my productivity (*denoted as C*), (4) Using a web-based expert (e-counseling) system for career counseling in my teaching job would increase my productivity (*denoted as D*), (5) Using a web-based expert (e-counseling) system for career counseling would make it easier to do my teaching job (*denoted as E*), (6) I would find a web-based expert (e-counseling) system for career counseling useful in my teaching job (*denoted as F*), (7) Learning to operate a web-based expert (e-counseling) system for career counseling would be easy for me (*denoted as G*), (8) I would find it easy to get a web-based expert (e-counseling) system for career counseling to do what I want it to do (*denoted as H*), (9) My interaction with a web-based expert (e-counseling) system for career counseling would be clear and understandable (*denoted as I*), (10) I would find a web-based expert (e-counseling) system for career counseling to be flexible to interact with (*denoted as J*), (11) It would be easy for me to become skillful at using a web-based expert (e-counseling) system for career counseling (*denoted as K*) and (12) It would be easy for me to become skillful at using a web-based expert (e-counseling) system for career development (*denoted as L*). Figures 5 and 6 below show the overall responses for the students and counselors respectively.

Exploratory Factor Analysis (EFA) Using Principal Components Analysis (Students)

Hogarty et al. (2005) stated that factor analysis is one of the numerous statistical techniques that has been used in most fields of study especially in the areas of social science (psychology, education and marketing). It is a multivariate statistical procedure that is used to reduce a large number of variables in a given dataset into a smaller set of variables (also referred to as factors) that could explain the variations in the original variables. The technique is able to establish underlying dimensions between measured variables and latent constructs, thereby allowing the formation and refinement of theory and finally, it provides construct validity evidence of self-reporting scales.

Before employing the technique, there are certain assumptions that the technique must follow. The results in Table 2 below were used to explain the assumptions underlying the technique. The first assumption is to test for suitability of the technique to fit the data gathered. The assumptions were tested using the Kaiser-Meyer-Olkin (KMO), Measure of Sampling Adequacy and Bartlett's Test of Sphericity. The KMO test ensures that the sample used is adequate for the study. The KMO index, in particular, is recommended when the cases to variable ratio are less than 1:5. The KMO values ranges from zero (0) to one (1). Hair et al. (1995); Tabachnick, Fidell, & Ullman (2007) indicated that KMO values of at least 0.50 is considered acceptable and suitable for factors analysis, which means that the sample used for the study is adequate.

In this study the estimated KMO is 0.68. This value was obtained after the model was modified to remove two (2) items from the analysis. The initial KMO was 0.64. The Bartlett's Test of Sphericity is

Figure 5. Overall responses from students

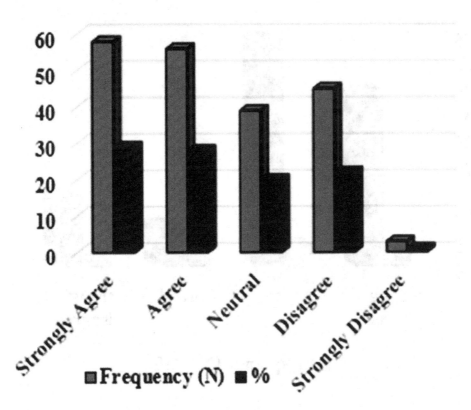

another test that must satisfied the usage of the EFA, the test result indicates that, p<0.05, which confirms that our example has patterned relationships. Indeed, these tests show that we do have patterned relationships amongst the variables since (p < .001). The implications of these test results are that if the assumptions are not met, distinct and reliable factors cannot be produced which means that, EFA would not be the best technique to be use for the study.

Factor Extraction and Rotation

In this study, the Principal Component Analysis (PCA) was used to determine the number of significant components necessary for the variables in the dataset. This extraction was done using the Varimax Rotation which is one of the common rotation techniques. Figures 7 and 8 show the results of the total variance explained which helps in the determination of the number of significant factors/components. Many researchers have accepted the general rule by Kaiser (1960) criteria, which states that eigenvalue must be greater than 1 (eigenvalue > 1 rule) i.e. Cumulative Percentage of Variance and Eigenvalue > 1. Hair et al. (1995) indicated that in natural sciences, factors should be stopped when at least 95% of the variance is explained within the origin variables. However, in the field of the humanities, the variance explained by the components show between 50-60% as indicated by Pett, Lackey, & Sullivan (2003).

In this study, the estimated cumulative percentage of variance is 63.78% and a total of five (5) components (factors) having an eigenvalue > 1 as indicted in the Figures 7 and 8. Having been able to determine

Figure 6. Overall responses from counselors

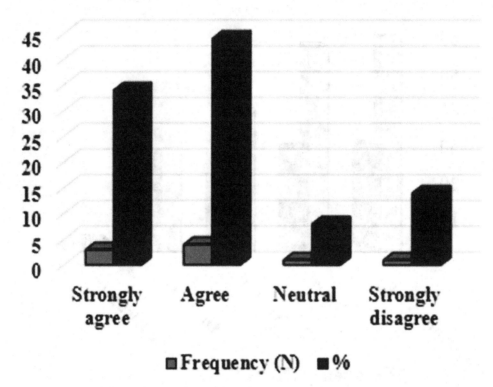

the variance explained by the variables, the communalities were estimated and after the removal of the two variables that were loading low. Item communalities are considered "high" if the items have communality value of at least 0.8, which is mostly not real in practical situations. More common magnitudes in the social sciences are low to moderate communalities of 0.40 to 0.70. If an item has communality of less than 0.40, it may either: a) not be related to the other items, or b) an additional suggested factor that should be explored.

Table 2. KMO and Bartlett's test results before and after modification for students

KMO And Bartlett's Test	Before Modification		After Modification	
Kaiser-Meyer-Olkin Measure of Sampling Adequacy.		0.643		0.682
Bartlett's Test of Sphericity	Approx. Chi-Square	144.682	Approx. Chi-Square	113.099
	df	66	Df	45
	Sig.	0.000	Sig.	0.000

Figure 7. Total variance before modification

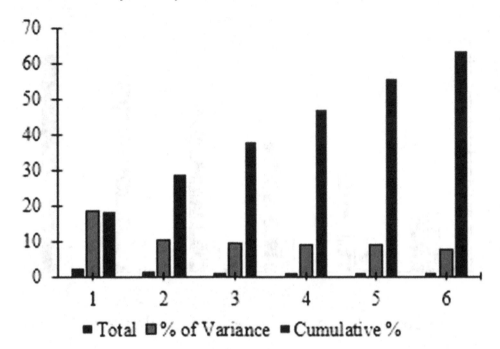

Rotated Component Matrix and Communalities

Table 3 shows the rotated component matrix and the items communalities. Ten items were retained in the analysis and 5 principal components were extracted as indicated in the Table 3. Item numbered 1-3 corelate well with component 1, with the highest correlated value being 0.74. Items numbered 4-6 correlate well with component 2, with the highest correlation value been 0.78. Item 7 correlates well with component three (3). Component four (4) has two items that it correlates high with. The last component has one item with a correlation value of 0.62. The results displayed in Table 3 shows that almost all the items have met the required cut-off point as indicated above. In the case of the communalities which determines the loading of each of the items, it can be observed that all items have communality values above 0.50, with minimum and maximum values of 0.56 and 0.74 respectively associated with item number 7.

SOLUTIONS AND RECOMMENDATIONS

The main philosophy behind the development of a web-based expert (e-counseling) system is to create a user-friendly platform that will be fully interactive and timely on decision making in the domain of tertiary programme selection for SHS students in Ghana to improve career development. As stated earlier, such e-counseling systems will enhance national development since students will have a clearer view of their intended university/tertiary programmes to rightfully select a future career.

Additionally, the issue of lack of counselors would be curbed as this system will be available on the internet for easy accessibility and availability to SHS students. The system will have a high response

Figure 8. Total variance before modification

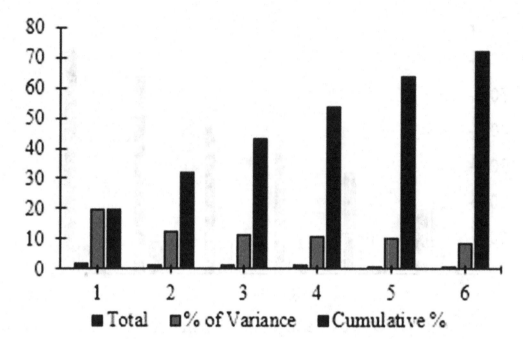

time (programme recommendation) and will as well assist many parents and teachers to support tertiary programme recommendation.

User Requirements

It is very important to get users of the web-based expert (e-counseling) system fully involved such that the problem of tertiary programme mismatch with career expectations does not arise. We therefore approached some SHS students to ask them what they expected as a user of the proposed system. The following are a list of user requirements we gathered from the initial procedure of software specification:

1. The system should be user friendly (attractive UI, easy navigation) easy to use and easily accessible from on the internet.
2. The system should be able to match student's interests and capabilities to the right tertiary programme.
3. The system that should be fast, effective and efficient in producing expert advice and results relating to the best university programme recommendation for particular SHS students.

Functional Requirements

Functional requirements capture the intended behaviour of the web-based expert (e-counseling) system. This behaviour may be expressed as services, tasks or functions the system is required to perform. Therefore, the proposed system is able to:

Table 3. Rotated component matrix and communalities

S/N	Item	1	2	3	4	5	Communalities
1	Using a web-based expert (e-counseling) system for career development in my learning and studying activities would increase my productivity.	0.74					0.61
2	It would be easy for me to become skillful at using a web-based expert (e-counseling) system for career development.	0.68					0.56
3	I would find a web-based expert (e-counseling) system for career development easy to use.	0.42					0.56
4	Using a web-based expert (e-counseling) system for career development would enhance my effectiveness on choosing a career path.		0.55				0.69
5	My interaction with a web-based expert (e-counseling) system for career development would be clear and understandable.		0.78				0.66
6	I would find a web-based expert (e-counseling) system for career development to be flexible to interact with.		0.43				0.63
7	Using a web-based expert (e-counseling) system for career development would improve my career prospects.			0.85			0.74
8	Using a web-based expert (e-counseling) system for career development in my learning activities would enable me to accomplish tasks more quickly.				0.71		0.65
9	I would find it easy to get a web-based expert (e-counseling) system for career development to do what I want it to do				0.70		0.66
10	Using a web-based expert (e-counseling) system for career development would make it easier to select a tertiary programme.					0.75	0.62

1. Captures the SHS student's input to each question field.
2. Make inference based on the captured input.
3. Expertly recommend a tertiary programme that suits student's career interest.
4. Expertly recommend the most appropriate university that offers the selected programme.

Non-Functional Requirements

Non-Functional Requirements are requirements which specify a criteria that can be used to judge the operation of a system rather than specific behaviours. Software quality attributes such as accuracy, performance, cost, security and modifiability as well as usability for the intended users represents the non-functional requirements of a system. Non-functional requirements of the proposed system include:

1. The system has user-friendly interfaces. This ensures the ease with which the system can be used.
2. The system is available and can be reached at any point in the day.
3. The system does not require any administrative privileges and is therefore easily accessible.

4.   The system can be reached from any part of the country with a device that has internet connectivity.

Knowledge Engineering Process

The decision rules (production rules) for our proposed web-based expert (e-counseling) system was constructed through a heuristic knowledge engineering procedure based on an interview with the School's Counselors (Domain Experts) at Amasaman Senior High/Technical School. The counselor indicated that the West African Senior Secondary Certificate Examination (WASSCE) is a prerequisite for admitting prospective SHS graduates into various higher educational institutions. Consequently, the decision rules should primarily contain programmes being offered in SHSs, the student's best elective and future career aspiration(s).

The counselor of at Amasaman Senior High/Technical School further added that the academic performance of the student also determines the programme that best suits the student. He further explained that the decision rules should include an option for students to enter their expected WASSCE results based on their current academic performance. He noted that financial constraints are a major limitation for most students and that the decision rules should as well include of an option for University fees for each programme of study. Finally, we also extracted information from the various University websites which consists of programmes offered and cut-off points. Factual knowledge from books were also utilized as rules in developing the production rules for the web-based expert system.

Development Tools

Development tools are hardware and software that were used in creating our proposed web-based expert (e-counseling) system. In this study, the development tools that were used include: Hypertext Mark-up Language (HTML) for creating the interface and linking relative pages, Cascading Style Sheets (CSS) for designing and decorating the interface, Hypertext Pre-processor (PHP) for designing inference and moving data between web pages and MySQL database as the knowledge base for storing expert knowledge.

Requirements for System Implementation

The implementation requirements depend on computer system specifications. These are the hardware and software requirements that the system runs on. The system supports all computer associated with Pentium IV microprocessors/CPUs and above, as well as Linux, Microsoft Windows and Mac Operating Systems with at least 3 GB of RAM, 32 GB of hard disk space and a 1.2 GHZ of the processor speed.

The client computer must have internet connectivity to have access to the web server through TCP/IP. Latest web-browsers with support for HTML 5 must be preinstalled. The system should be hosted on any server computer running on either Linux or Microsoft Windows architecture. The server should have at least 10 GB of RAM and 1 Terabyte of storage space and running on processor speed of at least 10 GHz.

Use Case Diagram (Decision Tree)

TPR represents the "Tertiary Programme Recommender" button found on the Home Page in Figure 10. When this button is clicked, the sessions shown in Figure 9 are initialized. User inputs are captured by these sessions respectively, as shown in Figure 9. The data captured through the respective sessions are

Figure 9. Use case diagram of our proposed web-based (e-counseling) expert system

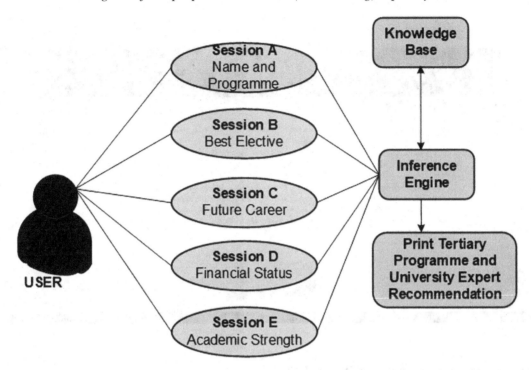

acted upon by the inference engine. The inference engine compares user choice of input in each session with the existing rules in the knowledge base and displays a matching-criteria for the user as the tertiary programme and university expert recommendation.

Functionality of the System

The system involves components that work together to see to the efficient functionality of the system. The following are briefly elaborated features of the proposed system. In Figure 10, the home page is the welcome page that introduces the user to the system. There is a button below the home screen which when pressed begins the student - expert session. This is the "Begin TPR" button. The home page also provides a brief description of user interaction with system. The system is divided into five steps:

Figure 11 represents the first page seen after the "Start TPR" button in Figure 10 has been clicked. This page is introduced as "STEP 1". STEP 1: allows the student to input his/her name and as well as selecting an SHS programme (Business and General Science for now). Figure 12 represents the system's second page. It appears after the "Next" button in Figure 11 has been clicked. This page is introduced as "STEP 2". STEP 2: allows the student to select his/her best elective subject for the chosen programme.

In Figure 13, the page is introduced as "STEP 3". STEP 3: allows the student to select a career stream. This is what the student intends to become in future. Figure 14 allows the student to choose their expected West African Senior Secondary Certificate Examination (WASSCE) grade which would be used by the system to determine the academic strength of the student. In Figure 15, the student selects a fee range based on his/her financial status. Finally, in Figure 16, a university and programme expert recommendation is generated for the student based on the student's choice of input in interacting with the system.

Figure 10. The home page

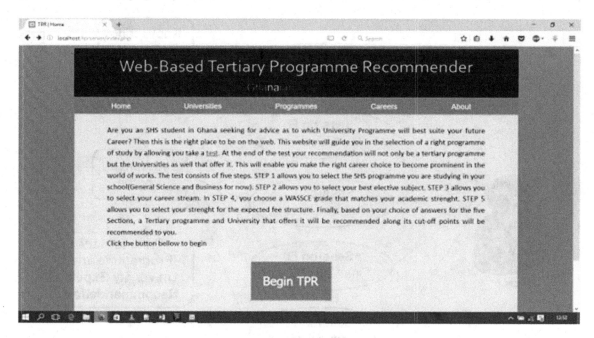

Summary of Research Results and Findings

Globally, advancements of technology through ICTs enables the beneficial adoption of computing applications and systems by various users. For instance, the web-based expert (e-counseling) system proposed in this chapter, cannot be implemented without both counselors and students willing to embrace technology and part of education in SHSs in Ghana. Initially, counselors have to familiarize themselves with ICT methods for counseling so that they transfer their knowledge to SHS students. Consequently, ICT proficiency and skills of both counselors and students should be upgraded (Asabere, 2013; Buabeng-Andoh, 2012; Asabere et al., 2017; Gati, Saka, & Krausz, 2001; Kolog et al., 2015).

In order to successfully develop and implement the web-based expert (e-counseling) system for SHSs proposed in this chapter, it was very necessary to review our research objectives and ascertain the preparedness of students and counselors in adopting technology as part of career guidance (counseling) activities. Furthermore, it was imperative to consider vital variables or needed resources that influence both counselors and students in the selected SHSs to encourage them to use ICTs for career guidance (counseling) activities.

Based on the research conducted, the findings revealed 59.5% (119 students) indicated that, they are been counseled by their teachers while 40.5% (81 students) indicated otherwise, however the mean and SD values in Figures 3 and 4 show that, there are currently no available web-based (e-counseling) expert systems for career guidance in the selected SHSs and the main stakeholders involving students and counselors are willing to embrace such technology to support their career guidance (counseling) activities in terms of *PU* and *PEOU*, which is a positive indication for successful implementation.

The students also noted that the availability of a computerized expert (web-based) expert system could assist them to make career related decisions through e-counseling. Furthermore, the counselors, also cor-

Figure 11. Enter student name and select SHS programme

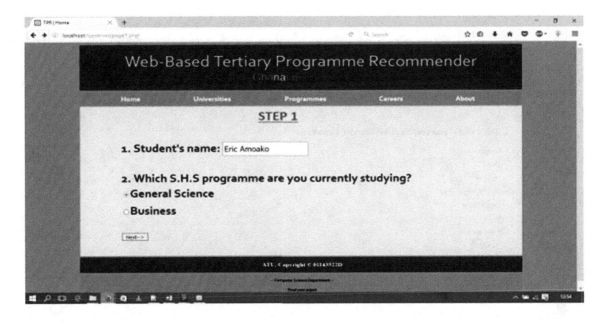

Figure 12. Select your best elective

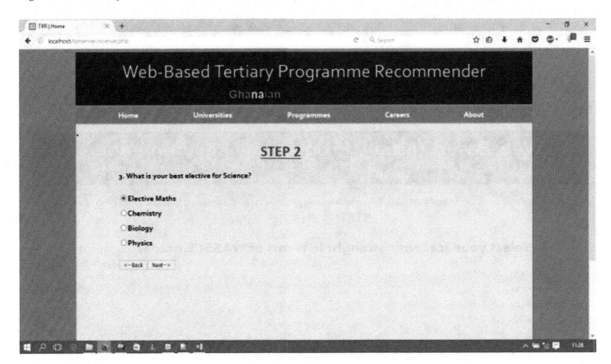

Figure 13. Select your Aspiring Future Career

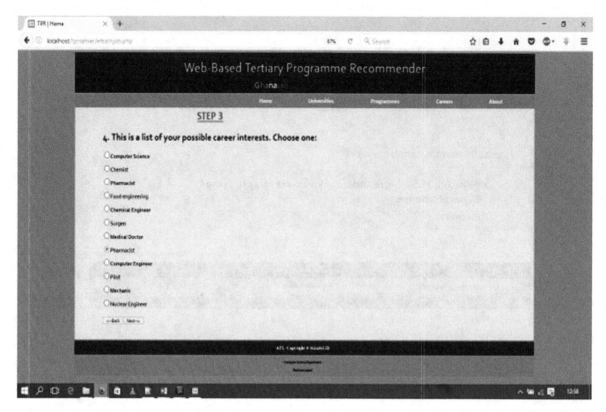

Figure 14. Select your expected WASSCE grade

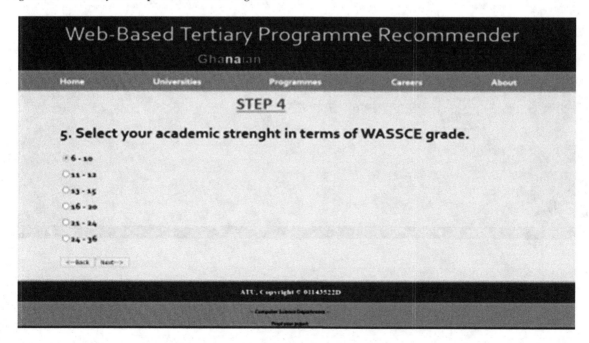

Figure 15. Fee range

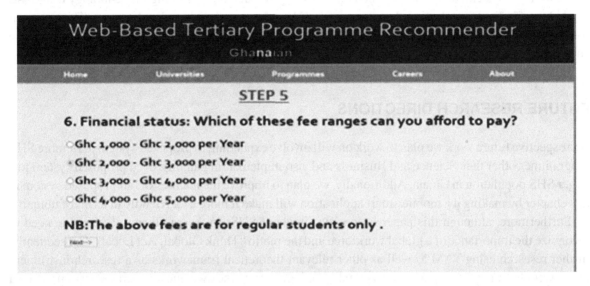

roborated that a web-based expert system directed towards career guidance e-counseling activities would help them in their work as counselors, since the expert system is driven by counselor expert knowledge.

The number of counselors and students used for evaluating our proposed web-based expert system were six (6) and one hundred (100) respectively. All the counselors (representing 100%) selected for user acceptance evaluation accepted the proposed web-based expert system and 80 out 100 students (representing 80%) selected for user acceptance evaluation accepted the same system.

Multimedia sources for explaining a practical method or concept for procedures/processes were also made accessible to the selected students and counselors. In the use of the proposed web-based expert

Figure 16. Expert recommendation for student's choice of input

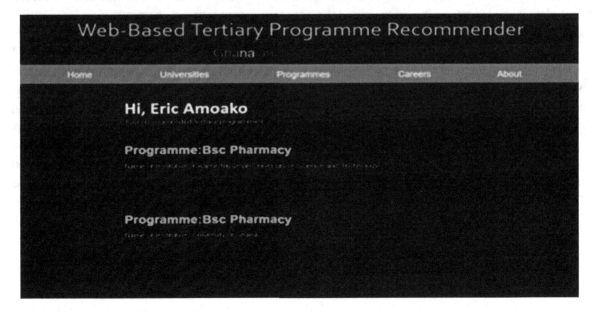

(e-counseling) system, both students and counselors agreed that more training of technology usage was needed to effectively implement the proposed web-based expert (e-counseling) system. The proposed web-based expert (e-counseling) system enabled opinions of both teachers and students to be taken into consideration for effective and successful implementation.

FUTURE RESEARCH DIRECTIONS

A prospective future work we plan to work on will involve expanding to proposed system to fit more SHS programmes other than Science and Business and also implementing an improved proposed system to a larger SHS population in Ghana. Additionally, we plan to improve the features of our proposed system in this chapter by making it a mobile/smart application will make it more user friendly in terms of ubiquity.

Furthermore, although this paper is specifically about SHSs in Accra-Ghana, there is the need to recognize the importance of a global workforce and the motto "Think Global, Act Local". Consequently, further research using TAM as well as other relevant theoretical frameworks as a research instrument component both in Ghana and Africa is vital in order to create the awareness of strategies to produce a global competent workforce, who are skilled to deal with systems, businesses, and technological economies which are currently growing rapidly.

CONCLUSION

As a result of the problems SHS students in Ghana encounter when making career choices in terms of tertiary programme selection, this chapter initially reviewed relevant literature and utilized a quantitative research methodology (questionnaires) to propose a web-based expert (e-counseling) system. Based on the findings and analysis, the implementation and usage of a web based expert system as shown in above is a venture worth investing in. There are a lot of benefits that can be realized through this system if taken seriously and embraced. Both the SHS students in Accra and the nation as a whole will benefit from it. If a student is guided by any means to choose the right tertiary programme, the productive contribution made by this student eventually contributes to national and career development.

The proposed web based expert (e-counseling) system provides this means by taking advantage of student's usage of the internet to deploy an interface of specified questions that the students answers about the programme he is studying in school, his best elective, future career aspiration, financial status and the location in which the student would like to school. Upon answering all questions, just like an expert, the system provides a recommendation of the best tertiary programme, the university that offers it as well as what to do in order to achieve future career aspirations. In a nutshell, with analysis, assessment and evaluation of the proposed system, it can be safely concluded that the proposed system is an efficient, usable and reliable student's tertiary programme advising expert system that is beneficial to the SHS student as well as the nation Ghana as a whole in the domain of national and career development.

REFERENCES

Aker, J. C., & Mbiti, I. M. (2010). Mobile phones and economic development in Africa. *The Journal of Economic Perspectives*, *24*(3), 207–232. doi:10.1257/jep.24.3.207

Al-Adwan, A., Al-Adwan, A., & Smedley, J. (2013). Exploring students' acceptance of e-learning using technology acceptance model in Jordanian universities. *International Journal of Education and Development Using Information and Communication Technology*, *9*(2), 4–18.

Al Ahmar, M. A. (2011). A prototype student advising expert system supported with an object-oriented database. *International Journal of Advanced Computer Science and Applications*, *1*(3), 100–105.

Athanasou, J. A., & Van Esbroeck, R. (Eds.). (2008). *International handbook of career guidance*. Springer Science & Business Media. doi:10.1007/978-1-4020-6230-8

Bordons, M., Zulueta, M. A., Romero, F., & Barrigón, S. (1999). Measuring interdisciplinary collaboration within a university: The effects of the multidisciplinary research programme. *Scientometrics*, *46*(3), 383–398. doi:10.1007/BF02459599

Cao, Y., & Zhang, L. (2011). Research about the college students' career counseling expert system based on agent. *Proceedings of the 2nd International Conference on Artificial Intelligence, Management Science and Electronic Commerce (AIMSEC)*, 3208-3211.

Covner, B. J. (1963). Engineers in midstream: A study of engineers seeking professional career guidance. *IEEE Transactions on Engineering Management*, *EM-10*(1), 15–18. doi:10.1109/TEM.1963.6449226

Cuseo, J. (2003). *Academic advisement and student retention: Empirical connections and systemic interventions*. University of Texas. http://146.85.50.73/retention/media/Academic-advisementv-and-student-retention.pdf

Dagger, D., O'Connor, A., Lawless, S., Walsh, E., & Wade, V. P. (2007). Service-oriented e-learning platforms: From monolithic systems to flexible services. *IEEE Internet Computing*, *11*(3), 28–35. doi:10.1109/MIC.2007.70

Davis, D. (1989). Perceived usefulness, perceived ease of use, and user acceptance of information technology. *Management Information Systems Quarterly*, *13*(3), 319–340. doi:10.2307/249008

Davis, F., Bagozzir, R., & Warshaw, P. (1989). User acceptance of computer technology: A comparison of two theoretical models. *Management Science*, *35*(8), 982–1003. doi:10.1287/mnsc.35.8.982

Deorah, S., Sridharan, S., & Goel, S. (2010). SAES-expert system for advising academic major. *Proceedings of the 2nd IEEE International Advance Computing Conference (IACC)*, 331-336.

Dogan, M. (1996). The hybridization of social science knowledge. *Library Trends*, *45*(2), 296–314.

Duan, Y., Edwards, J. S., & Xu, M. X. (2005). Web-based expert systems: Benefits and challenges. *Information & Management*, *42*(6), 799–811. doi:10.1016/j.im.2004.08.005

Essuman, J. K. (2001). A review of Educational studies in Guidance and counseling in schools in Ghana. *Ghana Journal of Psychology*, *1*(1), 22–43.

Gati, I., & Gutentag, T. (2015). The stability of aspect-based career preferences and of the recommended list of occupations derived from them. *Journal of Vocational Behavior, 87,* 11–21. doi:10.1016/j.jvb.2014.11.009

Gati, I., & Ram, G. (2000). Counsellors' judgments of the quality of the pre-screening stage of the career decision-making process. *Journal of Counseling Psychology, 47*(4), 414–428. doi:10.1037/0022-0167.47.4.414

Gati, I., Saka, N., & Krausz, M. (2001). Should I use a computer-assisted career guidance system? It depends on where your career decision-making difficulties lie. *British Journal of Guidance & Counselling, 29*(3), 301–321.

Gati, I., & Tal, S. (2008). Decision-making models and career guidance. In *International handbook of career guidance* (pp. 157–185). Springer. doi:10.1007/978-1-4020-6230-8_8

George, D., & Mallery, P. (2016). *IBM SPSS statistics 23 step by step: A simple guide and reference.* Routledge. doi:10.4324/9781315545899

Hair, J. F., Anderson, R. E., Tatham, R. L., & Black, W. C. (1995). *Multivariate data analysis with readings.* Petroleum Publishing.

Harris-Bowlsbey, J., & Sampson, J. P. Jr. (2005). Use of technology in delivering career services worldwide. *The Career Development Quarterly, 54*(1), 48–56. doi:10.1002/j.2161-0045.2005.tb00140.x

Hogarty, K. Y., Hines, C. V., Kromrey, J. D., Ferron, J. M., & Mumford, K. R. (2005). The quality of factor solutions in exploratory factor analysis: The influence of sample size, communality, and overdetermination. *Educational and Psychological Measurement, 65*(2), 202–226. doi:10.1177/0013164404267287

Ibrahim, M. E., Yang, Y., Ndzi, D. L., Yang, G., & Al-Maliki, M. (2019). Ontology-based personalized course recommendation framework. *IEEE Access: Practical Innovations, Open Solutions, 7,* 5180–5199. doi:10.1109/ACCESS.2018.2889635

Internet World Stats in Africa. (2019). https://www.internetworldstats.com/africa.htm

Jabbar, H. K., & Khan, R. Z. (2016). Survey on development of expert system from 2010 to 2015. *Proceedings of the Second ACM International Conference on Information and Communication Technology for Competitive Strategies.* 10.1145/2905055.2905190

Kaiser, H. F. (1960). The application of electronic computers to factor analysis. *Educational and Psychological Measurement, 20*(1), 141–151. doi:10.1177/001316446002000116

Kesson, A. B. (2013). *Students perception and utilization of counseling in Ghana: A case study of the Accra Metropolis* (Unpublished master's thesis). University of Ghana, Legon.

Kessy, D., Kaemba, M., & Gachoka, M. (2006). The reasons for under use of ICT in education. In the context of Kenya, Tanzania and Zambia. *Proceedings of the Fourth IEEE.*

Kevor, M. O. (2013). E-Counseling for Institutions of Higher Learning in Ghana: What are the Requirements? *International Journal of Research in Computer Application & Management, 3*(5), 131–134.

Khandelwal, T., Joshi, G., Singhania, A., & Dutta, A. (2013). Semantic Web-Based E-Counseling System. *International Journal of Computer Science and Electronics Engineering*, *1*(1), 2320–4028.

Khanna, S., Kaushik, A., & Barnela, M. (2010). Expert systems advance in education. *Proceedings of the National Conference on Computational Instrumentation*, 109-112.

Klein, J. T. (1996). Interdisciplinary needs: The current context. *Library Trends*, *45*(2), 134–154.

Kolog, E., Sutinen, E., & Vanhalakka-Ruoho, M. (2014). E-counselling implementation: Students' life stories and counselling technologies in perspective. *International Journal of Education and Development Using ICT*, *10*(3), 32–48.

Kolog, E. A., Sutinen, E., Vanhalakka-Ruoho, M., Suhonen, J., & Anohah, E. (2015). Using unified theory of acceptance and use of technology model to predict students' behavioral intention to adopt and use e-counseling in Ghana. *International Journal of Modern Education and Computer Science*, *7*(11), 1–11. doi:10.5815/ijmecs.2015.11.01

Lamar, M. M. (2012). Using and developing measurement instruments in science education: A Rasch modeling approach. *Science Education*, *96*(1), 183–185. doi:10.1002ce.20477

Lederer, A., Maupin, D., Sena, M., & Zhuang, Y. (2000). The technology acceptance model and the world wide web. *Decision Support Systems*, *29*(3), 269–282. doi:10.1016/S0167-9236(00)00076-2

Li, D., Fu, Z., & Duan, Y. (2002). Fish-Expert: A web-based expert system for fish disease diagnosis. *Expert Systems with Applications*, *23*(3), 311–320. doi:10.1016/S0957-4174(02)00050-7

Litwin, M. S., & Fink, A. (1995). *How to measure survey reliability and validity*. Sage Publications. doi:10.4135/9781483348957

Liu, X. (2010). *Using and developing measurement instruments in science education: A Rasch modeling approach*. Information Age Publishing (IAP).

Lule, I., Omwansa, T., & Waema, T. (2012). Application of technology acceptance model in m-banking adoption in Kenya. *International Journal of Computing and ICT Research*, *6*(1), 31–43.

Nambiar, A. N., & Dutta, A. K. (2010). Expert system for student advising using JESS. *Proceeding of the IEEE International Conference on Educational and Information Technology*, V1-312. 10.1109/ICEIT.2010.5607701

Pett, M. A., Lackey, N. R., & Sullivan, J. J. (2003). Making sense of factor analysis: The use of factor analysis for instrument development in health care research. *Sage (Atlanta, Ga.)*.

Pokrajac, D., & Rasamny, M. (2006). Interactive virtual expert system for advising (InVEStA). *Proceedings of the IEEE 36th Frontiers in Education Annual Conference*, 18-23. 10.1109/FIE.2006.322295

Porter, C., & Donthu, N. (2006). Using the technology acceptance model to explain how attitudes determine internet usage: The role of perceived access barriers and demographics. *Journal of Business Research*, *59*(9), 999–1007. doi:10.1016/j.jbusres.2006.06.003

Razak, T. R., Hashim, M. A., Noor, N. M., Halim, I. H. A., & Shamsul, N. F. F. (2014). Career path recommendation system for UiTM Perlis students using fuzzy logic. *Proceeding of the 5th IEEE International Conference on Intelligent and Advanced Systems (ICIAS)*, 1-5. 10.1109/ICIAS.2014.6869553

Sahin, Y. G., Balta, S., & Ercan, T. (2010). The use of internet resources by university students during their course projects elicitation: A case study. *The Turkish Online Journal of Educational Technology*, *9*(2), 234–244.

Seng, K., & Zeki, A. M. (2014). Career Guidance and Employment Management System. *Proceedings of the 3rd IEEE International Conference on Advanced Computer Science Applications and Technologies*, 73-78.

Srivathsan, G., Garg, P., Bharambe, A., Varshney, H., & Bhaskaran, R. (2011). A dialogue system for career counseling. *Proceedings of the ACM International Conference & Workshop on Emerging Trends in Technology*, 630-634. 10.1145/1980022.1980159

Tabachnick, B. G., Fidell, L. S., & Ullman, J. B. (2007). *Using multivariate statistics* (Vol. 5). Pearson.

Tate, D. F., Jackvony, E. H., & Wing, R. R. (2003). Effects of Internet behavioral counseling on weight loss in adults at risk for type 2 diabetes: A randomized trial. *Journal of the American Medical Association*, *289*(14), 1833–1836. doi:10.1001/jama.289.14.1833 PMID:12684363

The Gale Group Inc. (2002). Academic Disciplines. In *Encyclopaedia of Education*. Author.

Thomson, A. J., & Willoughby, I. (2004). A web-based expert system for advising on herbicide use in Great Britain. *Computers and Electronics in Agriculture*, *42*(1), 43–49. doi:10.1016/S0168-1699(03)00085-1

Venkatesh, V., & Davis, F. (2000). A theoretical extension of the technology acceptance model: Four longitudinal filed studies. *Management Science*, *46*(2), 186–204. doi:10.1287/mnsc.46.2.186.11926

Wang, Z., Chen, H., Xin, R., & Yi, C. (2010). Peer counseling. *Proceedings of the International Conference on Educational and Information Technology*.

Wondoh, J. (2012). Career choices and national development. *Ghana Web*. https://www.ghanaweb.com/GhanaHomePage/NewsArchive/Career-Choises-and-National-Development-257460

Yebowaah, F.A. (2018). Internet use and its effect on senior high school students in Wa Municipality of Ghana. *Library Philosophy and Practice*, 1817.

Yesilyurt, M. E., Basturk, R., Yesilyurt, F., & Kara, I. (2014). the effect of technological devices on student's academic success: Evidence from Denizli. *Journal of Internet Applications & Management*, *5*(1), 39–47. doi:10.5505/iuyd.2014.83007

Yu, J., Liu, C., & Yao, J. (2003). Technology acceptance model for wireless internet. *Internet Research*, *13*(3), 206–222. doi:10.1108/10662240310478222

Zetian, F., Feng, X., Yun, Z., & Xiaoshuan, Z. (2005). Pig-vet: A web-based expert system for pig disease diagnosis. *Expert Systems with Applications*, *29*(1), 93–103. doi:10.1016/j.eswa.2005.01.011

Zimmermann, H. J. (2012). *Fuzzy sets, decision making, and expert systems* (Vol. 10). Springer Science & Business Media.

Chapter 5

Challenges and Opportunities of Information Management in Disaster Preparedness:
The Case of Legazpi City, Albay Province

Sherwin E. Ona
De La Salle University, Philippines

Emmanuel C. Lallana
Ideacorp, Philippines

ABSTRACT

The need to improve local disaster risk reduction (DRR) capacities in the Philippines is crucial in mitigating and responding to future disaster events. Despite being one the most disaster-prone countries in the world, national protocols remain inefficient, marred by corruption and poor inter-agency coordination. In addition, the current top-down and reactive practices have proven to be inadequate in responding to the needs of various stakeholders. The chapter examined these disaster preparation practices through a qualitative-descriptive research design and by using disaster information management (DIM) as the framework. In particular, the authors focused on the disaster preparedness practices of selected parishes of the Diocese of Legazpi and their partner organizations. The study also examined their information management practices and the current information and communications technology (ICT) tools in disaster preparedness.

INTRODUCTION

The Philippines is considered as one of the most disaster-prone countries in the world. With an average of 15 to 20 typhoons hitting the country annually, national policies and programs created to address the adverse effects of these natural events. In particular, the landmark 2010 legislation on disaster risk reduction management (Republic Act 10121), resulted in a paradigm shift on how disaster management

DOI: 10.4018/978-1-7998-3468-7.ch005

is conducted in the country. The law empowers local governments to allocate resources to enable it to respond to disaster events. It also institutionalized disaster risk reduction management (DRRM) in governance through the creation of regional, provincial level disaster offices as well as the integration of DRR in the planning process of the local governments. However, a closer examination of the current Philippine disaster risk reduction management (DRRM) practices reveal its traditional civil defense-oriented nature. This nature is characterized by top-down (unidirectional) programs and information that are focused on disaster response and rehabilitation. Furthermore, it has a centralized nature that places much responsibility on the shoulders of the national government, thus treating local governments and its constituents as disaster aid recipients rather than active partners. On the other hand, a closer examination of the prevailing literature reveals a myriad of new practices that highlights the importance of determining demands, needs and on how to leverage indigenous information sources from local communities. These practices are often governed by social relations, use of information communications technology (ICT) and community data being managed at the village and local government levels.

In this paper, we examined the current community DRR practices using the disaster information management (DIM) perspective. In this view, our efforts focused on the following DIM concepts: a) Information flow and use; b) Identification of data sources and c) ICT tools used by the community and parish-based DRR actors.

To further understand the needs and practices, we adopted a qualitative-descriptive research design focusing on the Diocese of Legazpi and selected participants from the city government of Legazpi, Albay and selected members of the academe. At the end of the paper, we presented recommendations on how to further enhance DIM practices and discussed the future directions of our work.

BACKGROUND OF THE STUDY

Viewing the Phenomenon Using the Disaster Information Management (DIM)

Recognizing disaster-related data/information as a vital resource, the Hyogo Framework of Action (HFA) (2011) stressed the importance of information management (IM) and the use of relevant technologies to address DRRM challenges. The HFA cites the need for IM practices to support the phases of the DRR cycle. These IM practices are the following: (a) collection/storage of data- this includes the sorting, digitization of indigenous data and use of cloud technologies; (b) Use of information to produce new knowledge through data analytics, digital mapping among others; (c) Promoting collaboration and the opening of new communication channels through the use of ICT mediums (e.g. Social media, mobile, etc.). The HFA also cites the importance of building capacities through the presence of the right skills set and policy development (UN APCICT, 2011).

Similarly, the disaster information management (DIM) concept supports this HFA call by ensuring that emerging technologies and practices ensure accessible, timely and useful data as well as its high degree of integrity. DIM aims to transform disaster information (e.g. Vulnerabilities, history, risk, impact and early warning) into vital resources (Mutasa, 2013). This can be done by integrating crowd-sourced information to the traditional sources, enabling communities to collaborate, strength information flows, and generate/share information to purposeful recipients (Quiang et al 2014) (Zheng et al, 2013). Similarly, Li et al (2014) stressed that an effective DIM should be capable of collecting, organizing, analyzing and sharing disaster-related information. It must also respond to users' needs and extract patterns and trends from historical data. However, DIM practices are often characterized as ambiguous, often coming from various sources and channels as well as having different formats. Bolton and Stolcis (2008) stressed that these conflicts with traditional DRR management practices often lead to limited information sharing and horizontal communication among DRR actors and stakeholders. This view also leads to the inability of decision makers to account for wicked problems often missing the multi-faceted nature of the phenomenon that can affect the quality of the intervention (Lassa, 2012).

In addition, further examination of the literature suggests the dynamic, non-linear and discontinuous nature of a disaster environment, highlighting the need to further understand the phenomenon (Bolton and Stolcis, 2008) (Bergstrom et al, 2016) (Day, 2014). For instance, in studies examining the use of social media, Starbird et al (2015) and Palen (2008) highlights the occurrence of misinformation and describes the current information flow as unidirectional, arguing that these issues often lead to the failure to integrate information coming from such sources. While Carney and Weber (2015) point to trustworthiness of social media sources that inhibits its acceptability in DRR related activities.

Another issue affect DIM is heterogeneity of information sources. This phenomenon further adds to the difficulties of using and managing DRR-related information. Zheng et al (2013) acknowledged these difficulties in information and dissemination and exchange due to its multiple sources which is made more complicated with the occurrence of redundancy, problems of accuracy and a variety of reports. In addition, Li et al (2017) argues that these concerns on accuracy and redundancy can be traced to how information are captured and evaluated as well as identifying their sources. In addition, Hristidis et al (2010) further dissects the heterogenous nature of information sources by highlighting the nature of disaster information as having the following: a) Large number of users and producers with varying degree of trustworthiness; b) Lack of a common or standard terminology; c) Time bounded and sensitive and d) Disaster information as having both static and dynamic (streaming) characteristics. Lastly, Mutasa (2013) suggests the need to view disaster information as a relationship between the disaster event, the people involved and their environment. This view includes the issues on access to information, power relations and the need for an appropriate intervention to ensure the efficiency of the management process.

Philippine DRRM and the use of ICT

The enactment of RA 10121 (known as the "Philippine Disaster Risk Reduction Management Act of 2010") was seen as a major legislative accomplishment for the Philippines. Adhering to the principles of the Hyogo framework of action, the intention of this law was to strengthen the practice of disaster management. Furthermore, the law defined new responsibilities of national agencies as well as enabling local governments to address the adverse effects of natural events. Specifically, it empowered local governments to develop their own organizational structures, allocate resources and capacitate various stakeholders. The law also gave civil society organizations and community-based (barangay) peoples organizations roles in local DRRM efforts.

On the national level, the government was at the forefront of using information and communications technology (ICT) for DRRM. For instance, the Project NOAH (Nationwide Operational Assessment of Hazards) of the Department of Science and Technology (DOST) provided real time weather-related forecast and warnings using on-line and mobile applications. It also aimed to provide communities with hazard maps to assist local governments in their DRR planning. The government also acquired Doppler radars to improve its ability to track weather disturbances (Crisologo, 2013). There were also plans to provide villages (known locally as "barangays") with tablets to facilitate their access to Project NOAH information. Known as the Mobile Operational System for Emergency Services (MOSES) tablet, the plan was launched in Marikina city, but was eventually shelved due to lack of resources (NOAH, 2014).

However, despite these investments in ICT, reports coming from government agencies reveal the inability of civil defense agencies as well as local government units to collect, compile and disseminate DRR-related information. This is further exacerbated by the absence of electronic databases that can act as repositories of data, thus highlighting the absence of knowledge management practices (SEPO, 2017).

These practices clearly show a top down approach with regard to how ICTs are used. Mainly seen as tools for pushing information from national sources to the local recipients (top-down). This unidirectional flow limits information exchange and fails to harness community-based data. This limitation contributes to the inability of civil defense agencies to aggregate data and apply knowledge management techniques.

Legazpi City as a Best Practice in DRRM

The City of Legazpi is a first-class component city and the capital of Albay province. Located 527 kilometers south of Metro Manila, it is considered as the largest city of the Bicol region with a population of 196,639 (2015). Its proximity to Mayon Volcano and having its fair share of typhoons (approximately 3-5 typhoons every year), the province of Albay is considered a one of the disaster-prone areas in the Philippines. Recognizing this vulnerability, the provincial government of Albay adopted a zero-casualty policy and established the Albay Public Safety and Emergency Management Office (APSEMO) in 1995. The aim of APSEMO is to adopt a pro-active stance in responding to the challenges of climate change. In terms of the use of ICT in DRRM, the province in cooperation with the SMART telecommunications company, launched a mobile application known as "Tudlo". The application serves as an information dissemination tool for both local and provincial governments of Albay. Similarly, the city government of Legazpi is known for its innovative DRR programs. Aside from adopting the zero-casualty policy, constituent communities of the city have integrated DRR and climate change activities in their development plans. The city is also known for having an emergency management structure that includes all its villages (barangays) and other DRR partners. It has also developed disaster resilient infrastructure related to evacuation sites among others.

For its part, the Roman Catholic Diocese of Legazpi, through the Social Action Committee (SAC), serves as a DRR partner for both the province and the Legazpi city government. With local parishes of the Diocese as their main constituents, the SAC coordinates DRR activities with APSEMO and the City Disaster Risk and Response Office of Legazpi.

Problem Statement and Research Design

With this, we focused on how information management is practiced in communities, particularly in the selected parishes of the Diocese of Legazpi. To further understand this phenomenon, we put forward the following questions: (a) *What are the local information practices related to disaster preparedness?* And (b) *What are the ICT tools that are being used to support these indigenous practices?*

To answer these questions, discussed below are the phases of the research design.

1. **Phase 1:** This phase of the design involves the planning and preparation activities which started with the review of existing Philippine DRR policies and best practices as well as an extensive literature survey on disaster informatics. Our interest in best practices led us to the province of Albay, which

has a nationally recognized DRR program known for its goal of achieving a zero-casualty rate. In the interest of scoping, we decided to focus on Legazpi city, Albay Province due to the openness of the local diocese and the local government of the city. We also coordinated with the Commission on Higher Education (CHED) Regional Office-5 (CHEDRO-5) for participants from local state universities and colleges.

2. **Phase 2**: The second stage of the research involved data gathering. Activities within this phase included the development of questionnaires for the key informants as well as the conduct of the actual interviews and FGDs. Documents pertaining to the existing DRR programs and activities were also collected and review by our team. An expert in developing qualitative research questionnaires from the University of the Philippines assisted our team. Lastly for this phase, we also examined the websites and social media accounts of the local government and the diocese.

3. **Phase 3**: The third stage of the design focused on data analysis by using the critical incidence technique (CIT). This approach enabled the team to establish patterns and themes in the existing DRR practices of Legazpi City. The results were validated in a workshop with the SAC, parish participants and representatives from the local academic community. Another validation meeting was held with research partners from the UK-Newton research network.

Analysis of Results

Our results confirmed the existence of a unidirectional information flow during disaster events. Although acclaimed as one of the best practices in Philippine DRR, the interaction among key city actors remains formal (hierarchical) and top down in general (See figure 1).

Figure 1.

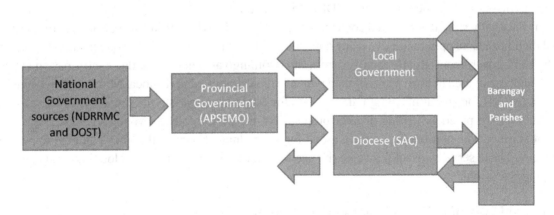

In the practice of disaster preparedness, our results showed that this top down flow can be categorized into 3 types of information: disaster preparedness practices (awareness and training), weather advisories, and community hazards/risks. For the disaster preparedness practices, these are usually sourced from the national government through the National Disaster Risk Reduction Management Council (NDRRMC). The NDRRMC is under the supervision of the Department of National Defense. This is the same with weather advisories, wherein the Philippine Atmospheric, Geophysical and Astronomical Service Administration (PAGASA) and Project NOAH are considered as the primary sources of news and weather-related information. Both sources are attached agencies of the Department of Science and Technology (DOST), a national government line agency. These information and practices are mainly pushed by the APSEMO to the local governments of Albay and its partners. In this case, because of the strong partnership between the government and the Catholic church, these information and practices are received by the Diocese and pushed to the parishes.

In addition, there is also limited feedback coming from the communities and parishes. This bottom up flow is usually in the form of a survey about hazards and risks in the community. As part of a training program, data pertaining to hazards and risks are collected and then aggregated at the city and provincial level

Parish-Based Disaster Preparedness Practices and the use of ICT

Table 1 shows the current disaster preparedness practices of selected parishes in Legazpi City. The table also presents the current ICT use in relation to disaster preparedness.

Overall, it can be seen in the above mentioned disaster preparedness practices that most of the activities are related to awareness and training. Considered as common practices in all surveyed parishes, these activities are usually sourced from the provincial government through the Albay Public Safety Management Office (APSEMO). For disaster related information, these are usually sourced by the parishes through the local governments, APSEMO and national sources (e.g. NDRRMC announcements). While training activities are given by NDRRMC and then coursed through the APSEMO and local governments.

Regarding disaster related information and the use of ICT in all the parishes, information sourced from national and tri media sources are disseminated through SMS (text message) blast and local radio announcements. In both Sto. Domingo and St. Raphael parishes, social media (in particular Facebook), is used to disseminate announcements of DRR-related activities.

Our data gathering also revealed some robust practices in DRR. For instance, Sto. Domingo parish cited their hazard mapping initiative using data coming from the community-based management system of the local government. Representatives from Sto. Domingo also noted that these information are collected and aggregated to form a hazard map which is then submitted to the local Mines and Geosciences Bureau (MGB) for digital mapping purposes. As for St. Michael parish, the project Harong stood out as an innovative practice. During disaster preparation, the parish calls for volunteer households to be part of Harong. The households are then asked for any volunteer service that they can give to possible evacuees. These services usually involve the use of bathrooms, free temporary lodging, meal sharing, and prayer sessions.

Common Uses of ICT and Related Challenges

In our FGDs, participating parishes confirmed the limited use of ICT. This finding was confirmed in our key informant interviews with members of the Social Action Committee (SAC) of the Diocese of Legazpi. In general, the data gathering results reiterated the use of ICTs as a dissemination tool, with the current practices involve dissemination (push) of nationally sourced DRR information. Provincial and city level information are also disseminated through a top-down fashion. This push process is usually for

Participating Parishes	Disaster Preparedness Practices	Use of ICT
Sn. Vincent Ferrer Parish	- Community training and organizing - Information dissemination and collection - Camp management	- SMS blast - Use of tri-media information for dissemination
Sn. Raphael Parish	- Planning: Convening of the Barangay-Parish Committee - Awareness campaign: through seminars (identification of hazards & risks; identification of evacuation area/routes) - Organize volunteers - Coordinate with local public schools	- Information dissemination using collected information from APSEMO and tri-media plus the internet (social media) - Use of SMS blast and handheld radios
Sts Michael and Stephen Protomartyr	- Planning using prioritization of community sectors - Information dissemination - Mapping of community volunteers through Project Harong	- Information dissemination using collected information from APSEMO and tri-media plus the internet (social media) - Use of SMS blast and handheld radios
Sto. Domingo Parish	- Awareness campaign and continuous monitoring of weather updates - Hazard mapping and coordination with the Mines and Geosciences Bureau, DENR - Access to community profile through the Community-based Management System	- Information dissemination using collected information from APSEMO and tri-media plus the internet (social media) - Use of SMS blast - Use of Social Media (e.g. Facebook) for announcement of training events

warnings (weather related or volcanic related) using mobile phones (called as SMS blast). Dissemination is also supported through Facebook.

In summary, the current uses of ICT tools in Disaster Preparation are seen in the following:

- Use of SMS and Social media for disseminating disaster information

- Use of PAGASA website for information
- Traditional Media (e.g Radio and TV) as additional sources of information
- Digital maps for area profiling

In addition, participants and key informants cited the challenges that are usually encountered in the use of ICT in disaster preparation. These are the following:

- **Inadequate SMS Load**: It was pointed out that most of the mobile users are pre-paid subscribers. Therefore, the cost of SMS, usually shouldered by the mobile owner, hinders the full dissemination of disaster warnings;
- **Poor Signal Quality of Mobile and Internet:** Intermittent mobile and internet signals hamper the dissemination of information
- **No Electricity During Disaster Events**: Additional weather warnings are not disseminated due to power failure caused by precedent adverse weather/ volcanic events.
- **Challenges in the use of the Digital Maps**: Participants narrated that the MGB initiated a number of digital mapping activities in the past. However, they pointed out that the results of the mapping were not cascaded back to the communities. In instances wherein, communities were given access to the digital maps, they were unable to use the maps due to the inadequate skills on how to use and interpret the mapping outputs.

Common Themes

During our interactions with members of the SAC, the parishes, members of the local academic community and key officials from Barangay Dapdap of Legazpi City, thematic concerns surfaced regarding the use of ICT in DRR.

Table 2 shows disaster awareness as a common theme that emerged from our data gathering activities.

This theme was linked to the importance of pushing early warning information using traditional ICTs like mobile phones and social media. However, the participants also noted that are multiple sources of disaster-related information which results in difficulties in sorting and prioritizing. Another challenge is the inability to push (or target) sector-specific community information (e.g. PWDs, senior citizens, women, etc.) during pre or post disaster events. These findings are consistent with the observations of Zheng et al (2013) and Li et al (2017) on accuracy and capture of disaster-related information.

On the aspect of improving local capacities to use ICT, it was pointed out that aside from mobile-SMS blasts, the participants see the need for digital mapping that can be used by the community. Aside from creating hazard maps, the participants floated the idea of mapping participating households of project Harong (volunteer households for temporary shelter) and the integration of existing community data sources from the barangays and local governments. Participants also suggested that there should be a way to measure or assess the efficacy of these applications.

In addition, key informants cited the challenges that are usually encountered in the use of ICT in disaster preparation. These are the following: (a) *Inadequate SMS load*- it was pointed out that most of the mobile users are pre-paid subscribers. Therefore, the cost of SMS, usually shouldered by the mobile owner, hinders the full-dissemination of disaster warnings; (b) *Poor signal quality of mobile and internet*- intermittent mobile and internet signals hamper the dissemination of information; (c) *Absence of electricity during disaster events*- additional weather warnings are not disseminated due to power

Participating Parishes	Disaster Preparedness Practices	Use of ICT
Sn. Vincent Ferrer Parish	- Community training and organizing - Information dissemination and collection - Camp management	- SMS blast - Use of tri-media information for dissemination
Sn. Raphael Parish	- Planning: Convening of the Barangay-Parish Committee - Awareness campaign: through seminars (identification of hazards & risks; identification of evacuation area/routes) - Organize volunteers - Coordinate with local public schools	- Information dissemination using collected information from APSEMO and tri-media plus the internet (social media) - Use of SMS blast and handheld radios
Sts Michael and Stephen Protomartyr	- Planning using prioritization of community sectors - Information dissemination - Mapping of community volunteers through Project Harong	- Information dissemination using collected information from APSEMO and tri-media plus the internet (social media) - Use of SMS blast and handheld radios
Sto. Domingo Parish	- Awareness campaign and continuous monitoring of weather updates - Hazard mapping and coordination with the Mines and Geosciences Bureau, DENR - Access to community profile through the Community-based Management System	- Information dissemination using collected information from APSEMO and tri-media plus the internet (social media) - Use of SMS blast - Use of Social Media (e.g. Facebook) for announcement of training events

failure caused by precedent adverse weather/ volcanic events; (d) *Challenges in the use of the digital maps*- participants narrated that the MGB initiated a number of digital mapping activities in the past. However, they pointed out that the results of the mapping were not cascaded back to the communities. In instances where communities were given access to the digital maps, they were unable to use the maps due to the inadequate skills on how to use and interpret the mapping outputs.

Finally, the participants also suggested that the mapping application be integrated with the existing vulnerability and threat assessment initiative of the Diocese of Legazpi as well as the local and provincial governments. The idea of a common-single DRR digital map that is accessible and understood by all DRR stakeholders can help avoid confusion and misinformation.

DIM and its uses

The results of the study also showed that disaster information management (DIM) practices in the sample parishes are in its nascent stage. The existing practices point to information dissemination (information push) and lacks the collection of data/information (information pull) from relevant sources in the communities/parishes. Although these surveys done about the vulnerabilities of the villages/parishes, the results of these surveys remain static, usually reflected in paper-based reports and is seldom converted into a digitized format. Such electronic information can be integrated into digital maps, which can serve as a planning tool for disaster preparedness.

Overall, the current disaster preparedness practices show the need to re-examine information management methods and tools. We believe that DIM can further enhance the ability of DRR planners to allocate resources and address vulnerability challenges. It can also provide a venue for communities to directly participate in the DRR cycle instead of being passive recipients of information from the local governments. Aside from communities, a robust DIM practice can complement existing practices and provide new opportunities for other DRR stakeholders (e.g. Private sector, the academe, and civil society organizations) to be part of the DRR effort.

RECOMMENDATIONS AND FUTURE WORK

Our findings showed that most of the DIM practices in Legazpi city are mainly about pushing disaster-related information during the preparation phase of DRRM. This is done using SMS messages (text blast) and through social media. This technique relies on a general list of mobile numbers and does not customize information according to the needs of recipients. This technique is also one-way, thus lacks the needed feedback mechanism. Furthermore, there are existing practices of collecting community information, however, these were made using physical forms and are seldom digitized. Using the DIM as our lens, we characterized these practices as being in its initial stages and are thus inadequate to realize information sharing, and collaboration. Furthermore, the DIM process was also hampered due to the existence of multiple and voluminous information sources as well as capacity gaps.

For our recommendations, we see that importance of reexamining DIM practices and how data/information can be sourced, stored, and used to address the information needs of all DRRM phases and stakeholders. In addition, we see the need to enhance digital/ICT capacities through a data literacy program designed to harness DRR-related data/information.

As for our future work, intend to continue our study on DIM practices by looking at studies on complex adaptive systems and the DIM-related practices of other communities. In addition, we will also examine how innovative ICT applications can be used to address the challenges of DRRM in communities. The possible applications are crowdsourcing, data analytics and block chain technologies. As part of our adherence to the idea of complex systems, we believe that an examination of the governance aspect through of the existing local policy environment and programs is also important to complete our understanding of community-level DRRM.

REFERENCES

Bergstrom, J., Uhr, C., & Frykmer, T. (2016, September). A Complexity Framework for Studying Disaster Response Management. *Journal of Contingencies and Crisis Management*, *24*(3), 124–135. doi:10.1111/1468-5973.12113

Bolton, M., & Stolcis, G. (2008). Overcoming failure of imagination in crisis management: The Complex Adaptive System. *Public Sector Innovation Journal, 3*(3).

Carney, T., & Weber, D. J. (2015). Public Health Intelligence: Learning from the Ebola Crisis. *American Journal of Public Health*, *105*(9), 1740–1744. doi:10.2105/AJPH.2015.302771 PMID:26180978

Cilliers, P. (1998). *Complexity and Postmodernism: Understanding complex systems*. Routledge.

Crisologo, I. (2013). *The Philippine radar network*. Project NOAH. Retrieved from https://center.noah.up.edu.ph/the-philippine-radar-network/

Day, J. (2014). Fostering emergent resilience: The complex adaptive supply network of disaster relief. *International Journal of Production Research*, *52*(7), 1970–1988. doi:10.1080/00207543.2013.787496

Hristidis, V., Chen, S. C., Li, T., Luis, S., & Deng, Y. (2010). Survey of data management and analysis in disaster situations. *Journal of Systems and Software*, *83*(10), 1701–1714. doi:10.1016/j.jss.2010.04.065

Lassa, J. (2012). *Post disaster governance, complexity and network theory: Evidence from Aceh, Indonesia after the Indian Ocean Tsunami in 2004*. IRGSC working paper. NTT, Indonesia.

Li, T. (2017). Data-driven Techniques in Disaster Information Management. ACM Computing Survey, 50(1). doi:10.1145/3017678

Mutasa, M. (2013). Investigating the significance of disaster information management. *Jàmbá. Journal of Disaster Risk Studies*, *5*(2), e1–e6.

NOAH. (2014). *DOST pilots MOSES project*. Retrieved from https://center.noah.up.edu.ph/dost-pilots-moses-project-in-marikina-business-mirror/

Palen, L. (2008). Research in Brief: Online social media in crisis event. *EDUCAUSE Quarterly*, (3), 2008.

Quiang, L., & Ying, C. (2014). Study on Disaster Information Management Systems compatible with VGI and Crowdsourcing. *IEEE Workshop on Advanced Research and Technology in Industry Applications*.

Starbird, K., Huang, Y., Orand, M., & Stanek, S. (2015). *Connected through crisis: Emotional proximity and the spread of misinformation online*. ACM.

UN-APCICT. (2011). ICT for Disaster Risk Management. Academy of ICT Essentials for Government Leaders. Asian Disaster Preparedness Center.

Zheng, L. (2013). Study on Disaster Information Management Systems compatible with VGI and Crowd-sourcing. *IEEE Workshop on Advanced Research and Technology in Industry Applications (WARTIA).*

Chapter 6
The Role of Mobile Learning in Developing Employability and Job–Related Skills at VTET Programs

Ahmed Mokhtar Abdelaziz
Saudi Aramco, Saudi Arabia

ABSTRACT

This chapter focuses on the role of mobile learning in developing employability and job-related skills in vocational and technical education and training (VTET) contexts. It is hoped that this chapter will contribute to the academic discussion on this topic by identifying a list of skills and discussing how mobile technologies can play a role in developing them. This chapter will also provide some insights and practical examples for instructors and program designers on effective utilization of mobile technologies for developing both the technical and soft skills. Finally, this chapter will provide some insights on the future direction of research in this area of study.

INTRODUCTION

Vocational and Technical Education and Training (VTET) plays a significant role in the development of human resources - especially in developing countries - by providing a means for creating and developing skilled manpower (Powell & McGrath, 2019; Akshay, Sreeram, Anand, Venkataraman, & Bhavani, 2012). VTET programs do not only equip trainees with the required skills, knowledge, and attitudes to perform a specific job, but also improve labour mobility, adaptability and productivity; thus, contributing to enhancing firms' competitiveness and redressing labour market imbalances (Baartman & De Bruijn, 2011; Stasz, 2001; Hillage & Pollard, 1998). Basically, VTET outcomes are "framed in terms of skills or competencies relating to particular vocational domains with, recently, a greater interest in what are increasingly referred to as twenty-first century or wider skills" (Lucas, 2014, p. 4).

DOI: 10.4018/978-1-7998-3468-7.ch006

In this respect, King and Palmer (2010) defined *skill* as the "capability of accomplishing something with precision and certainty and the ability to perform a function acquired or learned with practice" (p. 32). Yet, evidence suggests that an identification of a list of the skill-sets needed to perform a specific job is a complex task because there appears to be a limited agreement amongst educationalists on what this list should include (Rao, 2014; Rodzalan & Saat, 2012). Arguably though, researchers often used to base their evaluation of the required skill-sets by distinguishing between *technical* and *generic* skills. In this sense, it can be argued that the following skills are the most commonly cited skills that VTET training programs focus on (Abdelaziz, 2018):

- Craftsmanship Skills (Technical Skills)
- Safety Skills
- Teamworking, Cooperation, and Collaboration Skills
- Creativity, Problem Solving, and Critical Thinking Skills
- Presentation Skills
- Communication Skills (Verbal and Written Communication)
- Independent, Self-Development, and Lifelong Learning Skills
- Searching Skills
- ICT Skills
- Typing Skills

Evidence-based research confirms that the acquisition and development of the above-mentioned skills require effective training programs, such as Community of Practice (CoP)-based, Information and Communication Technology (ICT)-based, and hands-on based programs (Brixiová, Kangoye & Said, 2020; Johnson & Proctor, 2017; Harrison, 2015). However, perhaps the question that might arise is: In the age of highly advanced and digital technology, what may be the most optimal approach to deliver effective VTET training programs? Perhaps it is possible to argue that *Mobile Learning* (M-Learning) can provide an ideal approach for effective VTET training programs (Vaidya, 2020; Ricky & Rechell, 2015). Yet, existing research on the role of M-Learning in delivering VTET training programs with focus on developing employability and job-related skills is limited, and a more in-depth understanding for its potential is still needed. Accordingly, this study is focused on answering the following research question:

Ø How does M-Learning impact the development of employability and job-related skills at VTET Programs?

The following sections will present a background on the issue followed by the methodology employed, the findings, discussion, and conclusion.

BACKGROUND AND LITERATURE REVIEW

This section introduces a focused background on research on Vocational and Technical Education and Training (VTET) with a brief overview on M-Learning utilization for developing employability and job-related skills.

Vocational and Technical Education and Training (VTET)

VTET has been conceptualised in the literature and introduced under different themes by different researchers. The major concepts that have been recognized in the literature about VTET include:

- **Vocational Education and Training (VET)** (Wilke & Magenheim, 2017; Bacca, Baldiris, Fabregat & Sabine Graf, 2015; Ricky & Rechell, 2015; Skills Australia, 2011)
- **Vocational and Professional Education and Training (VPET)** (Ng, R., Lam, Ng, K., & Lai, 2016)
- **Technical and Vocational Education** (Rus, Yasin, Yunus, Rahim, Ismail, 2015; King & Palmer, 2010)

Although the terms *'vocational'* and *'technical'* are used interchangeably in literature, vocational education is broader and contains all types of technical and non-technical occupations. Lucas (2014) introduced three categories of vocational education, emphasising the medium through which the work is expressed:

1. Physical materials – *for example, bricklaying, plumbing, hairdressing, professional make-up.* **2. People** – *for example, financial advice, nursing, hospitality, retail, and care industries.* **3. Symbols (words, numbers and images)** – *for example, accountancy, journalism, software development, graphic design. (P. 3)*

For the sake of this study, VTET has been utilized to serve two main purposes: First, it is in line with existing research in this field (Rus et al., 2015; King & Palmer, 2010). Second, although the context of this study is primarily technical, where trainees study specialisations related to operational and maintenance jobs in the field of oil industry, findings of this study have the potential to impact a wide range of vocational training programs which are non-technical.

In this sense, VTET is defined as "education programmes that are designed for learners to acquire the knowledge, skills and competencies specific to a particular occupation, trade or class of occupations or trades" and this is the key difference between this type of education and the other forms of education (Bacca et al., 2015, p. 49). According to the European Centre for the Development of Vocational Training (2011), VTET benefits can be clustered using a classical typology based on the nature of results as in Figure 1 "VTET Benefits, (European Centre for the Development of Vocational Training, 2011)". "Two main categories can be identified: economic benefits and social benefits. Both can be analysed on three different levels: the micro level (the benefits for individuals); the meso level (benefits for enterprises/groups); and the macro level (benefits for society as a whole)" (European Centre for the Development of Vocational Training, 2011, p. 4).

Similarly, Hoeckel (2008, p. 4) summarized the short-term and long-term benefits of VTET for the trainees, employers, and the society in Table 1.

Thus, it can be concluded that there are several and widely-documented benefits of VTET training programs; the most important of which is developing manpower with improved skills, *technical* and *generic* skills (Masadeh, 2012).

Figure 1. VTET benefits, (European Centre for the Development of Vocational Training, 2011)

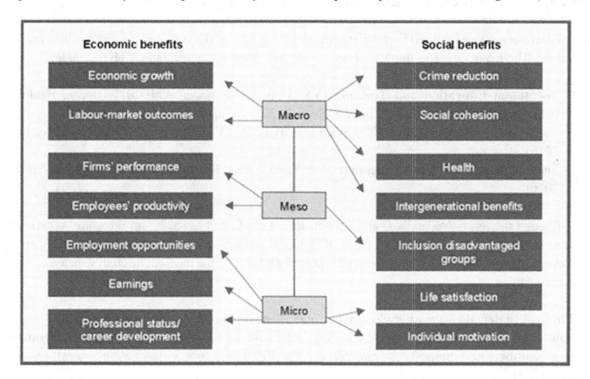

Technical and Generic Skills

Technical skills (also called *hard skills*) are simply defined as discipline- or role-specific skills while *generic skills* (also called *soft skills*) are overarching, meta skills, abilities, and traits that pertain to personality, attitude, and behaviour, and which are common to a range of occupations (Bryson, 2017; Lucas, 2014; Rodzalan & Saat, 2012). Generic skills are "generally understood as socio-emotional, intra-personal and inter-personal skills" (Vaughan, 2017, p. 2). They may enable introspection or self-examination, and they include creativity, analysis, problem solving, self-development, information literacy, working with technology, written and verbal communication, working in teams, critical thinking, and collaboration (Garwood, 2013; Bridgstock, 2009). It is worth mentioning that developing generic skills provides better chances for employability and job stability. Rao (2014) clarified that

Although a few successful students from educational institutions demonstrate adequate skills and get into corporate, they are fired subsequently due to lack of soft skills as they find it tough to get along within the corporate ambience... It is rightly said that people rise in organizations because of hard skills and fall due to dearth of soft skills. The hard skills are nothing but the core skills, domain skills, and technical skills. The soft skills complement the hard skills in evolving students as successful professionals. (p. 43)

As the researcher draws together the evidence presented above, he argues that the following skills form the most commonly cited employability and job-related skills that VTET training programs focus on (Abdelaziz, 2018):

Table 1. Short-term and long-term benefits of VTET, (Hoeckel, 2008)

	Individual	Employer	Society
Short-term benefits	• Employment chances • Earning levels • Work satisfaction • Drop out less likely from vocational than general courses (US data)	• Higher productivity from well trained workforce • Saved costs from recruiting external skilled workers (incl. time for integration and risk of hiring a person not known to the company)	• Saved expenses for social benefits (unemployment as consequence of failed transition from education to work)
Long-term benefits	• Flexibility and mobility • Lifelong learning (more likely to receive training and upgrade skills later in life)	• Supply benefits (e.g. image improvement) • Less turnover (no need for retraining of new workers)	• Externalities from productivity gain due to better education • Increase in tax income from higher earnings

- Craftsmanship Skills (Technical Skills)
- Safety Skills
- Teamworking, Cooperation, and Collaboration Skills
- Creativity, Problem Solving, and Critical Thinking Skills
- Presentation Skills
- Communication Skills (Verbal and Written Communication)
- Independent, Self-Development, and Lifelong Learning Skills
- Searching Skills
- ICT Skills
- Typing Skills

In the following section, the researcher will provide an overview on the suitability of M-Learning as an effective approach for delivering VTET training programs.

Mobile Learning in VTET

Evidence-based research indicates that there is a suitability for technology-enabled and M-Learning in VTET contexts. Noe, Clarke, and Klein (2014) reported that "in 2012, technology-based learning, which includes e-learning, online learning, and M-Learning, was used on average in 39% of organizations' formal learning hours" (247). They argued that providing formal training and development programs using advanced technology is one way that organizations are attempting to overcome the difficulties of learning in today's workplace. Other researchers highlighted the pedagogical value and effectiveness of M-learning in learning and training. For example, it was argued that mobile technologies have the potential to promote active learning (Dyson, Litchfield, Lawrence, Raban, & Leijdekkers, 2009), enable trainees to apply academic theories into practices (Ricky & Rechell, 2015), move learning outside classrooms and into students' real and virtual environments, (Mango, 2015; Sung, Chang, & Yang, 2015; Ozdamli & Cavus, 2011), and support authentic learning activities (Dyson et al., 2009).

Moreover, Ng et al. (2016) advocated M-Learning as an innovative pedagogical practice for VTET which has the potential to benefit both instructors and students. More specifically, Pimmer and Pachler (2013) argued that "the particular value of work-based M-Learning lies in connecting learning across different contexts, thereby bridging typical dichotomies of educational science" (p. 195). For example, mobile devices have the potential to enable bridging creation and sharing of content, bridging learning at work, bridging individual and social learning, bridging informal and formal learning contexts, and bridging (socio-) cognitive, cultural and constructivist perspectives.

Conversely, M-Learning has been criticized for various technical and pedagogical concerns. Challenges pertaining to connectivity, screen size, compatibility between devices, lack of properly-developed learning content have been documented by many researchers (Vaidya, 2020; Clarke & Svanaes, 2014; Kaalberg, 2014). It has been argued that multi-tasking on mobile technologies may impair learning by the distractions caused by phone ringing, texting, and constant visits to social medial platforms (Serah, 2014; Zhao, Reimer, Mehler, D'Ambrosio, & Coughlin, 2013). Moreover, despite the benefits of mobility, Gikas and Grant (2013) and Traxler (2010) warned against the pitfalls that learning across different contexts and at different times may produce fragmented knowledge and incomplete schemata. Finally, Shuib, Shamshirband, and Ismail (2015) argued that addiction to technology can lead to problems "such as emotional stress, damaged relationships and attention deficit disorder" (p. 240).

Nonetheless, the effectiveness and the role of mobile and flexible technologies to develop employability and job-related skills and facilitate the specific needs in VTET programs remains uncertain (Wilke & Magenheim, 2017; Ng et al., 2016; Mingyong, 2015). In light of this, the aim of this study is to explore the role of M-Learning in the field of VTET with focus on developing employability and job-related skills.

METHODOLOGY

This section provides a brief account on the study context; methods of data collection, sampling, and data synthesis and analysis.

Study Context

This study was conducted at one of Saudi Aramco's Industrial Training Centres (SA ITCs) in Saudi Arabia, specifically at Ras Tanura ITC. SA ITCs adopted the use of the iPads for its training programs which include *Academic* (English, Math, and Science) and *Job Skills* (Electrical, Welding, Mechanical, and other craft specializations). A completely new digital content was designed for the iPad training programs at SA ITCs, and all instructors and trainees were given iPads with the standard digital content installed on them. Further to that, instructors had received on-the-job training on using the iPad for teaching and learning purposes, and the trainees received adequate orientation on using the devices for learning before commencing on the pilot program. Trainees at SA ITCs are generally recent high school and vocational college graduates, ranging in age from 18 to 23 years. SA ITC training programs, which aim at graduating trainees with basic technical and soft skills, span over one to two years based on the program (high school or vocational), craft, and placement test scores. Upon completing the training program, SA ITC graduates join the company workforce as regular technicians. These features made SA ITCs an ideal context to conduct research on M-Learning environments and to explore its emerging affordances and challenges more in-depth.

Data Collection

Commencing on this study, a case study approach was adopted, where quantitative and qualitative data from trainee and instructor questionnaires, semi-structured interviews with trainees and instructors, onsite observations, and program documents were collected respectively. Open-ended items in the questionnaires enabled the researcher to identify some emerging and premature themes that needed further exploration and validation. The statistical analysis of the quantitative part of the questionnaires, on the other hand, helped to capture some trainees' and instructors' tendencies towards the role M-Learning in developing employability and job-related skills.

The researcher conducted interviews with 14 trainees and 20 instructors in order to listen to their unique points of view and to examine how mobile devices helped them to develop their technical and generic skills. Each participant was interviewed once for approximately 35 minutes. Data saturation, that is no new themes, perspectives or perceptions were evident in the data, was achieved at script 29. The researcher realized that saturation was achieved at this stage because participants in the sample were similar in their experiences with respect to the research domain (Guest, Bunce, & Johnson, 2006).

Besides, the observations were collected during the period of conducting the questionnaires and interviews, and they were not bound by a specific time (unstructured observations). The observations generated complementary data which led to further insights and a better understanding of the phenomenon under study.

Finally, documentary evidence such as email messages and reports on the implementation and evaluation of the iPad program as well as screenshots of some content pages and videos were employed as a method to cross-validate information gathered from the questionnaires, interviews, and observations.

This mixed method approach enabled the researcher to collect systematic data and to develop his findings in a coherent and robust way.

Sampling

The entire population participating in the iPad pilot program at Ras Tanura SA ITC (133 trainees and 29 instructors) took part in and responded to the questionnaire. For the interviews, non-probability purposive sampling was adopted. Despite the disadvantages that may arise from its non-representativeness, non-probability sampling is employed to deliberately and purposely recruit knowledgeable, interested, uninterested, and unbiased participants (Ary et al., 2010; Cohen et al., 2007). Therefore, interview participants (trainees and instructors) were selected based on some desired characteristics which included trainees who achieved the highest and the lowest in their academic and job skills courses, trainees with a high and low degree of motivation to participate in the iPad program based on instructors' observations, instructors who had been involved in the iPad program since the beginning of the initiative, instructors who gave presentations and workshops for in-house training programs, and senior instructors who coordinated the implementation of the iPad program. The researcher assumed that participants of these characteristics could give a full image of the role of M-learning at the context of this study.

Data Synthesis and Analysis

Synthesizing data which means combining, integrating, and summarizing the findings was carried out on an inductive basis. Broad generalizations, conclusions, and themes were generated from the transcripts, participants' discussions, observations, and the quantitative data (Gale et al., 2013; Fereday & Muir-Cochrane, 2006). Thomas (2006) explained that the "primary purpose of the inductive approach is to allow research findings to emerge from the frequent, dominant, or significant themes inherent in raw data, without the restraints imposed by structured methodologies" (p. 238). This researcher also adopted Hancock and Algozzine's (2016) framework (questions below) to synthesize the large amounts of data generated from different resources. Answering these questions facilitated the process of data synthesis:

- What information from different sources goes together?
- Within a source, what information can be grouped?
- What arguments contribute to grouping information together?
- What entities bounded by space and time are shared?
- How do various sources of information affect findings?
- What information links various findings together?
- What previous work provides a basis for analysis?
- What questions are being answered?
- What generalizations can be made? (Hancock & Algozzine, 2016, p. 63)

To answer these questions, the researcher followed a process of four steps (Ary et al., 2010, p. 565) which included:

- **Stage 1-Data Reduction:** The researcher printed out all the qualitative data, sorted them by questions, and color-coded them by theme. He gathered similar ideas and comments and used relevant quotations from participants to support the emerging themes.

- **Stage 2-Data Display:** The researcher displayed the quantitative data in percentages to enable readers to immediately recognize, compare and contrast the data. Qualitative data was displayed in a thematic manner where a concept or a theme was introduced, and description followed.
- **Stage 3-Data Consolidation:** The researcher combined both sets of data quantitative and qualitative to create a new set of findings.
- **Stage 4-Data Integration and Reporting**: The researcher integrated the data and interpretations into a coherent whole.

The researcher bracketed his understanding of the phenomenon - as much as he could - throughout the different stages of data analysis by consciously subduing the tendency to integrate the descriptions by research participants into existing theoretical structures, and by giving a clear description of the process of analysis to allow the reader to evaluate the attempt to achieve bracketing (Ashworth & Lucas, 2000).

FINDINGS

In this section, the researcher will introduce the findings of this study in a tabulated style in order for the readers to easily capture the themes and the factors at play.

Summary of the Main Themes for Each Skill

Table 2 below summarizes the key findings of this study in the form of parentages that participants (133 trainees and 29 instructors) felt that M-Learning plays an important role in developing each skill as well as the main themes and factors impacting the development of the skill.

DISCUSSION AND RECOMMENDATIONS

The data collected for this research indicated that M-Learning has the potential to play an important role in developing trainees' key employability and job-related skills. The key features of mobile technologies such as portability, connectivity, resourcefulness, ubiquity, instant feedback, entertainment, and novelty together with a well-designed digital content provide ample opportunities for an effective learning environment. Textbooks and stationary computers can provide a medium of learning similar to mobile technologies; however, features of learning at anywhere and at anytime, immediate access to rich resources, interactive and engaging learning content, and the different types of social interactions are all features that make M-Learning stand distinguished; especially in the field of VTET. The following is a discussion of the findings relevant to each skill with a linkage to existing research.

Craftsmanship Skills

This study showed that M-Learning plays an important role in developing trainees' theoretical and practical craftsman skills (*Hard skills*). Access to extra resources such as tutorial videos, 3D models, and animated designs can play a role in developing trainees' theoretical and practical knowledge about their specific disciplines. Other studies came to a similar conclusion. For example, Ng et al. (2016) and Ricky and

Table 2. Summary of the main themes for each skill

	Skill	Quantitative data of the questionnaires	Factors impacting the development of the skill based on the qualitative data
1	Craftsmanship Skills	· 71.5% trainees and 62.5% instructors think that **Mobile Technologies (MTs)** helped trainees to gain new technical skills more easily. · 68.5% trainees and 82.5% instructors think that the MTs increased trainees' job skills performance. · 76% trainees think that the MTs helped to prepare them for the practical work in workshop.	· Provision of simplified and interactive digital resources (such as tutorial videos, animated models, and virtual designs) motivate trainees to learn. · Multimodal online resources and animated representations of learning materials facilitate comprehension and retention of technical processes. · Learning from 'compressed information' and from different resources and 'nodes' increase trainees' content knowledge. · Mental preparation through the visual aids and continuous exposure to tutorial videos and animated models play a massive role in facilitating trainees' learning of complex technical processes and tasks.
2	Safety Skills	· 75% trainees and 65.5% instructors think that MTs helped to improve trainees' safety skills more easily.	· Exposure to interactive and entertaining safety videos and tutorials. · Access to various exciting safety videos that were produced by top specialized institutions. · Access (inside and outside the classrooms) to documentaries and series of investigations done on safety incidents. · Easy development of safety presentations. · Provision of various types of training resources in different modalities such as information, images, videos, and stories. · Easy and constant access to enjoyable, engaging, and interactive safety content and learning materials and the easy sharing of them. **Debates:** · Safety is a living thing that needs to be promoted during real work, not via online resources. · Digital content sometimes misses some important safety videos and tips, which makes it obligatory for instructors to fill these gaps using resources which do not - sometimes - meet the corporate standards.
3	Teamworking, Cooperation, and Collaboration Skills	· 84% trainees and 65.5% instructors think that MTs helped trainees to improve their teamworking skills.	· More opportunities for trainees to work on collaborative and cooperative activities through interaction and teamworking on innovative digital tools and online platforms. · Device portability, which does not obtrude conventional face-to-face interaction. · More resource sharing on various online platforms. · Flexible division of work roles. **Debates:** · Some trainees became more alone and more isolated than before and tend to learn arbitrarily on their own. · Instructors' interventions to make cooperation and collaboration happen is critical. · Proper training and awareness for trainees and instructors on how to promote teamworking skills through using MTs is required.
4	Creativity, Problem-Solving, and Critical Thinking Skills	· 64% trainees think that MTs helped them to improve their creativity skills. · 62.5% trainees think that MTs helped them to improve their problem-solving skills. · 36% trainees think that MTs helped them to improve their critical thinking skills (37.5% took a neutral position).	· Curiosity is accommodated on MTs as trainees are sure to find answers or clues to answers for whatever questions they may raise. · Learning from different resources and from others' experiences increases trainees' higher order thinking skills. · Trainees play more active roles when using MTs, which increases creativity, problem-solving, and critical thinking skills. · Searching for and using new applications and websites enhances these skills. · Trainees' designing their own drawings and technical processes using different applications helps them to be more innovative. · Rich resources and tools which are available at anytime and at anywhere facilitate problem-solving. · Ubiquity and connectivity encourage trainees to look for innovative and 'other methods' of doing things.
5	Presentation Skills	· 69% trainees think that MTs helped them to improve their presentation skills.	· Availability of different applications for creating presentations. · Device portability facilitate data collection and development instantly. · Taking notes and adding up to the content of the presentation possible at any stage of the presentation, at anytime and anywhere · Constant access to resources for content development (such as learning materials, images, and videos). · Cosmetics such as presentation backgrounds and animations have been improved. · Doing and delivering presentations on MTs makes trainees more creative. **Debates:** · Presentation content and delivery are still not impacted very much with the introduction of MTs.
6	Communication Skills: (Verbal and Written)	· 69% trainees think that the MTs helped them to improve their written communication skills. · 79.5% trainees think that the MTs helped them to improve their verbal communication skills.	· The easy access to and engagement on social media, various online groups, online chatting rooms and platforms, and instant messaging applications make trainees more connected and provide them with more opportunities for communication. · The increased amount of watching and listening to movies, songs, and online news on MTs develop trainees' communication skills. · Trainees' self-audio and video recordings help them to reflect on their communication styles and skills. · Quick access to online dictionaries and translators facilitates communication as trainees can find the meanings of words they do not know more easily. **Debates:** · There are doubts on the role MTs play to develop the verbal communication skills. · There is a need for more instructors' intervention to make communication happen.

continued on following page

Table 2. Continued

	Skill	Quantitative data of the questionnaires	Factors impacting the development of the skill based on the qualitative data
7	Independent, Self-Development, and Lifelong Learning Skills	· 76.5% trainees and 89.5% instructors think that the MTs helped trainees to improve their independent learning skills. · 64% trainees and 79.5% instructors think that the MTs helped trainees to improve their lifelong learning skills.	· The digital content design – with its interactive multimodal features – facilitates independent learning by helping trainees to study, review, or prepare their lessons and learning materials independently. · Content features of auto-correct and auto-check enable trainees to advance with their learning independently. · Resourcefulness: the aid applications and supplementary resources such as tutorial videos, translators, calculators, and other learning tools help trainees to proceed with their learning independently and instill the concept of lifelong learning in their minds. · Constant connectivity and resourcefulness encourage trainees to voluntarily complete more formal and informal online courses at their convenience.
8	Searching Skills	· 91.5% trainees think that MTs helped them to improve their searching skills.	· Constant searching for and engagement with online resources, extra learning materials, and information through navigating different websites and applications further enhance trainees' searching skills. **Debates:** · There is a need for more in-depth research on how MTs play a role in developing searching skills.
9	Information and Communication Technologies (ICT) Skills	· 92% trainees think that their ICT skills have improved with the use of MTs.	· The availability of mobile devices around the clock and the constant engagement with them help trainees to develop their ICT skills. · Trainees learn more about the software and the hardware of their devices and about information collection, storage, processing, and presentation due to the constant engagement with the devices. · Frequent downloading, trying, and using of different applications on the devices improves trainees' ICT skills. **Debates:** · There is a need for more in-depth research on the type of relationship between MTs and ICT.
10	Typing Skills	· 91% trainees think that the iPad helped them to improve their typing skills.	· Typing answers to questions and exercises, notes, emails, and chatting messages all day on mobile devices improves trainees' typing skills. · Setting the devices on typing *English only* improves trainees' skills of typing in English. · The auto-checking and auto-correct features of the keyboards help trainees to type faster. · Disadvantages of typing on touch screens; more with devices with small screens such as mobile phones, and less with devices with larger screens such as tablets are absent when trainees are provided with attachment physical keyboards. **Debates:** · The auto-correct feature of the keyboards impact spelling skills negatively.

Rechell (2015) reported that M-Learning best connects theories and practices to enrich situated learning experiences in VTET. They argued that effective means of pedagogies that take advantages of the mobile and flexible technologies can help trainees "to apply academic theories into practices and collaborate with peers and workplace mentors for a better understanding of tasks" (Ricky & Rechell, 2015, p. 97).

Thus, based on the findings of this research, it is recommended that program designers, curriculum developers, and instructors consider inserting and using, as much as possible, various kinds of media and content of multiple representations, such as 3-D models, animations, interactive dynamic visuals, graphs, and videos.

Safety Skills

This study suggests that mobile technologies can play an important role in developing safety skills as they have the potential to increase exposure to safety videos that were produced by top specialized institutions as well as documentaries and series of investigations conducted on safety incidents. These can increase trainees' awareness and knowledge about various safety concepts and practices. Similarly, Kenny, et al. (2009) argued that the impact of exposure to digital learning materials on mobile devices can increase trainees' confidence in their safety practice. Schofield, Hollands, and Denby (2001) confirmed that "the capacity to remember safety information from a three-dimensional computer world is far greater than the ability to translate information from a printed page" (p. 155).

Hence, it can be recommended that instructors increase trainees' exposure to safety videos, documentaries, and series of investigations on safety incidents that were produced by specialized institutions. Such videos have the potential to entertain trainees and increase their awareness and knowledge about safety. However, Burke, et al. (2006) found that video-based safety training is the least engaging method.

At this point, it can be argued that more research on engaging safety training methods and the role of videos and documentaries is required.

Furthermore, this study suggested that mobile devices facilitate the provision of interactive safety tutorials which help trainees to retain more information. Likewise, Reychav and Wu (2014) and Douphrate and Hagevoort (2015) argued that mobile technologies' capability to present high quality multimedia is a factor that can attract learners of safety training programs and help them to retain more information; thus, improving their learning and performance and allowing them to apply the skill effectively.

Moreover, this study suggested that mobile devices can positively impact trainees' safety culture over time as they facilitate trainees' access to safety tutorials, shares, and messages at anytime and at anywhere; a feature which can make trainees more connected with safety tutorials, discussions, and feedback. Likewise, Peters (2007) highlighted the significance of accessing safety information in a quick and efficient way on mobile devices as it may have a positive influence in changing the whole culture of safety.

Finally, this research proposes that the use of mobile devices has the potential to increase trainees' *safety awareness*; however, there may be a better chance for an in-depth investigation of whether and how mobile technologies can play a role in changing trainees' *safety convictions* and *modifying their unsafe behaviours*.

Teamworking, Cooperation, and Collaboration Skills

According to this research, mobile technologies provide opportunities for trainees to work together more than before because they provide additional platforms where different forms of interaction are enabled. Many existing studies came to similar findings (Atawneh, Al-Akhras, AlMomani, Liswi & Alawairdhi, 2020). For example, Ng et al. (2016) argued that mobile technologies allow VTET trainees to participate more in cooperative and collaborative activities and would share their views in their own time and spaces. They concluded that mobile technologies "enhance peer collaborative learning activities for information sharing, discussion and mutual supports" (p. 104). Hence, it is recommended that instructors encourage their trainees to utilize the affordances of mobile technologies by creating platforms where more types of interaction and communication can be facilitated.

Furthermore, this study confirmed that mobile technologies - with their portability feature - do not constrain face-to-face types of interaction. Trainees can still cooperate and collaborate face-to-face as in conventional textbook-based environments, but with the extra features that allow constant connectivity, they can work together more on the online groups and communities. Similarly, Naismith et al. (2004) argued that mobile devices can provide "another means of coordination without attempting to replace any human-human interactions, as compared to say online discussion boards which substitute for face-to-face discussions" (p. 17). In fact, M-Learning facilitates more types of interactions than other learning environments as in Figure 2 "Types of Interaction at M-Learning Environments". Conventional learning environments facilitate only face-to-face types of interactions, online learning environments facilitate only online types of interactions through the different synchronous and asynchronous tools, and blended learning environments facilitate both types of interactions (face-to-face and online) at limited timings and specific places such as the computer laboratories. But M-Learning environments facilitate all of these types of interactions at anytime and at anywhere; thus, enriching the learning environment with more dynamics and features.

However, some study participants highlighted that instructor's intervention to make cooperation and collaboration happen is critical. Some trainees may tend to learn arbitrarily on their own, and some

Figure 2. Types of interaction at m-learning environments

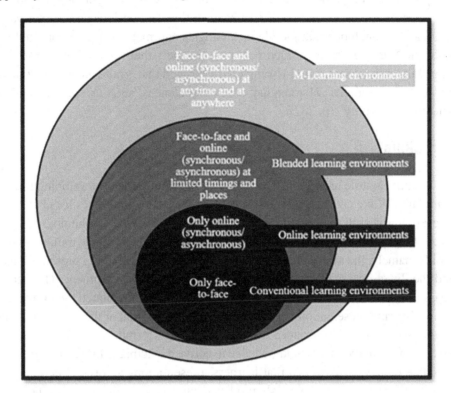

trainees are more alone than before. Therefore, it is recommended that the instructors ask their trainees to work together and see an evidence of teamworking, corporation, and collaboration happening. Accepting learners' autonomy in technology-enhanced learning environments does not mean that instructors can let learners learn anything arbitrarily (Naismith et al., 2004).

Creativity, Problem Solving and Critical Thinking Skills

This study showed that mobile technologies can play an important role in developing trainees' creativity, problem solving, and critical thinking skills. Similarly, in their study to investigate the effect of M-Learning on critical thinking skills, Cavus and Uzunboylu (2009) found that the students' creativity improved significantly with the use of mobile technologies for extended periods of time. Also, Garwood (2013) confirmed that new technologies can enable students "to learn to use a more advanced skill set including the ability to process the ever-increasing amount of available information, become flexible thinkers and creative problem-solvers" (p. 25).

This study suggested that searching for and using new applications and websites that help trainees to design their own drawings, presentations, and models impacted their creativity, problem solving and critical thinking skills positively. Furthermore, mobile technologies can ignite original and fresh ideas and help trainees to handle problems in an analytical style. With mobile technologies, curiosity can be more accommodated because trainees are confident that whatever questions they raise, they may find answers (or clues) to them in the rich resources available on their devices and with a sense of immediacy. In this respect, Lin et al. (2008) argued that mobile devices have the potential to support seamless learning which means that trainees "could learn whenever they feel curious and be motivated to learn" (p. 1). Hence, it can be concluded that mobile technologies can make trainees more inclined to adopt an active role in the learning process which positively impacts their creativity, problem solving and critical thinking skills. Likewise, Lai and Hwang (2014) argued that "more engagement in M-Learning activities could improve students' 21st century core competences, such as communication, complex problem-solving, and creativity" (p. 287).

Presentation Skills

According to this study, mobile technologies can play an important role in developing trainees' presentation skills. Similarly, Wilke and Magenheim (2017) reported that apprentices listed presentations and the use of PowerPoint as a skill that was improved with the use of mobile technologies.

This study identified three key features of mobile technologies which enable trainees to improve their presentation skills; namely, the availability of several applications for creating presentations, the device portability, and the direct access to limitless resources for content development. Thus, the process of individual and collaborative content creation for the presentations is facilitated by mobile technologies. Moreover, when delivering presentations as part of the training program or the assessment model, learners' presentation skills are further enhanced in terms of content, format, and delivery, and their role is further change from passive recipients of knowledge to active participants in the creation of knowledge. Similarly, Yousafzai et al. (2016) argued that learners' presentations and reproduction of multimedia content in a different format from a previously produced single version is related to the idea of content adaptation. This is a feature that makes trainees co-authors of knowledge with an active role as knowledge producers rather than consumers. Based on this, perhaps it can be recommended that institutes adopting M-Learning should increase the scope of presentations in the curriculum and assessment model as they offer valuable opportunities for learners' participation in the knowledge creation and content adaptation (Pimmer & Tulenko, 2016).

Conversely, although presentation visuals such as backgrounds and animations are improved, some trainees still read from the screens and do not interact with the audience during their presentations. Similarly, Simona (2015) argued that mobile technologies are disadvantageous, particularly, with low-achieving learners who tend to copy/paste content from the internet without considering copyright issues, reproduce the information they find online, and focus more on the visuals and less on learning the content or message that they have to deliver. Hence it can be argued that instructor's intervention and timely feedback on the trainees' presentations in terms of content, format and delivery is also critical to the development of this skill.

Communication Skills (Verbal and Written Communication)

This study showed that mobile technologies can play an important role in developing trainees' written and verbal communication skills. The features of audio and video recording together with the continuous access to social media and online chatting rooms and platforms help trainees to be better communicators as they have more chances to communicate at various levels inside and outside the classroom (Alajmia, et al. 2019).

Besides, the plethora of communication tools on mobile devices enable trainees to create various online groups where they can collaborate, discuss ideas, and share files and information. Similarly, Ng et al. (2016) found that mobile technologies can develop learners' communication skills as students preferred peer collaborative activities and social media chatting, and they prefer to establish various platforms for discussion and materials sharing.

However, this study also showed that there are doubts on the role mobile technologies play to develop, especially, the *verbal* communication skills. The iPad made some trainees more isolated and, thus, worse communicators. Other studies also warned against too much involvement with the devices in a way that increases withdrawal and affects communication negatively (McNaughton and Light, 2013).

Hence, it is recommended that curriculum developers and instructors should develop strategies and teaching methods that ensure more oral communication and encourage trainees to speak and interact at M-Learning environments. Presentations, recorded dialogues, and other communication-based activities have to be more incorporated in the training programs. Holland (2014) concluded that "we may be doing our students a disservice if we ask them to communicate only via one or two mediums" (para 4).

Independent, Self-Development, and Lifelong Learning Skills

It is impossible to equip learners with all required knowledge and skills during the institutional education; therefore, lifelong learning has emerged as a complement to institutional education, and as an entire lifetime process. In this respect, mobile technologies are argued to support this type of learning since they "offer the opportunity to learn and study at anytime and anywhere in different ways - according to the user's preferences" (Abfalter et al., 2004, p. 4).

This study showed that this type of learning can be further supported by the digital content design. Content features that facilitate self-study and independent learning such as the incorporation of interactive materials and exercises that have auto-correct and auto-check capabilities extend learning beyond the classroom. Furthermore, mobile technologies provide trainees with a direct access to a plethora of online courses and resources that enable them to learn additional subjects or enhance their standard learning materials. In this respect, Liu (2015) confirmed that students of Higher Vocational Colleges "are very much looking forward to the online course materials which they can obtain at anytime and anywhere. They expect their personal digital devices can play a role in learning outside the classroom" (p. 600).

Hence, it can be recommended that program designers consider shortening the training program period by converting some parts of the training program into a self-study mode. Fast tracks for high-performing trainees can be created; and thus, a more effective utilization of resources can be achieved. Also, high-performing trainees will have better chances of quick promotion in the training programs; thus, increasing trainees' autonomy and creating a highly-motivating learning environment for them.

Ricky and Rechell (2015) argued that full exploitation of mobile technologies for independent and lifelong learning "requires learners to have a higher degree of self-directness, self-management, persistence and independency" (p. 98). In light of this, it can be recommended that program developers and practitioners may consider appending lists of relevant online courses or training programs that offer additional professional development opportunities in different vocational specializations for trainees. This type of guidance has the potential to make trainees more focused and able to build the skills of independent and lifelong learning.

Searching Skills

According to this study, mobile technologies, with the continuous connectivity feature, play an important role in promoting trainees' searching skills. Trainees are often in search for online materials. This is becoming more and more important for successful learning which results from learners being able to "solve contextual, real-world problems through collaboratively exploring, evaluating, manipulating and integrating available information from an array of sources, as opposed to passively acquiring information from texts selected by the teacher" (McLoughlin & Lee, 2008, p. 647). Baran (2014) reported that mobile technologies increased searching capabilities; which "have further increased their versatility by promoting situated learning experiences and allowing exploration within authentic settings, particularly supporting inquiry-based learning" (p.18).

Trainees of this study reported that they look for relevant and up-to-date information on Google, Wikipedia, YouTube, and on other platforms to further understand a topic under study or to create their own projects and presentation. Such practices need to be supported at M-Learning training programs as learning is no longer 'content-driven'; otherwise, it would lead to a disaster if it continues with the current situation of the huge amount of available knowledge and information facilitated and availed by ICTs (Appiah & Cronjé, 2013). Learners have to be equipped with the skill of searching for relevant and up-to-date information effectively (Brown & Mbati, 2015; Strong & Hutchins, 2009). Furthermore, they "need to be able to make new connections through information analysis and synthesis and to create associations between thoughts, feelings, ideas, or sensations" (Armatas, Spratt, & Vincent, 2014, para. 7). This is where searching skills gain their importance.

However, according to this study trainees may have the basic searching skills, but they lack effective searching strategies. Hence, it can be recommended that especial training courses for developing searching skills and strategies be designed for trainees. The role of searching skills in developing effective learning and building knowledge in a world where knowledge doubles every 12 to 13 months is critical (Lewis, 2016; Egelhoff, 2014; Lundell, 2014).

Information and Communication Technologies (ICT) Skills

This study showed that interaction with the devices for longer periods of time facilitated the development of trainees' ICT skills as they started to learn more about the software and the hardware of their devices and about information collection, storage, processing, and presentation.

In fact, there is also a lack of research on how the adoption of mobile technologies may enhance learners' ICT skills. Many researchers looked at the relationship between mobile technologies and ICTs from an opposite stance, which is how ICT literacy impacts the adoption of mobile technologies. Mac Callum and Jeffrey (2014) argued that "ICT literacy is the measure of an individual's ability to use digital technology, communication tools, and/or networks to access, manage and integrate digital resources" (p. 9). Likewise, Mac Callum and Jeffrey (2013) assumed that "the perceived ease of use and usefulness of mobile technology would mediate the relationship between ICT skills and the intention of students to adopt mobile learning" (p. 303).

Hence, it can be argued that the relationship between mobile technologies and ICTs is a dialectical one. That is, basic ICT literacy decreases ICT anxiety and helps both instructors and learners to accept and adopt M-learning. Conversely, adopting M-Learning has the potential to enhance learners' ICT skills as they learn more about the software and the hardware of their devices and about information collection, storage, processing, and presentation. However, more research is required to explore this skill in more depth.

Typing Skills

According to this research, mobile technologies facilitate the development of trainees' typing skills. Trainees learn to type faster because they have to type all day inside and outside the classrooms on their mobile devices. In fact, it is because of this requirement - typing all day - that mastering this skill is indispensable as the ability to type efficiently impacts trainees' learning processes. For example, it impacts their speed and accuracy in completing learning tasks and activities, and it impacts their answers in the tests and quizzes.

However, this specific skill is rather neglected by researchers of M-Learning although it is a key skill for the success of mobile-based training programs. Trudeau, Catalano, Jindrich, and Dennerlein (2013) confirmed that "it has not yet been determined whether keyboard design affects performance and usability measures during functional tasks such as thumb typing (p. 2). However, there are a few studies that reported the difficulty of working on touch screens. For example, Rodrigues et al. (2016) indicated that touch screen devices have the disadvantage of "lacking the haptic feedback of physical buttons" (p. 393). Likewise, Rahmati and Zhong (2013) confirmed that tablets, with their bigger screen size than other devices such as smart phones, may overcome some of the problems such as buttons being too small, which may lead to improved typing skills. However, there should be more focus on "understanding and developing more appropriate solutions to improve typing performance on virtual keyboards for tablet devices" (Rahmati & Zhong, 2013, p. 1425).

In this regard, many of these difficulties were not identified by the participants of this study because each trainee was provided with - or was allowed to bring - a physical keyboard and a mouse as attachments to their iPads. In this sense, it could be suggested that providing these peripheries or allowing learners to have them in M-Learning environments may eliminate the limitations of typing on touch screens.

FUTURE RESEARCH DIRECTIONS

The importance of this research lies in paving the way towards more in-depth exploration of the role of mobile technologies in developing employability and job-related skills. There appears to be limited research in this area (Lucas, 2014; Liu et al., 2010; Pimmer, et al., 2010); the thing which makes the findings of this study very important for educationalists, researchers, and practitioners in the field of M-learning in general and VTET in particular. Previous studies have found mobile and flexible learning best connects theories and practices to enrich situated learning experiences in VTET (Ng et al, 2016; Ricky & Rechell, 2015); however, this research has provided some important illustrations and practical examples on some conceptual issues in the research field. Finally, this research was focused on many skillsets; thus, it may be recommended that future research focuses on individual skills with more in-depth exploration of all factors and aspects impacting them. Finally, it would be interesting to see if researchers at other contexts would agree on this list of skillsets or add further to it.

CONCLUSION

This research contributes to the academic discussion on the role of M-Learning at VTET programs with focus on the development of employability and job-related skills in many ways. A key contribution of this study is extending the theory and practice of VTET by identifying and exploring the key employability and job-related skills; specifically, craftsmanship skills, safety skills, teamworking, cooperation, and collaboration skills, creativity, problem solving and critical thinking skills, presentation skills, communication skills (verbal and written communication), independent learning, self-development, and lifelong learning skills, searching skills, information and communication technologies (ICT) Skills, and Typing Skills. These skills have been identified through the literature review and from the professional practice at the context of this study.

According to this research, mobile technologies have the potential to play an important role in developing these skills. The features of portability, connectivity, resourcefulness, ubiquity, instant feedback, entertainment, and novelty together with a well-designed digital content provide ample opportunities for an effective learning environment.

Finally, there is limited research on the role of M-Learning in this area although M-Learning is increasingly used in workplaces, museums, and schools; enabling a wide spectrum of possibilities (Lucas, 2014 and Liu, et al., 2010). This makes the findings of this study unique and lays the foundations for more research in this field. Further, this study highlighted some future directions for research into the use of mobile technologies for the development of the above skills at industrial training environments. It would be interesting to see if the results of this research were similar at other contexts.

REFERENCES

Abdelaziz, A. (2018). *Developing Employability and Job-Related Skills at Mobile Learning Environments: a case study at an industrial training centre* (Doctoral Thesis). Lancaster University, UK, 2018.

Akshay, N., Sreeram, K., Anand, A., Venkataraman, R., & Bhavani, R. (2012). MoVE: Mobile vocational education for rural India. *2012 IEEE International Conference on Technology Enhanced Education (ICTEE)*, 1-5. 10.1109/ICTEE.2012.6208644

Alajmia, N., Khambarib, M. N. M., Luanc, W. S., & Ahd, N. A. (2019). Mobile Learning in the Workplace: Employee's Perspectives on Readiness, Acceptance, Benefits and Limitations of Training with Mobile Technology in Kuwait. *International Journal of Innovation, Creativity and Change, 10*(9).

Appiah, E., & Cronjé, J. (2013). ICT, ideation pedagogy and Innovation Education: setting a new paradigm in graphic design education. In *Proceedings of the 2nd International Conference for Design Education Researchers* (pp. 2-14). Oslo: ABM-media.

Armatas, C., Spratt, C., & Vincent, A. (2014). Putting Connectivist Principles Into Practice: A Case Study of an Online Tertiary Course. *American Journal of Distance Education, 28*(2), 81–91. doi:10.1080/08923647.2014.901782

Atawneh, S., Al-Akhras, M., AlMomani, I., Liswi, A., & Alawairdhi, M. (2020). Collaborative Mobile-Learning Architecture Based on Mobile Agents. *Electronics (Basel)*, *9*(1), 162. doi:10.3390/electronics9010162

Baartman, L. K., & De Bruijn, E. (2011). Integrating knowledge, skills and attitudes: Conceptualising learning processes towards vocational competence. *Educational Research Review*, *6*(2), 125–134. doi:10.1016/j.edurev.2011.03.001

Bacca, J., Baldiris, S., Fabregat, R., & Graf, S. (2015). Mobile augmented reality in vocational education and training. *Procedia Computer Science*, *75*, 49–58. doi:10.1016/j.procs.2015.12.203

Baran, E. (2014). A review of research on mobile learning in teacher education. *Journal of Educational Technology & Society*, *17*(4), 17–32.

Bridgstock, R. (2009). The graduate attributes we've overlooked: Enhancing graduate employability through career management skills. *Higher Education Research & Development*, *28*(1), 31–44. doi:10.1080/07294360802444347

Brixiová, Z., Kangoye, T., & Said, M. (2020). Training, human capital, and gender gaps in entrepreneurial performance. *Economic Modelling*, *85*, 367–380. doi:10.1016/j.econmod.2019.11.006

Brown, T., & Mbati, L. (2015). Mobile Learning: Moving Past the Myths and Embracing the Opportunities. *International Review of Research in Open and Distributed Learning*, *16*(2). Advance online publication. doi:10.19173/irrodl.v16i2.2071

Bryson, J. (2017) Disciplinary Perspectives on Skill. In The Oxford Handbook of Skills and Training. Oxford University Press.

Burke, M. J., Sarpy, S. A., Smith-Crowe, K., Chan-Serafin, S., Salvador, R. O., & Islam, G. (2006). Relative effectiveness of worker safety and health training methods. *American Journal of Public Health*, *96*(2), 315–324. doi:10.2105/AJPH.2004.059840 PMID:16380566

Cavus, N., & Uzunboylu, H. (2009). Improving critical thinking skills in mobile learning. *Procedia: Social and Behavioral Sciences*, *1*(1), 434–438. doi:10.1016/j.sbspro.2009.01.078

Douphrate, D., & Hagevoort, R. (2015). *Using mobile devices to offer safety training to dairy workers.* Retrieved August 18, 2017, from https://www.progressivedairy.com/topics/management/using-mobile-devices-to-offer-safety-training-to-dairy-workers

Dyson, L., Litchfield, A., Lawrence, E., Raban, R., & Leijdekkers, P. (2009). Advancing the m-learning research agenda for active, experiential learning: Four case studies. *Australasian Journal of Educational Technology*, *25*(2), 250–267. doi:10.14742/ajet.1153

Egelhoff, T. (2014). *How Fast Is Knowledge Doubling?* Retrieved April 2017, From: https://kmmsam.com/how-fast-is-knowledge-doubling/

European Centre for the Development of Vocational Training. (2011). *The benefits of vocational education and training*. Publications Office of the European Union.

Garwood, J. E. (2013). *One-to-one iPads in the elementary classroom: Measuring the impact on student engagement, instructional practices, and teacher perception*. Western Illinois University.

Harrison, D. (Ed.). (2015). *Handbook of Research on Digital Media and Creative Technologies*. IGI Global. doi:10.4018/978-1-4666-8205-4

Hillage, J., & Pollard, E. (1998) *Employability: Developing a Framework for Policy Analysis*. London: DfEE.

Hoeckel, K. (2008). Costs and benefits in vocational education and training. Paris: Organisation for Economic Cooperation and Development.

Johnson, A., & Proctor, R. W. (2017). *Skill Acquisition and Training: Achieving Expertise in Simple and Complex Tasks*. Taylor & Francis.

Kenny, R. F., Park, C., Van Neste-Kenny, J. M., Burton, P. A., & Meiers, J. (2009). Using Mobile Learning to Enhance the Quality of Nursing Practice Education. In M. Ally (Ed.), *Mobile Learning: Transforming the Delivery of Education and Training* (Vol. 1, pp. 25-47). Edmonton, Alberta: AU Press. http://www.aupress.ca/index.php/books/120155

King, K., & Palmer, R. (2010). *Planning for technical and vocational skills development*. UNESCO, International Institute for Educational Planning.

Lai, C. L., & Hwang, G. J. (2014). Effects of mobile learning time on students' conception of collaboration, communication, complex problem–solving, meta–cognitive awareness and creativity. *International Journal of Mobile Learning and Organisation*, *8*(3-4), 276–291. doi:10.1504/IJMLO.2014.067029

Lewis, P. (2016). *Is knowledge doubling - or halving?* Retrieved April 2017, From: http://mobile.wnd.com/2016/05/is-knowledge-doubling-or-halving/

Liu, Y., Han, S., & Li, H. (2010). Understanding the factors driving m-learning adoption: A literature review. *Campus-Wide Information Systems*, *27*(4), 210–226. doi:10.1108/10650741011073761

Liu, Z. (2015). Study on Accessing to and Sharing of Media Mobile Learning Resources In Higher Vocational Colleges. In *2015 7th International Conference on Information Technology in Medicine and Education (ITME)* (pp. 598-600). IEEE. 10.1109/ITME.2015.171

Lucas, B. (2014). *Vocational pedagogy: what it is, why it matters and what we can do about it*. UNESCO-UNEVOC e-Forum. Retrieved June 2017, From: http://hdl.voced.edu.au/10707/321698

Lundell, P. (2014). *The Knowledge Doubling Curve*. Retrieved April 2017, From: https://www.peterlundell.com/the-knowledge-doubling-curve/

Mac Callum, K., & Jeffrey, L., (2013). The influence of students' ICT skills and their adoption of mobile learning. *Australasian Journal of Educational Technology, 29*(3), 303-314.

Mac Callum, K., Jeffrey, L., & Kinshuk. (2014). Comparing the role of ICT literacy and anxiety in the adoption of mobile learning. *Computers in Human Behavior*, *39*, 8–19. doi:10.1016/j.chb.2014.05.024

Mango, O. (2015). iPad Use and Student Engagement in the Classroom. *The Turkish Online Journal of Educational Technology*, *14*(1), 53–57.

Masadeh, M. (2012). Training, education, development and learning: What is the difference? *European Scientific Journal*, 8(10), 62–68.

McLoughlin, C., & Lee, M. J. W. (2008). Mapping the digital terrain: New media and social software as catalysts for pedagogical change. *Hello! Where are you in the landscape of educational technology? Proceedings ascilite Melbourne 2008,* 641-652. http://www.ascilite.org.au/conferences/melbourne08/procs/mcloughlin.html

McNaughton, D., & Light, J. (2013). The iPad and Mobile Technology Revolution: Benefits and Challenges for Individuals who require Augmentative and Alternative Communication. *Augmentative and Alternative Communication*, 29(2), 107–116. doi:10.3109/07434618.2013.784930 PMID:23705813

Mingyong, Z. (2015). Investigation into the use of mobile technology in English teaching and learning in institutes of higher vocational education in Hubei province in China. In *Futuristic Trends on Computational Analysis and Knowledge Management (ABLAZE), 2015 International Conference on* (pp. 505-509). IEEE. 10.1109/ABLAZE.2015.7155037

Naismith, L., Sharples, M., Vavoula, G., & Lonsdale, P. (2004). *Literature review in mobile technologies and learning*. Retrieved October 22, 2017, from: https://telearn.archives-ouvertes.fr/hal-00190143/document

Ng, R. Y. K., Lam, R. Y. S., Ng, K. K., & Lai, I. K. W. (2016, July). A Cross-Institutional Study of Vocational and Professional Education and Training (VPET) Students and Teachers' Needs of Innovative Pedagogical Practices. In *Educational Technology (ISET), 2016 International Symposium on* (pp. 101-105). IEEE.

Noe, R. A., Clarke, A. D., & Klein, H. J. (2014). Learning in the twenty-first-century workplace. *Annual Review of Organizational Psychology and Organizational Behavior*, 1(1), 245–275. doi:10.1146/annurev-orgpsych-031413-091321

Ozdamli, F., & Cavus, N. (2011). Basic Elements and Characteristics of Mobile Learning. *Procedia: Social and Behavioral Sciences*, 28, 937–942. doi:10.1016/j.sbspro.2011.11.173

Peters, K. (2007). m-Learning: Positioning educators for a mobile, connected future. *The International Review of Research in Open and Distributed Learning*, 8(2). Advance online publication. doi:10.19173/irrodl.v8i2.350

Pimmer, C., & Pachler, N. (2013). Mobile learning in the workplace. Unlocking the value of mobile technology for work-based education. In M. Ally & A. Tsinakos (Eds.), *Mobile Learning Development for Flexible Learning*. Athabasca University Press.

Pimmer, C., Pachler, N., & Attwell, G. (2010). Towards work-based mobile learning: What we can learn from the fields of work-based learning and mobile learning. *International Journal of Mobile and Blended Learning*, 2(4), 1–18. doi:10.4018/jmbl.2010100101

Pimmer, C., & Tulenko, K. (2016). The convergence of mobile and social media: Affordances and constraints of mobile networked communication for health workers in low-and middle-income countries. *Mobile Media & Communication*, 4(2), 252–269. doi:10.1177/2050157915622657

Powell, L. J., & McGrath, S. (2019). *Skills for human development: Transforming vocational education and training*. Routledge. doi:10.4324/9781315657592

Rahmati, A., & Zhong, L. (2013). Studying smartphone usage: Lessons from a four-month field study. *IEEE Transactions on Mobile Computing, 12*(7), 1417–1427. doi:10.1109/TMC.2012.127

Rao, M. S. (2014). Enhancing employability in engineering and management students through soft skills. *Industrial and Commercial Training, 46*(1), 42–48. doi:10.1108/ICT-04-2013-0023

Reychav, I., & Wu, D. (2014). Exploring mobile tablet training for road safety: A uses and gratifications perspective. *Computers & Education, 71*, 43–55. doi:10.1016/j.compedu.2013.09.005

Ricky, Y. K. N., & Rechell, Y. S. L. (2015, December). Using mobile and flexible technologies to enable, engage and enhance learning in Vocational Education and Training (VET). In *Teaching, Assessment, and Learning for Engineering (TALE), 2015 IEEE International Conference on* (pp. 96-101). IEEE.

Rodrigues, É., Carreira, M., & Gonçalves, D. (2016). Enhancing typing performance of older adults on tablets. *Universal Access in the Information Society, 15*(3), 393–418. doi:10.100710209-014-0394-8

Rodzalan, S., & Saat, M. (2012). The Effects of Industrial Training on Students' Generic Skills Development. *Procedia: Social and Behavioral Sciences, 56*, 357–368. doi:10.1016/j.sbspro.2012.09.664

Rus, R. C., Yasin, R. M., Yunus, F. A. N., Rahim, M. B., & Ismail, I. M. (2015). Skilling for job: A grounded theory of vocational training at industrial training institutes of malaysia. *Procedia: Social and Behavioral Sciences, 204*, 198–205. doi:10.1016/j.sbspro.2015.08.139

Sampson, D. (2006). Exploiting mobile and wireless technologies in vocational training. In *Wireless, Mobile and Ubiquitous Technology in Education, 2006. WMUTE'06. Fourth IEEE International Workshop on* (pp. 63-65). IEEE. 10.1109/WMTE.2006.261347

Schofield, D., Hollands, R., & Denby, B. (2001). Mine safety in the Twenty-First century: The application of computer graphics and virtual reality. In M. Karmis (Ed.), *Mine Health and Safety Management* (pp. 153–174). Society for Mining, Metallurgy, and Exploration.

Simona, C. E. (2015). Developing Presentation Skills in the English Language Courses for the Engineering Students of the 21st Century Knowledge Society: A Methodological Approach. *Procedia: Social and Behavioral Sciences, 203*, 69–74. doi:10.1016/j.sbspro.2015.08.261

Skills Australia, M. (2011). *Skills for prosperity: a roadmap for vocational education and training*. Canberra: Commonwealth of Australia.

Stasz, C. (2001). Assessing skills for work: Two perspectives. *Oxford Economic Papers, 53*(3), 385–405. doi:10.1093/oep/53.3.385

Strong, K., & Hutchins, H. (2009). Connectivism: A theory for learning in a world of growing complexity. *Impact: Journal of Applied Research in Workplace E-learning, 1*(1), 53–67.

Sung, Y., Chang, K., & Yang, J. (2015). (2015). How Effective are Mobile Devices for Language Learning? A Meta-Analysis. *Educational Research Review, 16*, 68–84. Advance online publication. doi:10.1016/j.edurev.2015.09.001

Trudeau, M. B., Catalano, P. J., Jindrich, D. L., & Dennerlein, J. T. (2013). Tablet Keyboard Configuration Affects Performance, Discomfort and Task Difficulty for Thumb Typing in a Two-Handed Grip. *PLoS One, 8*(6), e67525. doi:10.1371/journal.pone.0067525 PMID:23840730

Vaidya, C. V. (2020). Mobile Learning. *Our Heritage, 68*(9), 925–930.

Vaughan, K. (2017). The role of apprenticeship in the cultivation of soft skills and dispositions. *Journal of Vocational Education and Training, 69*(4), 540–557. Advance online publication. doi:10.1080/1363 6820.2017.1326516

Wilke, A., & Magenheim, J. (2017, April). Requirements analysis for the design of workplace-integrated learning scenarios with mobile devices: Mapping the territory for learning in industry 4.0. In *Global Engineering Education Conference (EDUCON)* (pp. 476-485). IEEE. 10.1109/EDUCON.2017.7942890

Yousafzai, A., Chang, V., Gani, A., & Noor, R. M. (2016). Multimedia augmented m-learning: Issues, trends and open challenges. *International Journal of Information Management, 36*(5), 784–792. doi:10.1016/j.ijinfomgt.2016.05.010

ADDITIONAL READING

Ada, M., Stansfield, M., & Baxter, G. (2015). Using mobile learning and social media to enhance learner feedback: Some empirical evidence. *Journal of Applied Research in Higher Education, 9*(1), 2017. doi:10.1108/JARHE-07-2015-0060

Alrasheedi, M. & Capretz, L. (2014). An empirical study of critical success factors of mobile learning platform from the perspective of instructors. *Procedia - Social and Behavioral Sciences, 176*(2015), 211-219. doi:. doi:10.1016/j.sbspro.2015.01.463

Dubey, M. (2015). 5 Best practices of mobile learning for skill based vocational training. Retrieved October 2017, From: https://www.nationalskillsnetwork.in/mobile-learning-vocational-training/

Keengwe, J. (Ed.). (2014). *Advancing Higher Education with Mobile Learning Technologies: Cases, Trends, and Inquiry-Based Methods: Cases, Trends, and Inquiry-Based Methods.* IGI Global.

Rikala, J. (2015). *Designing a mobile learning framework for a formal educational context.* University of Jyväskylä.

Rodríguez, A. I., Riaza, B. G., & Gómez, M. C. S. (2017). Collaborative learning and mobile devices: An educational experience in Primary Education. *Computers in Human Behavior, 72,* 664–677. doi:10.1016/j.chb.2016.07.019

Shuib, L., Shamshirband, S., & Ismail, M. (2015). A review of mobile pervasive learning: Applications and issues. *Computers in Human Behavior, 46,* 239–244. doi:10.1016/j.chb.2015.01.002

KEY TERMS AND DEFINITIONS

Generic (Soft) Skills: Overarching, meta skills which are common to a range of occupations. They are skills, abilities, and traits that pertain to personality, attitude, and behaviour.

Learning Environment: The medium where learning and teaching take place. It is the sum of the internal and external circumstances and influences surrounding and affecting a person's learning.

Mobile Learning: A type of learning that allows learners, as individuals or groups, to gain knowledge, ideas, skills, or concepts not already known or recognised from formal or informal contents using mobile technologies at anytime and anywhere.

Role-Specific (Technical) Skills: The hard or technical skills for a specific major or specialization.

Vocational and Technical Education and Training (VTET): Education programmes that are designed for learners to acquire the knowledge, skills, and competencies specific to a particular occupation, trade, or class of occupations or trades.

Chapter 7
Managing Information Technology Projects Using Agile Methodology:
The Case of Books for Africa Project

Alice S. Etim
Winston Salem State University, USA

Chandra Prakash Jaiswal
Winston Salem State University, USA

Marsheilla Subroto
Winston Salem State University, USA

Vivian E. Collins Ortega
Winston Salem State University, USA

ABSTRACT

The management of information technology (IT) projects has experienced a shift from predictive and traditional project management methodology to more adaptive practices like Agile. Agile method and its developmental stages are a response to current business-changing trends and computing needs of society. The process assists in accelerating product delivery with rapid feedback and cost-conscious, consecutive iteration, distinguishing it from other traditional practices like the waterfall method. This chapter contributes to the existing literature by discussing agile project management for IT projects, with a specific case of the Africa IT project – the Books for Africa Project (hereafter called, Book Project). The first part of the chapter is used to review the literature on Agile IT projects. The Book Project as a case is an IT project, and it is discussed in detail in the chapter. The chapter concludes with transferable lessons for projects in developing countries, specifically those located in Sub-Saharan Africa.

DOI: 10.4018/978-1-7998-3468-7.ch007

INTRODUCTION

Project Management, to an extent, has been present since the beginning of human civilization. The construction of such complicated architectural masterpieces like the Great Pyramid of Giza in 2570 BC, or The Great Wall of China in 208 BC, could hardly have been accomplished without at least a rudimentary standardization of project management principles; some could even argue that it would have been impossible without highly advanced technical project planning and management expertise (Haughey, 2010).

Through the evolutionary stages of project management, the field has been exposed to a shift from more traditional project methods like waterfall to the less conventional and current methods like agile. Two important reasons for the changes have been technological advancements and the on-demand IT products and services. The shift has revolutionized project management and contemporary agile method of managing projects have significantly affected the financial (cost) and schedule (time) variables of project operations. Unlike the predictive methods which suggest concrete planning before execution, the development of agile, lean, and related method have allowed for project activities to be done iteratively without completing any specific phase, such as the planning phase (12th Annual State of Agile Report, VisionOne, 2018).

The Book Project utilized the agile method of project management to collect books for the Main Library at the University of Jos, Nigeria, West Africa. Included in the chapter are some of the challenges and benefits encountered during the process of the book collection. The case is discussed to illustrate how the project was successfully initiated and implemented using the agile project methodology. The team involved in the Book Project discovered that when implementing projects using agile methodology, there were common variables that were relevant and the chapter discusses these variables and concludes with best practices to implement related projects in developing countries.

LITERATURE

Software Project History

The history of modern software project management can be traced back to the late 1950s. Software companies adopted the already well-known waterfall model, which was primarily used for hardware production as a model for its software projects. However, with developing systems, companies realized that this linear approach of product development was less than optimal for software (Mens, 2008).

The two major limitations of this linear model were the lack of flexibility for the separation of phases and a lack of requirements' clarity especially at the start of a project. The main causes for software project failures were expanded to incomplete or unclear requirements, inadequate user involvement, inadequate resources, unrealistic time demands, unclear or unrealistic project goals, poor estimates, inadequate executive support, changing requirement, and inadequate planning (Wells & Kloppenborg, 2019)

Project Success Definition

The identification of causes or obstacles that led to software project failures led to engineering of other methodologies like agile method. The preference for agile practices was mainly to achieve project success. There are several ways to determine the success of projects and many definitions of project success. According to Muller & Jugdev, 2012, p. 757, "project success is a multi-dimensional construct that undergoes influence from the interaction of personal, project, team and organizational success." Mir & Pinnington, 2014, on the other hand, indicate that project success measurement criteria differ from project to project. Project success has always been measured by meeting objectives, time, and budget. This evaluation is the most common way for many organizations to determine the success of the projects (Frese & Sauter, 2003; Bannerman, 2008). For development projects, success outcomes are not only determined by budget and time but also how the project will be able to deliver the benefit and meet the expectations of the various stakeholders like the sponsor and customers (Cavarec, 2012).

Two primary categories that an organization should focus on are project success and project management success. Project success is determined by the level of effectiveness and the project deliverables for stakeholders' satisfaction. On the other hand, project management success should focus on the level of efficiency of how the project achieves the objectives that were set in the beginning. Efficiency is related to how the project manages its limited resources to meet the goals while developing good relationships with internal and external stakeholders (Wells & Kloppenborg, 2019).

Waterfall Methodology

Waterfall methodology or traditional methodology has been in use for many years. Introduced by Winstow W. Royce in 1970, the waterfall method tends to emphasize a "logical progression of steps that is taken for software development life cycle, much like the cascading steps down an incremental waterfall" (Powell-Morse, 2016).

Waterfall methodology is a linear and sequential life cycle approach to software development in project settings. As shown in Figure 1, each phase in the method has to be completed before moving to the next phase to avoid overlapping in the phases.

Figure 1. Waterfall project phases
Adapted from (Westfall, 2010)

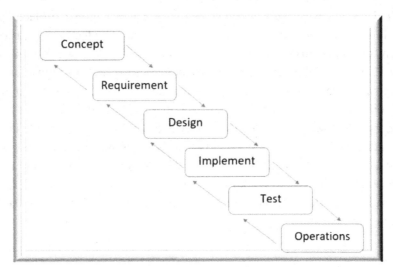

The waterfall method begins with the project concept. After the project is approved, the requirement gathering step is lauched followed by the systems design, implementation and test. The entire project must be completed using a predetermined project schedule, cost and resources. The last phase is the operations. The main problem with this method is that there is no flexibility or ability to adapt to emerging circumstances, changing competition and systemic risks. In present day business and project scenarios, things change and stakeholders are to adapt quickly. For example, when this chapter was being written, a pandemic called COVID-19 struck the entire global communities and many businesses shut down or asked employees to work from home in order to comply with the social distancing order to reduce the spread of the virus. In a waterfall project environment, it would be difficult to adapt or be flexible with an unfinished project. Waterfall method are completed in sequence whearas the project using Agile methodolody is completed iteratively. (Maassen & Dima, 2018).

AGILE PROJECT MANAGEMENT

The Agile Manifesto (Beck, et al., 2001), states that agile practitioners have shared values of:

1. Individuals and interactions over processes and tools
2. Working software over comprehensive documentation
3. Customer collaboration over contract negotiation
4. Response to change over following a plan.

According to Gustavsson (2016), there are some benefits from agile method that can also be applied for non-software development projects. A few of the benefits deal significantly with team-work, customer interaction, productivity, and flexibility. The greatest benefits reported correspond to the first value of the Agile Manifesto - Individuals and interactions over processes and tools. Some of the reported benefits are concepts that are not explicitly stated in the Agile Manifesto or the accompanying principles, such as the impediment removal on processes or better focus.

The agile method is a process that creates an advantage when managing a project, especially through the process of sectioning the project into different stages and obtaining feedback and collaboration from the stakeholders and customers to develop necessary improvements for new releases/ iterations at every stage of the project. One crucial aspect of the agile methodology that distinguishes it from the other traditional project management methods is its potential to determine the issues that may arise during the progression of a project. Adjustment is very significant; that is why agile will create a greater benefit to users, by allowing them to reach goals more efficiently and within budget and schedule.

The process of agile begins with finding the customer's needs and expectations for the project. The stages of the project comprise of 4 segments, starting with the initiation phase and moving through to project planning phase, then the executing phase, and finally the evaluation phase. A fundamental aspect of this process is continuous collaboration among team members and their project stakeholders to deliver fully-informed and accurate results.

Success Factors in Agile Practices

"The key intent of Agile Solution delivery is to provide value to an organization in increments, which are adjusted and built over time into a scalable solution" (Kruchten & Gorans, 2014, 4). They discuss that the factors that make agile processes successful are flexibility, anticipation of change, and ability to deliver working, tested features without huge consequences to the timeline or resources of a project.

According to (Cao & Chow, 2008), there are five groups of critical success factors for agile software: Organizational factors, people factors, process factors, technical factors, and project factors. Table 1 shows the five critical success and sub-success factors for agile methodology. All five groups are dependent on using reliable historical data to deliver business value early and continuing to satisfy the client and other stakeholders throughout the project.

The agile method is effective for meeting project demands because it greatly focuses on the Agile Manifesto, which suggests that individuals and interactions, working software, customer collaboration, and response to change be prioritized over processes and tools, comprehensive documentation, contract negotiation and following a plan. These guidelines are relevant to the ever-changing pace of technology which creates frequent changes to the scope of a project.

Table 1. Five factors critical success for agile methodology

Critical Success Factors	Main Success Factors	Sub Success Factors
Organizational	Corporate Culture	• Support from top management • Team Environment
People	User Involvement	• Handling commercial pressure • Stakeholder politics
	Team Capability	• Effective project management skills • Ability to handle the project complexity • Decision time • Effective communication and feedback
Process	Project management process	• Minimum change in requirements • Simplicity in process • Good reporting of project status
	Project definition process	• Risk management • Time allocation • Accurate estimates of project resources
	Active testing	• Code review
Project	Clear objectives and goals	• Project type • Project nature
	Realistic schedule	
	Realistic budget	• Team distribution • Team size
	Clear requirement and specifications	
Technical	Selecting proper agile method	• Configuring the necessary tools and infrastructure
	Using advance technology	• Familiarity with technology

Source: Retrieved from https://medium.com/pnr/critical-success-factors-of-agileprojects-65acd133a402

The focusing on business value also requires that features (discrete units of product functionality) be prioritized and delivered (PRNewswire, 2002). The measuring and running of tested software and requiring teams to focus on product features as the primary unit of planning, tracking & delivery, as well as tracking how many running and tested features are being delivered, are necessary to build a foundation of practical tasks.

Additional success factors include continuous planning occurring on the release level, iteration level, and the just-in-time approach. Just-in-time approach to planning is much more successful and simpler to use than large-scale upfront planning as in the case of waterfall method. It allows for there to be an equivalent amount of information output and details necessary for input. In addition, the agile process is very conservative with regards to resources and time management, allowing customers to test and approve the product as it progresses.

Agile methodology is adopted in over 800 companies around the globe. Some adopters include Dell, Behr, Alps and Texas Instruments. A few of the benefits to their guaranteed business results are that they "help companies reduce material costs, rapidly introduce the product to meet demand, and substantially improve productivity and product quality" (PRNewswire, 2002, 4)

In comparison to the waterfall project method, agile project is twice more likely to succeed and one third less likely to fail (Vcwebdesign, 2013). Figure 2 shows a comparison between agile and waterfall success rates captured in 2015 using constraints like schedule, cost and scope.

A successful project is defined as one with an outcome that meets the project goal based on all the critical constraints. Challenging projects are have outcomes that meet one or two out of three key constraints of schedule, cost and scope. A failed project is defined as the project that do not meet the three constraints of schedule, cost and scope or is canceled before meeting the project goal. (Sweeney, 2014).

Figure 2. Agile vs waterfall success rate, 2015
Source: Jhttp://blog.standishgroup.com

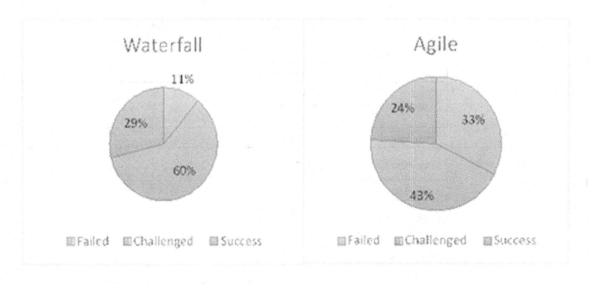

Table 2 is the resolution of all software projects from 2011-2015 as provided in the CHAOS Resolution database.

Table 2. CHAOS resolution - agile versus waterfall

Size	Method	Successful	Challenged	Failed
All Size Projects	Agile	39%	52%	9%
	Waterfall	11%	60%	29%
Large Size Projects	Agile	18%	59%	23%
	Waterfall	3%	55%	42%
Medium Size Projects	Agile	27%	62%	11%
	Waterfall	7%	68%	25%
Small Size Projects	Agile	58%	38%	4%
	Waterfall	44%	45%	11%

Source: The Standish Group International, Inc, 2015 https://www.standishgroup.com/sample_research_files/CHAOSReport2015-Final.pdf

Agile methodology is utilized more often now than traditional methods such as waterfall. Agile development projects typically involve more sophisticated planning than waterfall projects. Some critics may say that waterfall is successful if it delivers what is demanded as a requirement, and not what the stakeholders discover they need as the project progresses. (Cao & Chow, 2008) ; (Lotz, 2018); (Stankovic, Nikolic, Djordjevic, & Cao, 2013). In the next section, Agile and one of its important framework, called *Scrum* is discussed.

AGILE METHODOLOGIES AND FRAMEWORK

Scrum

Scrum is a framework. It enables people to address complex adaptive problems productively and creatively while delivering products of the highest possible value.

History of Scrum

Scrum was developed around the 1990s. However, it came to popularity after the Agile Alliance was founded in 2001. In 1986, a paper titled, *The New Product Development Game,* by Hirotaka Takeuchi and Ikujiro Nonaka in the Harvard Business Review discussed the sport of Rugby as an example of the benefits of self-organizing teams. Jeff Sutherland, Ken Schwaber, and Mike Beedle were so inspired by this paper that they took the idea of self-organizing teams and applied to software development. The term Scrum was first used by the trio, and was derived from an ordered formation of players usually a circle in Rugby where a player goes for the ball to get it back into the game again. Their first implementation of this method was at Easel Corporation in 1993 (Slinger, 2011). In 2002 Schwaber and Beedle published a book titled "Agile Software Development with Scrum" to share their experience. (Slinger, 2011).

Usage of Scrum

The Scrum framework is defined around a set of activities, roles, events, artifacts and rules (Griffiths, 2012). A list of thirteen items with their descriptions on Scrum practices is provided in Exhibit A.

The Scrum framework has three key roles: *Scrum Master, Product Owner,* and *Team Member.* The Scrum Master is the controller/regulator that makes sure that the Scrum process is being followed and resolves any impediments. The Product Owner controls the product *backlog.* Team Members are other members in the project team like analysts, designers, developers, testers, etc. The sprint is the heart of Scrum. It is a time-box of 2-4 weeks during which a potentially releasable product increment is created based on an agreed-upon task. Sprints consist of four events: *Sprint planning, daily standup, sprint review* and *sprint retrospective.* Theses events help in the checking of daily progress and constant flow of information between all team members and external stakeholders.

The Scrum artifacts are product backlog, sprint backlog, and product increment. The product backlog contains an ordered list of requirements to be developed in a future sprint. The sprint backlog contains requirements as part of the current live sprint. The product increment is the result of the functioning work which was done during a sprint; actually, it is the sum of all the product backlog items completed during a sprint combined with all previous sprints increments.

According to (Alexander, 2018), Scrum has been the most popular agile method in years. Scrum focused particularly on managing software development through the means of the iterative approach. Figure 3 shows the Scrum Process and the relationship between the listed factors with a sprint time-box of 1-4 weeks. For each sprint, the product owner and the team decide on a subset of items from the product backlog to be added to the sprint backlog. The team works throughout the sprint (time-boxed) to create a potentially working product increment based on the listed items in the sprint backlog. Each day, the team holds a daily scrum meeting for collaboration and catering of information as well as discussing defects or problems.

It is evident that Scrum is widely used in the Software industry. However, the use of Scrum is not limited to the software industry. As per The Scrum Guide™(2017), Scrum was developed primarily for developing products. Starting in the early 1990s, Scrum has been used extensively for (i) research and identify viable markets, technologies, and product capabilities; (ii) developing products; (iii) frequent release of prototypes, products and enhancements; (iv) developing and sustaining Cloud infrasturctures and services (online, secure, on-demand) and other operational environments for product use; (v) s ustain and renewing products. Scrum has been used to develop software, hardware, embedded software, networks of interacting function, autonomous vehicles, schools, government, marketing, managing the operation of organizations and almost everything we use in our daily lives.

Advantage and Disadvantages of Scrum

Scrum is an iterative, incremental development process. It offers various advantages that include:

1. It helps to get started on fuzzy grounds when the business requirements are hard to be determined completely and the less likelihood of having a successful project.

Figure 3. Scrum process
Source: Retrieve from https://www.vectorstock.com/royalty-free-vector/scrum-agile-process-workflow-with-stages-vec-tor-22575698

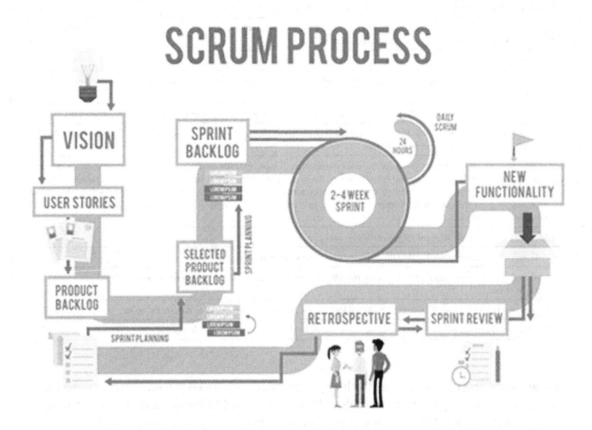

2.   It is fast-paced and uses cutting edge technologies for product development and quick implemention. Such as web development or media-related projects.
3.   It is easier for the team to cope up with the changes due to short sprint and constant feedback. Mistake can be easily rectifiable.
4.   Improvement in productivity is one of the significant factors in Scrum as daily meetings make it possible to track individual productivity.
5.   It increases the market potential of the organization by enabling them to release multiple versions of software at a much faster pace.

There are a few limitations posed by the nature of Scrum implementation and they include:

1.   Scope creep is one of the major issues of Agile in general and Scrum in particular. A stakeholder is tempted to keep demanding the additional functionalities unless there is a definitive end date.
2.   If the task is not well defined, it can roll over to multiple sprints and create a problem for project cost and effort variance.
3.   Scrum is very useful for small teams and fast-moving projects. However, there is less evidence of success for bigger teams.

Box 1. Exhibit A: Commonly Accepted Scrum Terminology and Practices

1. *Burndown chart* – It shows the implementation progress base on what is complete in a sprint.
2. *Daily standup* - 15-minute time-boxed event for the Scrum team to meet and/or collaborate and create a plan for work day.
3. *Definition of Done (DoD)* – A set of acceptance criteria. The correctness of implementation tested and verified for a user story to be completed and considered done based on the acceptance criteria.
4. *Iterative development* –Small time-boxed iterations called sprints. Each sprint usually lasts for two to four weeks.
5. *Product backlog* - The most critical evolving artifacts that include all features, requirements, enhancements, functions, and fixes and changes to be made to the product in future releases.
6. *Product owner* – A person responsible for the product backlog and decides the priority of individual tasks in the product backlog.
7. *Scrum Master* – The person responsible for making sure the scrum process is followed, and the project is running smoothly. The Scrum Master is often the person that leads the daily standup.
8. *Scrum of Scrums* – An approach to project planning and coordination that successfully employs Scrum-based organizations. Since the production-ready software is being delivered in every iteration, the success of teams is highly dependent on cross-functionality. What this means is that an agile development team must incorporate team members according to the skillset demanded by successful software delivery, including analysis, design, coding, testing, writing, user interface design, planning, and management. This is necessary because each iteration is its mini-project.
9. *Sprint backlog* – Action items selected for the current sprint.
10. *Sprint planning* – Selection of the backlog items for the sprint backlog by the team.
11. *Sprint retrospective* - Team looks back and brainstorm what could have been better and improved at the end of each sprint, and before the start of a new sprint,
12. *Sprint review* - After each sprint is complete, Stakeholders review and provide feedback for the current sprint.
13. *Team members* – Team members are the rest of the team except Product Owner and Scrum Master.

There are a few less known agile methodology frameworks such as Kanban, Extreme Programming, Dynamic Systems Development System (DSDM), Crystal Clear Method, Feature Driven Development (FDD). Kanban and Extreme Programming are discussed briefly as part of this chapter.

Kanban

Kanban is another flavor of the Agile methodology. The term Kanban originates from Toyota's "Just-in-Time" production system, which means doing "only what is needed, when it is needed, and in the amount needed." (Barolli, Nishino, & Miwa, 2019, 92) The main principle of the Kanban system is better communication through visualization and visual management (Poppendieck & Poppendieck, 2013). Kanban is more of a mindset than a methodology. While it does not offer a particular rule on how to follow a process, it focuses on having the right attitude (Poppendieck & Poppendieck, 2013)

(Griffiths, PMI-ACP Exam Prep, 2012) identifies five principles meant to support Kanban behavior in a project:

1. Visualize workflow
2. Limit Work-in-Progress (WiP)
3. Manage flow
4. Make process explicit
5. Improve collaboratively

Each item selected for development displays on a prioritized backlog called a Kanban whiteboard. A simple Kanban board can have three columns where each column represents a status. Each item is located in a designated column and flows from left to right as the work is being performed on it. A maximum WiP limit is set for each column, indicating the maximum item a column can hold. If there is any single column where items are clustered more than its maximum limit, the whole team will try to solve the bottleneck and make the flow smooth again. Figure 3 shows an example of a Kanban whiteboard. The higher priority items are placed higher in a column. Kanban method is a good choice for supporting projects that priorities change very frequently.

Figure 4. Kanban whiteboard
Source: Retrieved from https://www.cleverism.com/how-to-use-kanban-to-improvebusiness-productivity/

Extreme Programming

The extreme programming (XP) method focuses on improving software quality and responsiveness to changes in customer requirements (Yasvi, Yadav, & Shubhika, 2017). This method provides checkpoints during the development process where the developers can check the quality, and on the other hand, customers can redefine or adopt new requirements in order to improve quality of product. The XP method has five core values: (i) Simplicity (ii) Communication (iii) Feedback (iv) Respect and (v) Courage. In addition to the core values, XP has many practices. Figure 4 shows the XP framework.

Agile Best Practices

One of the best known practices of agile is the involvement of stakeholders during the extensive planning process to deliver what they need as the project progresses. This is unlike other processes such as waterfall that deliver what was initially requested and planned for in the requirements document with limited continuous interaction with stakeholders (Collabnet Version One, 2018). Agile method allows for planning to be continuous and new details are incorporated as they are discovered. It emphasizes

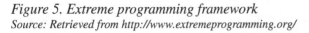

Figure 5. Extreme programming framework
Source: Retrieved from http://www.extremeprogramming.org/

on iterations as part of continuous planning and task estimation. Agile development projects quickly prioritize and estimate features and then refine details when necessary (Turk, France, & Rumpe, 2002).

By implementing continuous testing and encouraging customer participation, Agile allows for progress measurement and prevention of defects, ultimately reducing the risk of failure in projects (Kruchten & Gorans, 2014). Table 3 shows a list of selected agile practices and the estimated percentage of reduction of risk of failure.

CHALLENGES AND LIMITATIONS IN AGILE

Some of the limitations of agile processes were identified based on a study (Turk, France, & Rumpe, 2014)

- Software development did not focus on documentation and software models.
- Requirements and environment in which software were being developed to evolve with the incremental iterations.
- Consecutive Iteration produced high-quality products.
- Developers were highly skilled to adapt define and adapt the process.
- Incremental product delivery and project metrics were sufficient to track project visibility.
- Frequent informal reviews and testing would be sufficient to keep track of the software artifacts.
- Application-specific software did not focus on software code reusability and generality.
- The cost of change did not increase dramatically over time.

Table 3. A list of selected practices of agile method and reduction of failure/risk (percentage)

Agile Practice	Reduction of Failure (%)
Daily standup	90
Sprint/iteration planning	88
Retrospectives	85
Sprint/iteration review	80
Release planning/team estimation, Kanban	65
Frequent releases	51
Product road mapping	46
Story mapping	44
Agile portfolio planning	35
Agile/Lean UX	30

Source: https://entwickler.de/online/agile/state-of-agile-report-579797161.html

- The software can be developed in iteration and incrementally.

APPROACH TO OVERCOME ENVIRONMENT LIMITATION IN AGILE

The traditional agile method was developed for a team that is collocated where the parent organizations work to reach global markets, encourage virtual teams in software development. The benefit from these dispersion of teams means faster completion of production procedure, reduction in time-to-market, lower materialization cost, more affordable workforce, opportunities for new collaborations, and access to specialized professionals.

According to Amber (2018), the management of such teams, can be considered one of the most challenging things when implementing agile methodologies.

Challenges in distributed and diversified agile teams are:

1. Effective communication
2. Cultural differences
3. Coordination
4. Time zone differences
5. Trust

Using Cutting Edge Technologies to Manage Distributed Team Challenges

New technologies can be used to help overcome the challenges that could be encountered in distributed agile software development. A few of such technologies for project teams: (a) Web and video conferencing software allows for application sharing (b) Communication is further facilitated by instant messaging software (c) E-mail sharing allows for daily communication among team members, including daily objectives and tasks sharing, understanding priorities and improving collaboration among team members. Some of the agile project management tools include:

- VersionOne
- Atlassian JIRA
- CA Agile Central
- Lean Kit
- Bugzilla
- Collab Net Team Forge
- IBM Rational Team Concert
- Axosoft
- Google Docs
- Microsoft TFS
- Microsoft Excel
- Microsoft Project
- HP Quality Center/ALM
- HP Agile Manager
- Pivotal Tracker

Social Media and Social Networking and Project Collaboration/Team Work

Social media platforms can also be used to improve communication, build team trust, increase knowledge sharing, and facilitate management. (Anantatmula V. & Thomas, 2010); (Etim A. &., 2015); (Kauppila, Rajala, & Jyrama, 2011). Social media use can help to improve communication strategies in the software system development processes. The use social media and collaborative communication tools can boost team productivity, improve learning opportunities, decrease gaps between distributed sites, build trust among team members and even reduce project costs (Etim A. S., 2016) (Hysa & Spalek, 2019) (Sarker, Ahuja, Sarker, & Kirkeby, 2011). However, Social media platforms are to be used with care since potential benefits come with inherent risks in the form of data and information security breaches, privacy issues that can derail productive work, focus, and interpersonal relationships.

What are popular social media sites that can be leveraged within the restriction of organizational policy to improve project management collaboration and communication in distributed teams? The platforms listed below are used by global project teams.

Popular Social Media Sites for Leveraging Project Communication/Team Work:

- Facebook™ (https://www.facebook.com/)
- Twitter™ (https://twitter.com/)
- Instagram™ (https://www.instagram.com/?hl=en)
- LinkedIn® linkedin.com

Professional Networking Sites with Rich Resources to Support Projects Personnel/Team Work:

- Project Management Institute, pmi.org
- Project Management, projectmanagement.com
- Project Connections, projectconnections.com

THE CASE OF BOOKS FOR AFRICA PROJECT

The case for the Books for Africa Project, "Book Project" was an initiative taken by the MBA Project Management instructor, Dr. Alice Etim as a response to the rebuilding effort for the Main Library at the University of Jos (UNIJOS) in Nigeria that was guttered by fire in 2017. The Project became a field research project work in "MIS-6321 Project Management" class for the MBA students at Winston-Salem State University.

Based on the review of literature, the team decided on agile methodology for the Book Project. The Scrum method was the first choice for the Project. However, there were particular challenges that led to not using the strict sprint approach but a modified version to use the incremental iteration approach. Two of the notable challenges were:

1. All the team members were working professionals with different job shifts. This did not allow the team to follow the Daily Scrums but members met before or after classes every week.
2. To complete the project in the semester that it was assigned, team members needed to own and drive different work items in the Project Plan; for example, some used online, personal visits, and book drive to collect books. All the book collection modes were being done in concurrently, so this did not fit the time box sprint approach of Scrum.

The project planning was done in multiple iterations. The case is reported to show project initiation that included the Project Overview Statement (POS), Project Plan, key deliverables/accomplishments and lessons learned.

Project Initiation

The project initiation step required certain preliminary administrative activities, such as obtaining administrative approval from Winston-Salem state University (WSSU), and providing the opening information to WSSU Advancement Office and the Student Government Association (SGA). A project Kick-Off meeting was held and all project stakeholders participated.

Following the Kick-Off meeting was the creation of the Project Overview Statement (POS) to establish the Book Project's high-level goals, results and challenges, risks and opportunities. A sample of the POS is found in *Exhibit B*. Next was the creation of the outline for the project objectives to define the accomplishments sought for in the project. Two of such objectives were:

1. Make an educationally meaningful contribution to the rebuilding of the Main Library Collection at the University of Jos, Nigeria by collecting, cataloging and delivering at least 100 hard copy books in many disciplines by April 8th, 2019.
2. Supplement the Collection of donated books with historically valuable, poetical, philosophical and music theory material unlikely to be donated from other sources.

The project scope was developed based on a clear understanding of the client's needs and vision and was managed effectively to avoid scope creep. Project scope creep can occur when there are additional features or functions and requirements, or work that was not authorized or initially planned into the project. According to (PMI, 2018 in PMBOK®Guide), the top 5 reasons for scope creep include:

Box 2. Exhibit B: Project Overview Statement – Books for Africa Project, 2017 – 2019

Project Overview Statement	Project Name: Books for Africa	Project Sponsor: Dr. Alice Etim	Project Manager: Chandra Jaiswal
Problem/Opportunity: ● In 2017, Dr. Alice Etim learned that the library in the University of Jos in Nigeria was destroyed by a fire. The University of Jos was her alma mater, and in response to this incident, Dr. Etim began collecting books to help rebuild the main library. The "Books for Africa" Initiative was born and has become an annual, worldwide movement. ● This Project will help reconstruct the main library at the University of Jos, by collecting college-level books of all fields. This activity will help the students from a different stream in Nigeria to keep getting the source of knowledge (books) to build their career path and future endeavor. ● This project also creates an opportunity for the WSSU Graduate student Team to follow the Project management practices from Initiation to closing.			
Goal: ● To help the University of Jos repopulate their Main Library with useful books. ● To obtain a minimum of 100 books by April 9, 2019 ● To establish an organized plan for the collective of the books ● To improve the lives of collegiate level students ● To create the reputation and encourage donations year-round We hope to provide some relief to the Nigerian academics of Jos University by enabling them to continue their studies. Our contribution serves as an influencer to other organizations in the Winston Salem area and can yield much more significant results than the one we can provide			
Objectives: ● Collect at least 100 educational books sufficient for inclusion in the University of Jo's main Library. These books ideally will be as current as possible, with no textbooks published before 2010. ● Additionally, collect at least 20 philosophical, poetic, and musical texts. These may be published from any era, but the content must be of the historically accepted value. ● Present information regarding the project to staff at WSSU and other locations ● Strategically organize book collection among members to meet the deadline ● Collect relevant texts to expand the education at Jos University, Nigeria ● Spread knowledge of the project goal throughout every academic year ● Set up at least one book drive per month ● Review literature on Agile Projects and Communications Management to achieve the goal of being a better performer in Agile Projects and adaptive project environments			
Success Criteria: ● Proof of collected books successfully delivered to University of Jos library ● Collect academic books from science, social studies, politics, law and other majors that will help to rebuild the library ● Interactive communication among team members of groups and sponsor ● Following the project plan ● Share a flyer or poster that contain information about the project and book's requirement among friends, coworker, family, and social media ● Ensure all the books meet the requirement for the donation which is academic college-level books ● Setting up and monitor the book drive in a different location. ● A minimum of 100 books (no maximum).			
Assumptions, Risk, and Obstacles ● We assume that the books will be suitable for the university's curriculum. ● There is an educational need for books in Africa. ● Multiple units of the same book are acceptable from the book donor. ● The team will try to cover all majors. However, books from any major at the college and/or graduate level are acceptable. ● Books related to core sciences such as Biology, Anatomy, Physics, Chemistry, and Mathematics are acceptable even if they are dated prior to 2010 printed version. (Based on the fact that these core concepts do not change drastically over a period of time) ● We risk sending books that are outdated or irrelevant to the education system in Nigeria. ● Lack of motivation by the public to donate to this cause (not enough participants) ● Lack of time for team members to brainstorm ● Lack of adequate funding from WSSU fundraiser program ● No team member is 100% allocated to this project (As everyone is working a part-time or full-time job) so possibility that 50 books will not be collected by deadline. ● The weather could delay the delivery of the books; this would need to be dealt with by the client ● Time coordination for the physical meeting with the donor to collect the book could be a significant obstacle as each member of the team is working during the day time and would not able to meet the book donor. ● Miscommunication among team members of the goals of the project can hinder the progression of the project. ● We could get slow donations of books, this would need to be dealt with by creating advertisements (flyers, website, social media posts) asking for donations.			
Prepared by:	Date:	Approved by:	Date:

1.   Ambiguous or unrefined scope definition
2.   Lack of any formal scope or requirements management

Table 4. Project scope for the 2019 books for Africa project

Project scope is broken down into three overall components Deliverables, Functionality /Data, and Technical Structure.
Deliverables: Deliverables for the Books for Africa project are a minimum of 100 books of a subject matter appropriate for the repopulation of the JOS Library post-fire. The appropriate subject matter would be any conventionally relevant material commonly considered suitable for inclusion in a modern university library. Example subject fields could include but are not limited to disciplines such as Accounting, Finance, Economics, Literature, etc. Additionally, subject matter relevance will be constrained by book publication dates ideally not to precede 2010, except on a case by case basis, subject to senior project manager approval.
Functionality/Data: Functionally the deliverables will be executed in a three-part process. First, the books will be collected using the project work plan strategies. Second, the books will be recorded in the textbook project database file on an item by item basis either by the collector or a mutually agreed upon designee in the group. Third, the books will be delivered to and shelved in the designated storage area on the campus of Winston Salem State University.
Technical: From a technical perspective, the successful execution of the deliverables will rely on the accurate and timely documentation of the books collected in the Textbook Project Database file. Without this real-time information, the project will not have a clear picture of completion relative to the scope goal of a minimum of 100 books meeting the project specifications. In this sense, the Textbook Project Database file will be a primary and an iterative resource both to measure work to complete percentages as well as evaluate current strategy in the project execution and craft timely corrective responses to strategy and execution deficiencies.

3. Inconsistent process for collecting product requirements
4. Lack of sponsorship and stakeholder involvement
5. Project length.

Table 4 shows a summarized scope for the Book Project.

Table 5. Project Stakeholders' matrix for the books for Africa project

Internal Stakeholders	Project Roles
Project Manager Chandra Jaiswal	• Develop project and implementation plans • Initiate and schedule meetings related to the project • Monitor and review all project activities • Lead and manage the project team • Assign tasks to project team • Provide regular updates for sponsor and customers
Project Team Marsheilla Subroto Vivian Collins	• Complete all the tasks and responsibilities assigned by the project manager based on WBS • Contribute to overall project objectives • Practice excellent communication between all team members and project manager • Brainstorming ideas between team members • Documenting changes and updates
Sponsor Organization Winston Salem State University	• Approve project selection • Ensure the availability of resources • Communicate the project goals throughout the organization • Provide funding for books shipment to Africa
Suppliers Book Donor	• Donate or supply the used college books • Participate in raising funding through WSSU website
Client or Customers The University of Jos Main Library and the students in that University in Nigeria	• Providing the information to the project team about their needs and expectations • Provide feedback during the project process

All the stakeholders involved directly and indirectly were identified by the project team with their roles and responsibilities, and a Project Stakeholders' Matrix was prepared. Table 5 shows the Project Stakeholders' Matrix:

Project Planning

As part of Project Planning, the following activities were performed:

1. Define the detailed activities
2. Layout the activities or tasks as a WBS (Work Break down structure)
3. Create the WBS and sequence the activities
4. Schedule the tasks in a Project Plan after the team had completed task duration estimation
5. Identify the resources to perform all tasks and schedule them in the Project Plan

Figure 6. A section of the project plan for the book project

🛈	Task Mode	Task Name	Duration	Start	Finish	Pre	Resource Names
		⁴ **Preliminary Activities for Book Project in MIS 6351 - Spring 2019**	**66.25 days**	**Mon 1/7/19**	**Tue 4/9/19**		
✓		Project Writeup and Inclusion in Course	3 days	Mon 1/7/19	Wed 1/9/19		Dr. Etim
✓		Inform/Meet with Stakeholders - University Advancement & SGA	2 days	Thu 1/10/19	Fri 1/11/19	1	Dr. Etim
		Locate Room, Move Shelves Into Space	2 days	Mon 1/14/19	Tue 1/15/19	2	Facilities
✓		Share Project Information with Students in the Course	1 day	Tue 1/15/19	Tue 1/15/19	1	Dr. Etim
✓		Preliminary Activities Complete	0 days	Tue 1/15/19	Tue 1/15/19	4	
✓		▷ Project overview statement	5 days	Wed 2/27/19	Tue 3/5/19		
✓		▷ Project execution	46.25 days	Mon 2/4/19	Tue 4/9/19		
✓		▷ Project Closeout	1.25 days	Mon 4/8/19	Tue 4/9/19		

Figure 7. A section of the books for Africa database

Book_ID	No	Name of Book	Author	Publishing Year	Edition	Resource Subject Matter (ACC, MIS, MKT	ISB Number	Status, A=Av	Donated To (Univ.)	Donated To (Contact Person)	Donated Date
A1	1	Microeconomics	McCONNEL Brue Flynn	2009	18	Eco	978-0073365954	Donated		Vivian Collins	2/20/2019
A2	2	Business Essentials	ld J. Ebert, Ricky W. G	2005	5	Bus	978-0131441582	Donated		Vivian Collins	2/21/2019
A3		Rudolf Carnap	Paul Aurthur Schilpp	1991	NA	Phil		Donated		Vivian Collins	2/22/2019
A4		Cities and People	Mark Girouard	1985	NA	His	978-300039689	Donated		Vivian Collins	2/23/2019
A5	3	Intermediate accounting	eso Weygandt Warfie	2014	15	Acc	978-1118985311	Donated		Vivian Collins	2/24/2019
A6	4	Health care management	Ivan J. Barrick	2009	NA	Mgt	978-0763744502	Donated		Vivian Collins	2/25/2019
A7	5	Business law today	Roger LeRoy Miller	2014	10	Bus	978-1133191353	Donated		Vivian Collins	2/26/2019

Figure 5 shows a section of the Project Plan developed in Microsoft Project 2016 with scheduled tasks/duration, start and finish dates and the resource to complete each task.

Project Execution, Monitoring and Controlling Activities

Actual project execution, monitoring and controlling of activities were done based on the Project Plan. The tracking of the books that were collected was done using a Microsoft Excel database (known as *Books for Africa Database*). Figure 6 is a section of the Books for Africa Database with many fields that allow recording of all books with key metadata like the title, author information, ISBN number, year of publication, subject and the contact individual that received the donation. The database could be searched, queried for different things including the number of books that have been collected by a

Table 6. Selected activities successfully monitored/controlled for the book project

Book Collection from Individuals and Library 1. Schedule meetings with the Book Donor(s) 2. Meet with the Book Donor in Person 3. Document discussions with the Book Donor and take evidence if possible (video/photo). Show how you are spreading the awareness and encouraging your Book Donor to do the same 4. Collect the Book from the Book Donor 5. Verify and Validate the collected book 6. In case of a suitable book add an entry for each book to database journal or dispose of the unused book 7. Bring the Book to the storeroom and store it to the Team's designated area
Book Drive 1. Meet the Institution and obtain authorization for a book drive. 2. Create Pamphlet and bin for the book drive. 3. Find a suitable place as permitted by the authority in the institution premises. 4. Display the Pamphlet and Bin for the donation of the book. 5. Weekly visit the institution to check the book donation collection. 6. Verify and Validate the book and create an entry for each book in the database journal, dispose of all unnecessary collections. 7. Bring the Book to the storeroom and store it to the Team's designated area. 8. Brainstorm with the team about the performance of the book drive and see if any additional activity is required to meet the expectation.
Donation Website 1. Spread Awareness about the donation website. 2. Receive a copy of receipt for a donation and send to donor 3. Send appreciation letters or thank you notes to donors

specific team member or the number of books for a subject area in the Collection.

Project teams monitored and controlled the collection using tools like WhatsApp and Google Documents. The WhatsApp tool was very effective for team communication, coordination of collections/donations and sharing of ideas. Team members that had to travel during the project implementation period could be reached and contributed to documents using Google Documents. Using these technologies saved time and enabled team cohesion. Table 6 shows some of the tasks from the Project Plan that were successfully monitored/controlled and completed during the project monitoring & controlling phase.

SUMMARY, CONCLUSION AND TRANSFERRABLE LESSONS TO PROJECT COMMUNITIES

As discussed throughout the chapter, the key project objective was to make an educationally meaningful contribution to the rebuilding of the Main Library Collection at the University of Jos, Nigeria by collecting and cataloging at least 100 hard copy books in many disciplines by April 8th, 2019. After the review of literature on the relevant project methodologies, agile method was picked for the Book Project. Using the agile method, the project was initiated, scoped and planned iteratively and resource utilization was at its best. A key lesson lessoned very early in the initiation phase of the project was that agile is people focus; that means that it is driven by people and stakeholders including the project sponsor and the team. It was necessary to have clear objectives and expectations from the onset of the Book Project. The entire project experience was well coordinated by the team leadership to allow completion of project tasks, within budget and on schedule.

Project communication was important as the team were at different locations and met face-to-face once a week. The team developed a project plan using Microsoft Project and depended on collaborative communication tools such as WhatsApp, other instant messaging apps, Google Documents for effective communication and team documentation. Meetings, including weekly Scrums (had limitations in doing daily Scrums) were held through video conferencing. Electronic mailing was important for exchanging information with all stakeholders.

The project Work-Breakdown Structure (WBS) and Project Plan with Microsoft Project allowed scheduling and tracking of tasks completion and overall progress during the monitoring and controlling of the project. After collecting many books, team members were able to check with the course instructor and the ambassador for the University of Jos, Dr. Alice Etim to confirm the changing requirements that included books needed for subject areas. The use of Microsoft Excel database to manage the collection was crucial, as it allowed proper documentation of stored books and the management of the Collection.

In conclusion, the Book Project Case discussed in this chapter could guide other project teams particularly those that are located in Sub-Saharan African countries and other less-resource accessible countries at various stages of their projects.

Detail information on how the project succeeded have been shared. However, it will not be complete without sharing the lessons learned. The project monitoring and controlling was a challenge to the success of this project. Every team meeting revealed the need to restructure to meet the needs of book donors, team members' schedule and the customer. A project team that seeks to use the chapter information should plan very early during project initiation on how to mitigate risk factors that could arise from having a diverse team that is also dispersed. One of the suggestions for a future project is having an online web portal that could link the customer to the project team. For example, if there was an online web portal, the University of Jos community could have shared ideas easily that could have influenced the type of resources that were needed and should be collected, especially when people or organization offered to donate them. One lesson that was learned very late in the monitoring and controlling phase was that there could have been an arm of the Collection for electronic books (E-books) and media artifacts. Publishing houses could have been brought in as stakeholders to support electronic resource donation that could have been directly delivered through the customer's learning management system (LMS). These items could be investigated in future research projects.

REFERENCES

12th Annual State of Agile Report. (2018, April 8). Retrieved from Collabnet Version One: https://www.stateofagile.com/#ufh-i-423641583-12th-annual-state-of-agile-report/473508

Alden, B. (n.d.). *Limitations of Agile Methodologies- Agile Methodologies.* Retrieved April 1, 2019, from https://www.umsl.edu/~sauterv/analysis/Fall2013Papers/Buric/limitations-of-agile-methodologies-1.html

Alexander, M. (2018, June 19). *Agile project management: 12 key principles, 4 big hurdles.* Retrieved from CIO United States: https://www.cio.com/article/3156998/agile-project-management-a-beginners-guide.html

Ambler, S. W. (2018). *Communication on Agile Software Teams.* Retrieved from Agile Modeling: http://www.agilemodeling.com/essays/communication.htm

Anantatmula, V., & Thomas, M. (2010). *Managing global projects: A structured approach for better performance. Project Management Journal* , 41.

Bannerman, P. (2008, July 16). *Defining Project Success: a multilevel framework.* Retrieved from https://www.pmi.org/learning/library/defining-project-success-multilevel-framework-7096

Barolli, L., Nishino, H., & Miwa, H. (2019). *Advances in Intelligent Networking and Collaborative Systems: The 11th International Conference on Intelligent Networking and Collaborative Systems (IN-CoS-2019).* Springer.

Beck, K., Beedle, M., Van Bennekum, A., Cockburn, A., Fowler, M., Grenning, J., . . . Thomas, D. (2001). *Manifesto for Agile Software Development.* Retrieved from http://agilemanifesto.org/

Cao, D.-B., & Chow, T. (2008). *A Survey Study of Critical Success Factors in Agile Software Projects.* Academic Press.

Cavarec, Y. (2012, October 23). *Revisiting the definition of project success.* Retrieved from https://www.pmi.org/learning/library/revisiting-definition-project-success-6098

Characteristic of Agile Development Success. (2018, September 28). Retrieved from Collabnet Versionone: https://resources.collab.net/agile-101/agile-development-success

Collabnet Version One. (2018). *Characteristics of Agile Development Success.* Retrieved from https://resources.collab.net/agile-101/agile-development-success

Etim, A., & Huynh, K. (2015). The use of social media and collaborative tools for virtual teaming – a global market reach out by Navibank. *International Journal of Management & Information Systems, 19*(1), 1–6. doi:10.19030/ijmis.v19i1.9054

Etim, A. S., Huynh, K., Ramaswamy, S., Greer, A., Higdon, T., & Guevara, I. (2016). Educating project managers in the 21st-century economy: A field study on the adoption of social and collaborative tools as low-cost alternatives for project communication. *International Journal of Education Economics and Development, 7*(1/2), 79–94. doi:10.1504/IJEED.2016.079240

Frese, R. (2003, December 16). *Project Success and Failure: What is Success, What is Failure, and How Can You Improve Your Odds For Success?* Retrieved from http://www.umsl.edu/~sauterv/analysis/6840_f03_papers/frese/

Griffiths, M. (2012). *PMI-ACP Exam Prep*. RMC Publications Inc.

Gustavsson, T. (2016, August). *Benefits of Agile Project Management in A Non-Software Development Context- A Literature Review*. Retrieved from https://pmworldjournal.net/wp-content/uploads/2016/08/pmwj49-Aug2016-Gustavsson-benefits-of-agile-in-non-software-context-second-edition.pdf

Haughey, D. (2010, January 2). *A Brief History of Project Management*. Retrieved from Project Smart: https://www.projectsmart.co.uk/brief-history-of-project-management.php

Hysa, B., & Spalek, S. (2019, April 11). *Opportunities and Threats Presented by Social Media in Project Management*. Retrieved from https://www.ncbi.nlm.nih.gov/pmc/articles/PMC6465589/

Kauppila, O.-P., Rajala, R., & Jyrama, A. (2011). Knowledge sharing through virtual teams across borders and boundaries. *Management Learning, 42*(4), 395-418. Retrieved from https://research.aalto.fi/en/publications/knowledge-sharing-through-virtual-teams-across-borders-and-boundaries(c213160d-eca5-448e-a18a-26a2e6bb0abe).html

Kruchten, P., & Gorans, P. (2014). *A Guide to Critical Success Factors in Agile Delivery*. Retrieved from IBM Center for The Business of Goverment: http://www.businessofgovernment.org/sites/default/files/A%20Guide%20to%20Critical%20Success%20Factors%20in%20Agile%20Delivery.pdf

Lampropoulus, G., & Siakas, K. (2018, March). *Communication in Distributed Agile Software Development: Impact of Social Media-Social Networking*. Retrieved from Research Gate: https://www.researchgate.net/publication/327580426_Communication_in_Distributed_Agile_Software_Development_Impact_of_Social_Media_-_Social_Networking

Litchmore, K. A. (2016, July). *Comparative Study of Agile Methods, People Factors and Process Factors In Relation To Project Success*. Retrieved from http://152.12.30.4:2048/login?url=https://search.proquest.com/abicomplete/docview/1823291748/739BA3AA87BC4BBAPQ/2

Lotz, M. (2018, November 21). *Waterfall vs. Agile: Which Methodology is Right for Your Project?* Retrieved from https://www.seguetech.com/waterfall-vs-agile-methodology/

Maassen, M. A., & Dima, A. M. (2018). From Waterfall to Agile Software: Development models in the IT sector, 2006 to 2008. Impacts on company management. *Journal of International Studies*.

Mersino, A. (2018, April 1). *Agile Project Success Rates vs. Waterfall Projects*. Retrieved from Vitality Chicago: https://vitalitychicago.com/blog/agile-projects-are-more-successful-traditional-projects/

Mir, F. A., & Pinnington, A. (2014). *Exploring the value of project management: Linking Project Management Performance and Project Sucess*. Academic Press.

Muller, R., & Jugdev, K. (2012). *Critical success factors in projects: Pinto, Slevin, and Prescott – the elucidation of project success*. Academic Press.

Odedra, M., Lawrie, M., Bennett, M., & Goodman, S. (n.d.). *Information Technology in Sub-Saharan Africa.* Retrieved August 2019, from University of Pennsylvania- African Studies Center: http://www.africa.upenn.edu/Comp_Articles/Information_Technology_117.html

Poppendieck, M., & Poppendieck, T. (2013). *The Lean Mindset.* Addison Wesley.

Powell-Morse, A. (2016, December 8). *Waterfall Model: What is it and When you should use it?* Retrieved from https://airbrake.io/blog/sdlc/waterfall-model

PRNewswire. (2002, August 13). *Agile Software Launches Industry-First Guaranteed business Results Program.* Retrieved from Proquest: http://152.12.30.4:2048/login?url=https://search.proquest.com/docview/447496132?accountid=15070

Sarker, S., Ahuja, M., Sarker, S., & Kirkeby, S. (2011). The Role of Communication and Trust in Global Virtual Teams: A Social Network Perspective. *Journal of Management Information Systems, 28*(1), 273–309. doi:10.2753/MIS0742-1222280109

Saylor Academy. (2012). *Chapter 7: Subsaharan Africa.* Retrieved from https://saylordotorg.github.io/text_world-regional-geography-people-places-and-globalization/s10-subsaharan-africa.html

Schwaber, K., & Sutherland, J. (2017). *The Definitive Guide to Scrum: The Rules of Game.* Retrieved from https://www.scrumguides.org/docs/scrumguide/v2017/2017-Scrum-Guide-US.pdf

Slinger, M. (2011). *Agile Project Management with Scrum.* Paper presented at PMI® Global Congress 2011—North America, Dallas, TX.

Stankovic, D., Nikolic, V., Djordjevic, M., & Cao, D.-B. (2013, June 6). A survey study of critical success factors in agile software projects in former Yugoslavia IT companies. *Journal of Systems and Software, 86*(6), 1663–1678. doi:10.1016/j.jss.2013.02.027

Sweeney, M. (2014, December 2). *Agile vs Waterfall: Which Method is More Successful?* Retrieved from https://clearcode.cc/blog/agile-vs-waterfall-method

The Standish Group International. (2013). *Chaos Manifesto 2013: Think Big, Act Small.* Retrieved from https://www.immagic.com/eLibrary/ARCHIVES/GENERAL/GENREF/S130301C.pdf

The Standish Group International, Inc. (2015). *CHAOS Report 2015.* The Standish Group International, Inc.

Turk, D., France, R., & Rumpe, B. (2002, May). Assumptions Underlying Agile Software Development. *Journal of Database Management, 16*(4), 62–87. doi:10.4018/jdm.2005100104

Turk, D., France, R., & Rumpe, B. (2014, September). *Limitations of Agile Software Processes.* Retrieved from Research Gate: https://www.researchgate.net/profile/Robert_France/publication/266024162_Limitations_of_Agile_Software_Processes/links/00463526ed3341d25b000000/Limitations-of-Agile-Software-Processes.pdf?origin=publication_detail

Vcwebdesign. (2013, August 5). *What is Agile Methodology? and Why Do We Use It?* Retrieved from Visual Compass: http://vcwebdesign.com/uncategorized/what-agile-methodology-why-do-we-use-it/

Veneziano, V., Rainer, A., & Haider, S. (2014). *When Agile Is Not Good Enough: an initial attempt at understanding how to make ot right.* Retrieved from dblp: https://dblp.uni-trier.de/pers/hd/v/Veneziano:Vito

Wells, N., & Kloppenborg, T. J. (2019). *Project Management Essentials* (2nd ed.). Business Expert Press, LLC.

Westfall, L. (2010). *The Certified Software Quality Engineer Handbook*. Quality Press.

Yasvi, M., Yadav, K., & Shubhika. (2017, April 9). *Review On Extreme Programming-XP*. Retrieved. from https://www.researchgate.net/publication/332465869_Review_On_Extreme_Programming-XP/ citation/download

Chapter 8
A State-of-the-Art Review of Nigerian Languages Natural Language Processing Research

Toluwase Victor Asubiaro
https://orcid.org/0000-0003-0718-7739
University of Ibadan, Nigeria & Western University, Canada

Ebelechukwu Gloria Igwe
https://orcid.org/0000-0002-5180-5621
University of Ibadan, Nigeria

ABSTRACT

African languages, including those that are natives to Nigeria, are low-resource languages because they lack basic computing resources such as language-dependent hardware keyboard. Speakers of these low-resource languages are therefore unfairly deprived of information access on the internet. There is no information about the level of progress that has been made on the computation of Nigerian languages. Hence, this chapter presents a state-of-the-art review of Nigerian languages natural language processing. The review reveals that only four Nigerian languages; Hausa, Ibibio, Igbo, and Yoruba have been significantly studied in published NLP papers. Creating alternatives to hardware keyboard is one of the most popular research areas, and means such as automatic diacritics restoration, virtual keyboard, and optical character recognition have been explored. There was also an inclination towards speech and computational morphological analysis. Resource development and knowledge representation modeling of the languages using rapid resource development and cross-lingual methods are recommended.

INTRODUCTION

The inclusion of countries in the information society is importantly determined by their ability to access, create, and use information on the global information highway. Most prominent in the global report on measuring the information society is the annual report of the International Telecommunication Union

DOI: 10.4018/978-1-7998-3468-7.ch008

(ITU) which is pivoted on gadget and infrastructure-focused metrics such as internet use, telephone penetration, mobile telephone use, access to computer and other ICTs, broadband access, mobile signal availability, internet bandwidth size and internet traffic. Recent reports show that developing countries, which also belong to the *have-nots* in the digital divide, are improving on the ITU's information society metrics, though questions arise about the impact of the recorded progress on the developing countries' socio-economic development. Studies have suggested that the problem of inequalities in access to information have continued, even in the information era and despite the progress made by the developing countries as reported in the annual *Measuring the Information Society* reports of the ITU. Jansen and Sellar (2008) for instance, noted that, "… despite all the advances made in promoting access" through "… ICT and internet -the same familiar inequalities persist". Perhaps, the present metrics and efforts at bridging the digital divide do not include the most important type of access to information, which is in the mothers' language of the developing countries.

The importance of information access in the mothers' languages of the developing countries on bridging the digital divide has been expressed by earlier researchers using different terms and concepts. In explicit terms, Yu (2002), stated that "…barrier to digital participation is language". Adegbola (2017) described access to information in languages that are spoken by the local population of the developing countries as "the last six inches" of the digital divide bridge. Osborn (2010) recommended glocalization which is "the adaptation of digital information and contents to the local modes of communication, culture and standards", with much emphasis on provision of services and content creation in local languages (language access) as a panacea to bridging the digital divide. Borgman (2000) in "thinking locally, acting globally", suggested the development of customized or human-centered information systems that is dependent on age, expertise, language and other socio-demographic characteristics of individuals. These studies and others have recommended that language access to information is sacrosanct to bridging the digital divide.

Languages that are spoken by the countries in the *have-not* of the digital divide are regarded as resource-scarce languages. Resource-scarcity for languages in the digital age is used in tandem with other terms such as low-resource, resource-poor, under-resourced, resource-limited and resource-constrained to describe the dearth of computer resources such as large and accurate text and speech corpora, analytical tools (part-of-speech (POS) tagger, chunking systems, parsers, stemmers, lemmatizers syllabicators), inputting tools (keyboards, speech-to-text systems) and knowledge tools (models, machine translation (MT) models, computational grammar, morphology rules, etc) for the natural language processing (NLP) of such languages. NLP refers to the interdisciplinary field that draw knowledge from computer science, artificial intelligence, linguistics, statistics, and machine learning, and it focuses on analyzing and studying human languages (text and speech) with the aim of developing computer programs that can process human languages in human-like format. Availability of resources for a language, and subsequently the intensity of its NLP research, strongly correlates with the availability of digital application and contents for and in the language. Better still, languages in the *have* divide of the digital world have plenty of resources and relatively high number of NLP research than those in the *have-nots*. One of the gaps in literature is the review of NLP research of the Nigerian languages to evaluate the progress in bridging the digital language divide. This book chapter, therefore, provides a state-of-the-art review of the developments that have been made on the NLP of Nigerian languages by thematically analyzing the content of publications on the NLP of the languages.

Nigeria is the most populous African country with over 200 million population and 400 indigenous languages, though only four (Hausa/Fulani 29%, Yoruba 21%, Igbo 18% and Ijaw 10% (CIA, 2016)) of the languages are spoken by over 78% (153 million people) of the population. Nigeria is also caught in the conundrum of one of the realities of globalization called "multilingualism by English" (Rehbein 2015), a situation where indigenes of developing countries learn and speak English language apart from their mothers' language because it is regarded as the elites' language.

Objectives and Contributions of the Book Chapter

The objective of this book chapter is to provide an up-to-date overview of research on the NLP of Nigerian languages by reviewing relevant journal articles and conference proceedings. Aims of the study include identifying Nigerian languages that have been studied in NLP research and the extent to which the languages have been studied. This study provides an insight into the extent to which these languages have developed in the information age, beyond the rhetoric about their resource scarcity. Presently, studies only report the unavailability of NLP research on the Nigerian languages and scarcity of resources for the NLP of the languages, this research intends to fill the research gap on "what NLP research has been done" on Nigerian languages.

METHODOLOGY

Study Design

This study is a state-of-the-art review, which is aimed at providing a descriptive narrative on the Nigerian languages NLP research. This study employed a systematic and comprehensive search of the literature, this is imperative so that this review will present an accurate state-of-art review of the languages NLP. To achieve this, a systematic search of literature from three online search engines was carried out. It is acknowledged that ignoring other sources of literature is a limitation of the study. Potential sources of harvesting grey literature such as white papers, dissertations, theses, seminars etc on Nigerian languages are the institutional repositories of Nigerian universities, they were not considered because studies have shown that most (85%) of the academic libraries in Nigeria do not have full functional library websites (Asubiaro, 2017) that can host online repositories and in fact only about 10% of the libraries own online repositories (Kari & Baro, 2016). This study relied on evidence from journal articles and conference proceedings, which are available and indexed online. Synthesizing knowledge from journal articles and conference proceedings alone is acceptable because the core of research in Computer and Information Sciences are published in journal articles and conference proceedings. Many studies have considered journal articles and conference proceedings as data source for studying scholarly communication patterns in Computer and Information sciences (e.g. Asubiaro, 2019; Kim & Jeong, 2006; Fiala & Tutoky, 2017). This study included only the top ten most popular Nigerian languages (Eberhard, Simons & Fennig, 2018) (details on Table 1 below).

Search Strategy for Retrieving Relevant Articles

Google, Web of Science (WoS) and Scopus search engines were searched for relevant publications. A structured query which included the ten Nigerian languages, Natural language processing and computer related terms such as digital and electronics was implemented for searching each of WoS and Scopus.

Table 1. Top 10 languages in Nigeria by population from the Ethnologue

S/N	Language	No of speakers
1	Hausa	48,300,000
2	Igbo	27,000,000
3	Yoruba	39,500,000
4	Ibibio	5,470,000
5	Ijaw	2,000,000
6	Kanuri	7,862,500
7	Ebira	1,820,000
8	Efik	2,400,000
9	TIV	4,000,000
10	Fulfulde	7,610,000

The WoS and Scopus queries included Boolean operators "AND" and "OR" between keywords and wild cards (asterisks *) on terms like electronic to capture variants terms like electronics and electronically. Unlike WoS and Scopus that accepted one complex query, several queries were repeated for each of the ten languages on the Google search engine. Google search engine was searched to complement the shortcomings of the WoS and Scopus which have been reported in past studies to be biased against publications from Africa (Nwagwu, 2008). The details of the search queries and number of articles retrieved are displayed on Table 2 below.

Identifying Relevant Articles and Quality Assessment

After searching the three search engines, 586 articles were retrieved (without counting duplicates) and were subjected to cleaning and quality assessment. The first round of screening was aimed at removing irrelevant articles, this was done by reading the title, abstracts and/or full texts of the retrieved articles, only 178 articles were identified to be relevant to NLP of the Nigerian languages after the first screening. The second round of screening was intended to conduct quality assessment, this was achieved by carefully reading the full text of all the 178 articles and applying inclusion criteria. The following inclusion criteria were applied:

- Article must either be a conference proceeding or journal article,
- The full text of the article must be available and accessible online,
- The article must discuss the NLP (relevance) of at least one of the Nigerian languages.
- The methodology of the publication must be relevant to computation of at least one of the Nigerian languages.

Only 101 articles were included in the study after the quality assessment step. 15 additional relevant articles were found by searching the references of the 101 articles. All the 116 articles were reviewed.

The articles were classified and discussed under the major themes that were identified in the articles.

Figure 1. Literature search and quality assessment process

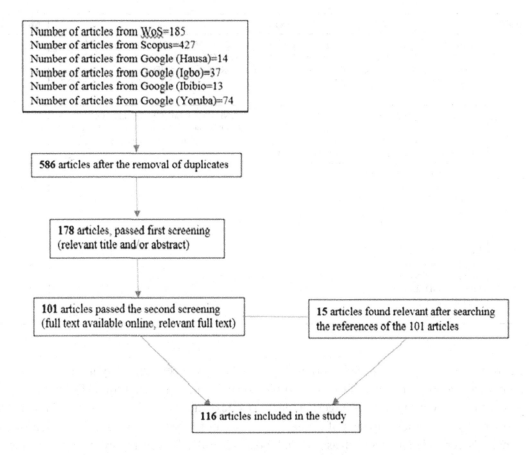

THE REVIEW

The result of the knowledge synthesis of the research on Nigerian languages' NLP of is presented on Table 3. The most popular research areas are morphological analysis, alternatives to language-dependent keyboard and speech analysis. The first three themes on the Table 3 constituted 67.24% of all the articles. The analysis shows that speech language technology is the most active research area, with Ibibio, Yoruba and Hausa featuring more. The research areas with the second and third highest number of articles are he computational morphology and development of alternatives to language-dependent computer hardware keyboards respectively. Papers on these research areas are reviewed succinctly in this section.

Alternatives to Language-Dependent Keyboard

Inputting texts of Nigerian languages into the computer is one of the problems that the NLP research have attempted to solve. Currently, there are no language-dependent computer hardware keyboards that accommodate the Nigerian languages' alphabets. This theme covers all the categories of research which have attempted at providing alternatives to language-dependent hardware keyboards. The first group of studies is the automatic diacritics restoration (ADR) research which is concerned with automatically

Table 2. Queries posed to the search engines and the number of results returned

Database	Query	No of results
Scopus	TITLE-ABS-KEY (((("*natural language processing*") OR ("*information*" AND ("*retrieval*" OR "*storage*" OR "*processing*" OR "*extraction*")) OR "*comput**" OR "*corpus*" OR "*machine*" OR "*automatic**" OR "*electronic**" OR "*internet*" OR "*web*" OR "*digit**") AND ("*yoruba*" OR "*hausa*" OR "*igbo*" OR "*fulfulde*" OR "*ijaw*" OR "*Ibibio*" OR "*ebira*" OR "*tiv*" OR "*kanuri*" OR "*efik*"))	427
Web of Science	**TS=** (((("natural language processing") OR ("information" AND ("retrieval" OR "storage" OR "processing" OR "extraction")) OR "comput*" OR "corpus" OR "machine" OR "automatic*" OR "electronic*" OR "internet" OR "web" OR "digit*") AND (yoruba OR hausa OR igbo OR fulfulde OR ijaw OR Ibibio OR ebira OR tiv OR kanuri OR efik))	185
Google	"natural language processing" AND lang "Information retrieval" AND lang "information processing" AND lang "information extraction" AND lang "information storage" AND lang Computer AND lang Corpus AND lang Electronic AND lang Automatic AND lang Internet AND lang Web AND lang Digital AND lang	Hausa-14 Ibibio-13 Igbo-37 Yoruba-74

restoring diacritics on the texts of the Nigerian language that have been originally inputted without diacritics. Another category of research focused on the optical character recognition (OCR) for Nigerian languages, which converts images of Nigerian languages' texts into textual computer readable formats. Another alternative is the development of virtual keyboards for the Nigerian languages, which are available for major Nigerian languages such as Hausa, Igbo and Yoruba, however, they are not convenient for typing large volume of texts and most of them are poorly implemented (Enguehard & Naroua, 2009).

ADR remains the most popular, effective and efficient alternative to hardware keyboards for many reasons. The implementation of diacritics restoration does not require the use of language-dependent keyboards which are currently not available. Secondly, it is economically and ergonomically friendly, unlike the virtual keyboards. Thirdly, it does not require special training like some virtual keyboards. With the ADR, texts of the Nigerian languages can be typed with the conventional keyboards while the ADR system automatically appends the appropriate diacritics on the alphabets.

Table 3. A description of the NLP research landscape

S/N	Classification	Languages					Total number of Articles
		Hausa	Ibibio	Igbo	Yoruba	others	
1	Speech analysis	5	12	0	20	0	37
2	Computational morphology	5	0	11	7	0	23
3	alternatives to language-dependent hardware keyboard	3	1	6	11	3	18
4	Others	13	1	8	23	2	
Total		26	14	25	61	5	

Three methods of automatic restoration of diacritics have been implemented for the Nigerian languages, which are: at the grapheme, syllabic and word levels. One of the earliest studies on ADR is De Pauw, Wagacha, & De Schryver, (2007) which applied memory-based machine learning approach at the grapheme and word-levels and considered Yoruba as one of its languages of interest. The study noted that the accuracy of grapheme and word-level diacritics restoration for other languages like Gĩkũyũ, Kĩkamba, Sesotho sa Leboa, Czech, Romanian and Vietnamese was reasonably high, while the results for Yoruba was low. Scannell, (2011) presented a follow-up to the De Pauw et al., (2007) by applying the Naïve Bayes machine learning approach to the word and grapheme-levels' diacritics restoration problem, by considering fifty-five African languages including Hausa, Igbo and Yoruba. The results of the study showed a significant improvement, especially on the trigram model which performed better. Another word-based diacritic restoration research for Yoruba text is Adegbola & Odilinye, (2012) which considered trigrams and produced better results than the De Pauw et al., (2007). Orife, (2018) is a more recent study which focused on ADR as a language translation problem at word-level and applied sequence-to-sequence neural MT approach, this study created a more state-of-the-art computing method and reported better results than the earlier studies.

Another ADR method is at the syllabic level, which was used in Oladiipo, Odejobi, Adagunodo, & Olubode-Sawe, (2017) and Oladiipo, Odejobi, & Adagunodo, (2017), focusing on Yoruba texts. The advantage of this method is its potential for solving "the twin challenges of resource scarcity and contextual insufficiency for tone mark restoration in Yorùbá text" (Oladiipo et al., 2017) by incorporating syllabication and concatenation of syllables based on probability modelling. With this method, the possibility of restoration tone marks on out-of-vocabulary (OOV) texts is higher and because more syllables are modelled with fewer words, insufficiently contextual words are captured.

Studies on diacritics restoration of Igbo texts have all used word-based methods, apart from Scannell, (2011). For instance, Ezeani, Hepple, & Onyenwe, (2016, 2017) applied the word-based methods using the maximum estimation of bi-grams and trigrams and later, five machine learning classification algorithms -Linear Discriminant Analysis(LDA), K Nearest Neighbors(KNN), Decision Trees, Support Vector Machines (SVC), and Naïve Bayes (MNB). The DTC performed best, followed by KNN while the unigrams and bigrams produced the best models for prediction. Ezeani, Hepple, Onyenwe, & Enemuoh, (2018a, 2018b) and Ezeani, Onyenwe, & Hepple, (2018) used the embedding models for diacritics restoration of Igbo texts. Two classes of word embeddings models were used: projected from the English embedding space and trained with Igbo bible corpus. Few studies such as Ekpenyong, Udoinyang, & Urua, (2009) focused on the ADR of Ibibio language by applying the dictionary look-up and morphological analysis methods. In another study, Ekpenyong, Inyang, & Umoren, (2016) worked on the modelling of Ibibio tonal pattern using the Hidden Markov Model (HMM) for ADR.

OCR is another alternative to language-dependent computer hardware keyboard for inputting texts, only Yoruba language has featured in OCR research. Research in this category include Oladayo, (2015) and Ajao, Olawuyi, & Odejobi, (2018) which used correlation and template matching techniques, and KNN respectively.

Computational Phonology, Speech Synthesis and Related Studies

This theme presents studies that are related to analyzing speech sounds of the Nigerian languages. Research in this category includes studies on computational phonology, text-to-speech (TTS) synthesis and automatic speech recognition (ASR). While Ibibio and Yoruba languages feature more prominently in this section, all the research on Ibibio also fall under this theme. Analysis of speech sounds of the Nigerian languages require the consideration for tonality in addition to the duration or phone features to cater to their linguistic peculiarity. This is often necessary for the phoneme pattern (pronunciation dictionary, letter or TTS modelling), prosody pattern (phrase break and accents, pitch accents, boundary tones), vowel duration pattern and, pitch modelling.

Earliest studies on the TTS and ASR of Yoruba started with Connel & Ladd, (1990) which modelled the fundamental frequencies of Yoruba tones. Other early studies were undertaken in Odéjobí, Beaumont, & Wong, (2004) and Odéjobí, Beaumont, & Wong, (2006) which presented a model for the analysis, design and computing of TTS intonation for Yoruba language using a combination of relational tree (RT) and fuzzy logic (FL) technologies. A duration model for Yoruba TTS was presented in Odejobí, Wong, & Beaumont, (2007) as a follow-up to Odéjobí, Beaumont, & Wong, (2006). Odejobí, Wong, & Beaumont followed up their previous studies with Odejobí, Wong, & Beaumont, (2008) which integrated the intonation and duration aspects of speech signals in its TTS system for Yoruba language. The system for TTS was based on RT for multi-dimensional waveform representation which integrated a framework that supported the independent implementation of intonation, duration and intensity. The RT and stem machine learning (Stem-ML) models were executed for the TTS where the Stem-ML method was reported to perform better for Yoruba language.

More recent studies applied artificial neural network (ANN), a machine learning approach to TTS modelling. ANN and FL were employed by Àkànbí & Odéjobí, (2011) in a system that integrated the phone and tonal aspects of vowel speech sounds in Yoruba language. The FL method provided more accuracy on the test set, with fewer text size with requirements for experts' knowledge. Other studies such as Afolabi, Omidiora, & Arulogun, (2013) and Adetunmbi, Obe, & Iyanda, (2016) focused on TTS for Yoruba using the syllable-based methods. The fundamental frequency contour of Yoruba language was modelled by van Niekerk & Barnard, (2012, 2013, 2014) by predicting the syllable of pitch targets for pitch realization. A strong correlation between the pitch level and pitch change was established for predicting the pitch targets.

Next to Yoruba language is Ibibio which recorded the highest number of studies on ASR and TTS. The earliest studies on the computation of Ibibio phonology, such as Gibbon, Urua, & Ekpenyong, (2005) focused on resource development by creating an experimental TTS prototype for Ibibio Language that included the tone–relevant morphophonemic and morphosyntactic contexts and the linguistic TTS component, a tone–oriented parsing and tagging system. Another pioneer research also developed speech corpus for TTS and speech synthesis (Ekpenyong, Urua, & Gibbon, 2008). With the challenge of resource-scarcity which subsisted, other related studies on Ibibio have specially considered its low-resource situation by creating models that are efficient and useful for resource development. For instance, Ekpenyong, Urua, Watts, King, & Yamagishi, (2014) employed a statistical parametric model and unsupervised learning of the relationship between acoustics of Ibibio sounds and their linguistic features using limited resources (a description of the resources is presented in Ekpenyong, Urua, & Gibbon, (2008)).

Other related studies on Ibibio include Ekpenyong & Inyang, (2016) which presented a method for modelling the Ibibio tone pattern for mining Ibibio speech corpus. Similarly, hybrid of FL and neural network (adaptive neuro-fuzzy Inference System) was used for modelling Ibibio speech prosody to improve synthetic speech quality (Ekpenyong, Inyang, & Udoh, 2016, 2018), the modelling of prosody features was undertaken to relate all the variations of prosodic features based on their structure, meaning and context of spoken languages. Ekpenyong & Udoh, (2013) also designed an intelligent fuzzy logic based (FL-B) framework for modelling prosody in Ibibio. Coombs (2013) focused on computing the phonological structure of Ibibio language's high tones processes using Hidden Markov's Model (HMM).

Next to Yoruba and Ibibio languages with the highest number of TTS and ASR articles is Hausa. Gauthier, Besacier, & Voisin, (2016a, 2016b) worked on reducing the word error rate in ASR systems for Hausa language, with a focus on the vowel length contrasts (long and short). The Multilayer Perceptrons (MLP), an application which is based on neural network, for feature extraction in place of the traditional MelFrequency Cepstral Coefficients (MFCC) was recommended for employed by Vu & Schultz, (2013) for the ASR of Hausa because its "features proved to be a high discriminative power and very robust against speaker and environmental variations". The MLP was applied to extract acoustic models of Czech, Vietnamese and Hausa, also regarded as the target languages, while source languages were English, French, German, Spanish, Bulgarian, Croatian, Polish, Russian, Chinese, Japanese, Korean and Thai. Another relevant study is Luka, Frank & Onwodi (2012) which applied pattern recognition ANN model to the development of an ASR system for Hausa language.

The speech analysis has been applied to problem solving in some of the NLP studies. One of the applications of TTS in Yoruba is Adeyemo & Idowu, (2015) which designed text to speech usability interface in Yoruba for the visually impaired. The speech engine was used to transform texts into speech through various processes including text, phonetic, prosodic analyses, and speech generation, which generated smooth and natural sounding speech. Another application of TTS was reported in Schlippe, Djomgang, Vu, Ochs, & Schultz, (2012) and Schlippe, Ochs, Vu, & Schultz, (2012) which created a cleaned manual speech dictionary using the rule-based method for Hausa language. Schlippe, Djomgang, et al., (2012) proposed a Language Vocabulary Continuous Speech Recognition (LVCSR) system for Hausa. The studies developed an ASR system from a large speech of Hausa language text corpus using the Rapid Language Adaptation Toolkit (RLAT). A system that supports distance education which integrated a search engine in extensible mark-up language (XML) and TTS technologies in Yoruba language was developed by (Ogwu, Talib, & Odejobi, 2006). A similar educative tool was implemented by Abdulkareem & Edet, (2016).

Computational Morphology and Related Studies

Computational morphology is sacrosanct to the accomplishment of many NLP tasks such as ASR, automatic language identification, MT, TTS computations, information extraction, automatic speech synthesis, spell checking, automatic summarization, and information retrieval (Iheanetu et al., 2017). This section focuses on computational morphology and related studies such as stemming, lemmatization and part-of-speech (POS) tagging. Igbo language has the highest number of studies in this section, followed by Hausa and Yoruba.

The most comprehensive computational morphology of Igbo language is Iheanetu et al., (2017) which used the data-driven approach to compute an exhaustive list of all the morphological structures of Igbo language. The data-driven method employed in this study was considered for computing the morphology of Igbo language because high accuracy was achieved with smaller corpus size, unlike the more popular unsupervised learning method which is more expensive and requires bigger corpus size which is not available for Igbo. The major setback for the data-driven method is the agglutinative nature of Igbo language, which makes it almost impossible to account for all morphological structures of the language. Other studies such as Iheanetu & Adeyeye, (2013) focused on computing the reduplication processes in verbs with prefixation, adverbs, prepositions, numerals, underived nominal words and ideophones of the Igbo language morphology. One study which have worked on stemming Igbo language is Enemuoh, Hepple, Onyenwe, & Ezeani, (2017) which developed "a method that can be used to detect morph-inflected words in a target language via alignment with a source language", in this case, Igbo was set as the target language while English was the source language.

Other studies have focused on the POS tagging of Igbo language, mostly developing methods that can achieve high accuracy and perform morphological decomposition so that OOV words can be correctly tagged automatically. Onyenwe et al., (2018) focused on the fundamentals, using manual POS tagging of Igbo corpus. Others such as Onyenwe, Hepple, & Uchechukwu, (2016) focused on the computational modelling of the morphological processes through morphological reconstruction and transformation-based learning methods of Igbo words so that POS tagging can be more accurate by increasing the chances of correctly tagging OOV words. The morphological reconstruction and transformation-based learning algorithm was also applied to Igbo POS systems in Onyenwe, Hepple, Uchechukwu, & Ezeani, (2015) and Onyenwe, Hepple, Chinedu, & Ezeani, (2019) to identify words that were likely incorrectly tagged so that human experts can accept, reject, or suggest tags. Onyenwe & Hepple, (2016) focused on improving the accuracy of POS taggers for Igbo language by incorporating the morphological analysis of morphologically-complex words (which are potentially sparsely used) into their stem and associated affixes, without considering their grammatical functions. The morphological reconstructions to their roots was successfully used to predict the tags of the OOV words by training the computer to learn the pattern of the morphological features of the known tags. A paradigm is the bootstrapping method which employs dual methods of cross-lingual and monolingual projections (Ikechukwu, Ebele, Godwin, & Ignatius, 2019). The cross-lingual method was used to automatically create an initial 'errorful' tagged corpus for a target resource-scarce language via word-alignment, using a parallel corpus between Igbo and English languages for the experiment. English language, a resource-rich language, was used as the source language, while Igbo, a resource-scarce language, was the target language. The monolingual method was applied to clean the induced noise from the initial cross-lingual method. This method proved useful for inducing the POS tags of resource-scarce languages.

Hausa recorded the highest number of articles in this section, after Igbo language. Hausa was considered as part of the project to develop morphological analyzer for resource-scarce languages by Kulick & Bies, (2016), it relied on existing reference texts for the morphological analysis of Hausa language. Crysmann, (2017) focused on reduplication in Hausa within the context of grammar by analyzing the feature structure of reduplicates using the integrative approach which combines syntactic, semantic and morphological knowledge. The framework which was termed the Head-driven Phrase Structure (HPSG) is based on the premise that "meaning representations are built up in tandem with syntactic analysis" (Crysmann, 2012). Studies such as Bimba, Idris, Khamis, & Noor, (2016) has worked on stemming of Hausa texts through affix-stripping using manual identification of stems and root words and creation of lexical database for reference look-up. Furthermore, the porter's stemming algorithm for English was modified for Hausa language by Bashir & Rozaimee, (2015). Salifou & Naroua, (2014) for designing a spell corrector for Hausa language using the dictionary look-up method.

Studies on Yoruba language focused mostly on different levels of computational analysis of Yoruba morphology, covering certain of parts of speech and length of words. The most comprehensive study of Yoruba computational morphology is Adegbola, (2016) which proposed a pattern-based unsupervised method for computational analysis of Yoruba morphology by clustering the morphological patterns in the language. The study used Yoruba corpus of about 210,000 words, 14,670 unique tokens and 1,282 representative clusters of morphological patterns. Earlier studies which worked on certain parts of Yoruba morphology include Finkel & Odejobi, (2009) which focused on the computational analysis of Yoruba verbs morphology using the KATR formalism. Oyinloye & Odejobi, (2015) worked on computing the morphological processes of monosyllabic and polysyllabic Yoruba verbs using the finite state automata (FST). The results of the study suggested that FST-based methods produced better results than KART for the computational morphological analysis of Yoruba. Eludiora & Ayemonisan, (2018) provided a computational morphological analysis of two to five letter Yoruba words using FSA. And lastly, POS tagger for Yoruba was developed by Ayogu, Adetunmbi, Ojokoh, & Oluwadare, (2017) using the Conditional Random Fields (CRF) and improved first-order hidden Markov model (HMM) that was improved with affix-derived information and use of Laplace and Kneser-Ney smoothing techniques.

Others

Research areas in which few studies have been recorded are presented on Table 4. The high number of research areas in NLP with little research also indicates that few has been done on the Nigerian languages. For instance, MT is an important research area which requires complex computation, whereby information from a language to another is translated without compromising the meaning and sentence structure of the target language. The most basic level of MT is at word-level, complex levels are at concept, phrase, sentence, and discourse levels. According to the information on Table 4, about 90% of research on MT was recorded on Yoruba language, and the studies were mostly at word-level.

CONCLUSION AND RECOMMENDATION

This book chapter provides an overview of the NLP literature on the ten most popular Nigerian languages, highlighting NLP areas that were covered and languages that have been studied. This review reveals that only four Nigerian languages (Hausa, Ibibio, Igbo and Yoruba) have been significantly studied in the published NLP studies. While in-depth study of Hausa language was not recorded in any of the research themes that were identified, other three languages recorded remarkable progress in few research areas. There is a significant progress around speech analysis, especially TTS, of Ibibio language; while tones of the language have been analyzed and TTS has been applied to its ADR. Igbo language NLP centered around morphological analysis, POS tagging, and ADR. Other highlight of the Igbo NLP research is the application of word embedding and POS tagging in ADR development; morphological deconstruction has also been applied to enhancing the accuracy its POS tags and morphological stemming. Most in-depth Yoruba language NLP studies focused on ADR, computational morphology, and speech analysis (TTS/ASR). Few studies were also recorded on the NLP of these languages outside the major research areas that were mentioned. Yoruba language NLP was the most widely studied with pockets of research on areas such as MT, document modelling, language identification, computational morphology, computational grammar, entity typing and sentiment analysis. Hausa language also recorded few studies on computational grammar, computational morphology, entity typing and language identification. Some studies on TTS/ASR, language identification and computational morphology of Igbo language was also recorded.

An emerging interesting research method is the cross-/multi-lingual methods which was applied to the POS tagging of Igbo language through word alignment (Ikechukwu, Ebele, Godwin, & Ignatius, 2019). These methods have also been applied to entity typing (Lu et al., 2016), ASR (Vu & Schultz, 2013) and MT, through word alignment (Pourdamghani, Ghazvininejad, & Knight, 2018). The cross-/multi-

Table 4. The minor classifications of the NLP literature

	Studies	Method	Scope	Languages covered
Machine Translation				
1	Safiriyu, Akindeji, & Isau, (2015)	Rule-based	Pronoun	Yoruba to English
2	Olufunminiyi & Adebayo, (2013)	Rule-based	words	Yoruba to English
3	Agbeyangi, Eludiora, & Popoola, (2016)	Rule-based	numerals	Yoruba to English
4	Akinadé & Ọdéjọbí, (2014)	context free grammar model	numerals	Yoruba to English
5	Oladayo, (2014)		numerals	Yoruba to English
6	Ninan, Iyanda, Elesemoyo, & Olamide, (2017)		numerals	Igbo to Arabic
7	Pourdamghani, Ghazvininejad, & Knight, (2018)	common alignment links	numerals	Yoruba
8	Adegbola, Owolabi, & Odejobi, (2011)	Word vector	words	Yoruba to English
Resource development and Capacity Building				
1	Adegbola, T., Owolabi, K., & Odejobi, T. (2011).	Capacity building		Yoruba, Igbo and Hausa
2	Dagba, Aoga, & Fanou, (2016	Manual	speech corpus	Yoruba language
Computational Grammar				
1	Adebara & Dahl, (2016)	Constraint Handling Rule Grammars (CHRG)	Noun phrases	Yoruba
2	Adebara, (2016)	Constraint Handling Rule Grammars (CHRG)	Noun phrases	Yoruba
3	Crysmann, (2015a)	Head-driven Phrase Structure Grammar (HPSG)		Hausa
4	Crysmann, (2015b)	Head-driven Phrase Structure Grammar (HPSG)		Hausa
Lexis and Lexical Analysis				
1	Enguehard & Mangeot, (2014)	Dictionary	XML format	Hausa-French
2	Asubiaro, (2013)	Stop words	Information Entropy	Yoruba
3	Ng'ang'a, (2010)	Dictionary	electronic	Igbo
4	Maitama et al., (2014)	Text normalization	Dictionary look up	Hausa
Narrative Computation				
1	Ninan, Ajíbádé, & Odéjobí (2016)	Folktales		Yoruba
2	Ninan & Odéjobí (2013)	Folktales		Yoruba
3	Ninan & Odéjobí, (2012)	Folktales		Yoruba
Language Identification				
1	Asubiaro, Adegbola, Mercer, & Ajiferuke, (2018)	Character trigrams		Hausa, Igbo and Yoruba
2	Selamat & Akosu, (2016)	Word-length information		Hausa, Igbo, Yoruba and Tiv
Sentiment Analysis and Feature extraction				
1	Orimaye, Alhashmi, & Eu-gene, (2012).	sentiment lexicon and absolute polarity score		Yoruba
2	(Bashir, Rozaimee, & Isa, 2017)	Feature extraction for text summarization		Hausa
Entity Typing				
1	Huang, May, Pan, & Ji, (2016)		Word embedding	Hausa and Yoruba
2	Huang et al., (2017)		Word embedding	
3	Lu et al., (2016).	Entity and events recognition	Entity Discovery and Linking (EDL)	Hausa
Document Modelling				
1	Ifeanyi-Reuben, Ugwu, & Adegbola, (2017)	Document similarity	n-grams models	Igbo
2	Ifeanyi-Reuben, Ugwu, & Nwachukwu, (2017)	Document similarity	n-grams models	Igbo
3	Asubiaro, (2015)	Heaps' and Zipf's model		Yoruba
4	Bashir, Rozaimee, & Isa, (2017)	Text summarization	Feature extraction	Hausa
Information Retrieval				
1	Asubiaro (2014)	Diacritics effect on retrieval		Yoruba

lingual methods depend on knowledge representation of source language (a resource-rich language) for the annotations of similar resources in a target language (a low resource language). Another interesting emerging method is the rapid development of resources, which is language-independent and optimized for low-resource languages (this method was used for creating Hausa morphological analyzer in Kulick & Bies, (2016)). It is recommended the researchers of the NLP of Nigerian languages should employ these cost-effective, language-independent methods for creating knowledge representation models and annotated resources for the languages. Similarly, research areas where few or no studies have been recorded are potential areas that intending NLP researchers of Nigerian languages can consider to study.

REFERENCES

Adebara, I. (2016). *Using Womb Grammars for Inducing the Grammar of a Subset of Yorùbá Noun Phrases* (Master of Science). Simon Fraser University. Retrieved from http://summit.sfu.ca/item/17390

Adebara, I., & Dahl, V. (2016). Grammar Induction as Automated Transformation between Constraint Solving Models of Language. *KnowProS@IJCAI 2016*, 7.

Adegbola, T. (2016). Pattern-based Unsupervised Induction Of Yorùbá Morphology. *Proceedings of the 25th International Conference Companion on World Wide Web - WWW '16 Companion*, 599–604. 10.1145/2872518.2890563

Adegbola, T. (2017). *Bridging the Last Six Inches of the Digital divide*. Nigeria Computer Society Conference. http://www.ncs.org.ng/wp-content/uploads/2017/08/Bridging-the-Last-Six-Inches-of-the-Digital-Divide-Tunde-Adegbola.pdf

Adegbola, T., & Odilinye, L. U. (2012). Quantifying the effect of corpus size on the quality of automatic diacritization of Yorùbá texts. In *Third Workshop on Spoken Language Technologies for Under-Resourced Languages*, (pp. 48–53). Cape Town, South Africa: International Speech Communication Association.

Adegbola, T., Owolabi, K., & Odejobi, T. (2011). Localising for Yoruba: Experience, Challenges and Future Direction. *Conference on Human Language Technology for Development*, 7-10.

Adetunmbi, O. A., Obe, O. O., & Iyanda, J. N. (2016). Development of Standard Yorùbá speech-to-text system using HTK. *International Journal of Speech Technology*, *19*(4), 929–944. doi:10.100710772-016-9380-2

Adewole, L. B., Adetunmbi, A. O., Alese, B. K., & Oluwadare, S. A. (2017). Token Validation in Automatic Corpus Gathering for Yoruba Language. *FUOYE Journal of Engineering and Technology*, *2*(1), 4. doi:10.46792/fuoyejet.v2i1.85

Adeyemo, O. O., & Idowu, A. (2015). Development and integration of Text to Speech Usability Interface for Visually Impaired Users in Yoruba language. *African Journal of Computing and ICT*, *8*(1), 87–94.

Afolabi, A., Omidiora, E., & Arulogun, T. (2013). Development of Text to Speech System for Yoruba Language. *Innovative Systems Design and Engineering*, *4*(9), 1–8.

Agbeyangi, A. O., Eludiora, S. I., & Popoola, O. A. (2016). Web-Based Yorùbá Numeral Translation System. *IAES International Journal of Artificial Intelligence*, *5*(4), 127–134. doi:10.11591/ijai.v5.i4. pp127-134

Ajao, J. F., Olawuyi, D. O., & Odejobi, O. O. (2018). Yoruba Handwritten Character Recognition using Freeman Chain Code and K-Nearest Neighbor Classifier. *Jurnal Teknologi Dan Sistem Komputer*, *6*(4), 129–134. doi:10.14710/jtsiskom.6.4.2018.129-134

Àkànbí, L. A., & Odéjobí, O. À. (2011). Automatic recognition of oral vowels in tone language: Experiments with fuzzy logic and neural network models. *Applied Soft Computing*, *11*(1), 1467–1480. doi:10.1016/j.asoc.2010.04.018

Akinadé, O. O., & Odéjobí, O. A. (2014). Computational modelling of Yorùbá numerals in a number-to-text conversion system. *Journal of Language Modelling*, *2*(1), 167. doi:10.15398/jlm.v2i1.83

Asubiaro, T. (2013). Entropy-Based Generic Stopwords List for Yoruba Texts. *International Journal of Computer and Information Technology*, *02*(05), 1065–1068.

Asubiaro, T. (2014). Effects of diacritics on Web search engines' performance for retrieval of Yoruba documents. *Journal of Library and Information Studies.*, *12*(1), 1–19.

Asubiaro, T. (2017). An Assessment of the Cyber Presence of Academic Libraries in Nigeria. *African Journal of Library Archives and Information Science*, *27*(1), 65–76.

Asubiaro, T. (2019). How Collaboration Type, Publication Place, Funding and Author's role affect Citations Received by Publications from Africa? A Bibliometric study of LIS research from 1996 to 2015. *Scientometrics*, *120*(3), 1261–1287. Advance online publication. doi:10.100711192-019-03157-1

Asubiaro, T., Adegbola, T., Mercer, R., & Ajiferuke, I. (2018). A word-level language identification strategy for resource-scarce languages: A Word-Level Language Identification Strategy for Resource-Scarce Languages. *Proceedings of the Association for Information Science and Technology*, *55*(1), 19–28. doi:10.1002/pra2.2018.14505501004

Asubiaro, T. V. (2015). Statistical Patterns of Diacritized and Undiacritized Yorùbá Texts. *International Journal of Computational Linguistics Research*, *6*(3), 77–84.

Ayogu, I. I., Adetunmbi, A. O., Ojokoh, B. A., & Oluwadare, S. A. (2017). A comparative study of hidden Markov model and conditional random fields on a Yorùba part-of-speech tagging task. *2017 International Conference on Computing Networking and Informatics (ICCNI)*, 1–6. 10.1109/ICCNI.2017.8123784

Bashir, M., Rozaimee, A., & Isa, W. M. W. (2017). Automatic Hausa LanguageText Summarization Based on Feature Extraction using Naïve Bayes Model. *World Applied Sciences Journal*, *35*(9), 7. doi:10.5829/idosi.wasj.2017.2074.2080

Bashir, M., & Rozaimee, A. B. (2015). A Word Stemming Algorithm for Hausa Language. *IOSR Journal of Computer Engineering*, *17*(3), 25–31.

Bimba, A., Idris, N., Khamis, N., & Noor, N. F. M. (2016). Stemming Hausa text: Using affix-stripping rules and reference look-up. *Language Resources and Evaluation*, *50*(3), 687–703. doi:10.100710579-015-9311-x

Borgman, C. L. (2000). *From Gutenberg to the Global Information Infrastructure: Access to Information in the Networked World*. MIT Press.

Chavez, C., Terceiro, A., Meirelles, P., Jr., & Kon, F. (2011). Free/Libre/Open Source Software Development in Software Engineering Education: Opportunities and Experiences. *Forum de Educacao Em Engenharia de Software (CBSoft'11-SBES-FEES)*, 8.

CIA. (2016). *The World Factbook — Central Intelligence Agency*. Retrieved from https://www.cia.gov/library/publications/the-world-factbook/geos/ni.html

Connel, B., & Ladd, R. (1990). Aspects of pitch realisation in Yoruba. *Phonology, 7*(1), 1–29. https://doi-org./ doi:10.1017/S095267570000110X

Coombs, A. L. (2013). High tone processes in Ibibio. *Proceedings of Meetings on Acoustics Acoustical Society of America, 19*, 060232–060232. doi:10.1121/1.4800734

Crysmann, B. (2012). HaG — A Computational Grammar of Hausa. In M. R. Marlo, N. B. Adams, C. R. Green, M. Morrison, & T. M. Purvis (Eds.), *Selected proceedings of the 42nd Annual Conference on African Linguistics (ACAL 42)*, (pp. 321–337). Academic Press.

Crysmann, B. (2015a). Representing morphological tone in a computational grammar of Hausa. *Journal of Language Modelling, 3*(2), 463. doi:10.15398/jlm.v3i2.126

Crysmann, B. (2015b). Resumption and Extraction in an Implemented HPSG of Hausa. *Proceedings of the Grammar Engineering Across Frameworks (GEAF) 2015 Workshop*, 65–72. 10.18653/v1/W15-3309

Crysmann, B. (2017). Reduplication in a computational HPSG of Hausa. *Morphology, 27*(4), 527–561. doi:10.100711525-017-9306-y

Dagba, T. K., Aoga, J. O. R., & Fanou, C. C. (2016). Design of a Yoruba Language Speech Corpus for the Purposes of Text-to-Speech (TTS) Synthesis. In N. T. Nguyen, B. Trawiński, H. Fujita, & T.-P. Hong (Eds.), *ACIIDS 2016: Intelligent Information and Database Systems* (pp. 161–169). doi:10.1007/978-3-662-49381-6_16

De Pauw, G., Wagacha, P. W., & De Schryver, G.-M. (2007). Automatic diacritic restoration for resource-scarce languages. *International Conference on Text, Speech and Dialogue*, 170–179. 10.1007/978-3-540-74628-7_24

Eberhard, D., Simons, G., & Fennig, C. (Eds.). (2018). Ethnologue: Languages of the World (twenty-first). Dallas, TX: SIL International.

Ekpenyong, M., Inyang, U., & Udoh, E. (2018). Unsupervised visualization of Under-resourced speech prosody. *Speech Communication, 101*, 45–56. doi:10.1016/j.specom.2018.04.011

Ekpenyong, M., & Udoh, E. (2013). Intelligent Prosody Modelling: A Framework for Tone Language Synthesis. Academic Press.

Ekpenyong, M., Udoinyang, M., & Urua, E.-A. (2009). A Robust Language Processor for African Tone Language Systems. *Georgian Electronic Scientific Journal: Computer Science and Telecommunications, 6*(23), 1–11.

Ekpenyong, M., Urua, E.-A., Watts, O., King, S., & Yamagishi, J. (2014). Statistical parametric speech synthesis for Ibibio. *Speech Communication*, *56*, 243–251. doi:10.1016/j.specom.2013.02.003

Ekpenyong, M. E., & Inyang, U. G. (2016). Unsupervised mining of under-resourced speech corpora for tone features classification. *2016 International Joint Conference on Neural Networks (IJCNN)*, 2374–2381. 10.1109/IJCNN.2016.7727494

Ekpenyong, M. E., Inyang, U. G., & Udoh, E. O. (2016). Adaptive Prosody Modelling for Improved Synthetic Speech Quality. In Z. Vetulani, H. Uszkoreit, & M. Kubis (Eds.), *Human Language Technology* (Vol. 9561, pp. 16–28). Challenges for Computer Science and Linguistics., doi:10.1007/978-3-319-43808-5_2

Ekpenyong, M. E., Inyang, U. G., & Umoren, I. J. (2016). Towards a Hybrid Learning Approach to Efficient Tone Pattern Recognition. In L. Rutkowski, M. Korytkowski, R. Scherer, R. Tadeusiewicz, L. A. Zadeh, & J. M. Zurada (Eds.), *Artificial Intelligence and Soft Computing* (Vol. 9692, pp. 571–583)., doi:10.1007/978-3-319-39378-0_49

Ekpenyong, M. E., & Udoh, E. (2014). Tone modelling in Ibibio speech synthesis. *International Journal of Speech Technology*, *17*(2), 145–159. doi:10.100710772-013-9216-2

Ekpenyong, M. E., Urua, E.-A., & Gibbon, D. (2008). Towards an unrestricted domain TTS system for African tone languages. *International Journal of Speech Technology*, *11*(2), 87–96. doi:10.100710772-009-9037-5

Eludiora, S. I., & Ayemonisan, O. R. (2018). *Computational Morphological Analysis of Yorùbá Language Words*. Academic Press.

Enemuoh, C., Hepple, M., Onyenwe, I., & Ezeani, I. (2017). Morph-Inflected Word Detection in Igbo via Bitext. *Proceedings of the 55th Annual Meeting of the Association for Computational Linguistics*, 4.

Enguehard, C., & Mangeot, M. (2014). Computerization of African languages-French dictionaries. Collaboration and Computing for Under Resourced Languages in the Linked Open Data Era, 121–128.

Enguehard, C., & Naroua, H. (2009). Evaluation of Virtual Keyboards for West-African Languages. *Language Resources and Evaluation*, 5.

Ezeani, I., Hepple, M., & Onyenwe, I. (2016). Automatic Restoration of Diacritics for Igbo Language. In P. Sojka, A. Horák, I. Kopeček, & K. Pala (Eds.), *Text* (Vol. 9924, pp. 198–205). doi:10.1007/978-3-319-45510-5_23

Ezeani, I., Hepple, M., & Onyenwe, I. (2017). Lexical Disambiguation of Igbo using Diacritic Restoration. *Proceedings of the 1st Workshop on Sense, Concept and Entity Representations and Their Applications*, 53–60. 10.18653/v1/W17-1907

Ezeani, I., Hepple, M., Onyenwe, I., & Enemuoh, C. (2018). Igbo Diacritic Restoration using Embedding Models. *Proceedings of the 2018 Conference of the North American Chapter of the Association for Computational Linguistics*. 10.18653/v1/N18-48008

Ezeani, I., Hepple, M., Onyenwe, I., & Enemuoh, C. (2018b). Multi-task Projected Embedding for Igbo. TSD 2018: Text, Speech, and Dialogue, 285–294.

Ezeani, I., Onyenwe, I., & Hepple, M. (2018). Transferred Embeddings for Igbo Similarity, Analogy, and Diacritic Restoration Tasks. In *Proceedings of SemDeep-3, the 3rd Workshop on Semantic Deep Learning*, (pp. 30–38). Association for Computational Linguistics.

Fiala, D., & Tutoky, G. (2017). Computer Science Papers in Web of Science: A Bibliometric Analysis. *Publications, 5*(4), 23. doi:10.3390/publications5040023

Finkel, R., & Odejobi, O. A. (2009). A computational approach to Yorùbá morphology. *Proceedings of the First Workshop on Language Technologies for African Languages - AfLaT '09*, 25. 10.3115/1564508.1564514

Gauthier, E., Besacier, L., & Voisin, S. (2016). Speed Perturbation and Vowel Duration Modeling for ASR in Hausa and Wolof Languages. *INTERSPEECH, 3529–3533*, 3529–3533. Advance online publication. doi:10.21437/Interspeech.2016-461

Gauthier, E., Besacier, L., & Voisin, S. (2016a). Automatic Speech Recognition for African Languages with Vowel Length Contrast. *Procedia Computer Science, 81*, 136–143. doi:10.1016/j.procs.2016.04.041

Gibbon, D., Urua, A., & Ekpenyong, M. (2005). Problems and solutions in African tone language Text–To–Speech. *MULTILING 2006 ISCA Tutorial and Research Workshop (ITRW)*, 6.

Hassan, S. T., Abolarinwa, J. A., Alenoghena, C. O., Bala, S. A., David, M., & Farzaminia, A. (2017). Intelligent sign language recognition using enhanced fourier descriptor: A case of Hausa sign language. *2017 IEEE 2nd International Conference on Automatic Control and Intelligent Systems (I2CACIS)*, 104–109. 10.1109/I2CACIS.2017.8239041

Huang, L., May, J., Pan, X., & Ji, H. (2016). *Building a Fine-Grained Entity Typing System Overnight for a New X (X = Language, Domain, Genre)*. Retrieved from https://arxiv.org/abs/1603.03112

Huang, L., May, J., Pan, X., Ji, H., Ren, X., Han, J., Zhao, L., & Hendler, J. A. (2017). Liberal Entity Extraction: Rapid Construction of Fine-Grained Entity Typing Systems. *Big Data, 5*(1), 19–31. doi:10.1089/big.2017.0012 PMID:28328252

Ifeanyi-Reuben, N., Ugwu, C., & Adegbola, T. (2017). Analysis and Representation of Igbo Text Document for a Text-Based System. *International Journal of Data Mining Techniques and Applications, 6*(1), 26–32. doi:10.20894/IJDMTA.102.006.001.005

Ifeanyi-Reuben, N., Ugwu, C., & Nwachukwu, E. O. (2017). Comparative Analysis of N-gram Text Representation on Igbo Text Document Similarity. *International Journal of Applied Information Systems, 12*(9), 1–7. doi:10.5120/ijais2017451724

Iheanetu, O., & Adeyeye, M. (2013). Finite state representation of reduplication processes in Igbo. *2013 Africon*, 1–6. doi:10.1109/AFRCON.2013.6757772

Iheanetu, O. U., Nwagwu, W. E., Adegbola, T., & Agarana, M. C. (2017). Corpus-size Quantification for Computational Morphological Analysis of Igbo Language. *Proceedings of the World Congress on Engineering and Computer Science*, 6.

Ikechukwu, E. O., Ebele, G. O., Godwin, E. A., & Ignatius, M. E. (2019). Bootstrapping Method for Developing Part-Of-Speech Tagged Corpus in Low Resource Languages Tagset- A Focus on an African IGBO. *International Journal on Natural Language Computing*, 8(1), 13–27. doi:10.5121/ijnlc.2019.8102

Jansen, R., & Sellar, M. (2008). Sustainable Access: An International Perspective. In D. Charbonneau (Ed.), *Global Information Inequalities: Bridging the Information Gap* (pp. 3–18). doi:10.1016/B978-1-84334-361-5.50001-8

Kari, K. H., & Baro, E. E. (2016). Digital Preservation Practices in University Libraries: A Survey of Institutional Repositories in Nigeria. *Preservation. Digital Technology & Culture*, 45(3), 134–144. doi:10.1515/pdtc-2016-0006

Kim, S.-J., & Jeong, D. Y. (2006). An analysis of the development and use of theory in library and information science research articles. *Library & Information Science Research*, 28(4), 548–562. doi:10.1016/j.lisr.2006.03.018

Kulick, S., & Bies, A. (2016). Rapid Development of Morphological Analyzers for Typologically Diverse Languages. *Proceedings of the Tenth International Conference on Language Resources and Evaluation*, 2551–2557.

Lu, D., Pan, X., Pourdamghani, N., Chang, S.-F., Ji, H., & Knight, K. (2016). A Multi-media Approach to Cross-lingual Entity Knowledge Transfer. *Proceedings of the 54th Annual Meeting of the Association for Computational Linguistics*, 54–65. 10.18653/v1/P16-1006

Luka, M. K., Frank, I. A., & Onwodi, G. (2012). Neural_Network_Based_Hausa_Language_Speech_Recognition. *International Journal of Advanced Research in Artificial Intelligence*, 1(2), 6.

Maitama, J. Z., Haruna, U., Gambo, A. Y., Thomas, A. B., Idris, N. B., Gital, A. Y., & Abubakar, A. (2014). Text Normalization Algorithm for Facebook Chats in Hausa Language. *The 5th International Conference on Information and Communication Technology for The Muslim World (ICT4M)*. 10.1109/ICT4M.2014.7020605

Ng'ang'a, W. (2010). Towards a Comprehensive, Machine-readable Dialectal Dictionary of Igbo. *Proceedings of the Second Workshop on African Language Technology*.

Ninan, O. D., & Odejobi, O. (2012). Towards a Digital Resource for African Folktales. Istanbul, Turkey: Association for Computational Linguistics.

Ninan, O. D., Ajíbádé, G. O., & Odéjobí, O. A. (2016). Appraisal of Computational Model for Yorùbá Folktale Narrative. *Schloss Dagstuhl - Leibniz-Zentrum Fuer Informatik GmbH*. doi:10.4230/oasics.cmn.2016.14

Ninan, O. D., & Odéjobí, O. A. (2013). Theoretical Issues in the Computational Modelling of Yorùbá Narratives. *Schloss Dagstuhl - Leibniz-Zentrum Fuer Informatik GmbH*. doi:10.4230/oasics.cmn.2013.153

Ninan, O. D. (2017). Computational Analysis of Igbo Numerals in a Number-to-text Conversion System. *Journal of Computer and Education Research*, 5(10), 241–254. doi:10.18009/jcer.325804

Nwagwu, W. (2008). Online journals and visibility of science in Africa: A role for African social science citation index. In *Proceedings of the Conference on Electronic Publishing and Dissemination: "Putting African Journals On Line: Opportunities, Implications and Limits"* (pp. 2–14). Dakar, Senegal: Academic Press.

Ọdẹ'jọbí, Ọ. A., Wong, S. H. S., & Beaumont, A. J. (2007). A fuzzy decision tree-based duration model for Standard Yorùbá text-to-speech synthesis. Computer Speech & Language, 21(2), 325–349. doi:10.1016/j.csl.2006.06.005

Ọdẹ'jọbí, Ọ. A., Wong, S. H. S., & Beaumont, A. J. (2008). A modular holistic approach to prosody modelling for Standard Yorùbá speech synthesis. Computer Speech & Language, 22(1), 39–68. doi:10.1016/j.csl.2007.05.002

Odejobi, O. A. (2008). Recognition of Tones in YorÙbÁ Speech: Experiments With Artificial Neural Networks. In B. Prasad & S. R. M. Prasanna (Eds.), *Speech, Audio, Image and Biomedical Signal Processing using Neural Networks.* Springer. doi:10.1007/978-3-540-75398-8_2

Odéjobí, O. A., Beaumont, A. J., & Wong, S. H. S. (2004). A Computational Model of Intonation for Yorùbá Text-to-Speech Synthesis: Design and Analysis. In P. Sojka, I. Kopeček, & K. Pala (Eds.), *Text* (Vol. 3206, pp. 409–416). Speech and Dialogue. doi:10.1007/978-3-540-30120-2_52

Ọdéjọbí, Ọ. A., Beaumont, A. J., & Wong, S. H. S. (2006). Intonation contour realisation for Standard Yorùbá text-to-speech synthesis: A fuzzy computational approach. *Computer Speech & Language, 20*(4), 563–588. doi:10.1016/j.csl.2005.08.006

Ogwu, E. J., Talib, M., & Odejobi, O. A. (2006). Text-to-speech processing using African language as case study. *Journal of Discrete Mathematical Sciences and Cryptography, 9*(2), 365–382. doi:10.1080/09720529.2006.10698085

Oladayo, O. (2015). Yoruba Language and Numerals' Offline Interpreter Using Morphological and Template Matching. *TELKOMNIKA Indonesian Journal of Electrical Engineering, 13*(1). Advance online publication. doi:10.11591/telkomnika.v13i1.6782

Oladayo, O. O. (2014). Yoruba Language and Numerals' Offline Interpreter Using Morphological and Template Matching. *IAES International Journal of Artificial Intelligence, 3*(2), 64–72. doi:10.11591/ijai.v3.i2.pp64-72

Oladiipo, A. F., Odejobi, O. A., Adagunodo, E. R., & Olubode-Sawe, F. O. (2017). Tone Mark Restoration in Standard Yoruba Texts: A Proposal. *INFOCOMP Journal of Computer Science, 16*, 8–19.

Oladiipo Asahiah, F., Ajadi Odejobi, O., & Rotimi Adagunodo, E. (2017). Restoring tone-marks in standard Yorùbá electronic text: Improved model. *Computer Science, 18*(3), 305. doi:10.7494/csci.2017.18.3.2128

Olufunminiyi, E., & Adebayo, S. (2013). Intelligent System for Learning and Understanding of Yoruba Language. *International Journal of Computer and Information Technology, 2*(5), 5.

Onyenwe, I., Hepple, M., & Uchechukwu, C. (2016). Improving Accuracy of Igbo Corpus Annotation Using Morphological Reconstruction andTransformation-Based Learning. *Actes de La Conférence Conjointe JEP-TALN-RECITAL, 2016*(11), 1–10.

Onyenwe, I., Hepple, M., Uchechukwu, C., & Ezeani, I. (2015). Use of Transformation-Based Learning in Annotation Pipeline of Igbo, an African Language. *Proceedings of the Recent Advances in Natural Language Processing.*

Onyenwe, I. E., & Hepple, M. (2016). Predicting Morphologically-Complex Unknown Words in Igbo. In P. Sojka, A. Horák, I. Kopeček, & K. Pala (Eds.), *Text* (Vol. 9924, pp. 206–214). doi:10.1007/978-3-319-45510-5_24

Onyenwe, I. E., Hepple, M., Chinedu, U., & Ezeani, I. (2018). A Basic Language Resource Kit Implementation for the Igbo *NLP* Project. *ACM Transactions on Asian and Low-Resource Language Information Processing, 17*(2), 1–23. doi:10.1145/3146387

Onyenwe, I. E., Hepple, M., Chinedu, U., & Ezeani, I. (2019). Toward an Effective Igbo Part-of-Speech Tagger. *ACM Transactions on Asian and Low-Resource Language Information Processing, 18*(4), 1–26. doi:10.1145/3314942

Orife, I. (2018). *Attentive Sequence-to-Sequence Learning for Diacritic Restoration of Yor\`ub\'a Language Text.* Retrieved from https://arxiv.org/abs/1804.00832

Orimaye, S. O., Alhashmi, S. M., & Eu-gene, S. (2012). Sentiment analysis amidst ambiguities in youtube comments on yoruba language (nollywood) movies. *Proceedings of the 21st International Conference Companion on World Wide Web - WWW '12 Companion,* 583. 10.1145/2187980.2188138

Osborn, D. (2010). *African Languages in a digital age; Challenges and opportunity for indigenous language computing.* Human Sciences Research Council, Cape Town.

Oyinloye, O. A., & Odejobi, O. A. (2015). Issues in Computational System for Morphological Analysis of Standard Yorùbá (SY) Verbs. *Proceedings of the World Congress on Engineering 2015.*

Pourdamghani, N., Ghazvininejad, M., & Knight, K. (2018). Using Word Vectors to Improve Word Alignments for Low Resource Machine Translation. *Proceedings of the 2018 Conference of the North American Chapter of the Association for Computational Linguistics: Human Language Technologies,* 524–528. 10.18653/v1/N18-2083

Rehbein, B. (2015). Globalization, Capitalism and Social Inequality. In A. Lenger & F. Schumacher (Eds.), *Understanding the Dynamics of Global Inequality* (pp. 149–157). Springer Berlin Heidelberg. https://link.springer.com/10.1007/978-3-662-44766-6_7

Safiriyu, I. E., Akindeji, O. A., & Isau, O. A. (2015). Computational modelling of personal pronouns for English to Yorùbà machine translation system. *2015 SAI Intelligent Systems Conference (IntelliSys),* 733–741. 10.1109/IntelliSys.2015.7361222

Salifou, L., & Naroua, H. (2014). *Design of A Spell Corrector For Hausa Language.* Academic Press.

Scannell, K. P. (2011). Statistical unicodification of African languages. *Language Resources and Evaluation, 45*(3), 375–386. doi:10.100710579-011-9150-3

Schlippe, T., Djomgang, E. G. K., Vu, N. T., Ochs, S., & Schultz, T. (2012). Hausa large vocabulary continuos speech recognition. *The 3rd Workshop on Spoken Language Technologies for Under-Resourced Languages (SLTU 2012)*, 11–14. Retrieved from http://www.research-karlsruhe.de/pubs/SLTU2012-Schlippe_Hausa.pdf

Schlippe, T., Ochs, S., Vu, N. T., & Schultz, T. (2012). Automatic Error Recovery for Pronunciation Dictionaries. *13th Annual Conference of the International Speech Communication Association*, 4. Retrieved from https://www.csl.uni-bremen.de/cms/images/documents/publications/Interspeech2012-Schlippe_DictFilter.pdf

Selamat, A., & Akosu, N. (2016). Word-length algorithm for language identification of under-resourced languages. *Journal of King Saud University - Computer and Information Sciences, 28*(4), 457–469. doi:10.1016/j.jksuci.2014.12.004

Sonnenburg, S., Braun, M. L., Ong, C. S., Bengio, S., Bottou, L., Holmes, G., & LeCun, Y. (2007). The Need for Open Source Software in Machine Learning. *Journal of Machine Learning Research, 8*, 2443–2466.

Sosimi, A., Adegbola, T., & Fakinlede, O. (2015). A Supervised Phrase Selection Strategy for Phonetically Balanced Standard Yorùbá Corpus. In A. Gelbukh (Ed.), *Computational Linguistics and Intelligent Text Processing* (Vol. 9042, pp. 565–582)., doi:10.1007/978-3-319-18117-2_42

Tucker, R., & Shalonova, K. (2005). *Supporting the Creation of TTS for Local Language Voice Information Systems. INTERSPEECH-2005*, 453–456.

van Niekerk, D. R., & Barnard, E. (2012). Tone realisation in a Yoruba speech recognition corpus. *Workshop on Spoken Language Technologies for Under-Resourced Languages*, 1–7.

van Niekerk, D. R., & Barnard, E. (2013). Generating Fundamental Frequency Contours for Speech Synthesis in Yoruba (F. Bimbot, C. Cerisara, C. Fougeron, G. Gravier, L. Lamel, F. Pellegrino, & P. Perrier, Eds.). Academic Press.

Van Niekerk, D. R., & Barnard, E. (2014). Predicting utterance pitch targets in Yorùbá for tone realisation in speech synthesis. *Speech Communication, 56*, 229–242. doi:10.1016/j.specom.2013.01.009

Vu, N. T., & Schultz, T. (2013). Multilingual Multilayer Perceptron For Rapid Language Adaptation Between and Across Language Families. In F. Bimbot, C. Cerisara, C. Fougeron, G. Gravier, L. Lamel, F. Pellegrino, & P. Perrier (Eds.), *INTERSPEECH 2013* (p. 5). Retrieved from https://www.isca-speech.org/archive/interspeech_2013

Yu, P. K. (2002). Bridging the Digital Divide: Equality in the Information Age. *Cardozo Arts and Entertainment, 20*(1), 1–52. doi:10.2139srn.309841

Chapter 9

Increasing Teacher Educators' Access and Use of Instructional and Web–Based Technologies in Sub–Saharan Africa:
Findings From a Mixed Method Study

Abdulsalami Ibrahim
https://orcid.org/0000-0001-7778-3582
Millersville University of Pennsylvania, USA

Crystal Machado
Indiana University of Pennsylvania, USA

ABSTRACT

While teacher educators in Sub-Saharan Africa have increased access to information and communication technology (ICT), there is a lack of empirical research that describes the detail of educators' use of technology. This chapter addresses the gap in the literature with an exploratory mixed method study in a region of Nigeria. Researchers developed a survey to collect quantitative data from 190 teacher educators and added data from 10 interviewees to verify and the survey findings. The survey assessed the types of technologies in use and the demographics of teachers who use them. As expected, use is dependent on access, and overall access was high. Demographic differences in use were not great, but women were slightly more accepting than men, and more recent graduates more accepting than older ones. Teachers overall were moderately comfortable with technology. Researchers did not collect data about enabling factors like technical support or professional development. This suggests that next steps would be to define instructional software and assess technical support needs.

DOI: 10.4018/978-1-7998-3468-7.ch009

INTRODUCTION

In recent decades, the information and communication technology (ICT) industry that has developed steadily since the 1970s has seen exponential growth. This growth has had positive effects in industry and government, not the least in the field of education. According to Thomas (2016), ICT growth has compelled educational leaders to adopt technology in education. To this end, the Nigerian government launched several initiatives to provide educators with access to technology across all levels of education (Garba & Alademerin, 2014). The focus of this chapter is to provide insight into how educators use ICTs for teaching and learning and to describe efforts of the Nigerian government and other education industry stakeholders to provide access to (ICT) infrastructure for sustained educational development throughout the country. We begin this chapter with a brief introduction to the background context of technology in Nigeria, followed by a synthesis of the literature on educators' access to ICTs, and the increased use of ICT tools for teaching. We then describe the goals, the research questions, and the methodology, followed by findings and discussion.

BACKGROUND AND CONTEXT OF TECHNOLOGY INTEGRATION IN NIGERIA

Over the course of history, Nigeria has faced challenges integrating technology into education. These challenges include lack of access to modern ICT equipment across all educational institutions (primary, secondary, and tertiary), educators' lack of knowledge and skills to use ICTs for learning, and limited access to technology-related professional development for educators (Garba, Ranjit-Singh, Yusuf, & Ziden, 2013; Onyia & Onyia, 2011; Owolabi, Oyewole, & Oke, 2013). These challenges are not unique to Nigeria; they are prevalent in other Sub-Saharan African countries as well. For example, Buabeng-Andoh (2012) reviewed teachers' adoption and integration of ICT in Ghana and found that limited access to ICTs and teachers' lack of ICT skills and confidence are among the major barriers to ICT use in teaching and learning.

Nigeria has a total of 95 public universities (NUC, 2019). To meet national development goals (Ibrahim, 2019), the federal government in 1993 Tax act and as amended in 1998, launched strategic initiatives through the Educational Trust Fund (ETF), Tertiary Education Trust Fund (TETFund), and National Information Technology Agency (NITDA). The aim of these initiatives was to improve the country's education system and enhance technology integration by providing access to ICT infrastructure which include computers, overhead projectors, optical fibres, fax machines, and high-speed Internet across campuses for educators and students (Apagu and Wakili, 2015). Additionally, setting up professional development venues like workshops and seminars to enhance educators' ability to integrate technology into teaching, and funding technology-related initiatives for the sum of N161bn in 2019 ("Buhari Approves N161bn," 2019, para.1). The following sections review literature on access to ICTs in education, and how some educators have made use of them for improved learning outcomes.

Review of Related Literature

The adoption of technology in education has the potential to empower educators and students across educational settings (Ibrahim, 2019). In Nigeria, there is a growing access to technology across all tiers of education, and educators make limited use of technology. However, this is changing recently, educators are accepting and using technology for teaching ever than before (Garba, Ranjit-Singh, Yusuf, & Ziden, 2013). This trend is evident in other countries in sub-Saharan Africa (Buabeng-Andoh, 2012).

Educators' Access to Information Communication Technology (ICT)

Technology access in the education sector is considered to be essential to contemporary learning methods. Fu (2013) explains that in the twenty-first century classroom, teaching and learning are no longer contingent on in-class, face-to-face, and traditional didactic methods. Teachers and learners can interact, access content, and learn online at any time. Ajoku (2014) explains that between the years of 2010 and 2014, Nigeria has made some progress in the use of technology for education. The federal government through the Education Trust Fund (ETF) equipped institutions of higher education (universities, colleges of education and polytechnics) with computers and academic software worth N4bn to provide a technology-rich learning environment (TETFund, 2016). Idowu and Esere (2013) describe nine national level ICT programs for educational interventions aimed at increasing access to technology across all tertiary institutions in Nigeria. They are Nigerian Universities Network (NuNet), Polytechnics Network (PolyNet), SchoolNet, Teacher Network (Teach Net) Project, National Open University of Nigeria (NOUN), Nigerian Education Academic and Research Network (NEARNet), National Virtual Library (Ministry of Science and Technology), and National Information Communication and Education program of the Presidency (p. 22). These intervention programs provide ICT-specific services to tertiary institutions across the country. The Nigerian University Networks (NuNet) project, and DigitNet project by ETF specifically provide Internet access and ICT facilities to universities, colleges, and polytechnics. Some of these programs that provide educators with research facilities and professional development include the National Virtual (Digital) Library, Nigerian Education Academic and Research Network (NEARNet), and National Open University (NOUN).

Access to high-speed Internet connection is a key factor in making use of technology tools in the classroom. Bushwater (2017) explains that "access to reliable, high-speed Internet connectivity has become an essential element of many digital tools and strategies. Yet, Internet access still varies widely from school to school, and district to district" (p.1). Ever since then, the Nigerian Federal Government (FG) has addressed this need by providing all tiers of society with access to high speed internet. Through the Nigerian Information Technology Development Agency (NITDA), the FG has established a Mobile Internet Unit (MIU). The MIU is a high-speed Internet service (hotspot) provider that is located at several centers across the country (Matthew, Joro, & Manasseh, 2015). The aim of the MIU is to provide access to the Internet for students within their residential areas (at homes), especially elementary and secondary students who may be excluded from the digital divide. As well, the Tertiary Education Trust Fund established several technology centers across higher education institutions (Onwuagboke, Singh & Fook, 2015). These centers are equipped with computers and high-speed Internet connections to provide access to online resources for educators and students (TETFund, 2016). With this increase in access, researchers can track technology use by educators and students.

Educators' Use of Information Communication Technology (ICT) for Teaching

Educators have used technology to support teaching and learning in novel emerging ways that are not possible with traditional classroom methods. In Nigeria, in order to attain the goal of creating a technologically literate society, the National Policy on Education (2004) emphasized the requirement for technology use in classrooms. Ibrahim (2019) posits that technology makes new ways of learning possible given proper access to web-based resources and opportunities collaboration, online simulation and open educational resources. A number of research articles describe the ways educational technology can enhance learning and student engagement. For example, Thaiposri and Wannapiroon (2015) used social networking and cloud computing to develop students' critical thinking skills with inquiry-based learning. They found that the use of social networking and cloud repositories for collaboration and sharing content expanded teaching and learning possibilities. Similarly, social networking provided students with new opportunities to communicate and collaborate with each other and with the educator during learning activities. Gan, Menkhoff, and Smith (2015) conducted a study to explore the impact of interactive digital media on college students' learning processes, using interactive technologies like Edmodo, Google Site, and others. This study also found that interactive digital media enhanced student learning, providing both educators and students with new opportunities to collaborate and communicate. Alwehaibi (2015) conducted a study of the effect of using YouTube in English as a foreign language (EFL) classrooms to enhance college students' learning of content. Using pre- and post-tests to collect data and t-tests for analysis, she found that students in the experimental group demonstrated a higher learning outcome than a control group after six weeks of using YouTube videos for learning content aligned with the curriculum.

Students of the control group were taught the same content through the usual lecture-based method. Instruction was provided to both groups by the researcher and took place throughout the second term of the academic year in 2011 for a period of 6 weeks, 2 hours per week. Statistical procedures were applied on the data obtained using a t-test, and major findings yielded results favorable to the use of the YouTube technology. (p.1)

Alwehaibi therefore recommends YouTube as an instructional technology for teaching EFL students.

Researchers have also investigated educators' use of technology in teacher preparation programs (Ajayi and Ekundayo, 2009; Garba, 2014), partly in response to the high levels of technology literacy among education students (Ibrahim 2019). Jude and Dankaro (2012) reported high technology utilization in teacher preparation colleges in North-Central Nigerian states. Ajayi and Ekundayo also identified educators' attitudes as a factor in their use of technology. Technology use for education is likely in its infancy (Garba, Singh, Yusuf, & Ziden, 2013; Owolabi, Oyewole, & Oke, 2013), and the literature on technology use in education is still a growing field in Nigeria. This chapter cites literature that supports key concepts relating to contemporary technology access and use for teaching across the global South.

METHODOLOGY

Context of the Study and Design

There are 85 teacher preparation colleges in Nigeria. Twenty-two are owned by the federal government, 47 by state governments, and 16 are privately owned (Ibrahim, 2019). We conducted the present study in the North-West region of Nigeria, which includes seven states and five federal teacher preparation colleges. We chose this region for the study because of time constraints and security challenges in other zones, but the results are transferable across all federal teacher preparation colleges in Nigeria, since they share similar curricula and program structures, and are all managed by the National Commission for Colleges of Education (NCCE) under the leadership of the executive secretary (ES). The NCCE sets the minimum standards for all colleges of education (federal, state, and private) in Nigeria (NCCE, 2016).

Research Design

We used an explanatory sequential mixed method approach to collect and analyze both quantitative and qualitative data (Creswell, 2012). Subedi (2016) explains that the explanatory sequential design involves collecting quantitative data and then using qualitative data to explore and understand the quantitative data. We found this design appropriate because we want to generate an in-depth data set to gain better understanding of educators' access and use of technology for teaching. The quantitative data provided frequencies while the qualitative data gave insight into participants' experiences (Creswell, 2013).

Purpose of the Study and Research Questions

This study was designed to understand Nigerian teacher educators' access, use, and comfort level with instructional and web-based technologies for teaching, as well as to describe efforts by government, policymakers, and stakeholders in education to make Nigerian education consistent with practices in the global information technology society. In this chapter we present data related to the following research questions:

1. Which instructional technologies do Nigerian teacher educators have access to and to what extent do they use them for teaching?
2. Which web-based technologies do Nigerian teacher educators have access to and to what extent do they use them for teaching?
3. What are Nigerian teacher educators' comfort levels regarding technology use for teaching?
4. Are there differences in Nigerian teacher educators' technology use based on gender, age, teaching experience, and level of education?

Phase One: Quantitative Phase

Survey Respondents

The five teacher preparation colleges located within seven states in the North West zone of Nigeria employ approximately 2100 teacher educators. We used a proportional sampling method to determine the finite population, then applied random sampling to identify subjects for the study (Salkind, 2010). There is unequal distribution of sample by gender. Of the 190 survey respondents, about ¾ (74%) were male and ¼ (25%) were female educators. About ⅔ (66.9%) of survey respondents were between the ages of 21 and 40, and about ⅓ (33.3%) survey respondents were over 40 years. In terms of educational qualification, there was some variability among survey respondents. The majority, ⅔ (67.9%) of survey respondents had a bachelor's degree, a smaller proportion had master's ⅓ (33.3%) and doctorate degrees (1.5%). Teaching experiences varied considerably. While 58% had one to five years, close to 40% had taught for six to ten years.

Procedures: Data Collection, Analysis, and Data Quality

Drawing on items from five other instruments, with permission, the lead author developed an instrument titled Educators' Technology Access, Attitudes, and Use (ETAAU) Survey. Six faculty at a mid-sized public university in the United States, five doctoral candidates from four different African countries, and the director of the Applied Research Lab at a medium size university in the east coast of the United States critiqued the instrument for face and content validity. The final instruments consisted of 19 items that aligned with the research questions. Some open-ended items provided respondents with the opportunity to describe their experiences. The instrument was deemed valid based on the coefficient of reliability for the following scale items: faculty attitudes ($\alpha = .80$), diffusion of innovation ($\alpha - .73$), technology acceptance model ($\alpha = .71$), and barriers to technology use ($\alpha = .71$).

Phase Two: Qualitative Phase

Interview Participants

Twenty faculty volunteered to participate in the qualitative phase of the study. Of these, ten participated in a recorded phone interview.

Procedures: Data Collection, Analysis, and Quality

We conducted all interviews via phone, using pseudonyms to conceal the identity of the interviewee during the transcription and data analysis phase. To enhance trustworthiness of the data, we shared transcripts with interviewees for member checking; they verified that their responses were accurate (Creswell, 2012). We used NVivo (v.25) to code the data, and generic (values) coding methods for categories in the data. The use of generic coding enabled us to adjust to interviewee language, perspective and worldviews (Saldana, 2016).

DATA ANALYSIS AND FINDINGS

Below we described the two types of data we collected and their analysis.

Access and Use of Instructional Technology for Teaching

Survey items one and two, relating to instructional and web-based technologies in use, were used to answer the first research question identifying technologies Nigerian teacher educators had access to and the extent to which they used them for teaching. We used the Statistical Software for Social Sciences (SPSS) to generate descriptive and inferential statistics.

We found that there was greater access to cell phones (n =182), laptops in classrooms (n = 179, 94.2%), Tablet (n = 177, 93.2%), VCR/DVD player (n = 172, 90.5%), and Internet connection in classrooms (n = 171, 90.0%) than to other tools. Cell phones (n = 175, 92.1%) and Tablets were said to be used daily (n = 170, 89.5%), and many survey respondents used laptops (n = 172, 90.5%) and VCR/DVD Players (n = 167) more frequently. We found that even though survey respondents have greater access to Clickers (n = 179, 94.2%), Instructor run computer stations (n = 179, 94.2%), LCD projector/computer projection systems (n = 179, 94.2%), overhead projector/document cameras (n = 179, 94.2%), and desktop computers in classrooms (n = 177, 93.7%). The latter are infrequently used for classroom and lecture hall teaching because educators used their laptops for projection of lecture materials.

Qualitative data generated from ten interviewees supplemented the quantitative findings. Educators revealed having more access to instructional technology within their colleges than ever before. Of the ten interviews participants, eight interviewees talk about the which technology they have access to in their schools, and how often they use them. They referenced to having increased access to several instructional technologies, mostly cell phones, laptops, projectors, sound systems, and social media. For example, one interviewee said, "I have access to a computer--desktop computer--and actually, we are using the smartboard, and rest of technologies." (Interviewee 3).

Access and Use of Web-based Technology for Teaching

Survey items five and six were used to answer research question two which identified the web-based technology Nigerian teacher educators had access to and the extent to which they used them for teaching. We used SPSS to generate descriptive and inferential statistics. Table 1 present the descriptive statistics related educators' access and use of web-based technologies.

Table 1. Educators access and extent of use of web-based technology

Web-Based Technology	Never n(%)	Rarely n(%)	Seldom n(%)	Occasionally n(%)	Frequently n(%)	Regularly n(%)
Content on Internet sites	4(2.1)	5(2.6)	1(.5)	3(1.6)	4 (2.1)	172(91.0)
Audio/podcast	16(8.4)	3(1.6)	--	--	169(88.9)	2(1.1)
Multimedia presentation	9(4.7)	--	2(1.1)	5(2.6)	173(91.1)	1(.5)
Sound system in the lecture room	12(6.3)	5(2.6)	--	2(1.1)	170(89.5)	1(.5)
Email	8(4.2)	3(1.6)	2(1.1)	5(2.6)	3(1.6)	169(88.9)
Social media tools	14(7.4)	1(.5)	1(.5)	169(88.9)	3(1.6)	2(1.1)
Photo/video sharing	186(97.9)	1(.5)	1(.5)	1(.5)	--	1(.5)
Videoconferencing/chatting systems	188(98.9)	1(.5)	--	1(.5)	--	--
Blogs	187(98.4)	--	--	1(.5)	--	1(.5)
Interactive quizzes	20(10.5)	1(.5)	--	--	--	169(88.9)
Google tools	12(6.3)	3(1.6)	--	2(1.1)	1(.5)	171(90.0)

Note. Rarely = 2 – 4 times a semester; Seldom = once a month; Occasionally = once every two weeks; Frequently = 1 – 2 times a week; Regularly = Daily.

We found that the majority of Nigerian teacher educators had used content on Internet sites (n = 176), email (n = 172), google tools (n = 171), and interactive quizzes (n = 169) for teaching and communication. While the majority of educators have used social media Tools (n = 126) for teaching occasionally, they used multimedia presentations (n = 174), audio/podcast (n =171), sound system in the lecture room (n = 171) frequently. Educators indicated that they have access to several web-based technologies but did not use them for teaching. However, they did not use photo/video sharing tools (n = 183), video conferencing/chatting systems (n = 180), blogs (n = 179), and social Media tools (n = 126) for teaching.

The qualitative data explained the numeric findings. Interviewees indicated that they had greater access to web-based technologies for teaching. For example, one interviewee said "now we have internet connection. We are able to use videos and collaborate on google documents. Without internet connectivity, we will not be able to do so" (Interview 6). Also, another interviewee said, "I give my students quiz and exams online that we don't have to be in class to do that like the olden days. I also use some presentation sites like Prezi to deliver content in class." Results supported the literature that indicates increased access to web-based technologies across Nigerian campuses as a result of government and stakeholders' continuing efforts to provide access to technology across all tiers of education (Ajegbelen, 2016; Udu & Nkwede, 2014).

Nigerian Teacher Educators' Comfort Levels with Technology Use for Teaching

Research question three explored Nigerian teacher educators' comfort levels regarding technology use for teaching. Survey item four and eight were used to answer this question. We ran a simple descriptive statistic to analyze data generated from these items. Findings revealed that educators demonstrated a moderate degree of comfort regarding the use of both instructional (M = 5.99, SD = .568) and web-based technologies (M = 5.77, SD = .624). The majority of respondents fall within the high comfort level for instructional (90%) and moderate for web-based (68.4%) technologies. In the qualitative phase, we asked interviewees to rate their comfort level in using technology from a scale of 1-10, considering one the lowest and the 10 the highest. Data obtained from open-ended items show that the majority of educators are comfortable using instructional (96.8%) and web-based (73.7%) technologies for teaching. For example, one interviewee said, "I can say I am very comfortable. I like it, and I enjoy using it. From that score, I can say 9. I really enjoy it, and I feel yes, I am very comfortable" (Interviewee 7). Another interviewee explained "Internet connection, you browse the internet to get information; that way, I am very comfortable. Even with the use of laptops, and projectors in the lab, from 1-10, I can say 7" (Interviewee 6).

Differences in Nigerian Teacher Educators' Technology Use Based on Gender, Age, Teaching Experience, and Level of Education

Survey Items 2, 6, and 14-18 elicited data to answer research question four, which examined the differences in Nigerian teacher educators' technology use based on gender, age, teaching experience, and level of education. We ran independent-samples t-tests for variables that had two categories and a one-way between groups analysis of variables (ANOVA) for variables that had three categories.

Differences in Educators' Technology Utilization by Gender

Results of the independent-samples t-test shows the mean scores between male (M = 34.5, SD = 5.24) and female (M = 35.4, SD = 3.00), t (150.5) = -1.48, p = .142 (two-tailed) for utilization of instructional technologies were not statistically significant. The magnitude of the difference in the means (mean difference = -.907, 95% CI: -2.12 to .308) was very small (eta squared = .01). Similarly, the mean scores for male (M = 48.7, SD = 7.96) and female (M = 49.8, SD = 5.10), t = (136.4) = -.1.14, p = .259 (two-tailed) for utilization of web-based technologies were not statistically significant. The magnitude of the difference in the means (mean difference = -1.13, 95% CI: -3.09 to .838) was very small (eta squared = .01). Table 2 presents the result of t-test and descriptive statistics for faculty technology utilization.

Table 2. Results of t-tests and descriptive statistics for educators' technology utilization by gender

Outcome	Levene's Test	Groups						95% CI for Mean Difference	t	df	p
		Male			Female						
		M	SD	N	M	SD	N				
Instructional Technologies	.012	34.5	5.24	139	35.4	3.00	50	-2.12, .308	-1.48	150.5	.142
Web-Based Technologies	.036	48.7	7.96	136	49.8	5.10	50	-3.09, .838	-1.14	136.4	.259

Differences in Educators' Technology Utilization by Age

The results of the two independent samples t-test presented in Table 3 show that the mean scores for survey respondents between ages 21-40 (M = 34.7, SD = 4.62) and those over 40 (M = 34.7, SD = 5.04), $t(187) = .004$, $p = .997$ (two-tailed) for utilization of instructional technology use were not statistically significant. The magnitude of the difference in the means (mean difference = .003, 95% CI: -1.42 to 1.43) was very small (eta squared = .01). A similar pattern was observed for survey respondents' utilization of web-based technologies. There was no statistically significant difference in the mean scores of survey respondents between the age of 21-40 (M = 48.7, SD = 7.56) and those of over 40 (M = 49.4, SD = 6.86), $t = (184) = -.624$, $p = .523$ (two-tailed) for utilization of web-based technologies. The magnitude of the difference in the means (mean difference = -.697, 95% CI: -2.90 to 1.50) was very small (eta squared = .01).

Differences in Educators' Technology Utilization by Level of Education

Results of independent-sample t-tests showed a statistically significant difference in mean scores for survey respondents' utilization of instructional technologies by level of education. Survey respondents

Table 3. Results of t-tests and descriptive statistics for educators' technology utilization by age

Outcome	Levene's Test	Groups						95% CI for Mean Difference	t	df	p
		21 - 40			Over 40						
		M	SD	N	M	SD	N				
Instructional Technologies	.872	34.7	4.62	121	34.7	5.04	68	-1.42, 1.43	.004	187	.997
Web-Based Technologies	.360	48.7	7.56	119	49.4	6.86	67	-2.90, 1.50	-.624	184	.534

with an undergraduate degree had a higher mean score (M = 35.6, SD = 2.85) than those with a graduate degree (M = 32.8, SD = 7.03), t (68.2) = 2.90, p = .005 (two-tailed). The magnitude of the difference in the means (mean difference = 2.73, 95% CI: .847 to 4.60) was moderate (eta squared = .10). Similarly, in terms of web-based technologies, there was a statistically significant difference in the mean scores. Survey respondents with an undergraduate degree had a higher mean score (M = 50.6, SD = 3.67) than those with a graduate degree (M = 45.4, SD = 11.1) t = (64.0) = 3.52, p = .001 (two-tailed) for utilization of web-based technologies. The magnitude of the difference in the means (mean difference = 5.20, 95% CI: 2.25 to 8.15) was moderate (eta squared = .10).

Table 4. Results of t-tests and descriptive statistics for educators' technology utilization by levels of education

Outcome	Levene's Test	Groups						95% CI for Mean Difference	t	df	p
		Undergraduate Degree			Graduate (MS, Ph.D./D.Ed., PGD)						
		M	SD	N	M	SD	N				
Instructional Technologies	.000	35.6	2.85	129	32.8	7.03	60	.847, 4.60	2.90	68.2	.005
Web-Based Technologies	.000	50.6	3.67	127	45.4	11.1	59	2.25, 8.15	3.52	64.0	.001

Differences in Educators' Technology Utilization by Years of Service

Findings from one-way between-groups ANOVA revealed a statistically significant difference at p < .01 across years of service for survey respondents' utilization of instructional technologies, F (2, 186) = 19.5, p < .01, d = .17, as well as their utilization of web-based technologies, F (2, 183), = 29.1, p < .01, d = .17. Table 5 shows the result of one-way between the groups ANOVA.

Post-hoc comparison tests using the Tukey HSD for utilization of instructional technology shows that survey respondents who had 1-5 years' experience (M = 35.6, SD = 2.44) had higher mean scores than

Table 5. One-way ANOVA for educators' technology utilization by years of service

Variables	Sum of Squares	df	Mean Square	F	Sig
Instructional Technologies					
Between Groups	737.951	2	368.976	19.507	.000
Within Groups	3518.250	186	18.915		
Total	4256.201	188			
Web-Based Technologies					
Between Groups	2383.373	2	1191.687	29.115	.000
Within Groups	7490.283	183	40.931		
Total	9873.656	185			

p < .05

those with over 11 years' experience (M = 34.2, SD = 10.1). The mean score for survey respondents who had 6-10 years' experience (M = 34.2, SD = 5.71) is higher than mean scores for those with over 11 years' experience (M = 25.3, SD = 10.1). However, the mean scores for respondents with 1-5 years' experiences (M = 35.6, SD = 2.44) and those with 6-10 years' experience (M = 34.2, SD = 5.371) did not differ significantly. For utilization of web-based technologies, the mean scores for survey respondents with 1 – 5 years' experience (M = 50.1, SD = 5.00) were higher than those with over 11 years' experience (M = 29.7, SD = 6.60). The mean scores for survey respondents with 6-10 years' experience (M = 48.8, SD = 8.20) were higher than mean scores for those with over 11 years' experience (M = 29.7, SD = 6.60). However, mean scores for survey respondents with 1-5 years' experience (M = 50.1, SD = 5.0) differs only slightly from those with 6 – 10 years' experience (M = 48.8, SD = 8.20).

Differences in Educators' Utilization of Instructional and Web-Based Technologies Across Years of Teaching with Technology

Findings from the first one-way between-groups ANOVA revealed that there was a statistically significant difference at $p < .01$ in the mean scores for survey respondents' utilization of instructional technologies, F (3, 184) = 62.6, $p < .01$, $d = .5$ by Years of Teaching with Technology. Also, there was a statistically significant difference in survey respondents' mean scores for utilization of web-based technologies, F (3, 181), = 66.2, $p < .01$, $d = .5$ by Years of Teaching with Technology. Table 6 shows the results of the two one-way ANOVA tests.

Table 6. One-way ANOVA for educators' technology utilization by years of college teaching with technology

	Sum of Squares	df	Mean Square	F	Sig
Instructional Technologies					
Between Groups	1888.679	3	629.560	62.622	.000
Within Groups	1849.805	184	10.053		
Total	3738.484	187			
Web-Based Technologies					
Between Groups	4837.911	3	1612.637	66.195	.000
Within Groups	4409.527	181	24.362		
Total	9247.438	184			

p < 0.05

Post-hoc comparison using the Tukey HSD test for instructional technology use showed that survey respondents with 1-3 years of experience of teaching with technology (M = 35.7, SD = 2.21) had higher mean scores than those with 4-6 years (M = 23.0, SD = 8.40), 7-9 years (M = 22.0, SD = 11.4), and over 10 years (M = 30.6, SD = 6.20). The mean score for survey respondents with 4-6 years of teaching experience with technology (M = 23.0, SD = 8.40) and 7-9 years category (M = 22.0, SD = 11.4) did not differ significantly.

DISCUSSION OF FINDINGS

The findings that emerged from analysis of both phases (quantitative and qualitative) addressed the four research questions and highlight implications for educators and stakeholders in education. This section presents a discussion of findings generated from this study.

As the integration of ICT in education has increased in recent years, scholars have identified factors that influence technology integration in both K-12 and college classrooms. Predictably, access has had an impact on faculty use of technology for teaching (Howard & Mozejko, 2015). Both access to and attitudes toward technology are determining factors in adoption (Ajoku, 2014). This is confirmed in studies of instructor use of instructional technologies in K-12 and higher education classrooms (Blackwell, Lauricella, & Wartella 2014; Ertmer, Ottenbreit-Leftwich, Sadik, Sendurur, & Sandurur, 2012; Howley, Wood, & Hough 2011; Pittman & Gaines 2015). Faculty use is increased when students also have direct access Pittman and Gaines (2015). Saxena (2017) argues that lack of technology access and teachers' low technological knowledge, along with lack of technical support are impediments to technology integration and the increase in student efficacy that goes with it. Thus access alone is not the only factor.

Among the issues faced by teachers when attempting to integrate ICT into their classrooms are gaps in ICT knowledge and skills, lack of training and inadequate support and scaffolding. Other issues include inability to translate training into pedagogical practice and curriculum design and lack of access to current hardware and software....Teachers are core to the integration of ICT in the classroom and hence are often under pressure, since ICT integration is not just about having the right hardware and software; it is deeper and covers many layers. (Saxena, 2017, p. 1)

The literature on Nigeria shows that government and other stakeholders have made efforts to increase technology access in the country's education sector (Onwuagboke, Singh & Fook, 2015; TETFund, 2016). Ajoku (2014) critically examines Nigeria's colleges' access to technology. Ajoku (2014) found that access to technology is the primary determinant of technology utilization in classrooms. Other scholars (Ajayi & Ekundayo, 2009; Jude & Dankaro, 2012; Onwuagboke, Ranjit-Singh, & Soon Fook, 2015) have documented that there is limited access to instructional and web-based technologies in Nigeria's colleges. Findings from this current study echoed the increase in access to technology across Nigerian tertiary institutions which stemmed from government and stakeholders' efforts to equip institutions with required technology.

Globally, researchers report high technology utilization in the classroom (Buchanan, Sainter, & Saunders, 2013; Marzilli, Delello, Marmion, McWhorter, Roberts and Marzilli, 2014; Strayhorn, 2007). Strayhorn (2007) and Jaschik and Ledeman (2018) found a high level of technology utilization among higher education faculty in the United States. According to Pew Research (2014), "in developing countries, there has been an increase in the number of social media users from 33% in 2013 to 42% in 2017" (p. 6). The researcher was unable to find studies describing Nigerian faculty use of web-based technologies for teaching. This study shows that web-based technology continues to be underutilized in Nigeria's teacher preparation program. Educators described that they have not used these web-based technologies photo/video sharing tools, video conferencing/chatting systems, blogs, and social Media tools for teaching.

As discussed in the findings, this could be due to educators' lack of technological skills that will enable them to effectively use instructional and web-based technologies across Nigeria's teacher preparation colleges.

The literature showed the interplay of several factors that determine faculty technology comfort level. These include technology skills and expertise, technology competence and training, self-efficacy, and confidence. Marzilli, Delello, Marmion, WcWhorter, Roberts, and Marzilli (2014) found that faculty technology skills have a significant correlation with technology use in the classroom. Buchanan, Sainter, and Saunders (2013) found a positive relationship between faculty internet self-efficacy and use of technology for teaching, and that this determines the comfort level in using technologies for teaching. Likewise, Owolabi, Oyewole, and Oke (2013) found that faculty technology comfort levels influenced their technology attitude formation, as does Buabeng-Andoh (2012).

This study supports prior literature; findings revealed that the majority of survey respondents were moderately comfortable regarding the use of instructional and web-based technologies for teaching. In terms of interviews, since the questions closely paralleled the survey questions, similar findings emerged. One interviewee observed that prior access to technology impacts comfort level that faculty would develop, which eventually determines faculty technology attitude formation. Faculty were comfortable with the technology to which they had access. In Nigeria and other developing countries, faculty have limited access to technology as compared with developed countries (Acılar, 2011; Cruz-Jesus, Oliveira, & Bacao, 2012; Garba, 2014).

Our study concurred with other studies showing that gender is not a factor in technology utilization (Mehdi & Al-Dera, 2013; Onwuagboke & Singh, 2016). In our study, results of an independent-samples t-test show that mean scores between male and female for the utilization of instructional and web-based technologies were not statistically significant. It is important to note that three quarters of faculty who participated in this study were male. This situation is likely comparable in all tertiary institutions in Nigeria because of unequal sample size could as pointed earlier in the quantitative data section. A further study might shed more light on how the issue of unequal distribution of samples could be addressed.

Levels of education and teaching experience are a factor in faculty technology utilization (Marzilli, Delello, Marmion, WcWhorter, Roberts, & Marzilli 2014). While Mehi and Al-Dera (2013) did not observe a group difference in technology use based on teaching experience, this study showed a statistically significant difference in the mean scores for faculty utilization of instructional and web-based technologies by level of education. Survey respondents with an undergraduate degree had a higher mean score than those with a graduate degree for both instructional and web-based technologies. This likely follows from the fact that faculty with 1-5 years of service were trained when technology became part of instruction across Nigeria's colleges and universities.

On the topic of faculty technological skills, competence, and experience, other researchers found that faculty technology skill level was significantly correlated with technology use in the classroom (Hassad, 2013, Marzilli, Delello, Marmion, WcWhorter, Roberts, and Marzilli, 2014; Morley, 2011). Georgina and Hosford (2009) studied the impact of faculty technology competence and training on technology adoption. They found a significant correlation between faculty technology competence and integration into teaching. Faculty who have just begun their careers are clearly more technologically savvy, since technology is part of everyday life, and they were trained when technology tools became more accessible. Therefore, this is a problem that time itself may help to solve. What remains to be solved are the actual instructional practices that make best use of technology.

IMPLICATIONS FOR STAKEHOLDERS AND EDUCATORS

Given the relatively low level of empirical studies in sub-Saharan Africa, this study has implications for stakeholders and educators in Nigeria and for their counterparts in other sub-Saharan countries. Stakeholders (government, administrators, and department of education) in education play a critical role. They are fundamental actors in educators' professional development. While funding for educators to attend conferences, workshops and seminars may increase awareness, it is critically important that administrators provide sufficient access to appropriately designed technologies for twenty-first century learning environments for educators and students. Training and localized technical support are essential to ease of use and encouragement, as well as to maintaining the state of the art in technology.

To participate in a digitally connected world, it is critical that educators be trained in the use of technology tools for teaching and learning. Educators and scholars should engage in ongoing evaluation of the technologies in use, and how these support learning. For educators in Nigeria and other sub-Saharan African countries to be able to use technology effectively and impart twenty-first century skills to our young generation in schools, they need to be committed to their professional development through attending conferences-local, regional and international. They can expand their technological skills by reading books written by experts, especially ones related to best practices in pedagogy. Open educational resources (OER) are also available to them. All of these practices must be supported by adequate technical support, training and government commitment to funding educational technology.

DIRECTIONS FOR FUTURE RESEARCH AND RECOMMENDATIONS

Sub-Saharan African countries have developed ICTs over the years. According to United Nations Educational, Scientific and Cultural Organization (UNESCO), "since the 1960s, various information and communication technologies have aroused strong interest in sub-Saharan African as a way to increasing access to education, and enhancing its quality and fairness" (2015, p. 54). This has accorded the region with opportunities to set aim for learning technology, learning with technology and learning through technology (UNESCO, 2015). Without access to ICTs, achieving these aims is difficult. We hope this study will provide an avenue for stakeholders to take seriously all the forms of investment required and act accordingly.

The topic of ICT integration for educational development covers a wide range of topics beyond access, use and comfort levels. It involves educators' attitudes, technology knowledge and expertise, educators' perceptions about ease of use and online education. Future research should focus on in-depth studies in these areas across sub-Saharan Africa. Researchers might look into basic technological needs regarding access, training and support for faculty and conduct studies to support the local needs of instructional methods and content delivery. Based on these needs, in the next sub-section, we provide some recommendations.

RECOMMENDATIONS

This study examined Nigerian teacher educators' access, use, and comfort levels with instructional and web-based technologies for teaching, as well as describing efforts by government, policymakers, and stakeholders in education to bring Nigerian education into the global information society. Based on findings from this study, we suggest that researchers in Nigeria and sub-Saharan Africa consider the following as directions for future research:

1. Researchers in Nigeria could replicate this study with a sample that includes all colleges across all six geopolitical regions.
2. Researchers should focus on the state of technology use in Nigeria. The specific focus could be placed on educators' technology needs and how to provide those services to them across campuses.
3. Researchers in sub-Saharan African countries could also replicate this study. This will deepen our understanding of the level of access and use of technology in the context of teacher preparation programs across the region and serve as a source of empirical findings across sub-Saharan Africa.
4. There is a need for educational researchers, educators, and policymakers in sub-Saharan Africa to look into information and communication for development (ICT4D) and design a development plan for this region for a specific time period. This could take the form of a task force that will identify the most desirable ICT tools for twenty-first century learning, and work to provide them across all tiers of education, as well as to provide adequate training for educators to develop their competencies for effective ICT integration.

CONCLUSION

There is the critical need for technology integration in all tiers of society, including education. According to Castro- Sanchez, and Aleman (2011) technology can transform teaching and learning into learner-centric environments. Educator ability to use technology for teaching and learning will enable students' mastery of twenty-first century skills and increase their relevance in the global information communication technology (ICT) society. Findings presented in this chapter have shown that Nigeria has made progress in technology access in schools-tertiary institution, and that educators report being comfortable with the ICTs they have for teaching and learning. The literature itemizes efforts put forward by Nigerian government and stakeholders in education to improve the state of ICT resources in the field of education. They include, the Nigerian Universities Network (NuNet), Polytechnics Network (PolyNet), SchoolNet, National Open University of Nigeria (NOUN), National Virtual (Digital) Library (NUC), Nigerian Education Academic and Research Network (NEARNet), Teachers Network (Teach Net), National Virtual Library (Ministry of Science and Technology), and National Information Communication and Education program of the Presidency. However, this progress is not substantial. There is need for stable high-speed Internet connectivity across all tiers of education-primary, secondary and tertiary because educators and students need the Internet to access abundant resources from around the world The recommendations above are meant to aid educators and stakeholders to plan for growth in educational ICT. We also hope that future research will benefit Nigeria and other countries throughout sub-Saharan Africa.

REFERENCES

Acılar, A. (2011). Exploring the aspects of digital divide in a developing country. *Issues in Informing Science & Information Technology*, 8, 231–244. doi:10.28945/1415

Ajayi, I. A., & Ekundayo, H. T. (2009). The application of information and communication technology in Nigerian secondary schools. *International NGO Journal*, 4(5), 281–286. http://citeseerx.ist.psu.edu/viewdoc/download?doi=10.1.1.933.9342&rep=rep1&type=pdf

Ajegbelen, A. J. (2016). Impact of education trust fund (ETF) on tertiary institutions in Nigeria, using college of education as a case study. *Journal of Research & Method in Education*, 6(3), 18–25. http://www.iosrjournals.org/iosr-jrme/papers/Vol-6%20Issue-3/Version-2/C0603021825.pdf

Ajoku, L. I. (2014). The place of ICT in teacher preparation and climate change curriculum at the tertiary education level in Nigeria. *Journal of Education and Practice*, 5(13), 2014185. https://www.iiste.org/Journals/index.php/JEP/article/view/12763/13072

Alwehaibi, H. O. (2015). The impact of using YouTube in EFL classroom on enhancing EFL students' content learning. *Journal of College Teaching and Learning*, 12(2), 121–126. doi:10.19030/tlc.v12i2.9182

Apagu, V. V., & Wakili, B. A. (2015). Availability and utilization of ICT facilities for teaching and learning of vocational and technical education in Yobe State Technical Colleges. *American Journal of Engineering Research*, 4(2), 113–118.

Blackwell, C. K., Lauricella, A. R., Wartella, E., Robb, M., & Schomburg, R. (2013). Adoption and use of technology in early education: The interplay of extrinsic barriers and teacher attitudes. *Computers & Education*, 69, 310–319. doi:10.1016/j.compedu.2013.07.024

Buchanan, T., Sainter, P., & Saunders, G. J. (2013). Factors affecting faculty use of learning technologies: Implications for models of technology adoption. *Journal of Computing in Higher Education*, 25(1), 1–11. doi:10.100712528-013-9066-6

Buhari Approves N161bn for 2019 TETFund. (2019, January 4). Retrieved from https://punchng.com/buhari-approves-n161bn-for-2019-tetfund-interventions-in-varsities-others/

Bushweller, G. (2017, June 12). Classroom technology: Where schools stand. *Education Week*. Retrieved from https://www.edweek.org/ew/articles/2017/06/14/tracking-20-years-of-change-in-ed-tech.html?intc=EW-TC17-TOC

Castro Sánchez, J. J., & Alemán, E. C. (2011). Teachers' opinion survey on the use of ICT tools to support attendance-based teaching. *Journal Computers & Education*, 56(3), 911–915. doi:10.1016/j.compedu.2010.11.005

Creswell, J. W. (2012). *Educational research: Planning, conducting, and evaluating quantitative and qualitative research* (4th ed.). Pearson.

Cruz-Jesus, F., Oliveira, T., & Bacao, F. (2012). Digital divide across the European Union. *Information & Management*, 49(6), 278–291. doi:10.1016/j.im.2012.09.003

Ertmer, P. A., Ottenbreit-Leftwich, A. T., Sadik, O., Sendurur, E., & Sendurur, P. (2012). Teacher beliefs and technology integration practices: A critical relationship. *Computers & Education*, *59*(2), 423–435. doi:10.1016/j.compedu.2012.02.001

Fu, J. S. (2013). ICT in education: A critical literature review and its implications. *International Journal of Education and Development Using ICT*, *9*(1), 112–125. https://www.learntechlib.org/p/111900/

Gan, B., Menkhoff, T., & Smith, R. (2015). Enhancing students' learning process through interactive digital media: New opportunities for collaborative learning. *Computers in Human Behavior*, *51*, 652–663. doi:10.1016/j.chb.2014.12.048

Garba, S. A. (2014). Impact of ICT course on preservice teachers' acquisition of ICT literacy skills and competence in Nigeria. *International Journal of Modern Education Research*, *1*(2), 37–42. https://www.researchgate.net/profile/Sani_Garba2/publication/273593700_Impact_of_ICT_course_on_pre-service_teachers_acquisition_of_ICT_literacy_skills_and_competence_in_Nigeria/links/5506a9bb0cf24cee3a05c4b8/Impact-of-ICT-course-on-pre-service-teachers-acquisition-of-ICT-literacy-skills-and-competence-in-Nigeria.pdf

Garba, S. A., & Alademerin, C. A. (2014). Exploring the readiness of Nigerian colleges of education toward pre-service teacher preparation for technology integration. *International Journal of Technology & Inclusive Education*, *3*(2), 335–342. doi:10.20533/ijtie.2047.0533.2014.0043

Georgina, D. A., & Hosford, C. C. (2009). Higher education faculty perceptions on technology integration and training. *Teaching and Teacher Education*, *25*(5), 690–696. doi:10.1016/j.tate.2008.11.004

Hassad, R. A. (2013). Faculty attitude towards technology-assisted Instruction for introductory statistics in the context of educational reform. *Technology Innovations in Statistics Education, 7*(2). Retrieved from https://escholarship.org/dist/wJD5zTgC2vrImRR/dist/prd/content/qt9k19k2f7/qt9k19k2f7.pdf

Howley, A., Wood, L., & Hough, B. (2011). Rural elementary school teachers' technology integration. *Journal of Research in Rural Education (Online)*, *26*(9), 1–14. https://jrre.psu.edu/articles/26-9.pdf

Ibrahim, A. (2019). Faculty access, attitudes, and use of instructional and web-based technologies in Nigeria's teacher preparation program: A mixed method study. *Theses and Dissertation (All)*. 1743. Retrieved from https://knowledge.library.iup.edu/etd/1743

Idowu, A. I., & Esere, M. (2013). ICT and higher educational system in Nigeria. *Educational Research Review*, *8*(21), 2021–2025. doi:10.5897/ERR09.044

Jaschik, S., & Lederman, D. (2018) 2018 survey of faculty attitudes on technology: A survey by inside Higher Ed and Gallup. *Inside Higher Ed Report*. Retrieved from https://mediasite.com/wp-content/uploads/2018/11/2018-Faculty-Survey-Mediasite.pdf

Jude, W. I., & Dankaro, J. T. (2012). ICT resource utilization, availability and accessibility by teacher educators for instructional development in College of Education Katsina-Ala. *New Media & Mass Communication, 3*, 1-6. Retrieved from https://www.iiste.org/Journals/index.php/NMMC/article/view/1766/1719

Marzilli, C., Delello, J., Marmion, S., McWhorter, R., Roberts, P., & Marzilli, T. S. (2014). Faculty attitudes towards integrating technology and innovation. *International Journal on Integrating Technology in Education*, *3*(1), 1–20. doi:10.5121/ijite.2014.3101

Matthew, D., Joro, I. D., & Manasseh, H. (2015). The role of information communication technology in Nigeria educational system. *International Journal of Research in Humanities and Social Studies*, *2*(2). http://www.ijrhss.org/pdf/v2-i2/8.pdf

Mehdi, H. S., & Al-Dera, A. S. (2013). The impact teachers' age, gender, and experience in the use of information and communication technology in EFL teaching. *English Language Teaching*, *6*(6), 57–67. doi:10.5539/elt.v6n6p57

Morley, G. (2011). Primary teachers and ICT: Is gender, age or experience important? *Systematics, Cybernetics, &. Informatics (MDPI)*, *9*(7), 5–9. doi:10.1504/ijiome.2010.034636

National Commission for Colleges of Education. (2016). *Colleges of education in Nigeria*. Retrieved from http://www.ncceonline.edu.ng

National Universities Commission. (2019). *Universities in Nigeria*. Retrieved from https://nuc.edu.ng/nigerian-univerisities/federal-univeristies/

Onwuagboke, B. B. C., & Singh, T. K. R. (2016). Faculty attitude and use of ICT in instructional delivery in tertiary institutions in a developing nation. *International Journal of Research Studies in Educational Technology*, *5*(1), 77–88. doi:10.5861/ijrset.2016.1428

Onwuagboke, B. B. C., Singh, T. K. R., & Fook, F. S. (2015). Need for ICT integration for effective instructional delivery in Nigerian colleges of education. *Journal of Education and Practice*, *6*(3), 51–56. https://files.eric.ed.gov/fulltext/EJ1083763.pdf

Onyia, C. R., & Onyia, M. (2011). Faculty perception for technology integration in Nigeria university system: Implication for faculty quality curriculum design. *International Journal of Business and Social Science*, *2*(12), 81–92. http://www.ijbssnet.com/journals/Vol._2_No._12%3B_July_2011/10.pdf

Owolabi, T. O., Oyewole, B. K., & Oke, J. O. (2013). Teacher education, information and communication technology: Prospects and challenges of e-teaching profession in Nigeria. *American Journal of Humanities & Social Sciences*, *1*(2), 87–91. doi:10.11634/232907811301314

Pew Research Center. (2018). *Social media use continues to rise in developing countries but plateaus across developing once*. Retrieved from http://assets.pewresearch.org/wp-content/uploads/sites/2/2018/06/15135408/Pew-Research-Center_Global-Tech-Social-Media-Use_2018.06.19.pdf

Pittman, T., & Gaines, T. (2015). Technology integration in third, fourth and fifth grade classrooms in a Florida school district. *Educational Technology Research and Development*, *63*(4), 539–554. doi:10.100711423-015-9391-8

Saldana, J. (2016). *The coding manual for qualitative researchers*. Sage.

Salkind, N. J. (Ed.). (2010). *Encyclopedia of research design* (Vol. 1). Sage. doi:10.4135/9781412961288

Saxena, A. (2017). Issues and impediments faced by Canadian teachers while integrating ICT in pedagogical practice. *The Turkish Journal of Educational Technology*, *16*(2), 58–70. https://files.eric.ed.gov/fulltext/EJ1137791.pdf

Strayhorn, T. L. (2007). Use of technology among higher education faculty members: Implications for innovative practice. *Student Affairs On-Line, 8*(2). Retrieved from https://www.studentaffairs.com/Customer-Content/www/CMS/files/Journal/Technology-Use-By-Faculty.pdf

Subedi, D. (2016). Explanatory sequential mixed method design as the third research community of knowledge claim. *American Journal of Educational Research*, *4*(7), 570–577.

TETFund. (2016). *ICT support intervention.* Retrieved from https://www.tetfund.gov.ng/index.php/component/search/#?Itemid=265

Thaiposri, P., & Wannapiroon, P. (2015). Enhancing students' critical thinking skills through teaching and learning by inquiry-based learning activities using social network and cloud computing. *Procedia: Social and Behavioral Sciences*, *174*, 2137–2144. doi:10.1016/j.sbspro.2015.02.013

Thomas, S. (2016). *Future ready learning: Reimagining the role of technology in education. 2016 National Education Technology Plan.* Office of Educational Technology, US Department of Education. Retrieved from https://tech.ed.gov/files/2017/01/NETP17.pdf

Udu, L. E., & Nkwede, J. O. (2014). Tertiary education trust fund interventions and sustainable development in Nigerian Universities: Evidence from Ebonyi State University, Abakaliki. *Journal of Sustainable Development*, *7*(4), 191. doi:10.5539/jsd.v7n4p191

UNESCO. (2015). *Digital services for education in Africa.* Retrieved from https://unesdoc.unesco.org/in/documentViewer.xhtml?v=2.1.196&id=p:usmarcdef_0000231867&file=/in/rest/annotationSVC/DownloadWatermarkedAttachment/attach_import_2b9960eb-b645-43cc-8b97-bfb7441a3dc0%3F_%3D231867eng.pdf&updateUrl=updateUrl3227&ark=/ark:/48223/pf0000231867/PDF/231867eng.pdf.multi&fullScreen=true&locale=en#%5B%7B%22num%22%3A83%2C%22gen%22%3A0%7D%2C%7B%22name%22%3A%22XYZ%22%7D%2Cnull%2Cnull%2C0%5D

KEY TERMS AND DEFINITION

Empowering Educators: This is the government and stakeholders' efforts to provided enormous access to technology and Internet across all tiers of education.

Instructional Technology: Any technology tool that is used for the purpose of teaching and learning, being it a communication or collaboration tool.

Sub-Saharan Africa: A geographic region in African continent that comprised of 46 countries. Countries within this region differ in their rich and diverse cultural heritage.

Teacher Education: A training undertaken by a preservice teacher that leads to obtaining teaching certification.

Teacher Preparation Programs: A specific area in teacher education where a teacher candidate gets certified. For example, English Education, Secondary Math Education, Early Childhood Education/Special Education, etc.

Technology Access: Availability of instructional and web-based technologies in an educational institution.

Technology Integration: The effective use of technology tool to enhance teaching and learning.

Web-Based Technologies: Any technology tools that can only be accessed on the internet and used for teaching and learning. It can be a website or a web-based tool (Web 2.0).

Chapter 10
Web 2.0 Technology in Libraries:
A Case Study of Engineering PG Student Preferences at Mekelle University, Ethiopia

Prakash Bhagwan Dongardive
University of Mekelle, Ethiopia

ABSTRACT

Progress in information communication technology (ICT) has become the backbone for every branch of knowledge in academic arena and library, and information centers are not apart from it. Social networking is playing a significant role in serving to the library users. The chapter examines libraries and their importance in accepting the Web 2.0 phenomenon of social networking sites like Facebook Twitter, YouTube, and a number of social networking tools to enable libraries to engage with students in the virtual environment to promote library event and services, teaching and learning, and humanizing the concept of library and librarians. This chapter also focuses on the importance of social networking sites, which improve the professional relationships within the library profession and across the boundaries of particular national library education systems across the world, which is increasingly sharing information that ensures libraries are the head of changes in demands and needs of their users.

INTRODUCTION

Web 2.0 is a term given to describe the second generation of World Wide Web, which focused on the ability to collaborate and share information online among the people. Web 2.0 basically refers to the transition from static HTML web pages to a more dynamic web which is more organized and is based on serving web applications for users. Other improved functionality of Web 2.0 includes open communication with an emphasis on web based communities of users and more open sharing of information. Graham, Paul (2005). People create their online profile on web 2.0 sites with biographical data, pictures, like, dislike and any other information they choose to post. The user can communicate with each other

DOI: 10.4018/978-1-7998-3468-7.ch010

by text, voice, chat, instant massages, video conferences, blogs which provide a way to the registered member for contact friends and permitting them to grow their network. The traditional SNS include; Bebo, blogs, Delicious, portfolios, face book, Friendster, Instant messenger, LinkedIn, Micro blogs, My space, Orkut, Podcasts, RSS, Social book marking, Twitter, wikis, You tube, etc. These Web 2.0 websites permit users to interact and collaborate with each other. This technology can be used in libraries to interact between users and library professionals for provision of fast library services. Richardson, Will (2009).

BACKGROUND OF THE STUDY

Social Networking Technologies and its inferences for transforming the library services through the web; Information literacy through web 2.0 integrated web OPAC: an experiment at Jaypee group of Institutes applications of web 2.0 the second generation of internet has become one of the fastest growing communication technology and being adopted by corporate and service sector. It is same in the case of library and information science services centers. Increasing popularity of web 2.0 technology provides a prime opportunity to engage patrons in the virtual age. It attracts the user to communicate with similar interest people through networking and present numerous of resources and information in the form of multimedia, blogging, tagging, and bookmarking, messaging and social networking. The primary objectives of this papers were to explore the concept of social search evaluate the performance of social networking tools and to understand the relationship between SNS and social search. The author intends to examine the possible social networking sites or tools present as the feature of online search and the implication for libraries.

SOCIAL NETWORKING

History of Social Networking

As a social networking tool Friendster was the first online social networking site. It was quickly followed one year later by MySpace. Two young friends started myspace, and it quickly becomes hugely popular. Its parent company, Intermix, was acquired by News Corporation for $580 million just after two years of its launch. Thus next face book in 2004, which initially followed by college students but now millions of people of all the age using it as a primary SNS to interface each other, as well as there, are some social networking sites are available online.

Defining Social Networking

A social networking is a network of people useful to create similar interests about any product, services and sharing it among the group. Every new user has to create his profile on social networking site and to create his/her own social link for getting number of service information for instance; career services, educational services, sport etc. Social networking is an effective mechanism for advertising and making publicity of any company product. It is convenient to send multimedia message and attract the user to the product via social networking tools on user mobile. Here internet and mobile technology playing important role.

Facilities of SNS

It is the most hopeful and accepted technology and networking as well as a social network itself, SNS allow users following services; (1) To interact but to share and change resources dynamically in an electronic medium, enable the user to create accounts with the library network. (2) Perceive what other users have in common to their information needs, recommended resources to one another and the system recommended resources to the user based on the similar profile. (3) Previously accessed sources and a host of data that user provides, enable the user to choose what is public and what is private that could help to avoid the privacy issues which Lib 2.0 raises. (4) Social networking enables the user to catalogue their books and view what other users share those books. (5) Social networking enables the users to recommended books to one another simply by viewing one another collection online. (6) SNS also allow users to communicate asynchronously; for instance, Asynchronous learning, a student-centered teaching method that uses online learning resources to facilitate information sharing outside the constraints of time and place among a network of people like the blog and tag as their source of information.

Types of Social Networks

Types of Social networking based on peoples need and objectives. Social networks exist in many areas for instance; organizations, geographical and social boundaries etc. Malaiya, Ritesh (2012)

The major types of social networks are given below:

1. **Social Contact Networks:** SCN are formed to keep contact with friends and family and are one of the most popular sites on the web today. It has all the components of Web 2.0 like blogging, tagging, wikis, and forums. Examples of these include Orkut, Face book, and Twitter.
2. **Study Circles:** These are social networks dedicated for students where they can have areas devoted to student education topics, placement related queries, and advanced research opportunity gathering. These have components like blogging and file sharing. Examples of these are Fledge Wing and College Tonight.
3. **Social Networks for Specialist Groups:** These types of social networks are specifically designed for core field workers like doctors, scientists, engineers, members of the corporate industries. A perfect example of this kind of network is LinkedIn.
4. **Systems for Fine Arts:** These types of social networks are dedicated to people connected with music, painting and related arts and have lots of useful networking information for all enthusiastic people of the same line.
5. **Police and Military Networks:** These types of networks are not on a public domain, these networks on a private sphere due to the confidentiality of information.
6. **Sporting Networks:** These types of social networks are dedicated to people of the sporting fraternity and have a scope of information related to this field.
7. **Mixed Networks:** Some social networks have a subscription of individuals from all the above groups and are heterogeneous social networks serving multiple types of social collaboration.
8. **Social Networks for the Inventors:** These are the social networks for the people who have invented the concept of social networks, the very developers, and architects that have developed the social networks.

Figure 1. Various social networks

9. **Shopping and Utility Service Networks:** The present world of vast consumerism has triggered people to invest in social networks which will try to analyze the social behavior and send related information for the same to respective marts and stores.
10. **Others:** Other social networks serve a huge number of the internet population in various ways. Some of these networks pass away very fast due to lack of constructive sustenance thoughts while others finally migrate to a more specialist system as shown above.

WEB 2.0 TOOLS

Blogging

A blog is an informational website published on the World Wide Web consisting of separate, often informal diary style text entries or posts. Posts are typically displayed in reverse chronological order, so that the most recent post appears first, at the top of the web page. Until 2009, blogs were usually the work of a single individual. Occasionally of a small group, and often covered a single subject or topic. In the 2010s, "multi-author blogs" have developed, with posts written by large numbers of authors and sometimes professionally edited. Blood and Rebecca (2000).

Podcasts

A Podcast is audio video) file. A podcaster solicit subscriptions from listeners, so that, when new podcasts are released, they are automatically delivered to a subscriber's computer or mobile device. The podcast features an audio show with new episodes that are served to the application at planned intervals, such as daily or weekly. Its format encourages listeners to subscribe and if you want to subscribe to a podcast "feed," you'll need to install podcatcher software on your computer. The most popular podcatcher software is iTunes. Millions of podcasts are currently available for free, and thousands of new podcasts are created every day. Joshua Stern (2015)

Social Networking

Social networking features provide a convenient platform to create a group of same preferences about any tool, product or services. Register users on the social networking sites create their online profile page with biographical data, pictures, likes, dislikes and any other information what they choose to post, these users can communicate with each other by text, voice, chat, instant message, videoconference, and blogs, and the services typically provide a way to contact friends of other users. Thus, millions and billions of people have joined one or more social networking sites. The most popular social networking Websites include: (1) MySpace (2) Face book (3) Friendster (4) LinkedIn etc.

Wikis

A wiki is a website on which users collaboratively modify content and structure directly from the web browser. In other words, wiki is a page or collection of Web pages designed to enable anyone who accesses them to contribute or modify the content quickly. A wiki engine is a type of content management system, wikis have little implicit structure, allowing structure to emerge according to the needs of the users. Wikis are used in business to provide intranets and knowledge management systems. Also wikis are used in education to allow students to co-create documents and research (co-citation, doc. proximity). Mitchell, Scott (2008).

EPortfolios

E-portfolio is a collection of electronic evidence assembled and managed by a user, usually on the Web. Such electronic evidence may include input text, electronic files, images, multimedia, blog entries, and hyperlinks. E-portfolios are both demonstrations of the user's abilities and platforms for self-expression. If they are online, users can maintain them dynamically over time. E-Portfolios can include a broad range of information and content for example: (i) Personal information (ii) Education history (iii) Recognition; awards and certificates (iv) Reflective comments (v) Coursework; assignment, projects (vi) Instructor comments (vii) Previous employer comments (viii) Goals, plans (ix) Personal values and interests (x) Presentations, papers, other work (xi) Personal activities; volunteer work, professional development. E-portfolios, like traditional portfolios, can facilitate students' reflection on their own learning, leading to more awareness of learning strategies and needs. Zimmerman, Eilene (2012)

Micro-Blogging

Microblogs allow users to exchange small elements of content such as short sentences, individual images, and audio-video links. Microblogging is a combination of blogging and instant messaging that allows registered users to create short messages to be posted and shared with an audience online. Especially on the mobile technology 'Twitter' has become very famous around the world as a new type of blogging software. Here users read microblog posts online or request that updates be delivered at the same time to their desktop as an instant message or sent to a mobile device as a SMS text message. Kaplan Andreas M. and Haenlein Michael (2011)

Social Bookmarking

Social bookmarking is a centralized online service which allows users to add, interpret, edit, and share bookmarks of online documents. Here users save links to web pages what they like or want to share, using a social bookmarking site to store these links. These bookmarks are usually public, and it can be viewed by other members of the site where they are stored. Examples of social bookmarking sites include; Delicious, Evernote, Pinterest, Bitly etc. Noll, Michael G. and Meinel, Christoph (2007)

LITERATURE REVIEWS

Luo, (2010) 'Social Networking websites: An exploratory study of student peer socializing in an online LIS program.' He presented a study a survey study investigating how students in an online MLIS program use social networking websites to socialize with their peers and to develop a professional network. Both general purpose social networking sites such as face book and a school wide social networking sites are studied. His finding indicates that social networking websites are the second most popular venue for student's peer socializing and are considered a productive channel for establishing social networks among students. However, the lacks of the time and the vast variety of social networking website choices have hindered student's engagement in social networking sites. In response to these roadblocks, the study proposes several initiatives that online LIS programs can make to streamline the process of involving social networking websites in community building efforts.

A. Click (2010) 'social networking and web 2.0 in information literacy. In this paper, he has discussed free online and internet tools that can be adapted by librarians for use with library instruction and information literacy training, with a focus on social media and web 2.0 technologies, including social networking website face book and Twitter, blogs, RSS, wikis, and video sharing. Many students already use this technology and are readily engaged with the library when the technology is incorporated into library websites and classes. There are challenges in using this technology, especially in countries with the tyrannical government this review is based, in part, on a presentation the author gave at the UNESCO training the trainers in the information literacy work shop at the bibliotheca Alexandrina, Egypt in November 2008.

Chua and Alton (2010) 'A study of web 2.0 applications in library websites' He states that web 2.0 represents and emerging suite of applications that hold enormous potential in enriching communication, enabling collaboration and fostering innovation. However, little work has been done previously to research web 2.0 applications in library websites. This paper addresses the following three research questions: (a) to what extent are web 2.0 applications prevalent in libraries? (b) In what ways have web 2.0 application been used in libraries? (c) Does the presence of web 2.0 applications enhance the quality of library websites? Divided equally between public and academic, 120 libraries web sites from North America, Europe, and Asia were sampled and analyzed using a three step content analysis method. The finding suggests that the order of popularity of web 2.0 applications implemented in libraries is: Blogs, RSS, instant messaging, social networking sites, wikis, and social tagging applications. Also, libraries have recognized how different web 2.0 applications can be used complementarily to increase the level of user engagement. Finally, the presences of web 2.0 applications were found to be associated with the overall quality, and in particular, service quality of library websites. This paper concludes by highlighting implications for both librarians and scholars interested in investigating deeper into the implementation of web 2.0 applications.

Aharony (2010) ' Twitter Use in libraries: An exploratory analysis' Aharony states that the micro blogging is a relatively new phenomenon in online social networking that has become increasing common for the last few years. This study explores the use of twitter in public and academic libraries to understand micro blogging patterns. Analysis of the tweets was concluded in two phases: descriptive statistical analysis and content analysis. The research finding shows that there are some differences between public and academic libraries including the number of tweets, linguistic differences and materials, states, and professional interests. The research findings are relevant for librarians and information scientists who wish to understand better and explore the phenomenon of library tweet.

OBJECTIVES OF THE STUDY

1. To explore how social networking can be used in libraries.
2. To access the information seeking behavior of users in the online era.
3. To evaluate the internet usage pattern of the users at different levels.
4. To undertake the comprehensive analysis of the objectives above mentioned.

SCOPE OF THE STUDY

The study attempts to understand the information seeking behavior and internet usage pattern by the students at Mekelle University Ethiopia. The study is based on engineering PG students at EIT, Mekelle University. The research has been carried out to understand the features of social networking in the context of libraries, which shows the social networking has gained the popularity over the years.

LIMITATION OF THE STUDY

Due to the wide spread, this study is restricted to only Engineering PG students at [EIT] Ethiopian Technical Institute, Mekelle University, Ethiopia as a case study. Therefore, the extent to which the findings of this study meet the need of all others departments, Colleges and Institutions at all the Ethiopian Universities are the limitation of this study.

STATEMENT OF THE PROBLEM

Use of Web 2.0 technology in libraries offers opportunities to obtain accurate and timely literature, as well as creating same preferences groups of peoples to sharing information, the fast transition of library services in users hand through the combination of mobile technology and web 2.0 technologies. Pilot survey observation shows that there was a high preference to use SNS among engineering PG students at Mekelle University and this was evidenced by informal meeting and interviews with Information Science students and their observation. Nonuse of SNS (web 2.0) was cited as a challenge to user satisfactions and library image.

RESEARCH QUESTIONS

(1) Do Engineering PG students have computer literacy to use web 2.0 technology? (2) Do Engineering PG students have awareness about Social Networking and Web 2.0 technology? (3) Do Engineering PG students prefer to visit frequently to social networking sites [SNS]? (4) Do there any registered social networking sites [SNS] which Engineering PG students prefer to use? (5) Do the Engineering PG students have any purpose of using social networking? (6) Do Engineering PG students have any preferred general search engine to access SNS? (7) Do Engineering PG students have created their blogs? (8) Do Engineering PG students have preferred frequency to updating blogs? (9) Does Mekelle University Libraries create library blogs for user feedback? (10) Do the SNS being used in Mekelle University Libraries services? (11) Do Engineering PG students prefer to access MU library services through SNS? (12) Do Engineering PG students want to join the library community through SNS?

ASSUMPTION OF THE STUDY

1. The use of advanced technology for instance; web 2.0 technology, ICT and Mobile technology can help libraries and its users to obtain their needed information quick and create same preference group peoples for sharing information and understanding information needs.
2. Advanced technology can change the image of libraries in the society.

RESEARCH METHODOLOGY

Research Design

The descriptive survey method has adopted because it seeks to explore the preferences of using social networking [web 2.0] by Engineering PG students at Mekelle University libraries. The data have been collected for information about the preferences about SNS social networking sites by Engineering PG students, students at Mekelle University libraries.

Population of the Study:

The estimated population for this study was 263 respondents drawn from Engineering PG students, EIT, Mekelle University, Ethiopia. The breakdown of the faculty population is as illustrated in table 1 below.

Table 1. Showing the year wise population breakdown for the study

EIT Departments	Population	Percentage population
Architecture and Urban Planning	23	8.74%
Chemical Engineering	00	0%
Civil Engineering	74	28.13%
Computing Engineering	56	21.29%
Electrical and Computer Engineering	33	12.54%
Industrial Engineering	40	15.20%
Mechanical Engineering	37	14.06%
Total	263	100%

Sample and Sampling Technique

Due to the small number of respondents involved the entire 263 populations have been used as the sample for the study and Snowball sampling has been used for the present study.

Research Instrument

The questionnaire titled Web 2.0 Technology in Libraries: A Case Study of Engineering PG Student's Preferences at Mekelle University, Ethiopia. Surveys have been used as the data collection instrument for this study. The surveys have provided data on students' preferences about using social networking in Mekelle University library services. It is aimed at answering questions on; the level of computer skills, preferences of social networking sites to use, library services like to access through social networking sites by the Engineering PG students from EIT, Mekelle University

Method of Data Collection

The questionnaires were sent out to the Engineering PG students at EIT, Mekelle University. The researcher employed the service of research assistants to administer the survey one-on-one to the faculties, and their response collected immediately. This method has been preferred to achieve a high response rate.

Method of Data Analysis

The simple percentage method has been adopted for calculation of the result. The result has been presented in the tabular and the frequencies of respondents were used to calculate the percentage of items 3-10 and 13- 16. The rates have been computed by using the following formula of Kothari, C.R. (2004).

$$N = \frac{X}{Y} \times \frac{100}{1}$$

$$\frac{\text{Number of Responses}}{\text{Total number of Responses}} \times \frac{100}{1}$$

Where N=simple percentage, x= Number of Responses, Y= total number of Responses, while the lickert method of, strongly agree"

Mekelle University Libraries a Profile

Mekelle University is found in the town of Mekelle in Tigray region of Northern Ethiopia, at a distance of 783 Kilometers from the Ethiopian capital. The merger of the two former colleges: Mekelle Business College and Mekelle University College established the University in May 2000 by the Government of Ethiopia (Council of Ministers, Regulations No. 61/1999 of Article 3) as an autonomous higher education institution. There are 6 Campuses at Mekelle university; Endayesus (Main Campus), Adihaki, Ayder, Kalamino, Aynalem and Quiha among this there are 7 Colleges, 8 Institutes, and 2 Schools, 1739 full-time Academic staff members, 26747 undergraduate students and 2052 graduate students. There are six university libraries established at different six campuses such as Endayesus (Main Campus), Adihaki, Ayder, Kalamino, Aynalem and Quiha. The Main Circulating collection refers to all publications that are found in the MU Library. DDC call numbers arrange all Circulation Books from 000-999. MU library has Institutional Repositories in which publications produced by MU community will be posted and accessed by users through the digital library system. Libraries provide the available library materials in print and electronic formats just in time based on user request and to serve the informational, educational and intellectual needs of MU's community. Circulation units at six libraries strive to offer fast, free and fair Library service as well as provide full access to Library materials for people with disabilities. Besides, the unit also provides a loan (short and long), reservation and document delivery services to users. Moreover, the unit provides fast and user friendly online service through which user check circulation information from their office and reserve, borrow as well as renew the material that they would like to use. The Library's mission is to provide comprehensive collections, quality services, and engaging spaces to support the education, research and community service mission of Mekelle University. The library promotes the development of self-learning and meets users' evolving needs and expectation through the provision of open access to cultural, intellectual, and informational resources both in print and digital format. The Library's physical and virtual spaces respond to the changing habits of its users to enrich the campus experience and to the dynamic information landscape in the 21st century.

DATA ANALYSIS AND INTERPRETATION

Figure 2. The gender ratio among engineering PG students

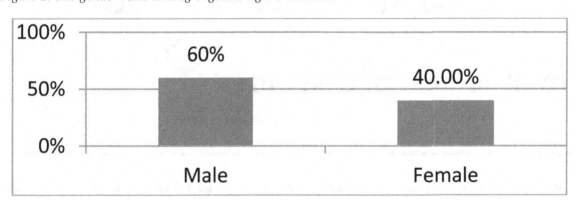

Data collected from the Engineering PG students by using questionnaires and a total of 263 questionnaires were distributed to respondents and were successfully retrieved giving a total 160 in a sense (100%) rate of return. Questionnaires were analyzed using frequency counts and simple percentage.

Research Question 1: What was the Gender Ratio Among Engineering PG Students?

The results of the analysis are presented in Figure 2

Figure 2 shows the perceived rate of gender among engineering PG EIT, Mekelle University. It was discovered that the majority 60% respondents were male and 40% were female among engineering PG students at EIT, MU.

Figure 3. Computer literacy ratio among engineering PG students

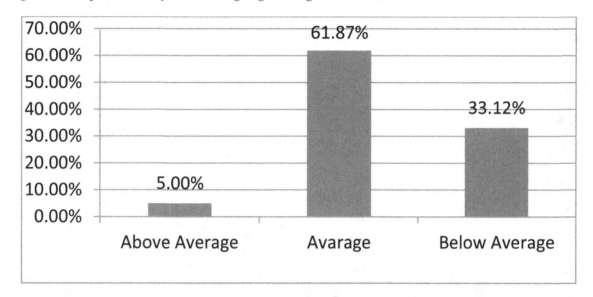

Research Question 2: What was the Level of Computer Literacy Among Engineering PG Students?

The results of the analysis are presented in Figure 3

Figure 4. Level of awareness about SNS or web 2.0

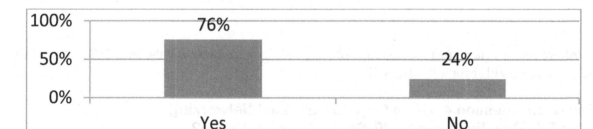

It was found that the majority 61.87% respondents had average computer literacy at EIT. It was also found that 33.12% students were having below average computer literacy and only 5% engineering PG students were having above average computer literacy at EIT, Mekelle University.

Research Question 3: What was the Level of Awareness About Social Networking or Web 2.0 Among Engineering PG Students?

The results of the analysis are presented in Figure 4

Figure 5. Level of preference about SNS among engineering PG students

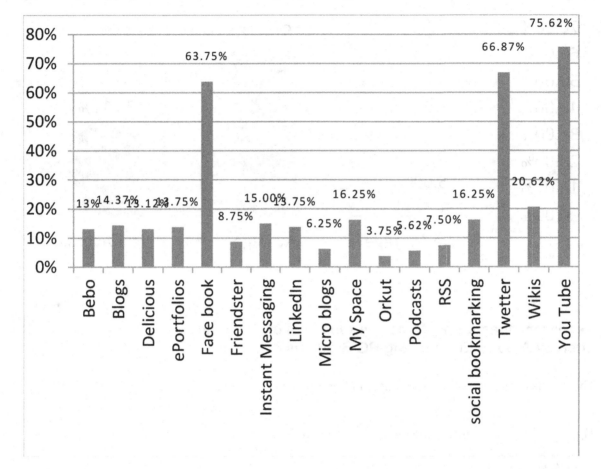

Above figure 4 shows that the majority 76% respondents were aware and the least 24% respondents were not aware still about web 2.0 at EIT.

Research Question 4: Witch Registered Social Networking Sites [SNS] do Engineering PG Students Prefer to use?

The results of the analysis are presented in Figure 5.

It was found that there are diversity preferences in using SNS [web 2.0] among engineering PG students. The above figure shows that the majority of 75.62%, 66.87% and 63.75% respondents were preferred you tube, Twitter, and Face book respectively. It was also discovered that the same majority of 16.25%, 13.75% and 13.12% respondents were preferred My Space, social book marking; e-portfolios, LinkedIn; Bebo, Delicious respectively. It was also found that 20.62%, 15%, 14.37%, 8.75% respondents preferred to use the wiki, Instance Massaging, Blogs, Friendster as web 2.0 tools respectively. The least 7.5%, 6.25%, 5.62% and 3.75% respondents were preferred to use RSS [gorgeous site summery], micro blogs, podcast, Orkut respectively.

Figure 6. Level of preferences to use SNS among 'engineering PG' students

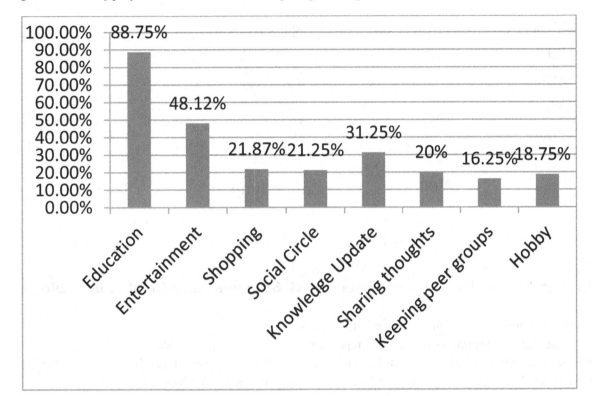

Research Question 5: What Purpose do the Engineering PG Students Prefer to use Social Networking?

The results of the analysis is presented in Figure 6

It was found that there was a diversity of preferences about web 2.0; below figure shows, the majority of 88.75% respondents were preferred web 2.0 for education purpose. It was also discovered that 48.12%, 31.25%, 21.87% and 21.25% respondents were preferred web 2.0 tools for entertainment, knowledge update, shopping, and social circles respectively. The least 20%, 18.75% and 16.25% respondents were preferred web 2.0 tools to share a thought, hobby and keeping peer groups respectively.

Research Question 6: What was the Level of Frequency to Visit Social Networking Sites [SNS] Preferred by Engineering PG Students at Mekelle University?

The results of the analysis are presented in Figure 7.

According to the responses of Engineering PG students at EIT Mekelle University, It was found that the majority 81.87% students preferred to visit social networking site 'some time,' and the least 13.75% and 4.37% engineering PG student marked for often and rarely visit SNS.

Figure 7. The level of preferred frequency to visit SNS

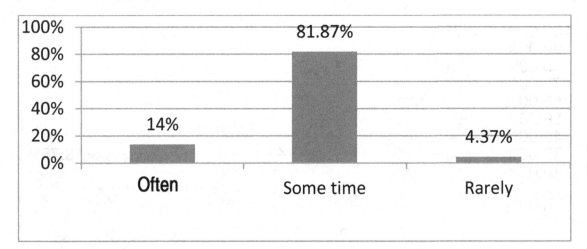

Research Question 7: Do Engineering PG' Students' have Created their Blogs?

The results of the analysis are presented in Figure 8.

Blogs are an essential online personal repository to create same preferences people groups to getting feedback and improvement as well as knowledge update. It was discovered that the 38.12% respondents were created their blogs and only 16.87% respondents were not created blogs.

Research Questions 8: What was the Level of Frequency to Update Blogs Among Engineering PG Students at EIT, Mekelle University?

The result of the analysis is presented in Figure 9.

Figure 8. Ratio of 'Engineering PG' students creating their blogs

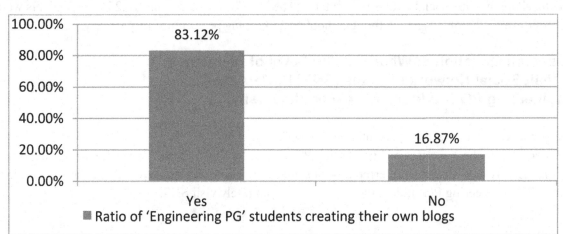

Figure 9. Level of frequency to update blog

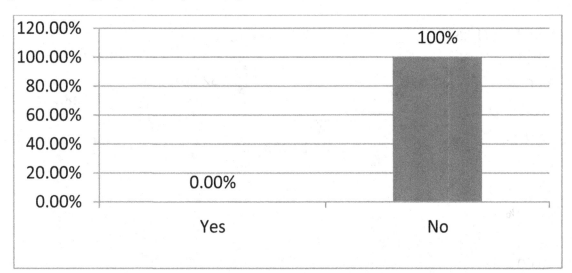

It was found that the majority 81.87% respondents were updating their blogs 'some time,' 13.75% were updating 'often, ' and the least 4.37% respondents were marked for 'rarely' to visiting the site and updating the blogs.

Research Questions 9: Does Mekelle University Libraries Created Library Blogs for user Feedback?

The result of the analysis is presented in Figure 10.

It was discovered that the majority 100% respondents were marked that, Mekelle University libraries were not using blogs to provide library services. Thus it was observed that 'engineering PG' students want blogs for pasting their feedback library service but MU libraries still not using blogs as a web 2.0 technology tool to provide services to their users.

Figure 10. Use of blogs in MU library services

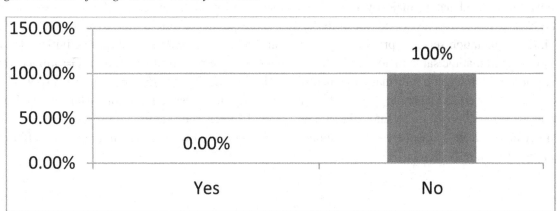

Figure 11. Use of web 2.0 Technologies in Mekelle University library services

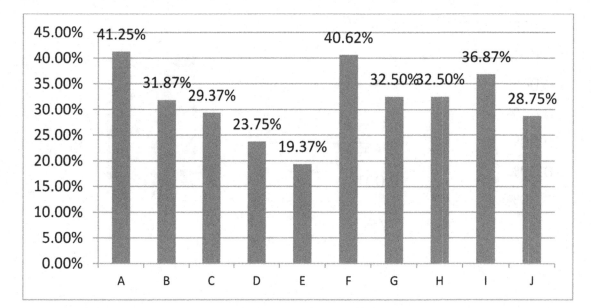

Research Question 10: Does the Mekelle University Libraries use Web 2.0 Technologies for Provision of Library Services?

The results of the analysis are presented in Figure 11.

It was discovered that the majority 100% respondents were marked that, Mekelle University libraries were not using blogs to provide library services. Thus it was observed that 'engineering PG' students want to use web 2.0 for giving their feedback about library service but MU libraries still not using blogs as a web 2.0 technology tool to provide services to their users.

Research Question 11: Which Services do you Prefer to Access Through SNS from Mekelle University Libraries?

The results of the analysis is presented in Figure 12.

It was discovered that the majority 41.25% respondents prefer to use web 2.0 for A= book reservation in the library. It was also found that the 40.62%, 36.87% respondents were preferred to use web 2.0 for F= library orientation services provided by library staff and I= reminders of library activities. It was also discovered that the same majority 32.50% respondents were preferred web 2.0 for G= library tour video and H= membership information respectively. 31.87%, 29.37%, 28.75% and 23.75% respondents were preferred web 2.0 technology for different library services respectively for instance; B= CAS current awareness services, C= Inter library link, J= SDI selective dissemination of information, and D= inter library loan. The least 19.37% respondents have preferred web 2.0 technology for E= library discussion forum respectively.

Figure 12.

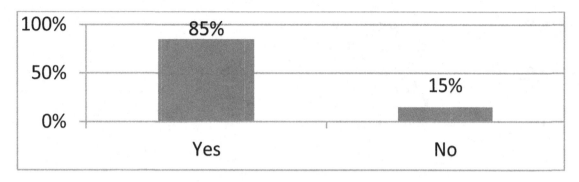

Research Question 12: Do 'Engineering PG Students' want to Join the Library Community Through Web 2.0 Technology?

The results of the analysis is presented in Figure 14.

It was invented that, the majority 85% students prefer to join library community through web 2.0 technology and the least 15% respondents were not preferred to join library community through web 2.0 technology.

Figure 13. Ratio of preferred library services access through SNS among engineering students

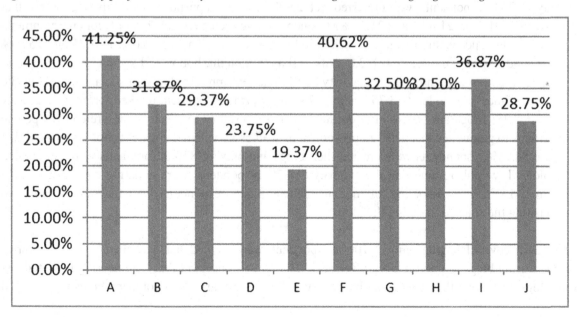

Figure 14. The ratio of preferences to join the library community through SNS

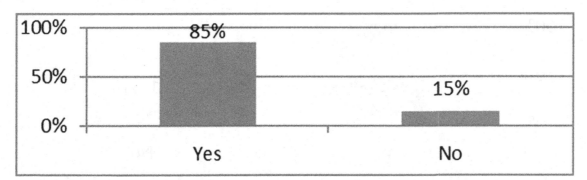

MAJOR FINDINGS

1. It was discovered that the majority 60% respondents were male and 40% were female among engineering PG students at EIT, MU. 61.87% respondents were having average computer literacy and 33.12% students were having below average computer literacy. The least 5% engineering PG students were having above average computer literacy. 76% respondents were aware, and the least 24% respondents were not aware still about web 2.0. It was found that there are diversity preferences in using SNS [web 2.0] among engineering PG students. 75.62%, 66.87% and 63.75% respondents were preferred you tube, Twitter, and Face book respectively. It was also discovered that the same majority of 16.25%, 13.75% and 13.12% respondents were preferred My Space, social book marking; e-portfolios, LinkedIn; Bebo, Delicious respectively. It was also found that 20.62%, 15%, 14.37%, 8.75% respondents preferred to use the wiki, Instance Massaging, Blogs, Friendster as web 2.0 tools respectively. The least 7.5%, 6.25%, 5.62% and 3.75% respondents were preferred to use RSS [rich site summery], micro blogs, podcast, Orkut respectively.

2. It was found that there was a diversity of preferences about web 2.0; below chart shows, the majority 88.75% respondents were preferred web 2.0 for education purpose. It was also discovered that 48.12%, 31.25%, 21.87% and 21.25% respondents were preferred web 2.0 tools for entertainment, knowledge update, shopping, and social circles respectively. The least 20%, 18.75% and 16.25% respondents were preferred web 2.0 tools to share a thought, hobby and keeping peer groups respectively. It was found that the majority 81.87% students preferred to visit social networking site 'some time,' and the least 13.75% and 4.37% engineering PG student marked for often and rarely visit SNS. Blogs are an essential online personal repository to create same preferences people groups to getting feedback and improvement as well as knowledge update. It was discovered that the 38.12% respondents were created their blogs and only 16.87% respondents were not created blogs. It was also found that the majority 81.87% respondents were updating their blogs 'some time,' 13.75% were updating 'often, ' and the least 4.37% respondents were marked for 'rarely' to visiting the site and updating the blogs.

(3) It was discovered that the majority 100% respondents were marked that, Mekelle University libraries were not using blogs to provide library services. Thus it was observed that 'engineering PG' students want blogs for pasting their feedback library service but MU libraries still not using blogs as a web 2.0

technology tool to provide services to their users. It was also discovered that the majority 100% respondents were marked that, Mekelle University libraries were not using blogs to provide library services. Thus it was observed that 'engineering PG' students want to use web 2.0 for giving their feedback about library service but MU libraries still not using blogs as a web 2.0 technology tool to provide services to their users. It was discovered that the majority 41.25% respondents prefer to use web 2.0 for book reservation in the library. It was also found that the 40.62%, 36.87% respondents were preferred to use web 2.0 for library orientation services provided by library staff and reminders of library activities. Ti was also discovered that the equal majority 32.50% respondents were preferred web 2.0 for library tour video and membership information respectively. 31.87%, 29.37%, 28.75% and 23.75% respondents were preferred web 2.0 technology for different library services respectively for instance; CAS current awareness services, Inter library link, SDI selective dissemination of information, and inter library loan. The least 19.37% respondents have preferred web 2.0 technology for library discussion forum respectively. It was also invented that, the majority 85% students prefer to join library community through web 2.0 technology and the least 15% respondents were not preferred to join library community through web 2.0 technology.

CONCLUSION

Information users in this fast transmission electronic age want their answer or information need quickly as possible as in the most convenient way. Unfortunately, the reality is that most of the students, who wish to find out about something, the first thing they would do, would be to search the internet and not think about the library as an option. No user would think about asking a reference librarian or even logging onto a library website to use the inquiry service. This is the new marketplace; this is where most people live and work. Thus, as libraries and information centers must recognize that the Internet and search engines are now the main ways in which people look for information. Therefore, rather than try to change users' habits, the library can change its approach and meet users where they are; on the Web, using the tools web 2.0 what they enjoy using. To libraries should use web 2.0 which is new tools of technology then the libraries can survive this new electronic environment.

SUGGESTIONS

1. According to the finding, it was suggested that the Mekelle University libraries should accept new web 2.0 technologies and should create library blog for user's feedback and improve their services accordingly.
2. According to the present survey, engineering PG students prefer to use social networking (web 2.0), and the students suggested that the Mekelle University libraries should use SNS for providing various library services which are more convenient and beneficial for users even for libraries to survive in the electronic era.
3. Finally, Mekelle University libraries should adapt new technology for instance; (SNS, web 2.0, and multimedia application), new trends in library and information science, to provide fast and convenient services which are more user interface.

REFERENCES

Aharony. (2010). Twitter Use in libraries: An exploratory analysis. *Journal of Web Librarianship, 4*(4), 333-350. http://eric.ed.gov/?id=EJ907467

Berendt. (2007). Tags are not metadata but just more content' to some people. International Joint Conferences on Artificial Intelligence. *Proceedings of the International Conference on Weblogs and Social Media (ICWSM)*. https://icwsm.org/papers/2--Berendt-Hanser.pdf

Blood, R. (2000). Weblogs: A History and Perspective. *The Weblog Handbooks*. Available at: http://www.rebeccablood.net/essays/weblog_history.html

Blood, R. (2013). Weblogs: A History and Perspective. *Rebecca's Pocket*. Available at: http://www.rebeccablood.net/essays/weblog_history.html

Buettner, R. (2016). The Weakness of Ties. In *49th Annual Hawaii International Conference on System Sciences*. Kauai, HI: IEEE. DOI: 10.13140/RG.2.1.3249.2241

Chua & Goh. (2010). A Study of Web 2.0 applications in library websites. *Library & Information Science Research, 32*, 203-211. Available at http://ejournals.library.ualberta.ca/index.php/EBLIP/article/.../9474/1513

Click, A., & Petit, J. (2010). Social Networking and Web 2.0 in Information literacy. *The International Information & Library Review*, *42*(2), 137–142. doi:10.1080/10572317.2010.10762855

Graham, P. (2005). Web 2.0. *Web 2.0 conference*. Available at: http://www.paulgraham.com/web20.html

Kaplan, A. M., & Michael, H. (2011). The early bird catches the news: Nine things you should know about micro-blogging. *Business Horizons, 54*(2). Retrieved 26/08/2019. http://michaelhaenlein.net/Publications/Kaplan,%20Andreas%20%20The%20early%20bird%20catches%20the%20...%20news.pdf

Keen, M. (2009). *Case Study: Web 2.0 SOA Scenario*. Red Paper IBM. Available at: http://www.redbooks.ibm.com/redpapers/pdfs/redp4555.pdf

Kothari, C. R. (2004). Research Methodology: Methods and Techniques. New Age Publishing Limited.

Libby, D. (1999). *RSS 0.91 Spies, revision 3: Netscape communication*. http://scripting.com/netscapeDocs/RSS%200_91%20Spec,%20revision%203.html

Lili, L. (2010). Social Networking Websites: An Exploratory Study of Student Peer Socializing in an Online LIS Program. *Journal of Education for Library and Information Science*. Available at: https://works.bepress.com/lili_luo/1/

Malaiya, R. (2012). *Cloud Computing: A case study*. https://cloudcomputingseminar.wordpress.com/

Mitchell, S. (2008). Easy Wiki Hosting, Scott Hansel man's blog, and Snagging Screens. *MSDN Magazine*. Available at: https://en.wikipedia.org/wiki/Wiki

Noll, M. G., & Meinel, C. (2007). *Web Search Personalization via Social Bookmarking and Tagging: Lecture Note in Computer Science*. Available at: https://link.springer.com/chapter/10.1007%2F978-3-540-76298-0_27

O'Reilly, T. (2005). *What is Web 2.0 Design Patterns and Business Models for the Next Generation of Software.* Available at: http://www.oreilly.com/pub/a/web2/archive/what-is-web-20.html?page=1 Retrieved on 15/02/2019

Richardson, W. (2009). Blogs, Wikis, Podcasts, and Other Powerful Web Tools for Classrooms. Corwin Press.

Saleh, S. (2015). IM Session Identification by Outlier Detection in Cross-correlation Functions. *Conference on Information Sciences and Systems (CISS).* https://www.researchgate.net/publication/274635819_IM_Session_Identification_by_Outlier_Detection_in_Cross-correlation_Functions

Shah, D. N. (2009). *A complete guide to Internet and web programing.* Dream Take Press. www.scribd.com/document/47763275/A-Complete-Guide-to-Internet-and-Web-Programming

Stern, J. (2008). *Introduction to Web 2.0 Technologies.* Available at http://www.wlac.edu/online/documents/Web_2.0%20v.02.pdf

Stern, J. (2015). *Introduction to web 2.0.* Available at: http://www.ictliteracy.info/rf.pdf/Web2.0_Introduction.pdf

Strickland, J. (2007). *How Web 2.0 Works.* Available at: www.computer.howstuffworks.com

WhatIs.Com. (n.d.). *Social Networking.* Available at: https://whatis.techtarget.com/definition/social-networking

Zimmerman, E. (2012). Career couch: Showcasing Your Work. Online Portfolio. *New York Times.* Available at: https://www.nytimes.com/2012/07/01/jobs/an-online-portfolio-can-showcase-your-work-career-couch.html

Chapter 11
Revolutionary Integration of Information and Communication Technology in Nigeria's Higher Education System:
Dimensions and Impacts

Okanlade Adesokan Lawal-Adebowale
Federal University of Agriculture, Abeokuta, Nigeria

Olalekan Oyekunle
Federal University of Agriculture, Abeokuta, Nigeria

ABSTRACT

Emergence and integration of information and communication technology (ICT) in the global education system has significantly enhanced intelligible teaching and learning, particularly in the developing countries. Among the developing countries, Nigeria has equally integrated ICT in its educational system. While the information driven technology has little or no integration in the lower level of education, it is intensively integrated in the higher education system. Although the Nigerian education system lacks integration of robust ICT tools to support virtual and in learning, the installed basic ICT tools such as computers, multimedia projectors, process, and internet have greatly changed the face of the country's educational administration and teaching and learning from the traditional practice. Effective and efficient use of ICT are however affected by extrinsic and intrinsic barriers. The need to strengthen the ICT framework and deployment for a more robust teaching and learning process in the country's education system is emphasized.

DOI: 10.4018/978-1-7998-3468-7.ch011

INTRODUCTION

In the drive to enhance teaching and learning in the global education system, several countries have leveraged on the potentials of ICT to accomplish these tasks of education. In the Nigerian education system is integration of ICT to complement the instructional delivery and enhance learning across the schools in the country. Consequently, this article reflects the extent of ICT integration and its impacts on Nigeria's education system. To guide the development of this article are the following salient research questions: What are the common ICT usage in the Nigerian education system? To what extent is ICT integrated in the country's education system? In what dimension is the ICT deployed in the Nigerian education system? What is the impact of ICT in the Nigerian education system? What are the challenges to effective use of ICT in the country's education system? What is the way out of the challenges?

Before providing answers to these questions, the article first gave insight to the concept of ICT in education, background to ICT deployment in the global education system, revolutionary ICT development in Nigeria, scope of the Nigerian education system and extent of ICT integration. Thereafter is the reflection of the dimensions of ICT in the Nigerian higher learning institutions, impacts of ICT on the Nigerian education system, challenges to ICT usage, solution and recommendations to overcoming the challenges, and rounding up with the conclusion.

Concept of ICT in Education

ICT in education, as opined by Linways (2017), refers to any electronic device that supports, enhances, and optimises instructional delivery and learning in a given teaching and learning situation. Taking this further, EduSys (2019), regarded the information-driven technology in education as a set of electronic devices that allow or enhance presentations, demonstrations, drills and practices, interactions, and collaborations to add value to teaching and learning, promote smart classroom, and simplify administration procedures and operations. These concepts, suggests that ICT in education exists in varying forms with each of them serving specific educational purpose. ICT in education could thus be in form of teaching aids, such as the convergence of computers and multimedia projectors, audio and video playing devices; or virtual learning tools, such as the teaching and learning apps, parent-teacher communication apps, mobile learning apps, lesson planning software, home-tutoring websites, revision blogs etc. (Wastiau et al., 2013; Huda, 2016; Hannah, 2018). The teaching aids, as expressed by Olakulehin (2007) are meant to complement teachers' instructional delivery for effective learning. The virtual or e-learning on the other hand is often aided by Internet-laden ICT applications, which allow for educational networking, web-based learning and mobile learning (Luo & Lei, 2012). These concepts of ICT thus guide the outlook of the expected ICT in the Nigerian education system.

BACKGROUND TO ICT DEPLOYMENT IN THE GLOBAL EDUCATION SYSTEM

Schools across the globe generally serve the purpose of providing educational service with the aim of imparting knowledge and understanding of certain subject matter in students who are officially enrolled for learning. The inculcated and acquired education provide the foundation for the learners' contributions to the development of societal social and economic wellbeing (Ozturk, 2001). According to the European University Association [EUA] (2007), creative thinking by graduates of higher education is a key to adequately addressing the emerging life challenges brought about by the rapidly changing human ecosystem and its attendant complexity. The need to make instructional education impactful on human society thus form the basis for redirecting the conventional teaching methods to innovative teaching strategies. Such innovative teaching strategies range through the use of inquiry-based learning, quick response (QR) codes, problem-based learning, wisely managed classroom technology, and jigsaws (Davis, 2017). Alongside these are integration of audio and visual aids, and the information and communication Technology (ICT) as innovative teaching resources.

Based on the revolutionary potentials of ICT in education, the information-driven technology has been extensively deployed for teaching, learning and administration of educational tasks. According to the United Nations Education, Scientific and Cultural Organisation [UNESCO] (2009), ICT integration in the administration of education system dated back to early 1970s when universities around the world began to use the information-driven technology to administrate staff and student records, create financial database, and management of information. An instance of ICT in school administration is the Student Information System (SIS) with which students' admissions, data building, record of assessment scores and other student-related data are facilitated by some universities in Hong Kong (Yuen et al., 2011). In addition to this is development of Human Resource Information System (HRIS) to support the process, practice and coordination of human resource functions in terms of staff selection, recruitment and appointment, performance management, staff development, and career progression and development (Yuen et al, 2011). Consequently, Cortese (2003); McClea and Yen (2005) stressed that ICT integration in education administration serves the useful purpose of improving the general admissions process and formatting profiles of staff as human resource information system.

In the teaching system, ICT is deployed to enhance teaching and learning process (Becta, 2004). Common ICT tools for teaching and learning ranged between the simple electronic audio-visual aids and the advanced computerised learning programmes or web-based learning tools. Singh (2005) describes audio-visual aids as any device that increase individuals' learning experience beyond what is, or could be acquired through reading. Electronic devices such as radio and television sets, audio and video players, multimedia projectors, interactive boards, internet and internet-based media constitute audio-visual aids basically because they have the potentials to enhance learning by appealing to both senses of sight and sound. According to Rasul, Bukhsh, and Batool (2011), teaching aids are undoubtedly used in the classroom basically because they arouse the interest of learners and stimulate effective learning. At the same time, the teaching devices help the teachers to explain taught lessons more easily or making it real to the learners. Effective use of audio-visual aids however depends, not only on the teachers' good understanding of the subjects or courses to be taught and their good teaching skills and techniques (Wilson & Peterson, 2006), but also on their ability to use the audio-visual aides for good and quality teaching.

Not only is ICT deployed for teaching and learning within the school environment, but also for facilitating teaching and learning over a distance. This mode of education practice, generally referred to as Distance Learning, entails the provision of educational training to everyone who desires knowledge acquisition in a formal school arrangement but could not be physically present in the school premises (Keegan, 1980; Naidu, 2019). This virtual learning, as indicated by Dede (1996), is made possible by the convergence of the new media, such as the internet, computers, hypermedia, multimedia, mobile learning devices or computer-supported collaborative learning. An instance of such open education or distance learning provision is the case of India's Symbiosis Centre for Distance Learning (SCDL) under which a university education is provided for whoever is interested in being developed intellectually. According to Mujumdar (2011), the service is provided from the main campus in Pune, Western India, with the use of world-class facilities such as video conferencing, an e-communication centre, well equipped laboratories and classrooms, library, audio-visual halls and conference hall for instructional delivery. With such installed facilities, all the distant learning centres are connected to the facilities through a virtual private network for enhancement of accessibility and delivery of quality of education to thousands of distant learners irrespective of their locations. Unlike the traditional schooling arrangement, distance learning education system is characterised by provision of self-learning materials, e-learning, online learning and faculty-based learning; with the learning materials saved either in flash/compact discs or online drives on downloading for later use.

REVOLUTIONARY DEVELOPMENT OF ICT IN NIGERIA

Transformational development of ICT and its deployment for social and economic endeavours in Nigeria began in August 2001 in the wake of the implementation of the telecom sector deregulation policy by the Federal Government of Nigeria (FGN). The reform not only halts the government's monopolistic control of the telecom sector, but also usher in a steady growth of the sector. Against the teledensity of 0.49% or per unit telephone line access to the Nigerian population, under the monopolistic control of the sector by the FGN, (Lawal-Adebowale, 2015), is an unimaginable teledensity of 94.50% as at October 2019, under the private sector control (Nigerian Communication Commission [NCC], 2019). Similarly, the country moved from about 200,000 active internet users back in the year 2000 to about 123.4million as at June 2019 to give a 61.6% rise in internet usage (Internet World Stats [IWS], 2019). Invariably, there is an increased accessibility and usage of mobile phone and internet services across the country.

The mobile telecommunication and internet services were though meant to enhance information and communication flow or exchange among Nigerians, and also with other people across the globe, dynamic utility of the information-driven technologies have been greatly explored and exploited beyond voice or text communication to effecting changes in all spheres of life in the country. An important sector of Nigeria's social and economic sphere with intensive ICT integration is the education sector.

THE SCOPE OF NIGERIA'S EDUCATION SYSTEM AND EXTENT OF ICT INTEGRATION

The Nigerian education system is classified as 9-3-4 with the implication that every child in the country is to have 6years of primary school education and 3 years of post-primary school education, often referred to as Junior Secondary School 1 to 3 (JS 1-3), to attain a 9-year basic or minimum education. Those with good learning abilities could take up additional 3years of post-primary school education, i.e. Senior Secondary School 1-3 (SS 1-3), to make a 12-year minimum attainable level of education. On completion of the 6-year post-primary school education, the intellectually gifted ones proceed to acquire, at least, additional 4years of post-secondary school education as the minimum attainable. The Nigerian higher education system comprises the universities and polytechnics with the mandate of developing the intellectual capacity, professional and technical skills of learners through teaching and learning process.

Teaching and learning in the Nigerian education system are traditionally characterised by theoretical teachings and practical demonstrations as a way of developing the intellectual capacity and competencies of the learners on various subjects and disciplines. These mode of teaching though based on direct teacher-student contacts, their effectiveness depend on the inspirational teaching approach adopted the teachers, and the inner drive of the students to learn. According to Ko, Sammons and Bakkum (2016); Davis (2017); direct or contact teachings in the global education system have been highly effective in effecting cognitive development of learners as a result of teachers' adoption of instructional strategies like inquiry-based learning, anchored instruction, quick response codes, discovery learning, problem-based learning, wisely managed classroom technology, and other evidence-based teaching techniques (Dunn, Saville, Baker, & Marek, 2013). Alongside this is integration of ICT to complement the teaching strategies (Olakulehin, 2007). According to Fu (2013), ICT tends to enhance instructional delivery, learning, assessment and expand access to education. Recognition of these ICT potentials in education certainly informed the integration of the information-driven technology in the Nigerian education system.

To guide the development and extensive integration of ICT in the Nigerian education, the FGN, through the Federal Ministry of Education [FME] enacted ICT education policy with clear directional goal of installing essential ICT infrastructure at all levels of education in the country; and as well encourage manpower development for quality and sustenance utilisation of the ICT to enhance learning and other educational activities (FME, 2019). Consequently, is the launch of a number education-driven ICT initiatives in the country. Among these are the computers for all schools, one child per laptop, School-Net, Teachers Network (TeachNet), Nigerian Universities Network (NuNet), National Virtual Library, Nigerian Education, Academic and Research Network (NEARNet), Polytechnic Network (PolyNet) etc. (Adomi & Kpangban, 2010; Idowu and Esere, 2013). In view of this, the questions at hand are: what types of ICT are in place for educational activities in Nigeria? In what dimensions are the ICT deployed for educational activities? In what way has the ICT impacted on the Nigerian education system?

ICT IN THE NIGERIAN EDUCATION SYSTEM AND DIMENSIONS OF DEPLOYMENT FOR EDUCATIONAL ACTIVITIES

Despite the laudable ICT initiatives for the Nigerian education system, the country is yet to have a well-developed ICT for its educational system. Most schools only have the ICT facilities the readily support direct teaching and information management in place with no ICT that supports virtual or e-learning in the real sense of web-based learning. Thus, ICT such as computers/laptops, multimedia projectors, audio and video recording/playing devices and Internet are common in the Nigerian education system. These ICT facilities are however obvious in the higher learning institutions, but grossly lacking in the primary and secondary schools. According to Adomi and Kpangban (2010), the computer for all schools initiative was not extensively implemented in the public primary and secondary schools and as such, computer is not a part of classroom technology in more than 90% of Nigerian primary and secondary schools (Okebukola, 1997). The higher learning institutions with a measure of ICT facilities have thus regularly deployed the information-driven technology in various dimensions to fast-tract various academic and administrative tasks of importance to them. The various dimension of ICT integration are thus highlighted as follows:

ICT DEPLOYMENT FOR IMAGE BUILDING AND PUBLIC ENGAGEMENT

1. **Universities' Websites for Publicity and Image Building:** Website creation constitutes the means by which a university's image is publicised globally. With the websites, each of the Nigerian universities and polytechnics could be readily found online by interested individuals within and outside the country. Plate 1 shows the webpage of the University of Jos (UNIJOS), Plateau State, from which information about the university and its academic programmes could be found or accessed by the public. According to Gehrke and Turban (1999); Cato (2001); Flavian, Gurrea, and Orús (2009), website design or creation is crucial to getting positive outcomes for a concerned organisation. The dexterity of webpage creation thus explored, not just to ensure timely and accurate information of its contents, but also to positively influence the users' perceptions and behaviours toward the organisation. In view of this, websites by the Nigerian universities are designed to be attractive and informative to users of the webpages, and for appropriate public and good image building.

2. **Deployment of Website for Admission Application:** Although, Nigerian Universities do advertise their calls for admission and/or application for vacant positions in the universities in newspapers as a matter of regulations or bureaucratic procedure, the webpage remains the substantive point of applications for admission and the vacant positions. Plate 2 shows the webpage of Landmark University (LMU), Omu-Aran, Kwara State, where advertisement for admission into the university for the 2017/2018 academic session is posted. According to DMI Daily Digest (2019); Whitehead (2019), official websites of educational institutions are essentially a driving force by which prospective students are attracted for application to be admitted, and as such, institutions need to update and optimise their websites to allow for easy access of information and contents. With the posted calls for admission, the prospective students could visit the website of the university or of any other preferred university for applications into desired programmes and course of study. To login to the application portal, candidates have to obtain vouchers or scratch cards from which certain digits are retrieved as codes to be keyed into portal. Once the admission process is launched, the candidates provide their bio-data and other required information for admission. With this step, database is created for each of the prospective students, and from the supplied information, recommendations are made on the candidates to be admitted. According to Belkin (2019), in the course of admission process, colleges track their prospective students' online for interaction and sort decision on whom to admit.

3. **Deployment of Webpage for Employment Application:** In a similar manner to the deployment of webpages for attracting candidates for admission by the Nigerian universities are placement of advertisements for vacant positions on the webpages. Plate 3 shows the advertised job opportunity on the webpage of Babcock University, Ilisan-Remo, Ogun State. The advertisement showcased staff vacant positions and the application eligibility. Consequently, interested and eligible applicants visit the university's website for application and provision of the required information. In the process a database is for each of the applicants. From the database, résumé of each candidate is accessed for evaluation and recommendation. Successful and shortlisted candidates are thus invited by means of text messages either sent through the supplied e-mails or phone number(s) for interviews or written tests, which could sometimes be computer-based. In the long run, successful applicants are contacted by electronic means to inform them of their appointment and eventual resumption.

ICT DEPLOYMENT FOR ADMINISTRATIVE MATTERS

1. **Education Portals for Administration of Students' Records:** For administration of students' academic records and monitoring of progression, most of the Nigerian universities have developed educational portals (edu-portals or e-portals) for this purpose. An instance in this regard is e-portal integration for online registration of students and database management by the Federal University of Agriculture Abeokuta (FUNAAB), Ogun State, Nigeria (Plate 4). With the e-portal, every student on admission has his/her bio-data and admission profiles uploaded onto the portal for creation of database to which the records of each of them is linked. Based on this, all the courses to be taken by each of the students are automatically synchronised with their names and/or matriculation numbers thereby making it possible to monitor the sequence of courses taken and passed by the students. An important utility of the e-portal, as observed by Lawal-Adebowale and Oyekunle (2014), is that the platform neither allow students to register below or beyond the limit of the total course units to be registered per semester nor leave any of the lower or pre-requisite courses undone while attempting to take the requisite courses.

2. **Staff Portal:** Like the e-portals for administration of students' records, the staff portal is used for documentation of staff records by the Nigerian universities. Plate 5 shows the staff portal from the webpage of the Kaduna State University (KASU), Kaduna State, by which the school administrators readily access and/or provide information on each staff on demand or within a relatively short period. From the portal, each staff could readily access their personal career information and/or upload their related job information as may be required by management of the university. In some cases, essential administrative forms are hoisted on the webpage as observed with the Lagos State University (LASU) Ojo, Lagos State (Plate 6). With this provision, staff could readily retrieve the needed forms and upload after filling. Similarly is hoisting of academic staff's bio-data, research focus and achievements on the webpages by the universities. From the staff portal, a link is created to the publications of each of the academic staff. This provision thus makes it possible for staffs desiring collaboration with fellow staff within the same university or in other universities to readily identify a fitting or eligible researcher for interaction and joint work.

ICT DEPLOYMENT FOR TEACHING AND CONDUCT OF EXAMINATIONS IN NIGERIA

1. **Audio-Visual Teaching Aids:** In an attempt to accomplish the task of effective teaching and learning the Nigerian universities have put electronic teaching aids in place for use by tutors and students. Commonly used electronic audio-visual aids for teaching include the convergence of laptops and PowerPoint projectors, megaphones or microphones and loud speakers (Plate 7). In some cases is the use of television and video set for playback of educational programmes such as documentaries, dramas, and features for experiential learning. With these devices, it becomes possible for tutors to clearly and precisely present thoughts in a fascinating and intriguing manner. According to Mohanty (2001), audio-visual aids enhance accomplishment of lesson plans and educational objectives on the ground that they allow for a more professional and consistent presentation such that students are given additional ways to process taught concepts for better understanding. In the same vein, Rasul et al. (2011) expressed that integration of audio-visual aids in teaching makes instructional delivery and learning effective, providing the learners with realistic experience that captures attention and stimulates better understanding of the taught subject matter.

2. **Computer-Based Test:** As a way to ascertain whether taught lessons are understood by students, they are subjected to written tests and examinations. Increasing population of students across the

country's universities has however necessitated the integration of computer-based test or examination (CBT/E) for conduct of continuous assessment test and school examinations. Plate 8 shows a number of students of the Olabisi Onabanjo University (OOU), Ago-Iwoye, Ogun State, deploying computers for writing school examination. This process calls for uploading of questions onto the examination portals or computer-based packages. The students thus access and respond to questions within the allotted time for any of the examinations. The examination questions, as expressed by Thelwall (2000), are either presented in multiple choice or fill-in-the-gaps, whereby students pick an option of right answer or provide the exact word or phrase that best fits the sentence-based questions.

3. **E-Portal for Result Processing:** On completion of examinations, be it computer-based or paper work, obtained scores by the students are forwarded to course lecturers for uploading into the result processing database. The uploaded scores are automatically synchronised with the records of each of the students by virtue of their matriculation numbers. While it is invariably impossible for any student that did not register for a particular course to have result, even when such wrote the examination, those that registered but did not sit for a particular examination paper will automatically be credited with a score of zero. To ascertain the successful uploading and allocation of scores to each of the students, the result portal gives a preview of the result outlook by indicating the matriculation numbers with found scores and those without scores for verification by the course lecturers. On careful checks and satisfaction with the displayed outlook of the results for each of the students, a click of the confirmation button proceeds to save the uploaded scores. Once the scores for all courses have been uploaded individual lecturers, Heads of Departments, as the Chief Examiners, go ahead to generate the cumulative results for all the students in their respective Departments; after which it is printed for public presentation. With approval of the result by Senate of the university, every student could then access their personal results from the result portal by means of their matriculation numbers and personally created passwords.

ICT DEPLOYMENT FOR SELF-LEARNING AND ACADEMIC INTERACTIONS IN NIGERIA

1. **Computer Deployment and Software Application in Education:** Given the value and utility of ICT in education, both students and faculties have personally deployed some ICT devices for educational activities. For instance, laptops or desktop computers have been deployed for word processing to fulfil the tasks of lesson notes and research reports preparation by faculties; while students readily use the device for typesetting notes, term papers and projects/dissertation/thesis. In addition to this is exploration of several software utility for fulfilment of other academic tasks. The Microsoft PowerPoint is largely explored for presentation of information during lectures and seminar presentations. The Microsoft Excel plays important role as spreadsheet for data management, particularly for analysis of data. Other specialised software package installed for data management by both students and faculty members are Statistical Package for Social Scientists (SPSS), Statistics and Data (STATA), Robert Ihaka and Robert Gentleman R programming (R), Statistical Analysis System (SAS), and Minitab etc.

2. **Integration of Educational Apps for Learning:** The revolutionary development of educational digital Apps has found useful applications for learning among students in the Nigerian universities. Common educational Apps are the inbuilt scientific computation application or calculator which enables the students to fast-track computation of figures in related mathematical tasks; and the

English dictionaries used for checking spellings and meaning of English words for better understanding and application. Depending on the interests and desires of each of the students, several other educational Apps are downloaded for use. In this regard are related English, Mathematics and Science Apps. For instance, the use of the 'Maths-Master-Maths Game App', enables the students of mathematics to improve their mathematical skills and ability to quickly count by mind. This in turn sharpens their intellects, logical thinking and analysis. English language Apps such as 'Improve English Speaking' is in use by students who intend to improve their grammar and fluency. On science disciplines are the use of Apps such as 'Science Facts', 'General Science Book' by the science students,, particularly in physics, chemistry, biology, zoology, ecology, and water, to gain better insight and understanding of the related science courses taking by them.

3. **Mobile Phone Deployment in Education:** Mobile phone has a wide usage in Nigeria and as such has been intensively integrated in the country's education system by both students and faculty members. The wide application of the device is largely due to its utility and mobility. The mobile phone ordinarily serves the useful purpose of communication, either by voice or text, among members of the university communities, emergence of android phones have changed the dimensional usage of the communication device into other computer-based utility thereby enhancing usage for educational activities. Observation among the students is the use of the phone for taking pictures of practical and field events, and pasted notices on information boards. With the internet utility of the phones, the device is used either as an internet-based phone or in convergence with laptops by tethering the hotspot for internet connection, to fast-track academic activities such as sourcing information from online, and uploading of research outputs for publicity. The mobile phone equally serves the useful purpose of communicating notice on seminars and meetings by text messages, or give notifications and reminders on issues of importance.

ICT INTEGRATION FOR ELECTRONIC AND VIRTUAL LIBRARY MANAGEMENT

1. **Library and E-Resources:** An important component of school curriculum is the library which provide support services for the core academic programmes across the globe. In Nigeria's universities are established libraries to support teaching and learning through the provision of relevant and up-to-date publications as may be required by students and faculty members. To fulfil this supportive role, relevant publications are provided both in print and electronic forms to the library users. According to Tenopir (2003), libraries will though continue to offer print collections for many years to come, all have now embraced digital collections with opportunity for users to access needed publications with convenience, be it at home, dormitory and/or office, whether or not the physical libraries are opened. A visit to a number of the universities in Nigeria reveals that they have ICT such as computers and internets well integrated in their library services. In the Federal University of Technology Akure (FUTA) Ondo State (Plate 9), electronic library services (E-Resources) or databases, is provided for use by members of the university community. The e-resources are either subscription-based or Open Access-based. As reflected on the university's webpage, the subscription-based databases include the 'EBSCOhost' – a database for all subjects and the 'Research4Life' resource comprising AGORA (Access to Global Online Research on Agriculture), HINARI (Access to Research Initiative on Health), OARE (Online Access to Research in the Environment), GOALI (Global Online Access to Legal Information) and ARDI (Access to Research Development and Innovation). The Open Access resources in the library include TEEAL

(The Essential Electronic Agricultural Library), which is a database of related agriculture publications/information in Compact Discs and Digital Video Discs (CDs/DVDs).

2. **Online Search for Publications and Publishers:** In addition to the e-library services across the Nigerian universities is online sourcing of publications and/or reputable publishers by students and faculties in the country. In view of the quantum of information available online, most of which are Open Access (Plate 10), both students and faculty members have found the Internet utility valuable to support their quest for new knowledge and to improve their research write-up by referencing the sourced online publications. In the same vein is the opportunity to locate reputable journals and publishing houses with which the faculties' could have their research outputs published. The Internet has also enabled individual researchers in the country to have a fair share of their knowledge or research outputs with other academia around the world; and also acquire new knowledge and research approaches via the online platform.

THE INTERNET PLATFORM FOR CONNECTIVITY AND DISTANCE LEARNING

1. **Internet Platform for Interconnectivity and Global Information Exchange:** With utility of the Internet for connectivity and information flow, the information-driven technology has enabled interconnectivity between students; and faculty members for fast-tracking information flow, teaching and learning. Specific trend of Internet usage include the electronic mail (e-mail) and social media for communication of academic related information. With this provision, electronic copies of class notes, notice of seminars, date and time of continuous assessment test (CAT) are communicated to students by the faculties. This medium also serve as the platform of correspondence on projects, thesis and dissertation write-ups between supervisors and supervisees. The e-mail also serve as means of receiving assignments or take home academic exercises from students by lecturers.

2. **Distance Learning:** Although, most academic programmes take place within the university environment in Nigeria, with the option of enrolling either as full time, part-time or weekend students. The National Open University of Nigeria (NOUN) is however providing distance learning education service for those who could not enrol in the conventional university system in the country. All prospective students thus apply online for their choice programmes and courses, using the indicated steps on the admission section of the university's webpage (Plate 11). To support the students' self-learning drives, lesson notes and publications are made available in the repository database of the university which could be retrieved by the students (Plate 12). Emphasising the value of distance learning, Mujumdar (2011) expresses that the use of ICT as innovative technology solutions have not only made it possible for distance learning to achieve academic and operational excellence, but has equally made it possible for education to be extended to a large number of people and doing so in a more flexible and cost effective manner.

3. **Online Learning and Tutorials:** Teaching and learning in the Nigerian education system are largely classroom-based with direct contacts between tutors and learners. Emergence of online videos have provided additional learning rooms for students and researchers in Nigeria. Among the several online video hosting services, such as YouTube, Vimeo, Netflix, Roku, Twitch, Amazon Prime, Youku, Momo etc., the Nigerian students and faculty members largely explore the YouTube as an online learning room for knowledge building or acquisition on subjects of interest. According to Jia (2019), YouTube, which is the most visited online video-sharing service, has become an educational tool with which instructors and students are improving their learning on subject of

interest. Interactions with members of the Nigerian university academic communities on the value and frequency of YouTube usage shows that the online video platform is regularly used and has greatly impacted on their learning. The accompanying pictures in the sought subjects made the taught subjects clearer and better understood. The platform was observed to have been deployed for learning subject matters of interest by both students and the faculties.

IMPACTS OF ICT USAGE ON THE NIGERIAN HIGHER EDUCATION SYSTEM

1. **Enhanced Publicity and Easy Access to University Communities:** Integration of ICT in the Nigerian education system has somehow transformed the mode of teaching and learning process, and administration of the school system. Unlike the era of using brochures to search for information on specific universities in Nigeria, website creation has made it possible for each of the country's universities to be readily located and reached for educational and other official matters. The web-pages made information on the mission and vision of the universities, and as well their available academic programmes, known to the public. It also serves as image building and attraction of more prospective candidates to the institutions for knowledge and skill acquisition. On the same note, the created websites made it possible for profiles of the academic staff of the universities to be accessible to any interested person for easy contact and interaction.

2. **Enhancement of Teaching and Learning Process:** Integration of ICT such as computers, PowerPoint projectors and audio devices are known to have enhanced teaching and learning as the devices made presentations audible and clearer, particularly to students in large classrooms. The devices equally enhanced presentations of research proposals and outputs by students to audience of faculties and fellow students. Integration of the internet platform, using the e-mails and social media, made information exchange possible and easier, be it for academic or social purpose, between staff and students and among peers/colleagues. In addition, deployment of educational Apps and online search engines for sourcing of academic information had given the students ample opportunities to acquire more information on a particular subject matter and to learn at own convenience. This is in line with Binghilams (2009) submission that, just as the new ICT can enhance the teachers' pedagogical practice, so it assists students' learning.

3. **Enhancement of Academic Record Keeping and Retrieval:** Development and use of e-portal serves the useful purpose of accurate keeping of students' academic records, enhance course registration and students' access to own academic records. It also helps to fast-track the administration of other non-academic engagement such that staff could readily access necessary and essential information to aid the quality of their daily routine and services; and to enhance the development of their career. Deployment of the ICT for examinations has also helped to reduce the stress of manual grading of scripts, particularly in classes with large number of students. The e-portal made the processing of results easy and convenient, and also ensures timely release of the results. It equally ensures secured storage of the result database from which transcripts can be readily generated at any point in time.

4. **Enhanced Access to University Education through Virtual Learning:** Distance learning provided by NOUN has equally made it possible for all who desired university education to have access to such level of education irrespective of the distance and geographical-base of the students in the country. With this service provision, a lot more of the Nigerians that could not attend or gain admission into the conventional universities have been able acquire university education for skill

and intellectual capacity development. Similarly, those that were gainfully employed but in need to further their studies have been able to do so through the distance learning education service provided by NOUN. With the ICT in place, students on distance learning programmes were able to study on their own by downloading course notes and/or sourcing needed academic information from online, databases and electronic sources created by the university's library.

CHALLENGES OF ICT USAGE IN THE NIGERIAN HIGHER EDUCATION SYSTEM

ICT in the Nigerian education system though reveals that the information driven-technology has been largely deployed in the context of teaching, learning, and administrative matters across schools in the country, the integration is certainly characterised by a number of challenges. A number of authors have classified challenges or barriers to effective ICT integration in teaching and learning into two major categories, namely extrinsic and intrinsic barriers (Binghilams, 2009). While the extrinsic barrier has to do with lack or inadequate provision of ICT and other supporting resources, the intrinsic barrier relates with individuals' capability and behavioural disposition to using the ICT resources. In as much as these two dimensions of challenges are important and worth consideration, the extrinsic challenge must hold before the intrinsic could be ascertained. Both extrinsic and intrinsic barriers to effective ICT integration in the Nigerian education system are thus highlighted as follows:

EXTRINSIC BARRIERS TO EFFECTIVE ICT USAGE IN THE NIGERIAN EDUCATION SYSTEM

1. **High Cost of ICT Acquisition:** Due to poor economic status of Nigeria, the cost of ICT facilities is still very high. Based on this, ICT becomes too expensive for most schools in Nigeria to acquire. While it is relatively easier for the universities to acquire some ICT facilities, it is extremely diffi-cult or even impossible for the public primary and secondary schools to do so due to poor funding of the schools and lack of opportunity to seek alternative funding source. Although, most of the higher learning institutions were able to acquire the basic ICT, such as desktop computers or lap-tops, multimedia projectors, audio sound systems (microphone and loudspeakers, or megaphone) and television set, for teaching and learning, the institutions have not been able to provide these basic ICT tools to all staff and students for use due to high cost of doing so. Consequently, staff and students in most cases personally acquire desktop computers or laptops for use. In the same vein, hardly is it possible for all staff to access multimedia projectors and sound systems simultaneously for teaching or seminar presentations.

2. **Lack of Robust ICT Teaching and Learning Tools:** The information driven-technology, though, exists in various forms, its application for teaching and learning in the Nigerian higher learning institutions is less robust owing to the fact that computers, PowerPoint projectors and sound sys-tems form the thrust of ICT facilities for teaching and learning in the country. In most cases, the institutions lacked e-learning opportunity due to non-availability of specialised education-driven ICT tools, such as text magnifiers, head wands audio books, flipped classrooms, and Wide Area Network (WAN) to allow for remote or virtual teaching and learning. Where an attempt is made for such provision, hardly is the complete package provided to allow for appropriate functional-

ity and utilisation. A practical experience in this regard is provision of interactive boards across the federal universities in the country but with no other supporting facilities to enable functional operation and usage of the devices. In addition, the schools lacked education-based programming and apps to enhance intelligible learning.

3. **Lack of Political-Will to Ensure Adequate ICT Resource Provision:** In reality, Nigeria has a robust policy on ICT for education (FME, 2019); the highlighted policy statements on ensuring a well-grounded ICT infrastructure at all levels of the education is yet to be implemented thereby making the use of ICT in the country's education system less robust. In the lower levels of education, particularly in the public primary and secondary schools, hardly is ICT facilities provided for the schools to enhance teaching and learning. In most cases, only a single desktop computer or laptop with a printer is available to a school, primarily for typesetting of documents. This could be letters for administrative correspondence between a particular school and other external bodies, or typesetting of questions and preparation of question papers for the school examination. Hardly is there any ICT provision for teaching and learning purpose in the public schools. According to Agyeman (2007), the one-child-per-laptop-ownership scheme; and the project of setting up computer laboratories at both primary and secondary schools have failed to materialise in the country. This could be attributed to poor funding of the lower levels of education, and lack of commitment to appropriately implement the institutionalised policy on ICT for education in Nigeria. The initial step of supplying 10 computers per school for digital training of pupil could not be up-scaled and sustained thereby leaving the schools out of the digital drive for effective teaching and learning. In addition, all the public primary and secondary schools had no internet facilities for digital activities.

4. **Poor Internet Network Service:** Internet service provision and usage in Nigeria is certainly on the increase, but the available bandwidth and servers are sometimes slow. According to King (2015), slow internet connectivity could be caused by factors such as types of Internet access, the state of computer in use, traffic jam on busy network or local Internet congestion, and proxy server. The slow internet connectivity thus makes its usage highly tasking or hectic in some cases. For instance, due to poor internet connectivity it could take longer time for the least file to be uploaded or downloaded. In the same vein, Office of the Auditor General [OAG] (2016) expresses that slow or unreliable internet discourages its usage, limits its regular access to the classroom, and delays academic tasks to be performed.

5. **Lack of Stable Electric Power Supply:** Utility of ICT largely depends on stable electric power supply. Irregular and outright lack of electric power supply thus constitute a major challenge to successful ICT usage in Nigeria. Most of the public and secondary schools across the country, particularly the classrooms, lacked provision of electricity thereby making it highly impossible to have ICT devices operated in the schools. For the schools with electricity, particularly the universities, irregular power supply greatly hinders intensive use of the available ICT facilities for teaching and administrative matters. Consequently, institutions spent a great deal amount of money on acquisition, operation and maintenance of generating sets or inverters as alternative sources of electricity supply in order to keep academic and administrative work running. Individuals at household level experience the same issue of poor and long-hours or days, and even months in some cases, of power outage thereby forcing nearly everyone in the country to source alternative electricity supply by the use of generating sets or inverters.

INTRINSIC BARRIER TO ROBUST USE OF ICT IN THE NIGERIAN EDUCATION SYSTEM

1. **High cost of ICT Operation:** Functional use of ICT such as the internet requires service charge, as may be contracted with Internet Service Providers. Failure to regularly fulfil this obligation often results in disconnection thereby leading to breakdown of connectivity for regular usage by members of the higher school communities. On another note, majority of members of the academic communities access internet at home by reliance on the internet service provided by the mobile telephony service providers in the country. This implies individuals have to subscribe for data plan from the mobile telephony service providers which is usually expensive. Based on market information on data plans, 1giggabite (1GB) cost N500 (US$1.42 @N350 per dollar) per month. With heavy usage of data by the academics, hardly could they subscribe for enough data for a long duration of academic exercise. Consequently, students and faculties subscribe and use data for internet service only when it becomes absolutely necessary and mandatory to get a particular task done online.

2. **Poor ICT Maintenance Culture:** The basic ICT tools for teaching may though be available across the Nigerian higher learning institutions, poor maintenance of the facilities have turned out to be a barrier to sustainable use of the facilities. With this situation, faulty multimedia projector(s), computers or any of the electronic teaching aids may remain unattended to for a considerable period of time due to bureaucratic procedure that often delay consideration and approval for either repairs or replacement of the electronic teaching tools. Consequently, academic activities that essentially rely on the use of such ICT for execution becomes delayed or hectic to accomplish.

3. **Ineptitude of Behaviour Toward the use of ICT for Educational Activities:** The less use or non-availability of ICT for educational activities in the lower level of the Nigerian education system can be attributed to lack of the drive for use of the technology by tutors and learners in both primary and secondary schools in the country. It is obvious that ICT tool is less or not provided for the lower level of education, there was never an agitation for such provision by students and staffs. This could be because they never saw a need for the ICT tools or do not understanding the values of the information-driven technology in teaching and learning. In addition, lack of personal drive for development of skilful and innovative use of ICT by students and faculties in the higher learning institutions also underscore inefficient use of the ICT for robust teaching and learning in the country's education system.

4. **Flair for ICT-Mediated Entertainment than Educational Activities:** In as much as the ICT is of great value to enhancing learning and other educational activities, the entertainment provided by the information-driven technology, particularly with use of smart phones, has become a serious source distraction to the students of higher learning institutions. Field observation shows that majority of the students with mobile phones often use it to socialise more with friends and families than for academic activities. They spent more time on chatting through the social media, watching films and video clips, playing games and listening to music than academic activities.

5. **Limited Competence of ICT Usage:** The issue of competence of ICT usage can only be ascertained where the ICT is available and accessible to an intending user. In view of this, most of the faculties and students have the skill to operate the ICT available to them. However, field observation shows that their competence is limited to certain aspect of the ICT and grossly lacking in some. For instance, quite a number of students and faculties can make use of computers for word processing but lacked skilful use of excel and/or PowerPoint. Consequently, they resort to seeking assistance of competent hands to execute the intending tasks that require the use of these computer-based software applications.

SOLUTIONS AND RECOMMENDATIONS

In as much as the basic ICT devices are crucial to enhancing teaching and learning in the classroom setting, and the internet for information management, there is a need for integration of robust computerised language learning for inspirational teaching and intelligible learning. According to Wong et al. (2006), in as much as the convergent ICT plays important role in supporting the face-to-face teaching, there is a need for extensive integration of computerised language learning, simulation-based learning, web courses, self-study net etc., just as it were in several other educational system around the world (Kanninen, 2008; Yazici & Cagiltay, 2009; Wieland & Ifenthaler, 2009). Internet access in the Nigerian higher education is largely within the environment of the higher learning institutions due to reliance on the Local Area Network (LAN) as the service point for internet service. The resultant effect of this is hindrance of virtual or e-learning in the country. To enhance virtual and interactive learning, there is a need for development of Wide Area Network (WAN) and even Metropolitan Area Network (MAN). Learning through online discussions, as opined by Hung, Tan and Chen (2005); Wang and Woo (2007), is an important instructional strategy to enhance students' critical thinking, knowledge construction and social relationship.

Consequently, it becomes essential to have the framework of ICT in the Nigerian education system further strengthened through conscientious implementation of the instituted education-based ICT policy. This will guide and ensure the installation and provision of robust ICT facilities, especially software and programming tools, to enhance effective teaching and intelligible learning across the entire Nigerian education system. In addition to this is the need for creating an enabling environment, in terms of providing electricity to all the schools in Nigeria and ensuring steady power supply to support efficient utilisation of the provided ICT for effective teaching and learning in the Nigerian education system. In addition, there is a need for regular training of students and faculties on different ICT tools for competence, creativity and dynamic applications in teaching, learning and management of information.

FUTURE RESEARCH DIRECTIONS

ICT in education remain crucial to enhancing wider access to education and stimulating quality teaching and learning in the global education system. Although, education-driven ICT is well entrenched in the developed countries, it is fast gaining ground in the developing countries, especially in the sub-Saharan Africa, where ICT facilities are gradually being integrated in the education system of the region. This suggests that new ICT in education development will continue to emerge in the developing countries. This calls for conscientious monitoring and evaluation for progressive documentation and exposition of the developing countries technology inclusion in the 21st century information society. Thus, attention needs to be given to the type of emerging ICT in the developing countries' education system, dimensions of application, impacts, challenges and motivation to effective usage. In addition, will be the need to assess the training and capacity development needs of tutors and learners for effective ICT usage, attitude and behavioural disposition to ICT usage in the education system.

CONCLUSION

Emergence of ICT and integration in Nigeria's education system has greatly changed the face of education administration and instructional delivery in the country. The information-driven technology though had little or no impact on the lower level of education (primary and secondary), it has wider application in the higher learning schools across the country. Dimensions of ICT integration in the Nigerian higher education system thus range through website creation for publicity and image building, administration of both academic and non-academic administrative matters, teaching and learning, and conduct of school examinations. The technology is equally deployed for social and educational interactions among faculties and students, self and distance learning, virtual library services and online sourcing of academic information or publications. With these dimensions of ICT integration, information driven technology has in one way or the other impacted on the Nigerian higher education system. Specific areas of impacts include enhanced publicity and easy access to information about a particular university in the country, enhancement of teaching and learning process, ease of academic and non-academic record keeping and retrieval, and enhancement of access to university education through distance learning.

In the core academic matters, the deployed ICT tools for teaching, mostly comprises computers, PowerPoint projectors, microphones and loudspeakers, have proven to be of value, particularly when teaching a large class of students. With these set of ICT tools, every student, irrespective of where they may be sitting in the lecture theatre, could readily see and hear what is being taught by a lecturer. Without the ICT devices, teaching of large classes has been hideous with easy loss of attention and interest by students in what is being taught in such a classroom condition. The Internet service has been of great value for promoting ready access to online educational apps, documents and videos for improved learning opportunities. In addition, the internet application made it possible for the institutionalised Open University in the country to be sustained and fulfil its mandate of providing a university education to every interested candidate through the distance learning service. This has in turn made it possible for a number of Nigerians to have access to university education as expected. In the administrative matters is efficient handling of tasks than when all activities were operated by hands-on-desk services. Unlike the era of searching through the shelves or store rooms for a file that may never be found; and if found may have become mutilated with loss of information, record keeping are now electronic-based. This development not only ensure that the records are up-to-date but also allows for easy retrieval of the documents or information on request at the click of a button on the computer-based stored files.

Effective and efficient use of ICT in the country's higher education system is however being challenged by a number of factors, which were termed extrinsic and intrinsic barriers. Among the extrinsic barriers are inadequate ICT resources, absence of robust teaching and learning ICT tools, poor internet network and irregular power supply; while intrinsic barriers include high cost of ICT acquisition and operation, lack of strong drive for its usage and competent skills. Consequently, ICT integration in the Nigerian education system remains at the rudimentary stage largely because ICT devices that readily support direct teaching in classrooms, facilitates information processing and communication, are the commonly deployed. The country thus needs to advance its educational ICT status to support interactive networking, web-based and mobile learning for attainment of inspirational teaching and intelligible learning.

REFERENCES

Adomi, E. E., & Kpangban, E. (2010). Application of ICTs in Nigerian secondary schools. *Library Philosophy and Practice*. Retrieved April 10, 2020, from https://www.uidaho.edu/~mbolin/lpp2010.htm

Aduwa-Ogiegbean, S. E., & Iyamu, E. O. S. (2005). Using information and communication technology in secondary schools in Nigeria. *Journal of Educational Technology & Society*, 8(1), 104–112.

Agyeman, O. T. (2007). *ICT for education in Nigeria. Survey of ICT and Education in Africa: Nigeria Country Report*. Retrieved November 8, 2019, from www.infodev.org/ict4edu-africa

Becta, H. (2004). *Enabling teachers to make successful use of ICT*. Retrieved August 15, 2019, from http://ww.becta.org.uk

Belkin, D. (2019). Colleges mine data on their applicants. *The Street Wall Journal*. Retrieved January 4, 2019, from https://www.wsj.com/articles/the-data-colleges-collect-on-applicants-11548507602

Binghilams, K. A. (2009). Barriers to the successful integration of ICT in teaching and learning environments: A literature review. Eurasian *Journal of Mathematics, Science & Technology Education*, 5(3), 235–245.

Cato, J. (2001). *User-Centered Web Design*. Pearson Education.

Cortese, A. D. (2003). *The critical role of higher education in creating a sustainable future*. Retrieved May 15, 2019, from http://old.syntao.com/Uploads/files/The%20Critical%20Role%20of%20Higher%20Education%20in%20Creating%20a %20Sustainable %20Future.pdf

Daily Digest, D. M. I. (2019). 6 digital strategies to attract international students. *DMI Daily Digest blog*. Retrieved February 16, 2020, from https://digitalmarketinginstitute.com/en-gb/blog/6-digital-strategies-to-attract-international-students

Davis, J. (2017). *Innovative teaching strategies that improve student engagement. Association for middle level education*. Retrieved November 8, 2019, from https://www.amle.org/BrowsebyTopic/WhatsNew/WNDet/TabId/270/ArtMID/ 888/ArticleID/876/Innovative-Teaching-Strategies-that-Improve-Student-Engagement.aspx

Dede, C. (1996). The evolution of distance education: Emerging technologies and distributed learning. *American Journal of Distance Education*, 10(2), 4–36. doi:10.1080/08923649609526919

Dunn, D. S., Saville, B. K., Baker, S. C., & Marek, P. (2013). Evidence-based teaching: Tools and techniques that promote learning in the psychology classroom. *Australian Journal of Psychology*, 65(1), 5–13. doi:10.1111/ajpy.12004

EduSys. (2019). *What is ICT in education? Advantage & disadvantage* [Blog post]. Retrieved January 5, 2020, from https://www.edusys.co/blog/what-is-ict-in-education

European University Association. (2007). *Creativity in higher education. Report on the EUA creativity project 2006-2007*. Retrieved December 18, 2019, from https://eua.eu/downloads/publications/creativity%20in%20higher%20education%20%20report%20on%20the %20eua%20creativity%20project%20 2006-2007.pdf

FAO. (1993). *The potentials of microcomputers in support of agricultural extension, education and training*. Food and Agriculture Organisation of the United Nations.

Federal Ministry of Education. (2019). *National implementation guidelines for ICT in education*. Abuja: Author. Retrieved January 3, 2020, from http://education.gov.ng/ wpcontent/uploads/2019/07/national-implementation-guidelines-for-ict-in-education-2019.pdf

Flavian, C., Gurrea, R., & Orús, C. (2009). Web design: A key factor for the website success. *Journal of Systems and Information Technology, 11*(2), 168–184. doi:10.1108/13287260910955129

Fu, J. S. (2013). ICT in education: A critical literature review and its implications. *International Journal of Education and Development Using Information and Communication Technology, 9*(1), 112–125.

Gehrke, D., & Turban, E. (1999). Determinants of successful website design: Relative importance and recommendations for effectiveness. *Proceedings of the 32nd Hawaii International Conference on System Sciences*. 10.1109/HICSS.1999.772943

Hannah, C. (2018). *The 92 hottest EdTech tools according to education experts*. Tutorful. Retrieved January 5, 2020, from https://tutorful.co.uk/blog/the-82-hottest-edtech-tools-of-2017-according-to-education-experts

Huda, M., Anshari, M., Almunawar, M. N., Shahrill, M., Tan, A., & Jaidin, J. H. … Masari, M. (2016). Innovative teaching in higher education: The big data approach. *The Turkish Online Journal of Educational Technology*. Retrieved December 2, 2019, from https://www.researchgate.net/ profile/Miftachul_Huda4/publication/311576765_Innovative_Teaching_in_Higher_Education_The_Big_Data_Approach/links/584e7f5f08ae4bc8993779eb/Innovative-Teaching-in-Higher-Education-The-Big-Data-Approach.pdf

Hung, D., Tan, S. C., & Chen, D. T. (2005). How the Internet facilitates learning as dialog design considerations for online discussions. *International Journal of Instructional Media, 32*(1), 37–46.

Idowu, A. I., & Esere, M. (2013). ICT and higher educational system in Nigeria. *Educational Research Review, 8*(21), 2021–2025. doi:10.5897/ERR09.044

IWS. (2019). *Top 20 country in internet users vs. rest of the world*. Internet World Stats. Retrieved January 12, 2020, from https://www.internetworldstats.com/ top20.htm

Jia, S. (2019). *Literature review of YouTube in teaching activities*. Paper presented at the Twenty-Third Pacific Asia Conference on Information Systems, China. Retrieved February 1, 2020, from http://www. pacis2019.org/wd/Submissions/ PACIS2019_paper_236.pdf

Kanninen, E. (2008). *Learning styles and e-learning*. (Unpublished Master of science thesis). Tempere University of Technology.

Keegan, D. J. (1980). On defining distance education. *Distance Education, 1*(1), 13–36. doi:10.1080/0158791800010102

King, C. (2015). *3 most common causes of slow internet connection*. Retrieved April 7, 2020, from https://www.linkedin.com/pulse/3-most-common-causes-slow-internet-connection-charlotte-king

Ko, J., Sammons, P., & Bakkum, L. (2010). *Effective teaching*. Education Development Trust.

Lawal-Adebowale, O. A. (2015). Mobile phone revolution and its dimensional social and economic impacts in Nigeria's context. In P. E. Thomas, M. Srihari, & S. Kaur (Eds.), *Handbook of research on cultural and economic impacts of the information society* (pp. 359–390). IGI Global. doi:10.4018/978-1-4666-8598-7.ch016

Lawal-Adebowale, O. A., & Oyekunle, O. (2014). Agro-students' appraisal of online registration of academic courses in the Federal University of Agriculture Abeokuta, Ogun State Nigeria. *International Journal of Education and Development Using Information and Communication Technology*, *10*(4), 139–154.

Linways. (2017). *ICT enabled education: The alchemy of mixing technology and education* [Blog post]. Retrieved November 16, 2019. From https://stories.linways.in/ict-enabled-education-d190bcc91bf0

Luo, H., & Lei, J. (2012). Emerging technologies for interactive learning in ICT age. In J. Jia (Ed.), *Educational stages and interactive learning: from kindergarten To workplace training* (pp. 73–91). Information Science Reference. doi:10.4018/978-1-4666-0137-6.ch005

McClea, M., & Yen, D. C. (2005). A framework for the utilization of information technology in higher education admission department. *International Journal of Educational Management*, *19*(2/3), 87–101. doi:10.1108/09513540510582390

Mohanty, J. (2001). *Educational Technology*. Rajouri Garden.

Mujumdar, S. (2011). ICT for distance learning symbiosis centre for distance learning, India. In C. Wing (Ed.), *ICT for higher education case studies from Asia and the Pacific*. United Nations Education, Scientific and Cultural Organisation/ Asia and Pacific Regional Bureau for Education.

Naidu, S. (2019). The idea of open education. *Distance Education*, *40*(1), 1–4. doi:10.1080/01587919.2018.1564622

NCC Database. (2019). *Subscriber statistics*. Nigerian Communication Commission. Retrieved January 12, 2020, from https://www.ncc.gov.ng/statistics-reports/ subscriber-data#monthly-subscriber-technology-data

Office of the Auditor General. (2016). *Information and communication technology (ICT) in education*. Report 19. Author. Retrieved May 7, 2020, from https://www.wa.gov.au/reports-and-publications/reports/information-and-communication-technology-ict-in-education/key-findings/internet-speed-bandwidth-agin-devices-impact-use-ict-schools/

Okebukola, P. (1997). Old, new, and current technology in education. *UNESCO Africa*, *14*(15), 7–18.

Olakulehin, F. K. (2007). Information and communication technologies in teacher training and professional development in Nigeria. *Turkish Journal of Distance Education*, *8*(1), 133–142.

Ozturk, I. (2001). The role of education in economic development: A theoretical perspective. *Journal of Rural Development and Administration*, *33*(1), 39–47. doi:10.2139srn.1137541

Rasul, S., Bukhsh, Q., & Batool, S. (2011). A study to analyze the effectiveness of audio visual aids in teaching learning process at university level. *Procedia: Social and Behavioral Sciences, 28*, 78–81. doi:10.1016/j.sbspro.2011.11.016

Singh, Y. K. (2005). *Instructional technology in education.* Darya Ganj.

Tenopir, C. (2003). *Use and users of electronic library resources: an overview and analysis of recent research studies.* Washington, DC: Council on Library and Information Resources. Retrieved July 18, 20219, http://webdoc.sub.gwdg.de/ ebook/aw/2004/pub120.pdf

Thelwall, M. (2000). Computer-based assessment: A versatile educational tool. *Computer Education, 34*(1), 37–39. doi:10.1016/S0360-1315(99)00037-8

UNESCO. (2009). *ICTs for higher education.* Paper presented at the 2009 World Conference on Higher Education (WCHE), Paris, France.

Wang, Q. Y., & Woo, H. L. (2007). Comparing asynchronous online discussions and face-to-face discussions in a classroom setting. *British Journal of Educational Technology, 38*(2), 272–286. doi:10.1111/j.1467-8535.2006.00621.x

Wastiau, P., Blamire, R., Kearney, C., Quittre, V., Van de Gaer, E., & Monseur, C. (2013). The use of ICT in education: A survey of schools in Europe. *European Journal of Education, 48*(1), 11–27. doi:10.1111/ejed.12020

Whitehead, F. (2019, November 13). Student recruitment strategy: four universities, five key questions. *The Guardian.* https://www.theguardian.com/higher-education-network/blog/2012/nov/13/student-recruitment-strategy-international-universities

Wieland, K., & Ifenthaler, D. (2009). Evaluating the effectiveness of a simulation-based collaborative learning environment and validating new ways to assess learning outcomes. *Proceedings of 32nd Annual Conference of the Association for Educational Communication and Technology, 2*, 243-250.

Wilson, S. M., & Peterson, P. L. (2006). *Theories of learning and teaching: What do they mean for educators?* National Education Association Research.

Wong, A. F. L., Quek, C.-L., Divaharan, S., Liu, W.-C., Peer, J., & William, M. D. (2006). Singapore students' and teachers' perception of computer-supported project work classroom learning environment. *Journal of Research on Technology in Education, 38*(4), 449–479. doi:10.1080/15391523.2006.10782469

Yazici, C., & Cagiltay, K. (2009). Evaluation of a university level computerized language learning architecture through the perceptions of students, instructors and administrators: A case study. *Proceedings of 32nd Annual Conference of the Association for Educational Communication and Technology, 2*, 251-259.

Yuen, A., Fox, B., & Park, J. (2011). The use of ICT for administration and management at the University of Hong Kong. In C. Wing (Ed.), *ICT for higher education case studies from Asia and the Pacific.* United Nations Education, Scientific and Cultural Organisation/Asia and Pacific Regional Bureau for Education.

Chapter 12
ICT Use in Higher Education in Eastern States of India:
An Analysis

Adwaita Maiti
 https://orcid.org/0000-0003-0838-9041
Prabhat Kumar College, Contai, India

Sebak Kumar Jana
 https://orcid.org/0000-0002-3532-4350
Vidyasagar University, India

ABSTRACT

Information and communication technology (ICT) cannot be separated from our daily needs. ICT helps in reducing the disparity in wealth of educational resources. The uses of ICT in education add value in teaching and learning by enhancing the effectiveness of learning or by adding a dimension to learning. ICT may also be a significant motivational factor in students' learning. Uses of ICT in eastern states in India are lagging behind all other regions of India. In this background, the authors review the use of ICT by higher education students of four states in eastern India. They have attempted to find the factors responsible for use of ICT by the students. As the findings suggest, region, gender, education levels of households, type of courses, possession of computer and internet facility, consumption levels of households, and whether students stay in institutional hostel or not are the influencing factors to use of ICT.

INTRODUCTION

In the modern age Information and Communication Technology (ICT) cannot be separated with our daily needs. Higher education is in the process of challenge, thereby challenging the traditional system of education. India's achievements in the field of higher education in post-independence period are remarkable. There has been a huge quantitative expansion of higher education in India in the post-independence period. In 2016-17, there were 864 universities, about 40 thousands colleges, 35.7 millions of students

DOI: 10.4018/978-1-7998-3468-7.ch012

and 1.365 million teachers in higher education in India (AISHE 2018). Higher education systems in India have grown exponentially in the last five decades to meet the demands of quality education for all. This aspect has further gained momentum due to swift advancements in ICT. Use of ICT in higher education is not only a technique for educational development but also a way of socio-economic development of the nation (Sarkar, 2012).

ICT infrastructure is one important way of stimulating growth in national innovation and economic productivity. It is clear from international evidence that there is a virtuous nexus and a clear link between ICT and productivity (OECD, 2012). Government of India has taken long-term initiatives like Digital India, Make in India, Smart Cities, e-Governance, push for digital talent through Skill India, drive towards a cashless economy and efforts to kindle innovation through Start-up India for making India a digitally empowered society and a knowledge hub (Karmakar and Jana, 2015). ICT is one of the economic development pillars to gain national competitive advantage. It can improve the quality of human life because it can be used as learning and education media. The boundaries between regular students and distance student diffuse with the use of ICTs (Jana & Maiti, 2020). The use of ICT in education add value in teaching and learning, by enhancing the effectiveness of learning, or by adding a dimension to learning, ICT may also be a significant motivational factor in students' learning, and can support students' engagement with collaborative learning. It increases its importance in people's lives, ICT literacy become a functional requirement for people's work, social, and personal lives.

Use of ICT by the students of higher education in eastern region is less compare to all others region and also the national average. In this background we propose to review the use of ICT by the students of higher education in eastern states in India based on following objectives.

Objectives

The major objectives of the present study are as follows:

1. To explore the status of the use of computer and internet by the students of higher education in eastern states of India.
2. To find the determinants of use information and communication technology (ICT) by the students in eastern region in India.

LITERATURE REVIEW

We mention here a brief review of literature on use of ICT in education. Alumu and Thiagarajan, (2016) explain how internet is becoming an integral part of Higher Education in the current scenario. E-learning is greeted all over the world, especially for academics, as the benefits are very satisfying, compared with face-to-face learning. According to Mondal and Mete (2016), the introduction of ICTs in the higher education has profound implications for the whole education process especially in dealing with key issues of access, equity, management, efficiency, pedagogy and quality. According to Irvin (2007) despite coming of age with the Internet and other technologies, many students in colleges lack the information and communication technology (ICT) literacy skills—locating, evaluating, and communicating information—necessary to navigate and use the overabundance of information available today. Krishnaveni and Meenakumari (2010) identify the various functional areas to which ICT is deployed for information administration in higher education institutions, as in General Administration, Pay Roll and Financial Accounting, Administration of Student Data, Inventory Management, Personnel Records Maintenance, Library System. According to Al-Alak (2009), during the twentieth century, education, skill and the acquisition of knowledge have become crucial determinants of people and nations' productivity. According to Hoy (2014), internet helps in democratization of education, by facilitating everyone to access knowledge that has been accumulated by mankind. Nowadays MOOCs are playing supportive role of traditional education system. Students should take benefit of free MOOCs all over the world. Working People and house wives who cannot join regular education, MOOCs provides learning opportunity to them to educate from their desired universities (Joshi, 2015).

The study by Abramovich & Bride, 2018n reveals that Open Educational Resources (OER) are equal or better than traditional course content, especially in helping students reach course learning objectives. Scott et al (2016) suggest that students practice self-regulated learning in ESN (Enterprise Social Network system) informal learning spaces, raising new possibilities for future development of online learning ecologies. University Grants Commission (2017) in India proposed that the education through digital mission holds promise since it is accessible to everyone, it is affordable, it can overcome the shortage of quality faculty and it can enhance the enrolment in higher education system. The digital learning platforms provide opportunities for lifelong learning. So many digital initiatives taken by the commission like, e-pg Pathshala, Swayam-Prabh etc. To an extent MOOCS, a newest technology supported educational programmes will be of great help to individuals irrespective of nation, social status and economic conditions (Ajithkumar, 2016). The problem of access, quality concerns of the prevailing education programmes etc. is a barrier to the right of the individual in obtaining higher education.

There is continuing debate regarding the impact of ICT on performance of students. Some researcher argues that ICT impact positively on the performance of the student of higher education. Kulik's (1994) meta-analysis study revealed that, on average, students who used ICT-based instruction scored higher than students without computers. The students also liked their classes more when ICT-based instruction was included. Youssef &Dahmani (2008) examine the relationship between the use of information and communication technologies (ICT) and student performance in higher education, ICT seems to have a impact on the process of learning in higher education by offering new possibilities for learners and teachers. These possibilities can have an impact on student performance and achievement. Fuchs and Woessman (2004) showed that while the bivariate correlation between the availability of ICT and students' performance is strongly and significantly positive, the correlation becomes small and insignificant when other student environment characteristics are taken into consideration.

Future higher education will look quite different in terms of the mission and functions of higher education institutions, modes of teaching and learning, pedagogical approaches, student-teacher relationships and the role of teachers. To stay competitive teacher educators should use ICT to support existing pedagogical practices, but be aware of its potential drawbacks. Only a coordinated effort by the teacher educators will ensure success of ICT in a reasonable manner (Koryuhina and Shamshina, 2018). Ritzhaupt and Liu (2013) examine information and communication technology (ICT) literacy of students and its relationship to a student's socio-economic status (SES) like gender, and ethnicity of students. Results show a digital divide between low and high SES, white and non-white, and female and male students on all measures of the Student Tool for Technology Measurement. Specifically, high-SES, white, and female students outperformed their counterparts. Boys held more favourable attitudes toward technology and considered them more competent than girls did (Cai et al., 2017). Siddiq and Schererb (2019) findings contrast those obtained from previous meta-analyses that were based on self-reported ICT literacy and suggest that the ICT gender gap may not be as severe as it had been claimed to be.

Disparities in access to and proficiency in information and communication technology (ICT), particularly between socio-economically advantaged and disadvantaged children, and between rural and urban residents, have long been a focus of public policy. The expression "digital divide" was coined to underline the fact that such disparities may threaten social and national cohesion, as they impede full participation in work and reduce political efficacy for population groups that are left behind on the analogue side of the divide (OECD, 2001). what students do with computers, from using e-mail to reading news on the Internet, is related to students' socio-economic difference in access in computer and internet, gender difference, rural –urban gap in Internet access, the role of institute to provide computer and internet access, computer use at home (OECD, 2015)

Some researchers argue that there is no clear relation or direct relation between ICT and performance of the students. Terry, Lewer and Macy (2003) surveyed some students in a programme offering courses in the three formats of online, on-campus, and hybrid. Using a standard regression model where final examination score is the dependent variable and student characteristics are the independent variables, they report that predicted exam scores for students in the online courses were significantly less than those of students in the on-campus and in the hybrid formats.

Per capita income of eastern region states of India (Bihar, Jharkhand, Orissa and West Bengal) are less than national average. The public spending on higher education across major states in India is found much below the desired level (Jana & Maiti, 2019). In Eastern India approximately 70% people are literate according to 2011 census data. Eastern states have above 15% share of enrolment in higher education In India. NSSO unit level data (2014) revealed that (table 1).

Table 1. Region-wise use of ICT by the students of higher education in India

Region	% of Students' Household has Computer	% of Students' Household has Internet Facility	% of students in Higher Education	
			Operate_ Computer	Internet_ search
Central	47.9	70.5	86.2	83.5
Eastern	*48.7*	*72.8*	*78.1*	*73.5*
North Eastern	57.5	73.0	79.7	74.3
Northern	53.5	74.8	79.3	75.9
Southern	56.0	89.8	95.4	92.2
Western	57.0	84.9	89.0	85.5
Grand Total	**54.0**	**79.6**	**85.4**	**81.6**

Source: Own Calculation based on NSSO 71st Round Unit Level Data on Social Consumption: Education.

DATA SOURCE

The present study uses the NSSO 71st Round Unit Level Data on Social Consumption: Education, survey conducted in January-June 2014 (71st round) and published in 2015. Here we only use data related to higher education (graduate and post graduate) of all eastern region states in India. The other sources of data are: All India Survey of Higher Education (AISHE), MHRD, GOI, Various years.

Data Source	Data Provide	URL
NSSO	National Sample Survey Office provides different socio economic data at household level.	http://www.mospi.gov.in/nsso
AISHE Report	All India Survey of Higher Education provide higher education data at disaggregate level in India.	(http://aishe.nic.in/aishe/home)

HYPOTHESIS

Whether different socioeconomic factors, like region, caste, gender, consumption class, parents occupation and education level, have significant effect on ability to use ICT.

METHODOLOGY

Econometric tools have been used for the analysis of data. We have used logit regression model for finding the determinants of use information and communication technology (ICT) by the students.

To find the factors of use of ICT in higher education, we have arranged the data by different categories like region, caste, gender, consumption class and have calculated the required percentages of ICT able students. To identify the determinants of use ICT, a binary logistic regression model has been employed. Logistic regression applies maximum likelihood estimation after transforming the dependent into a logit variable. In our analysis the dependent variable is Y is binary variable,

Y=1; when a student able to operate computer, know computer word, internet search and also know how to emailing then he is ICT able,

Y= 0, otherwise

Now, the Logit model may be presented as in equation (1).

$$L_i = \ln\left(\frac{P_i}{1-P_i}\right) = Z_i = \beta_0 + \beta_1 X_1 + \beta_2 X_2 + \ldots + \beta_n X_n + u_i \tag{1}$$

$P_i = E (Y_i = 1/X_i)$ means the students have ability to use ICT. $P_i/(1-P_i)$ is simply the odds ratio in favour of ability to use ICT – the ratio of the probability that a student is able to use ICT to the probability that not able to use ICT. L_i, the log of the odds ratio, is not only linier in X but also linier in the parameters. L is called the logit, and hence the name logit model (models like equation 1). X_i's are independent variables. The coefficients of the model β_i's represent the change in the value of the *logit* for a unit change in the covariate (when continuous) or the difference from one category to the next if the covariate is binary; u_i represents the error term. Selected explanatory variables for the analysis are presented in table 3.

Table 3. Independent variables selected for binary logistic regression model analysis

Explanatory Variables			Expected Sign
Categories	**Variables**	**Variables Label**	
1. State	Bihar	Bihar=1, Other States= 0	Negative
	West Bengal	West Bengal=1, Other States=0	Positive
2. Sector	Urban	Rural=0, Urban=1	Positive
3. Gender	Female	Female=1, Male=0	Negative
4. Course	Technical/Professional courses	Technical/Professional courses=1, General Course= 0	Positive
	Post Graduate	Post Graduate= 1, Graduate= 0	Positive
5. Institution Type	Private	Private=1, Govt.=0	Positive
6. Medium of Instruction	English	English Medium = 1, Others Medium=0	Positive
7. Occupation of Head of the household	Self Employed	Self Employed = 1, others=0	Negative
	Daily wage & salary	Wage and Salaried = 1, Others=0	Positive
8. Religion	Hindu	Hindu=1, Others=0	Positive
9. Social Caste	Non- Scheduled	Non Scheduled=, Scheduled=0	Negative
10. Household has Computer and Internet facility	Hhs comp. (Y=1, N=0)	Household have computer= 1, not have computer= 0	Positive
	Internet (Y=1, N=0)	Household have internet facility=1, not have internet facility=0	Positive
11. HHs Consumption Expenditure	UMPCE	Usual Monthly Per Capita Consumption Expenditure (in Rs.)	Positive
	Quintile 1	Quintle Class 1=1, Quintile Class 2-5= 0	Negative
	Quintile 4	Quintile Class 4=1, Quintile Class 1-3 and 5= 0	Positive
	Quintile 5	Quintile Class 5=1, Quintile Class 1-4= 0	Positive
12. Education Level of Head	Graduate and Above	Graduate and Above =1, otherwise= 0	Positive
	Up to Upper Primary	Up to Upper Primary =1, otherwise=0	Negative
13. Institutional Hostel	Hostel (Y=1, N=0)	Student stay in Institutional Hostel=1, Otherwise=0	Positive

Table 4 presents number of surveyed students in eastern states in India by various dimensions. This study only incorporates the students of higher education, pursuing graduation and post-graduation degrees with different general and technical/professional courses. The analysis is based on 1940 students from all the states in eastern region in India, out of those 821 students were from the rural area and 1119 from the urban area, and 1135 pursuing general courses and 805 pursuing technical/professional courses.

Table 4. State wise number of students in analysis by different dimension

States	Sector		Gender		Course		Total
	Rural	Urban	Female	Male	General	Technical/ Professional	
Bihar	331	296	225	402	401	226	627
Jharkhand	80	131	107	104	115	96	211
Orissa	133	143	131	145	168	108	276
West Bengal	277	549	367	459	451	375	826
Eastern Region	**821**	**1119**	**830**	**1110**	**1135**	**805**	**1940**

Source:Own Calculation based on NSSO 71st Round . 2015

RESULTS AND DISCUSSION

This section provides an analysis about the state wise disparity in use of ICT by the higher education students in India, by Sector, gender, castes, institutions type, subject/courses, household education level and by consumption quintile. At last by using binary logistic regression model we try to find out what are the determinants of use ICT by the students of higher education in eastern states in India. In table 5 we have present different aspects of variability in the data.

State Wise Disparityin Use of ICT

In this section we have tried to find state wise use of computer and internet by the students in higher education eastern states in India. We have emphasised here on four basic indicators of ICT needed for present day higher education: 1) Ability to operate computer, 2) ability to use computer word, 3) Ability to use internet for searching and, 4) Able to use internet for sending e-mails. These are defined as follows.

Able to operate computer (Operate_Computer): Ability to use the basic functions of computer processing, like creating a document, taking printouts, saving, naming/renaming of files, editing, using excel and so many basic work using computer.

*Ability to use computer word (Comp_Word):*Ability to write a text on Microsoft word and saving this as word document.

*Able to use internet for searching (Internet_Search):*Use of internet by using a search engine and advanced search for searching desired information, opening links in new windows, visiting websites, etc.

*Able to use internet for sending emails (Internet_email):*Communicate through internet by sending or reading emails, composing a message, attaching a file, deleting an e-mail etc.

Table 6 presents state wise percentage of students in higher education able to operate computer, able to operate computer word, able to search internet and able to e-mailing, separately.

In India, in higher education, 85.4% students are able to operate computer, 82.3% students able to operate computer word, 81.6% students are able to search internet and 78.2% students are able to e-

Table 5. Data structure

Categories	Variability in Data
States	Bihar = 7.3%, Jharkhand = 14.2%, Orissa= 9.5%, West Bengal= 42.6%
Sector	Rural= 42.3%, Urban= 57.7%
Gender	Female= 42.8%, Male= 57.2%
Course	Graduate= 81%, Post Graduate= 19%
	General= 58.5%, Technical/Professional= 41.5%
Institution Type	Private= 34%, Govt. = 66%
Medium of Instruction	English= 49.6%, Hindi= 27.7%, Bengali= 20.3%, Others= 2.4%
Occupation of Head	Self-Employed= 72.5%, Regular wage/salary earnings= 11.9%, Casual Labour= 3.8%, Others= 11.8%
Religion	Hindu= 86.4%, Muslim= 11.2%, others = 2.4%
Social Caste	Scheduled= 16.6%, Non-Scheduled= 83.4%
Households have Computer and Internet Facility	Students household have computer= 48.7%, not have computer=51.3%; Students household have internet facility= 72.8%, not have internet facility= 27.2%
HHs Consumption Expenditure	Quintile 1= 9.3%, Quintile 2= 16.1%, Quintile 3= 14.8%, Quintile 4 = 22.9%, Quintile 5= 36.9% Mean UMPCE=Rs. 2600, SD=1984.28, Max= Rs. 20625, Min= 250
Education Level of Head	Primary= 10.9%, Upper Primary= 29.1%, Secondary= 18.4%, Higher secondary= 12.8%, Graduation= 21.9%, Above Graduation= 7%
Institutional Hostel	Student stay in Hostel= 21.83%, Not stay in hostel= 78.17%

Source:Own Calculation based on NSSO 71st Round . 2015

mailing. But in eastern region these indicators respectively are 78.1%, 75.2%, 73.5% and 69.6%, it is clear that all indicators are less then national level.

State Wise Disparity of Operating Computer by Sector, Gender and Caste

Here we focus on different socio economic factorsthat affect use of ICT for all the states in eastern region in India. Table 7 presents sector, gender and social caste wise percentage of students operate computer

Table 6. State wise percentage of students in higher education who are able to operate ICT

Region	States	% of Students' Household has Computer	% of Students' Household has Internet Facility	% of students in Higher Education			
				Operate Computer	Compword	Internetsearch	Internet_ email
Eastern		**48.7**	**72.8**	**78.1**	**75.2**	**73.5**	**69.6**
	Bihar	51.7	71.8	71.9	65.7	68.4	65.4
	Jharkhand	36.0	60.7	75.4	72.5	71.1	68.2
	Odisha	35.9	70.3	75.0	73.6	72.1	70.3
	West Bengal	53.9	77.6	84.6	83.5	78.3	73.0
India		**54.0**	**79.6**	**85.4**	**82.3**	**81.6**	**78.2**

Source:Own Calculation based on NSSO 71st Round . 2015

Table 7. Region and state wise percentage of students operate computer

Region	States/UTs	Region		Gender		Social Caste	
		Rural	Urban	Female	Male	Non-Scheduled	Scheduled
Eastern		**67.6**	**85.9**	**71.2**	**83.3**	**79.8**	**69.7**
	Bihar	65.6	79.1	59.6	78.9	72.7	65.1
	Jharkhand	63.8	82.4	69.2	81.7	77.4	67.4
	Odisha	67.7	81.8	67.9	81.4	79.5	57.9
	West Bengal	71.1	91.4	80.1	88.2	86.6	76.3
India		**77.4**	**91.5**	**81.4**	**88.5**	**86.9**	**80.0**

Source:Own Calculation based on NSSO 71ˢᵗ Round . 2015

who are pursuing higher education at the time of survey. In rural regionof eastern India 67.6% higher education student and in urban region 85.9% student higher education student are able to operate computer, these values are far less from national average. In this region 71.2% female student and 83.3% male student operate computer also 69.7% scheduled student and 79.8% non-scheduled student in higher education are able to operate computer.

State wise Disparity of Using ICT by Institution Type

In eastern region in India the average percentage of the student for use ICT is higher for private institutions compared to public institutions. Those enrolled in private institutions for higher education are using more ICT. 89% of the student of private institutions have operated computers compare to 72.6% of the student of public institutions operate computer. 87.9% student in private institutions has used to know computer word but in public institutions, this is 68.8%. In private institutions, 84.6% of the students know how to sending email but in public institutions, only 62.1% of the student knows it. State-wise percentage present in table 8.

Table 8. Percentage of students able to use ICT by public and private institutions

Region	States/UTs	Operate Computer (%)		Comp_word (%)		Internet_email (%)	
		Public	Private	Public	Private	Public	Private
Eastern		**72.6**	**89.0**	**68.8**	**87.9**	**62.1**	**84.6**
	Bihar	64.9	86.3	56.7	84.3	57.4	81.7
	Jharkhand	72.7	85.7	68.9	85.7	64.0	83.7
	Odisha	73.3	76.7	71.2	76.0	67.1	73.6
	West Bengal	78.2	97.4	77.5	96.6	63.8	92.2
India		**79.2**	**89.7**	**75.1**	**87.3**	**69.8**	**84.1**

Source:Own Calculation based on NSSO 71ˢᵗ Round . 2015

ICT Ability of the Students in Higher Education by Different Courses/Subjects

Table 9 presents course wise ability to use ICT by the student of higher education for the respective states in India. We see that in all the states in eastern region, huge disparity in use of ICT have present between those are studied general courses and those who are studied in technical/professional courses. Technical/professional courses student have more able to use ICT compare to general courses student.

Table 9. Percentage of students able to use ICT by Course

State	Course	% HH Comp	% HH internet	% operate_ computer	% computer_ word	% Internet_ search	% internet_ email
Bihar	General	38.2	61.1	59.9	51.4	55.6	51.4
	Tech./Prof.	75.7	90.7	93.4	91.2	91.2	90.3
Jharkhand	General	33.9	57.4	66.1	63.5	59.1	53.9
	Tech./Prof.	38.5	64.6	86.5	83.3	85.4	85.4
Orissa	General	19.6	56.5	60.7	59.5	56.5	55.4
	Tech./Prof.	61.1	91.7	97.2	95.4	96.3	93.5
West Bengal	General	39.7	65.0	74.1	72.5	63.4	55.4
	Tech./Prof.	70.9	92.8	97.3	96.8	96.3	94.1

Source:Own Calculation based on NSSO 71st Round . 2015

NB: *HH Comp:* student household has computer,*HH Internet:* Student household has internet facility.

Household Education Level and Use of ICT

Do education levels of the household members of the student have any effect on use of ICT? It is expected that better educated families to value education more and accordingly to spend more on higher education also importance to ICT. The highest education level of any member of the household who is not necessarily the head of the household but the education level of the head of the household does matter more significantly. Table 10 presents use of computer and internet by the student for their respective household head education level in eastern states in India. Use of ICT more or less systematically increases by the educational level of the head of the household. The higher the education level of the head of the household, the higher will be the use of computer and internet.

Household Consumption Level and use of ICT

Household consumption levels measured by Usual Monthly Per capita Consumption Expenditure (UMPCE) prescribed by NSSO (National Sample Survey Organisation). In the Table 11, the different quintile classes are referred to simply as 1 (lowest quintile class), 2, 3, 4 and 5 (highest quintile class). Lower and upper limits of the quintiles to have an idea of level of living of the households belonging to these quintile classes.

We present quintile class wise status of ICT use by the students in higher education in eastern region in India and India as whole. Percentage of students' householdspossessing computer and have internet

Table 10. Status of ICT of the students in higher education by education level of households' head

Head Education Level	% Students' householdspossessing computer	% Students' households having Internet Facility	% of students who can Operate computer
Primary	23.1	52.4	60.8
Upper Primary	32.3	66.0	72.9
Secondary	48.9	70.5	76.1
Higher Secondary	56.0	78.2	83.5
Graduation	66.8	84.5	88.5
Above Graduation	85.9	93.3	90.4
Grand Total	*48.7*	*72.8*	*78.1*

Source:Own Calculation based on NSSO 71ˢᵗ Round . 2015

Table 11. Lower and upper limits of UMPCE in different quintile classes for each sector (Rs.)

Quintile class	Rural (UMPCE in Rs.)		Urban (UMPCE in Rs.)	
	Lower limit	upper limit	lower limit	upper limit
Quintile 1	0	786	0	1200
Quintile 2	786	1000	1200	1667
Quintile 3	1000	1286	1667	2250
Quintile 4	1287	1667	2250	3333
Quintile 5	1667	-	3333	-

Source: NSSO 71ˢᵗRound, 2015

facility increases from lower class to upper quintile class. From this discussion it is clear to understand that there is direct relation between consumption level of household and use of ICT. Different consumption quintile wise information of ICT use presents in table 12.

Table 12. Status of ICT by quintile class of household of the student

Quintile Class	% Students' household has computer		% Students' household has Internet Facility		% of students Operate computer	
	India	Eastern Region	India	Eastern Region	India	Eastern Region
Quintile 1	25.2	20.0	54.7	47.8	64.6	58.3
Quintile 2	33.4	29.7	66.0	63.6	73.0	68.1
Quintile 3	42.0	40.8	73.4	64.5	80.7	76.7
Quintile 4	50.1	48.0	78.9	73.9	85.5	79.1
Quintile 5	68.3	67.7	88.4	85.9	92.5	87.6
Grand Total	*54.0*	48.7	*79.6*	72.8	*85.4*	78.1

Source:Own Calculation based on NSSO 71ˢᵗ Round . 2015

Determinants of ability to use of computers and internet by the students in higher education in Eastern Region in India (Graduate and Post-Graduate Level) (Binary Logistic Model)

Table 12 presents the logistic regression results when modelling the effects of socio-economic determinants (Xi) on ability to use ICT as presented in equation 1. This analysis has been done at the unit level data on 1940 students who were pursuing higher education (Graduate & Post Graduate) in four eastern region states in India at the time of NSSO 71st round (2014) survey.

From the logistic regression results in table 12, we see that in *Bihar* region variables negatively and significantly influence the use of ICT. *Urban* sector positively and significantly affect dependent variable that means students belongs to urban sector have more ability to use computer and internet compare to the students belongs to rural sector. *Female* under gender category negatively affect dependent variable at 1% level of significant. That means males have more ability to use ICT compare to females. Variable

Table 13. Regression result (binary logistic regression)

Categories	Variables	B	S.E.	Wald	Sig.	Exp(B)
Region	*Bihar*	-.512	.185	7.71	**.005**	.599
	West Bengal	-.119	.176	.45	.500	.888
Sector	*Urban*	.582	.186	9.81	**.002**	1.789
Gender	*Female*	-.979	.139	49.51	**.000**	.376
Course	*Post Graduate*	1.016	.200	25.79	**.000**	2.762
	Tech/Professional	1.080	.175	38.23	**.000**	2.944
Institution type	*Private*	.077	.172	.19	.655	1.080
Medium of Instruction	*English*	.654	.165	15.71	**.000**	1.922
Occupation of the Head of the Household	*Self employed*	-.266	.190	1.95	.162	.767
	Daily wage & salary	-.530	.251	4.46	.035	.589
Religion	*Hindu*	.383	.185	4.28	.038	1.466
Social Caste	*Non scheduled*	.012	.171	.01	.943	1.012
Household has Computer and Internet Facility	*Hh comp(Y=1, N=0)*	.600	.162	13.69	**.000**	1.821
	internet(Y=1, N=0)	1.604	.156	106.29	**.000**	4.973
Consumption expenditure	*UMPCE (Rs.)*	.000	.000	2.16	.142	1.000
	Quintile1	-.639	.231	7.63	**.006**	.528
	Quintile4	.110	.189	.34	.561	1.116
	Quintile5	-.100	.274	.13	.715	.905
Education Level of Head	*Graduate and Above*	.039	.190	.04	.839	1.039
	Up to Upper Primary	-.238	.158	2.26	.133	.788
Institutional Hostel	*Hostel (Y=1, N=0)*	.983	.241	16.65	**.000**	2.673
Constant		-1.256	.350	12.86	.000	.285
Cox & Snell R Square	0.38					
Nagelkerke R Square	0.53					
-2 Log likelihood	1485.38*					

Source: Own Estimation based on NSSO 71st Round . 2015

post-graduate under course category are positively affect dependent variable at 1% level of significant, i.e. post graduate student have more use ICT compare to Graduate student in higher education. The variable, *Technical/Professional* under course category positively and significantly related with dependent variable, i.e. people studying technical and professional courses have more able to use ICT compare to people studying general courses in higher education. Institution type, whether it is government institute or private institute, does not matter for use of ICT, and not significantly affect ability to use ICT. But the medium of instruction is important factor influence ICT ability. Students who are studying English medium institutions are more able to use computers and internet compare to other medium. Variables under occupation of the Head of the Household are not significantly affect dependent variable. Also social caste does not matter for ability to use ICT. Households of the students having computer and internet facility, both positively affect use ICT at 1% level of significant. Students are more ICT able those household have computer and Internet facility. Household consumption expenditure is important influencing factor for use of ICT. Usual monthly per capita consumption expenditure positively affects dependent variable at 1% level of significant. Students belongs to lower consumption quintile (Quintile 1, 2) have low level of ability to use ICT compare to students belongs to upper quintile classes (Quintile 4, 5). Another influencing factor to use ICT is education level of head of the household of the student, ICT competence is low for students whose family heads have lower educational qualifications. A student whether staying in hostel or not, is important factor for ability to use ICT, with results thatstudents staying in hostels are more able to use ICT.

The binary logistic regression model has been estimated based on the data of 1940 higher education students. The classification table (table 14) shows us the sensitivity of prediction, that is, the percentage of occurrences correctly predicted 88.9%. We also see specificity of the prediction, which is the percentage of non occurrences correctly, predicted 65%. Overall our predictions were correct 1579 out of 1940, for an overall success rate 81.4%.

Table 14. The observed and the predicted frequencies for ability to use ICT, by logistic regression with the cut-off of 0.50

Observed	Predicted		Percentage Correct
	No	Yes	
No	397	214	65.0
Yes	147	1182	88.9
Overall Percentage			81.4

Source: Own Estimation based on NSSO 71st Round . 2015

CONCLUSION

ICT has made the economy with no boundary in time and space. It brings a lot of advantages for economic development including the development of the education sector. Many factors are found responsible for use of ICT by the students of higher education in eastern states in India as revealed in the present study. These factors are regional, rural-urban disparities, gender, education levels of households, type of courses pursued by the students, households having computer and internet facility or not, consumption levels of households and whether students staying in institutional hostel or not . Students from Bihar, have less ability to use ICT compared to other states of eastern India. Ability to use ICT for male students is greater than female students. The students from urban sector is more able to use it compared to the students those are from rural sector. Those studying in technical and professional courses are more able to use computer and internet compare to those who are studying in general courses. Students from upper consumption quintile are more able to use ICT. Post-graduate students are more able to use ICT compared to under-graduate students. Students staying in institutional hostels are found to have more ability to use it. 'English' as a medium of instruction is an influencing factor of ability to use ICT. The study reveals that there is enough scope of improving the skill for the use of ICT in higher education in India.

REFERENCES

Abramovich, S., & Bride, M. M. (2018). Open education resources and perceptions of financial value. *Internet and Higher Education*, *39*, 33–38. doi:10.1016/j.iheduc.2018.06.002

Ajithkumar, C. (2016). Transforming Indian Higher Education-Role of MOOCs. *International Journal for Innovative Research in Multidisciplinary Field*, *2*(9), 195–201.

Al-Alak, B. A. (2009). Measuring and evaluating business students' satisfaction perceptions at public and private universities in Jordan. *Asian Journal of Marketing*, *3*(2), 33–51. doi:10.3923/ajm.2009.33.51

Alumu, S., & Thiagarajan, P. (2016). Massive Open Online Courses and E-learning in Higher Education. *Indian Journal of Science and Technology*, *9*(6), 1–10. doi:10.17485/ijst/2016/v9i6/81170

Cai, Z., Fan, X., & Du, J. (2017). Gender and attitudes toward technology use: A meta-analysis. *Computers & Education*, *105*, 1–13. doi:10.1016/j.compedu.2016.11.003

Fuchs, T. & Woessmann, L. (2005). *Computers and Student Learning: Bivariate and Multivariate Evidence on the Availability and Use of Computers at Home and at School*. CES ifo Working Paper No. 8. https://www.ifo.de/DocDL/IfoWorkingPaper-8.pdf

Hoy, M. B. (2014). MOOCs 101: An introduction to massive open online courses. *Medical Reference Services Quarterly*, *33*(1), 85–91. doi:10.1080/02763869.2014.866490 PMID:24528267

Irvin, R. (2007). Information and communication technology (ICT) literacy: Integration and assessment in higher education. *Journal of Systemics, Cybernetics and Informatics*, *5*(4), 50–55.

Jana, S. K., & Maiti, A. (2019). State-wise Public Expenditure on Higher Education in India: An Empirical Analysis. *Arthashastra Indian Journal of Economics and Research*, *8*(2), 7–20. doi:10.17010/aijer/2019/v8i2/145222

Jana, S.K. & Maiti, A. (2020). Innovations in Higher Education in India. In *Theoretical and practical approaches to innovation in higher education*. IGI Global. Doi:10.4018/978-1-7998-1662-1.ch009

Joshi, N. M. (2015). *Acceptance of MOOCs for Engineering Education in India*. 10th International CALIBER-2015, HP University and IIAS, Shimla, Himachal Pradesh, India. https://nptel.ac.in/NPTEL_Media/pdf/inflibnet.pdf

Karmakar, A. K., & Jana, S. K. (2015, December). In What Direction is the Wind blowing? Education and Skill Development: The case of BRICS. *The Indian Economic Journal,* (Special Issue), 131–147.

Koryuhina, C., & Shamshina, T. (2018). *Challenges of ICT in education. In The 16th international scientific conference information technologies and management.* ISMA University. https://www.isma.lv/FILES/SCIENCE/IT&M2018_THESES/03_MDM/15_IT&M2018_Korjuhina_Shamshina.pdf

Krishnaveni, R., & Meenakumari, J. (2010). Usage of ICT for Information Administration in Higher education Institutions–A study. *International Journal of Environmental Sciences and Development, 1*(3), 282–286. doi:10.7763/IJESD.2010.V1.55

Kulik, J. A. (1994). Meta-analysis study of findings on computer-based instruction. In E. L. Baker & H. F. O'neil (Eds.), *Technology assessment in education and training.* Lawrence Erlbaum.

MHRD. (2018). *All India Survey of Higher Education 2017-18. Monistry of Human Resource Development.* Govt. of India.

Mondal, A., & Mete, J. (2012). ICT in higher education: Opportunities and challenges. *Institutions, 21*(60), 4.

NSSO, Government of India. (2015). Key Indicators of Social Consumption in India: Education. National Sample Survey Office, Ministry of Statistics and Programme Implementation, Government of India.

OECD. (2001). *Understanding the Digital Divide. OECD Digital Economy Papers, No. 49.* OECD Publishing. doi:10.1787/236405667766

OECD. (2015). *Students, Computers and Learning: Making the Connection. PISA.* OECD Publishing. doi:10.1787/9789264239555-

Ritzhaupt, A. D., Liu, F., Dawson, K., & Barron, A. E. (2013). Differences in Student Information and Communication Technology Literacy Based on Socio-Economic Status, Ethnicity, and Gender: Evidence of a Digital Divide in Florida Schools. *JRTE, 45*(4), 291–307. doi:10.1080/15391523.2013.10782607

Sarkar, S. (2012). The role of information and communication technology (ICT) in higher education for the 21st century. *Science, 1*(1), 30–41.

Scott, K. S., Sorokti, K. H., & Merrell, J. D. (2016). Learning "beyond the classroom" within an enterprise social network system. *Internet and Higher Education, 29,* 75–90. doi:10.1016/j.iheduc.2015.12.005

Siddiq, F., & Schererb, R. (2019). Is there a gender gap? A meta-analysis of the gender differences in students' ICT literacy. *Educational Research Review, 27,* 205–217. doi:10.1016/j.edurev.2019.03.007

Spiezia, V. (2012). ICT investments and productivity: Measuring the contribution of ICTS to growth. *OECD Journal: Economic Studies., 2012*(1). Advance online publication. doi:10.1787/eco_studies-2012-5k8xdhj4tv0t

Terry, N., Lewer, J. J., & Macy, A. (2003). *The Efficacy of Alternative Instruction Modes in Economics.* https://www.researchgate.net/publication/228289032_The_Efficacy_of_Alternative_Instruction_Modes_in_Economics

University Grants Commission. (2017). *National Convention on Digital Initiatives for Higher Education*. https://www.ugc.ac.in/pdfnews/9208605_Brochure-(National-Convention-on-Digital-Initiatives-for-Higher-Education).pdf

Youssef, A. B., & Dahmani, M. (2008). The impact of ICT on student performance in higher education: Direct effects, indirect effects and organisational change. RUSC. *Universities and Knowledge Society Journal*, *5*(1), 45–56.

Chapter 13

Adoption and Use of ICTs by Livestock Keepers for Improved Access to Livestock Information:
A Case of Selected Urban Areas in Tanzania

Consolata Kemirembe Angello
iD https://orcid.org/0000-0002-8768-6417
Sokoine University of Agriculture, Tanzania

ABSTRACT

Information and communication technologies (ICTs) are very important tools for economic development and poverty reduction when used effectively by individuals in all economic sectors including agriculture. Urban livestock keepers need ICTs in their activities so that they can make informed decisions that can lead to improvement of the livestock industry. Despite its importance, ICT use is hindered by several factors including unawareness of the radio and television programmes and lack of computer skills. This chapter reveals the extent of use of ICTs by urban and peri-urban livestock keepers whereby different types of ICTs are used by urban livestock keepers to access livestock information, though some ICTs, for example, mobile phones are used more than other ICTs (radio and television). Internet is used by very few livestock keepers due computer illiteracy. Policy implications include improvement of the telecommunications services by the government through relevant bodies in order to facilitate more access to information through mobile phones, radio, television, and the internet.

DOI: 10.4018/978-1-7998-3468-7.ch013

INTRODUCTION

The use of ICTs has increased dramatically since the 1990s; information can now be disseminated to different people more easily, faster and at a cheaper cost, regardless of the distance between the people. ICTs are often categorized based on how long they have been in common use, and to some extent the technology used for the transmission and storage of information. ICTs can be grouped as new (or modern), old (or traditional) and very old ICTs (Thioune, 2003). Computers, satellites, wireless, mobile phones, the Internet, e-mail and multimedia generally fall into the new ICT category. The concepts behind these technologies are not particularly new, but the common and inexpensive use of them is what makes them new. Most of these, and virtually all new versions of them, are based on digital communications. Old or Traditional ICTs include radio, television, fixed line telephones, and facsimile machines. These are technologies that have been in common use throughout much of the world for many decades. Traditionally, these technologies have used analog transmission techniques, although they too are migrating to the now less expensive digital format, which have been gradually ingrained in the daily habits and lives of people and communities. Newspapers, books and libraries fall into the very old ICTs category. They have been in common use for several hundred years.

In Africa, ICTs have a very great potential in enhancing access to agricultural information hence improving the agricultural sector. The ICTs have become important tools for recording livestock performance and production levels. Many commercial farmers in Africa run computer-based recording and management software that turns raw performance data into information that can be used immediately at the local farm level. In South Africa for example, most local livestock data is fed into a centralized information system called the Integrated Registration and Genetic Information System (INTERGIS), which sets national livestock productivity benchmarks, enables comparisons of all animals in terms of genetic potential, and provides policymakers and farmers with a reliable source of reference (Westhuizen, 2003). Farmers in Senegal are now better placed to receive accurate market information on their mobile phones. Small producers no longer have to accept the first price they are offered; with access to up-to-date market information, they can negotiate to try to get a better deal. They can also communicate with other farmers more easily, making it feasible for them to set up cooperatives that can explore new markets and sell their products to bigger buyers (CTA, 2009).

Various studies have indicated that ICTs have been used for accessing agricultural information in some East African countries including Kenya and Uganda (Ferris, 2004; Achora, 2009; Kiplagat, 2009; Gantt and Cantor, 2010). In Kenya, ICTs such as mobile phones have successfully been used by community animal health workers in disseminating information. The phones have enabled the animal health care service providers to keep one another updated on animal health issues and share information on availability of essential veterinary drugs. It has also contributed to a reduction in transaction costs (transport, time spent travelling and other miscellaneous costs involved in animal treatment), leading to increased access to and efficiency of animal health service delivery (Kithuka *et al*, 2001).

Background Information

Livestock production is one of the major agricultural activities in Tanzania. The sub sector contributes to national food supply, converts rangelands resources into products suitable for human consumption and is a source of income both to the farmers and to the country. It provides about 30 per cent of the Agricultural Gross Domestic Product (GDP). Out of the sub sector's contribution to GDP, about 40 percent originates from beef production, 30 percent from Milk production and another 30 percent from poultry and small stock (URT, 2007). Approximately 99 percent of the livestock in Tanzania belongs to small scale livestock keepers with big ranches and dairy farms constituting the remaining one percent. In Dar-es-Salaam urban farming is the second largest employer after petty trade and labor, and 74 percent of urban farmers keep livestock. Urban livestock keeping in Tanzania is regulated in practice and is commonly practiced as zero-grazing, as reguired by the by-laws of urban livestock keeping (Jacobi et al, 2005). Development of the livestock sector, therefore, could contribute to reducing poverty level substantially. The governmental development strategy to increase livestock production and productivity sector falls into the broader National Strategy for Agricultural Development. The main objective is the promotion of a market-driven livestock sector able to support the income levels of the poor livestock keepers (URT, 2005).

Livestock keepers need information on livestock diseases, nutrition, treatment and control of diseases, breeding techniques and markets for their products, among many other information needs. These information needs may be grouped into five headings: agricultural inputs; extension education; agricultural technology; agricultural credit; and marketing (Ozowa, 1995). All this information has to be made available, accessed and used by the livestock keepers in order to increase productivity and hence improve their livelihoods. There are various ICTs that can be used by urban livestock keepers in accessing information as opposed to rural livestock keepers. Examples of these technologies include; telephones/mobile phones, television, radio and the Internet. These technologies can be very useful in providing various types of information to the livestock keepers depending on their information needs.

Research has shown that lack of access to information is one of the serious obstacles to development, including agricultural development. Livestock husbandry faces lack of research and services provision: information access and adoption of improved technologies is limited for small scale urban livestock keepers. This is made worse by the fact that existing services are not tailored towards their needs and circumstances (CIRAD, 2009). One of the coping strategies of this problem is the organization and networking among small scale urban livestock keepers to improve access to information and other services: urban livestock keepers should become more aware of the potential benefits of organization and networking as a means to access information and services and improve marketing strategies (Guendel, 2002). According to Munyua (2008), emerging technologies and new materials are key success factors in addressing the challenges of small-scale farmers. Information and knowledge are considered prime productive resources and play a key role in ensuring food security and sustainable development. Kapange (2002) states that, development of networks and use of low-cost ICTs enhance timely access to accurate and reliable information. It therefore calls for investment of part of the country's limited resources for ICT development.

MAIN FOCUS OF THE CHAPTER

Issues, Controversies and Problems

In Tanzania there is still no clear evidence on how ICTs such as mobile phones, radio, television and the Internet help the urban livestock keepers to access livestock information. Despite the relatively well developed ICT infrastructure in the urban areas, urban livestock keepers still lack adequate information on livestock keeping practices (CIRAD, 2009). This is because they mostly rely on advice services as sources of information which are usually insufficient (Gakuru *et al*, 2009). Lack of timely information is well known to be the largest constraint on small-scale agricultural production, a sector that provides livelihood for 70-80% of Africa's population. The lack of information leads to poor husbandry practices, which in turn leads to poor production. Other information-related problems that face the livestock sector in Tanzania include; poor husbandry practices (e.g. poor nutrition of the animals, poor housing and un-hygienic conditions), poor disease control measures and lack of markets for the livestock products. This situation could probably be improved by making use of ICTs to get the required information on time, hence solve some of the information-related problems the livestock keepers face in livestock keeping. Jensen (2002) and African Connection, Strategic Planning (2002) state that, with improved information systems, it would be easier to obtain much better market-related prices, sell their produce directly to distributors and negotiate for better prices. However so far, the potential for ICTs to impact this sector has not yet received much attention.

According to Schilderman (2002), ICTs have not played their role in getting the required information to the urban people (especially the poor), though it is generally believed that ICTs have great potential to significantly improve the urban people's access to knowledge and information. There is little scientific evidence in specific urban communities about the ways in which individuals and communities exploit access to ICTs and the impact they have on livelihoods in urban communities (Souter et al, 2005). A study by Chilimo (2009) reported that, despite the strong belief in the role of ICTs for socio-economic development, clear evidence on how ICTs can be used to achieve this purpose in the Tanzanian context is still lacking. This research therefore investigates the extent of adoption and use of ICTs by urban livestock keepers and thus contributes to knowledge on how these ICTs are used in accessing livestock information and thereby improving the livestock keeping practices in urban and peri-urban areas of Tanzania.

Conceptual Framework

This study has adopted the work chart structure conceptual framework by Bystrom and Jarvelin (1995) that incorporates different information concepts and how these concepts are related with one another, these concepts include the terms; information, information need, information source, information channel and information and communication technology. This conceptual framework classifies tasks into different categories based on different individual's work roles. It also classifies different information categories based on the needs of different individuals, and finally it classifies different sources of information according to the category of information that is looked for. In combination, the three classifications suggest a set of hypotheses of the type: "*Tasks of complexity type X require information of type Y that is available from sources of type Z*" (Jarvelin and Wilson, 2003). Thus the classifications suggest analytical relationships between the variables, as shown in Figure 1.

ADOPTION AND USE OF DIFFERENT TYPES OF ICTS BY URBAN LIVESTOCK KEEPERS

The main objective in this chapter intends to reveal the perceptions of the livestock keepers on the adoption and use of different ICTs in accessing livestock information. The first question that the respondents were asked in order to fulfill this objective was whether they used any of the ICTs to access livestock information. The results of this study are presented in Table 1.

Figure 1. The work chart structure (Bystrom and Jarvelin, 1995)
Source: (Jarvelin and Wilson, 2003)

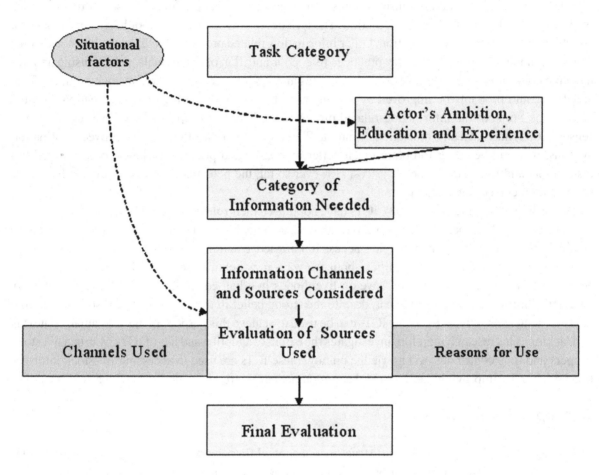

As indicated in Table 1, most of the respondents 239 (94.1%) admitted having used at least one of the ICTs to access livestock information as opposed to 15 respondents (5.9%) who did not use any of the ICTs to access livestock information. The results further indicate that 144 of the respondents in Kinondoni (94.7%) used ICTs as opposed to 95 (93.1%) in Morogoro urban district. This was probably because of the relatively well developed ICT infrastructure in Kinondoni compared to Morogoro urban

Table 1. Use of ICTs in accessing livestock information

ICT use	Kinondoni		Morogoro urban		Overall	
	Freq.	%	Freq.	%	Freq.	%
Yes	144	94.7	95	93.1	239	94.1
No	8	5.3	7	6.9	15	5.9

Source: (Author, 2013)
N=152 (Kinondoni), N=102 (Morogoro urban), N=254 (Overall)

district or because of the fact that many respondents in this study were from Kinondoni District. Only 15 (5.9%) respondents did not use any of the ICTs and 7 (6.9%) of these were from Morogoro urban while 8 (6.1%) were from Kinondoni district. These findings have revealed that ICTs are being used by many livestock keepers in urban areas to access livestock information, though the primary reason for acquiring ICTs was for communication purposes (for mobile phones and internet), news and entertainment (for radio and television). This is an indication that urban livestock keepers can now be more informed if they make proper use of ICTs to access livestock information. This can be through getting advice or help from veterinarians and/or extension officers through mobile phones, radio television and the Internet, and this may lead to quick solving of problems and improvement of the urban livestock keeping practice.

The respondents were then asked to mention the types of ICTs that they used in accessing livestock information. Findings reveal that different types of ICTs are mentioned by the livestock keepers including radio, television, mobile phone and the Internet. Most livestock keepers use at least one of the ICTs while some use more than one type of ICT and very few livestock keepers use all types of ICTs to access livestock information. These ICTs are used at different levels by respondents in each of the two districts. Table 2 shows the number of respondents who use each of the ICTs in the two districts.

Table 2. Types of ICTs used by urban livestock keepers

Type of ICT used	Kinondoni		Morogoro urban		Overall	
	Freq.	%	Freq.	%	Freq.	%
Mobile phone	141	92.8	93	91.2	234	92.1
Television	37	24.3	30	29.4	67	24.6
Radio	19	12.5	36	35.3	55	21.7
Internet	5	3.3	1	1.0	6	2.4

Source: (Author, 2013)
N=152 (Kinondoni), N=102 (Morogoro urban), N=254 (Overall)

The results in Table 2 indicate that mobile phone were used by most (234) of the livestock keepers (92.1%). It shows that respondents in Kinondoni (92.8%) used mobile phones slightly more than respondents in Morogoro urban (91.2%). Another type of ICT that was mentioned by the respondents was television 67 (24.4%). This was watched more by respondents in Morogoro urban (29.4%) compared to the respondents in Kinondoni (24.3%). Radio was also mentioned more by respondents in Morogoro urban (35.3%) compared to the respondents in Kinondoni (12.5%). Internet was used by the least; 6 (2.4%) number of respondents. Respondents who used the Internet were more in Kinondoni 5 (3.3%) than in Morogoro urban district 1 (1.0%).

Adejo and Haruna (2010) classified ICTs into conventional ICTs (radio, television) and contemporary ICTs (telephones, computer/internet). These results mean that mobile phone and the Internet (contemporary ICTs) are used more by respondents in Kinondoni compared to radio and television (Conventional ICTs) which are used more by respondents in Morogoro urban districts. This could probably be due to the fact that respondents in Dar es Salaam are busier with other economic activities hence they may be lacking time to watch television and listen to radio livestock programmes. The livestock keepers in Kinondoni District may also be ignorant on the importance of the livestock programmes or they may not have been aware of the livestock programmes in the radio and television. The well developed ICT infrastructure in Kinondoni may be the reason as to why mobile phones and the Internet are used more by respondents in Kinondoni. The livestock keepers explained how they used different types of ICTs in accessing livestock information, the usefulness of each of the ICTs in livestock keeping and reasons why they did not use some or all of the ICTs. The following section will discuss how different types of ICTs are used by urban livestock keepers to access livestock information and the perceptions of the livestock keepers on each of the ICTs. The reasons as to why some types of ICTs are not used by some of the respondents to access livestock information are also discussed.

Use of Radio in Accessing Livestock Information

The respondents were asked to explain how they used their radios to access livestock information. First they were asked to mention any livestock keeping programmes that they knew and the frequency of listening to these programmes. Various radio programmes were mentioned. The radio programmes included; 'Mfugaji wa Kisasa' (TBC Taifa), which was watched by 41 out of 55 (74.5%) of the respondents, 'PADEP' (TBC Taifa) which was watched by 19 out of 55 (34.5%) of the respondents and 'Inuka' (Radio Free Africa) which was watched by 12 out of 55 (21.8%) of the respondents.

Among the radio programmes that were mentioned, it was established that the 'Mfugaji wa Kisasa' programme was watched frequently by only 18 out of 41 (43.9%) respondents, the 'PADEP' programme was frequently watched by only 3 out of 19 (15.8%) respondents and the 'inuka' programme was frequently watched by only 1 out of 12 (8.3%) respondents. The respondents who had watched the programmes less frequently were more (i.e., 51.2% for 'mfugaji wa kisasa', 42.1% for PADEP and 50.0% for Inuka) than those who had watched the programmes frequently. Those respondents who had never watched some of these programmes were also relatively many (i.e., 42.1% for PADEP and 41.7% for Inuka) compared to those who had watched the programmes frequently. Table 3 shows the different radio programmes that were listened to by the livestock keepers and the frequency of listening to each of the programmes.

Table 3. Radio programmes listened to by urban livestock keepers

Radio programme		Frequency of listening					
		Frequently		Less frequently		Never watched	
		Freq.	%	Freq.	%	Freq.	%
Mfugaji wa kisasa	N= 41	18	43.9	21	51.2	2	4.9
PADEP	N= 19	3	15.8	8	42.1	8	42.1
Inuka	N= 12	1	8.3	6	50.0	5	41.7

Source: (Author, 2013)

From these results, it may be concluded that these radio programmes are not watched frequently by the livestock keepers. Most of these programmes are watched less frequently and some of them have never been watched by the respondents. This could have been because of many reasons including lack of awareness of the existence of such programmes, lack of time to listen to the programmes and lack of interest or ignorance on the importance of such programmes in livestock keeping (as seen in later discussions). As a policy implication, the broadcasting media should ensure that the radio programmes are beneficial to the intended audience and should take the necessary measures to improve the programmes so that the intended audience benefits from the programmes. A similar policy implication was stated by Nazari and Abu (2010) who suggested that since the radio plays a more important role in public education, producers should be familiar with the latest and newest programme structures to be able to meet the needs of people by employing appealing methods.

Perceptions of Livestock Keepers on Use of Radio

The respondents who listened to radio programmes on livestock keeping were then asked whether the programmes provided any useful information on livestock keeping. The findings of this question are presented in Table 4.

Table 4. Usefulness of radio programmes on livestock keeping

N=254					
Usefulness of radio programmes on livestock keeping		**listening to livestock keeping programmes in the radio**			**Total**
		Yes	**No**	**Not applicable**	
Very useful	Count	27	0	0	27
	% within usefulness	(49.1%)	(.0%)	(.0%)	(10.6%)
Satisfactory	Count	24	0	0	24
	% within usefulness	(43.6%)	(.0%)	(.0%)	(9.4%)
Not useful	Count	1	1	0	2
	% within usefulness	(1.8%)	(.5%)	(.0%)	(.8%)
Not applicable	Count	3	189	9	201
	% within usefulness	(5.5%)	(99.5%)	(100.0%)	(79.1%)
Total	Count	55	190	9	254
	% within usefulness	(100.0%)	(100.0%)	(100.0%)	(100.0%)

Source: (Author, 2013)

Table 4 shows that a total of 27 out of 55 respondents (49.1%) agreed that the programmes were very useful while 24 (43.6%) said that they were satisfactory. Very few (1.8%) respondents said the programmes were not useful at all and a total of 201 out 254 respondents (79.1%) did not respond to the question and these were labeled as "Not applicable". The respondents were then asked to explain why the radio programmes were useful, satisfactory or not useful. The explanations that were given are shown in Table 5.

As indicated in Table 5, the results show that 27 respondents (100%) admitted that the radio programmes were very useful because they offered a lot of advice on animal husbandry practices. Some of these respondents admitted that they had exercised what they had learnt from the programmes and they had benefited by improving their animal husbandry practices. Although the radio programmes were

Table 5. Perceptions of livestock keepers on the radio programmes

Perceptions on livestock keeping radio programmes		Usefulness of radio programmes in livestock keeping				Total
		Very useful	Satisfactory	Not useful	Not applicable	
A lot of advice	Count	27	2	0	0	29
	% within perception	(100.0%)	(8.3%)	(.0%)	(.0%)	(11.4%)
Inssufficient technical advice	Count	0	8	0	0	8
	% within perception	(.0%)	(33.3%)	(.0%)	(.0%)	(3.1%)
Lack enough time	Count	0	12	1	0	13
	% within perception	(.0%)	(50.0%)	(50.0%)	(.0%)	(5.1%)
Radio programmes are biased	Count	0	2	0	6	8
	% within perception	(.0%)	(8.3%)	(.0%)	(3.0%)	(3.1%)
Not applicable	Count	0	0	1	195	196
	% within perception	(.0%)	(.0%)	(50.0%)	(97.0%)	(77.2%)
Total	Count	27	24	2	201	254
	% within perception	(100.0%)	(100.0%)	(100.0%)	(100.0%)	(100.0%)

Source: (Author, 2013)
N=254

said to be useful by most of the respondents, some of the respondents (33.3%) said that the programmes were satisfactory because the programmes offered insufficient technical advice. Another 12 out of 24 respondents (50.0%) complained that the programmes were satisfactory because the respondents had no enough time of listening to radio and following up the programmes due to their tight schedules. Very few of these respondents (8.3%) complained that the radio programmes were biased to only some few animals and therefore not all the livestock keepers were benefitting from the programmes.

These results are an indication that radio programmes on livestock keeping are very important to the livestock keepers despite the fact that only a few livestock keepers accessed the programmes. The radio programmes are useful because some of the livestock keepers admitted that they could benefit from the programmes despite the fact that time was a limitation to listening the programmes. This means that the radio programmes could be very beneficial to the livestock keepers if only the programmes could be accessed by many or all the livestock keepers. These programmes could lead to access of relevant information which could help the livestock keepers improve their practice hence increase their income and reduce poverty. If these programmes were advertised and their broadcasting schedules improved, more livestock keepers could benefit from the programmes. The broadcasting media and the programme producers are therefore responsible in ensuring that more livestock programmes are introduced and the programmes are advertised frequently in order to increase the awareness of the livestock keepers on the existence and importance of these programmes. Yahaya and Badiru (2002) also recommended that more effort should be made in advertisement of the radio programmes for more access to relevant agricultural information.

Reasons for not Using Radio to Access Livestock Information

The respondents who did not listen to the radio programmes were asked to give their reasons as to why they did not listen to the programmes and the findings are presented in Table 6.

Table 6. Reasons for not listening to radio livestock programmes

Reasons for not listening to the programmes	Frequency	Percentage (%)
No time to listen to the programmes	90	47.4
Not aware of the radio programmes	82	43.2
Not aware of the programme schedules	59	31.1
The programmes are not useful	4	2.1

Source: (Author, 2013)

N=190

The results in Table 6 show that out of 190 respondents who did not listen to radio programmes, 90 of the respondents (47.4%) claimed that they had no time for listening to the radio programmes because they were tied up with other activities during the day hence could not listen to the programmes. 82 respondents (43.2%) said that they did not listen to the programmes because they were not aware of the existence of the programmes. These respondents complained that the programmes were not being advertised hence the reason why they were not aware of the programmes. A total 59 of 190 respondents (31.1%) claimed that they were not aware of the programme schedules, thus they could not listen to the programmes because they did not know when they were being broadcasted. Very few respondents (2.1%) said that they did not listen to the programmes because they did not find the programmes useful to them.

Despite the fact that most of the livestock keepers in urban and peri-urban areas own radios, finding of this study have revealed that the radios are used by few livestock keepers to access livestock information and they are used mostly to access information on entertainment, news and other social purposes. This is an indication that most of the urban and peri-urban livestock keepers still lack the awareness that they can use their radios to access important information on livestock keeping. Lack of time to access the radio programmes on livestock keeping and ignorance on the existence of these programmes are also reasons for not listening to the radio programmes on livestock keeping. The livestock keepers therefore need to be knowledgeable on the existence and importance of the programmes and sensitized (though extension services and advertisements) to use radio to access information that can help them improve their livestock keeping practices.

Use of Television in Accessing Livestock Information

The respondents were asked to mention the livestock keeping television programmes that they watched. 67 out of 254 respondents watched different livestock television programmes including; 'Mfugaji wa Kisasa' (TBC one) which was watched by 33 out of 67 (49.3%) respondents, PADEP which was watched by 30 out of 67 (44.8%), 'Kilimo cha Kisasa' (StarTV) which was mentioned by 9 out of 67 (13.4%) of the respondents and SUA TV programmes that were mentioned by 2 out of 67 (3.0%) of the respon-

Table 7. Television programmes watched by urban livestock keepers

Television programme		Frequency of watching television programmes					
		Frequently		Less frequently		Never watched	
		Freq.	%	Freq.	%	Freq.	%
Mfugaji wa kisasa	N= 33	19	57.6	13	39.4	1	3.0
PADEP	N= 30	20	66.7	9	30.0	1	3.3
Kilimo cha kisasa	N= 9	7	77.8	2	22.2	0	0.0
SUA TV	N= 2	2	100	-	-	0	0.0

Source: (Author, 2013)

dents. These respondents were then asked to indicate the frequency of watching each of the television programmes. The findings are presented in Table 7.

Results in Table 7 indicate that 'mfugaji wa kisasa' (TBC one) programme was watched frequently by 19 out of 33 respondents (57.6%), PADEP was watched frequently by 30 out of 30 (66.7%) and 'Kilimo cha Kisasa' programme was watched frequently by 7 out of 9 (77.8%) respondents. These television programmes had been watched less frequently by 39.4% respondents for 'Mfugaji wa Kisasa', 30.0% for PADEP and 22.2% for 'Kilimo cha Kisasa'. The SUA TV programmes had been watched only by the respondents in Morogoro and not those in Kinondoni because SUA TV is a local channel in Morogoro and could only be seen by Morogoro residents. These results show that urban livestock keepers access livestock information through television programmes more than they do for radio programmes.

Perceptions of Livestock Keepers on the Use of Television

The respondents were then asked on the usefulness of the television programmes on their practice of livestock keeping. Findings in Table 8 indicate that out of 67 respondents who watched the television

Table 8. Usefulness of television programmes

Usefulness of TV programmes on livestock keeping		Watching livestock programmes on Television			Total
		Yes	No	Not applicable	
Very useful	Count	46	0	0	46
	% within usefulness	(68.7%)	(.0%)	(.0%)	(18.1%)
Satisfactory	Count	18	0	0	18
	% within usefulness	(26.9%)	(.0%)	(.0%)	(7.1%)
Not useful	Count	1	0	1	2
	% within usefulness	(1.5%)	(.0%)	(9.1%)	(.8%)
Not applicable	Count	2	176	10	188
	% within usefulness	(3.0%)	(100.0%)	(90.9%)	(74.0%)
Total	Count	67	176	11	254
	% within usefulness	(100.0%)	(100.0%)	(100.0%)	(100.0%)

Source: (Author, 2013)

programmes, 46 (68.7%) respondents admitted that the programmes were very useful. 18 out of 67 (26.9%) respondents said that the programmes were satisfactory and one out of 67 (1.5%) respondents replied that the programmes were not useful to them. These results are an indication that television livestock programmes are very useful to the urban livestock keepers because the livestock keepers gain knowledge from the programmes.

When asked to explain their answers, 44 out of 46 respondents (95.7%) admitted that the television programmes were very useful because they offered a lot of technical advice to the livestock keepers and one out of the 46 respondent (2.2%) said that the programmes were important because the lessons were by demonstrations hence they were easily understood. Some of the respondents (18 out of 254) claimed that the programmes were satisfactory. The results show that 11 out of 18 of these respondents (61.1%) explained that the television programmes were satisfactory because the respondents had no frequent follow-ups of the programmes. Four out of 18 respondents (22.2%) said that the programmes were satisfactory because the respondents had no time to watch the programmes. Some few (three out of 18) respondents (16.7%) claimed that the programmes were satisfactory because they showed complicated and expensive equipment hence they could not be applied in our environment. Very few (two out of 254) respondents complained that the television programmes were not useful at all. These respondents claimed that they lacked time to frequently follow-up the programmes hence they did not benefit from them. These results are shown in Table 9.

Table 9. Perceptions on the usefulness of livestock keeping TV programmes

Perceptions on livestock keeping TV programmes		Usefulness of TV programmes on livestock keeping				Total
		Very useful	Satisfactory	Not useful	Not applicable	
I get a lot of technical advice	Count	44	0	0	1	45
	%	(95.7%)	(.0%)	(.0%)	(.5%)	(17.7%)
Lessons are by demonstrations	Count	1	0	0	0	1
	%	(2.2%)	(.0%)	(.0%)	(.0%)	(.4%)
No frequent follow ups	Count	1	11	1	0	13
	%	(2.2%)	(61.1%)	(50.0%)	(.0%)	(5.1%)
No time to watch the programmes	Count	0	4	0	4	8
	%	(.0%)	(22.2%)	(.0%)	(2.1%)	(3.1%)
Show complicated techniques	Count	0	3	0	0	3
	%	(.0%)	(16.7%)	(.0%)	(.0%)	(1.2%)
Not applicable	Count	0	0	1	183	184
	%	(.0%)	(.0%)	950.0%)	(97.3%)	(72.4%)
Total	Count	46	18	2	188	254
	%	(100.0%)	(100.0%)	(100.0%)	(100.0%)	(100.0%)

Source: (Author, 2013)

N=254

From the results above, it may be concluded that though the television programmes were said to be very useful by the majority of the respondents, these programmes were not watched by many livestock keepers because of limited time to watch the programmes. This is also a policy implication for the relevant bodies to increase the number of livestock programmes and the frequency of broadcasting so that many livestock keepers are able to watch and follow-up the programmes.

Reasons for not Using Television to Access Livestock Information

The respondents who did not watch the television livestock programmes were asked to give reasons why they did not watch the programmes and the findings are presented in Table 10.

Table 10. Reasons for not watching television livestock programmes

Reason for not watching television	Frequency	Percentage (%)
No time to watch the programmes	81	46.0
Not aware of the programmes	63	35.8
Not aware of the programme schedules	54	30.7
No electricity	19	10.8
No television	10	5.7
No satellite dish	2	1.1
Programmes not useful	2	1.1

Source: (Author, 2013)
N= 176

As shown in Table 10, several reasons were mentioned by the respondents. 81 out of 176 respondents (46.0%) gave the reason that they had no time to watch the television programmes due to being busy with many other socio-economic activities. Another reason for not watching the programmes was the unawareness of the existence of the television livestock programmes, a reason given by 63 out of 176 (35.8%) respondents. Another 54 out of 176 (30.7%) respondents gave their reason for not watching the programmes as not being aware of the time when the television programme were broadcasted. 10.8% of the respondents said that they had no electricity in their houses that is why they were not watching the programmes while others (5.7%) said that they had no television. A few livestock keepers (1.1%) complained of lack of satellite dishes as reasons for not accessing some of the channels e.g. TBC one which broadcasted the programmes and others (1.1%) claimed that they did not watch the livestock programmes because the programmes were not useful to them.

These results show that many urban livestock keepers do not watch television programmes because they are tied up with other economic activities during the day that they have no time to watch the programmes most of which are shown at day time. Many urban livestock keepers were also not aware of the livestock programmes and their broadcasting schedules. This situation could be improved by increasing the frequency of advertising the programmes in order to increase awareness of the respondents on the existence of the programmes, as opposed to the present situation whereby these programmes are advertised only once in a while. The programme schedules should also be improved and should be shown at night or during the weekends to enable the livestock keepers to watch the programmes and benefit from them. Hassan *et al,* (2011) emphasizes that if television (and radio) programmes need to be used as effective channels for agriculture information dissemination, efforts must be taken to guarantee that the airing times are suitable. This is supported by (Chhachhar *et al,* 2012) who points out that many farmers prefer to watch agricultural related programs in evening because they work in fields during the day and thus evening time is good and suitable for watching such programs on television.

Use of Mobile Phone in Accessing Livestock Information

The respondents were also asked to mention how they used their mobile phones and the frequency in each use. It was found out that the respondents used their mobile phones in different ways. Results show that out of the 234 respondents who used mobile phones to access livestock information, 210 (89.7%) respondents used their mobile phones for calling or communicating with veterinary/extension officers. 121 out of 234 (51.7%) of the respondents used their mobile phones to exchange ideas or communicate with clients. 79 out of 234 (39.8%) of the respondents used their mobile phones to communicate with fellow livestock keepers, while 5 out of 234 (5.1%) respondents used their mobile phones in availing chicks and the remaining 10 out of 234 (4.3%) secured feeds through their mobile phones.

These results are an indication that many livestock keepers use their mobile phones in different ways in their livestock keeping practice. Urban livestock keepers benefit from their mobile phones in that they can easily get relevant information or advice from veterinarians or extension officers. Urban livestock keepers are also able to communicate with their clients and exchange ideas with their fellow livestock keepers. The livestock keepers can also get chicks and feeds by using their mobile phones whereby they can call and press orders, which mean their needs are met through their mobile phones. These respondents were then asked to state the frequency of each use of their mobile phones and the findings are shown in Table 11.

Table 11. Uses of mobile phones by urban livestock keepers

Uses of mobile phone		Frequency of use of mobile phone					
		Frequently		Less frequently		Least frequently	
		Freq.	%	Freq.	%	Freq.	%
Calling extension officers	N= 210	200	95.2	4	1.9	6	2.9
Communication with clients	N=121	101	83.5	13	10.7	7	5.8
Communication with fellows	N= 79	51	64.6	17	21.5	9	11.4
Buying feeds	N= 10	10	100	-	-	-	-
Buying chicks	N=5	5	100	-	-	-	-

Source: (Author, 2013)

As presented in Table 11, it was found out that 200 out of 210 (95.2%) respondents frequently used their mobile phones to communicate with veterinary or extension officers. This was followed by 101 out of 121 (83.5%) of the respondents who frequently used their mobile phones to communicate with their clients and 51 out of 79 (64.6%) respondents who frequently used their mobile phones to communicate with their fellow livestock keepers. Other respondents used their mobile phones frequently in securing chicks and feeds. Mobile phones were used less frequently by a few respondents to communicate with extension officers (1.9%), to communicate with clients (10.7%) and to communicate with fellow livestock keepers (21.5%). This is an indication that mobile phones are very important to urban livestock keepers in many ways that have been discussed. This result implies that most urban livestock keepers can hardly do without mobile phones in their livestock keeping practice.

Perceptions of Livestock Keepers on use of Mobile Phones

The respondents who used mobile phones were asked whether the mobile phones were important to them in their livestock keeping practice. They were also asked to explain the reasons why they thought the mobile phones were useful or not useful. These findings are shown in Table 12.

Table 12. Importance of mobile phones in accessing livestock information

Explanation for importance of mobile phone in livestock keeping		Importance of mobile phone in livestock keeping			Total
		Yes	No	Not applicable	
Easy communication	Count	199	0	0	199
	%	(85.0%)	(.0%)	(.0%)	(78.3%)
Easy availability of feeds, chicks and markets	Count	22	0	0	22
	%	(9.4%)	(.0%)	(.0%)	(8.7%)
Quick solving of problems	Count	10	0	2	12
	%	(4.3%)	(.0%)	(10.5%)	(4.7%)
Save time and cost	Count	3	0	0	3
	%	(1.3%)	(.0%)	(.0%)	(1.2%)
Not applicable	Count	0	1	17	18
	%	(.0%)	(100.0%)	(89.5%)	(7.1%)
Total	Count	234	1	19	254
	%	(100.0%)	(100.0%)	(100.0%)	(100.0%)

Source: (Author, 2013)
N=234

The findings presented in Table 12 indicate all 234 respondents (100%) who used mobile phones in accessing livestock information agreed that the mobile phone was important to them. 1 out of 10 (10%) respondents who did not use mobile phones to access livestock information said that mobile phone was not important in the livestock keeping practice while 19 out of 254 (7.5%) respondents did not respond to the question. The respondents were then asked to give reasons why they thought mobile phones were important to them. 199 out of 234 respondents (85.0%) admitted that mobile phones enabled them to communicate easily with veterinarians, extension officers, clients and their fellow livestock keepers. 22 out of 234 respondents (9.4%) said that mobile phones enabled them to secure feeds, chicks and markets easily. 10 out of 234 respondents (4.3%) said that mobile phones enabled them to solve their problems quickly and 3 out of 234 respondents (1.3%) explained that mobile phones enabled them save time and costs.

Reasons for not Using Mobile Phones to Access Livestock Information

The findings from this study showed that only 10 out of 254 (3.9%) respondents did not use their mobile phones in accessing livestock information. These respondents claimed that they used their mobile phones in other activities including facilitating cultivation of their crops, businesses and social activities. Observations from this study revealed that almost all the respondents who did not use mobile phones did not also use any of the other ICTs. Observations also revealed that most of the respondents who did not use mobile phones to access livestock information were in either one or more of the following groups;

1.   Young in age (less than 30 years)
2.   Less experience in livestock keeping (beginners)
3.   Very old (more than 60 years)
4.   Illiterate.

Findings from this study also revealed that although very few respondents did not use mobile phones to access livestock information, most of these respondents admitted that mobile phones were important because they made communication easier.

Use of Internet in Accessing Livestock Information

The Internet was used by only 6 out of 254 of the respondents (2.4%) to access livestock information. Out of the 6 respondents who used the Internet, only 1 (16.7%) respondent used the Internet to send and receive e-mails with livestock information. All the 6 respondents (100%) used the Internet to search for relevant information on livestock keeping and there were no respondents who used the Internet to share ideas on livestock keeping with colleagues. Results presented in Table 13 shows that 1 respondent frequently used the Internet to exchange e-mails with extension officers. 4 out of 6 (66.7%) used the Internet

Table 13. Uses of Internet in accessing livestock information

Internet uses		Frequency of use					
		Frequently		Less frequently		Least frequently	
		Freq.	%	Freq.	%	Freq.	%
Searching	N= 6	4	66.7	2	33.3	0	0.0
E-mail	N= 1	1	100	-	-	0	0.0
Sharing	N= 6	-	-	-	-	0	0.0

Source: (Author, 2013)

frequently to search for relevant information and 2 out of 6 (33.3%) used the Internet less frequently to search for relevant information on livestock keeping.

From these results, it may be concluded that Internet users are very few compared to users of other ICTs. The low usage of the Internet is contributed to a large extent by lack of computer and Internet skills among the livestock keepers. The Internet however is a very good source of a lot and diverse amount of livestock information if only the IT skills are imparted to the livestock keepers to enable them use the Internet and access the information.

Perceptions of Livestock Keepers on Use of the Internet

The few respondents who used the Internet to access livestock information were asked whether the Internet was useful to them. Table 14 indicates that all of these respondents (2.4%) admitted that the Internet was very useful to them because it helped them to access a lot of relevant information on livestock keeping. The respondents who did not use the Internet were asked to give their reasons why they did not use the Internet. It was realized that 205 out of 238 (86.1%) of these respondents did not use the Internet because they did not have the computer skills. These were followed by 14 out of 238 (5.9%) of the respondents who had the computer skills but did not have the knowledge to use the Internet. Other 14 respondents (5.9%) had no interest of using the Internet to search for relevant livestock information though they had the Internet skills. Other reasons that were given by the respondents were; lack of time to use the Internet (3.8%), long distances to the Internet cafes' (2.9%), expensive Internet services (0.4%), ignorance of the usefulness of the Internet (0.4%) and lack of relevant websites to access livestock information (1.3%).

Table 14. Reasons for not using the Internet

Reason	Frequency	Percentage (%)
Lack of computer skills	205	86.1
Lack of Internet skills	14	5.9
Lack of interest to use the Internet	14	5.9
Lack of time	9	3.8
Long distances to Internet facilities	7	2.9
Lack of relevant websites	3	1.3
The Internet is not useful	1	0.4
Expensive Internet services	1	0.4

Source: (Author, 2013)
N=238

Responses from interviews revealed that most of the extension officers also lacked the basic computer skills nor did they have the necessary skills to use the Internet. Most of the extension officers had no e-mail addresses neither did they use the Internet to search for relevant livestock information. A few of the extension officers with Internet skills only used the Internet to exchange e-mails with friends.

Observations from this study revealed that there were no computers in almost all government offices for extension officers (except for one office in Morogoro- Bigwa Ward) and the computer was not connected to the Internet. The extension officers had to go out of their offices get the Internet services. Observations also revealed that there were a few Internet cafes most of which were located far from the livestock keepers.

RECOMMENDATIONS AND WAY FORWARD

Several recommendations have emanated from the findings of this study; some of which were given by the livestock keepers on how to improve the use of ICTs in accessing livestock information. Other recommendations have been brought forward as means to increase networking between the urban livestock keepers and improve access and usage of information among them in order to improve the urban livestock keeping practice. Most of these recommendations are for the government bodies and policy makers to implement. These recommendations include the following;

Improve use of Radio and Television in Accessing Livestock Information

Since ICTs are important tools of accessing livestock information, it is recommended that the broadcasting media should increase the frequency of broadcasting relevant livestock programmes. These radio and television programmes should be advertised frequently to increase the awareness of the livestock keepers on the existence of the programmes. The programmes should also be improved in order to include simple and affordable techniques that are relevant to our environment so that the knowledge obtained from the programmes is applied by all the livestock keepers. The programmes should also be sustainable to enable the livestock keepers to continue learning and benefitting from the programmes. The livestock keepers should also be sensitized though extension services to use radio and television to access livestock information. Community radio and television that are specifically for farmers should be introduced. These will be very useful for the livestock keepers who will learn and benefit from the programmes.

Enhance use of Mobile Phones and Internet to Access Livestock Information

The costs of using mobile phone and Internet services should be reduced so that all livestock keepers are able to use them. Relevant government bodies (e.g. TCRA) in collaboration with mobile phone service providers in Tanzania (e.g. Vodacom, Airtel, Tigo and Zantel) and Internet service providers should take into consideration the possibility of starting up ICT projects in urban areas to help specific urban communities gain easy access to information (as in rural areas). This can be through sending relevant short messages to the urban farmers especially on availability of markets and current market prices of various livestock products on demand in urban areas like meat, milk and eggs. These projects will enable the urban farmers to access relevant information through their mobile phones at cheaper prizes. Relevant websites on livestock keeping should also be introduced and advertised so that the livestock keepers are aware of them. These websites should be in Swahili language to enable many livestock keepers to benefit from them. The ICT projects can also provide computer and Internet skills to the farmers and extension officers; this will promote use of the Internet to access livestock information.

Form Organizations for Livestock Keepers

Information networking among urban livestock keepers is a very important pre-requisite for easy information access and usage among them. This study therefore recommends that urban livestock keepers should form small organizations in their areas (through supervision by the government extension officer); this will enable the extension/veterinary services to easily reach many livestock keepers and the livestock keepers will benefit from the extension services. Farmer organizations will enable the livestock keepers cooperate, share information and get treatment or vaccines in case of disease outbreaks; this will lead to control of many animal diseases.

Organizations will also help the livestock keepers get and share grazing areas in which the livestock keepers can graze their animals together in one area rather that each livestock keeper grazing his animals on his own. The availability of these grazing areas can be facilitated by the government by setting aside grazing areas for urban livestock keepers which currently is a big problem. Through these organizations, the livestock keepers can also benefit by getting seminars or meetings where they can get a lot of information that will help them in their activities. Formation of organizations can also enable the livestock keepers to get markets for their products and secure loans that will enable them improve their activities.

Introduce Livestock Information Centres

This study recommends that information centres that provide relevant information on farming should be introduced in urban areas (in addition to public libraries). These information centres can help the urban farmers to easily get all the relevant information that they need. The presence of these information centres can enable the livestock keepers access a lot of information without having to go to the libraries which are located far from most of the livestock keepers. The information centres can also enable the livestock keepers to access print information sources that have been revealed to be scarce from the finding of this study.

CONCLUSION

Different types of ICTs are used by urban livestock keepers to access livestock information. Mobile phone is used by the majority of livestock keepers whereby it helps them to get veterinary services easily and quickly, it enables availability of markets, feeds and chicks. It also enables the livestock keepers to exchange ideas with fellow livestock keepers. Radio and television are used by a few livestock keepers to access livestock information (though they are commonly used otherwise). This is due to unawareness of the existing livestock programmes. These programmes are very important to the few livestock keepers who access them because through the programmes, the livestock keepers are educated and learn a lot of experiences from other farmers. The Internet is used by very few livestock keepers to search for relevant livestock information. These livestock keepers admit that they get a lot of information in the Internet on different issues concerning livestock keeping. Internet use is hindered by lack of computer skills for the majority of the livestock keepers. Use of the Internet is also deterred by long distances to the Internet cafes, use of English language and ignorance on the importance of the Internet in accessing livestock information.

FUTURE RESEARCH DIRECTIONS

The literature review and findings from this study have revealed that there are some research and information gaps which need to be filled. This suggests that there are some areas that need to be researched on including the following.

A Participatory Action Research to Promote use of ICTs in Accessing Livestock Information

From the findings of this study, it was revealed that some of the urban livestock keepers were not aware of the fact that they can get a lot of information on livestock keeping through the use of ICTs. These livestock keepers need to be given the necessary knowledge and sensitized to use some of these ICTs like radio, television and the Internet, so that they can benefit by getting relevant information that could help them improve their livestock keeping practice. A participatory action research could therefore be a very useful study in ensuring that these livestock keepers are imparted with the necessary knowledge to enable them use the ICTs effectively in accessing livestock information.

Role of ICT Projects in Specific Urban Communities

This study has revealed that there are various ICT projects in Tanzania most of which are geared towards improving rural livelihoods, but little has been done on the role that these projects have played in improving the livelihoods of specific urban communities. Given the importance of ICT projects in rural areas of Tanzania and Africa at large, a study needs to be done to investigate the existence of ICT projects in urban areas and the extent to which specific urban communities benefit from these projects.

A Comparative Study on Role of ICTs Between Urban and Rural Communities

Findings of this study have revealed the importance of ICTs in accessing livestock information in urban areas and several other studies have been conducted to assess the role of ICTs in rural livelihoods in Tanzania. A comparative study therefore needs to be done to identify gaps of ICT use that exist between urban and rural communities in Tanzania and what can be done to fill the gaps and reduce the digital divide.

REFERENCES

Achora, J. C., & Ngolobe, B. (2009). Digital opportunities for change. ICT update: A current awareness bulletin for ACP agriculture, 50, 20.

Adejo, P. E., & Haruna, U. (2009). Access of farmers to ICTs for agricultural development in Bauchi local government area, Bauchi state. *Proceedings of the 43rd annual conference of the Agricultural Society of Nigeria*.

African Connection, Centre for Strategic Planning. (2002). *The Next Step: a rural ICT programme for Africa, Draft 2*. Prepared by Intelcom Research and Consultancy Ltd.

Asiedu, F., Gouro, A. S., Ndlovu, L., Nuru, H., & Lameta, K. (2009), *The role of Science, Technology and Innovation in addressing the challenges to food security and economic empowerment.* www.ypard. org/ypard/.../589_Livestock_Policy_Brief_Final_090529.pdf

Brodnig, G., & Mayer-Schönberger, V. (2000). Bridging the Gap: The role of spatial information technologies in the integration of traditional environmental knowledge and western science. *The Electronic Journal on Information Systems in Developing Countries, 1.* http://www.is.cityu.edu.hk/ejisdc.htm

Bystrom, K., & Jarvelin, K. (1995). Task complexity affects information seeking and use. *Information Processing & Management, 31*(2), 191–213. doi:10.1016/0306-4573(95)80035-R

Chhachhar, A. R., Hassan, M. S., Omar, S. Z., & Soomro, B. (2012). The Role of Television in Dissemination of Agriculture Information among Farmers. *Journal of Applied Environmental and Biological Sciences, 2*(11), 586-591.

Chilimo, W. L. (2009). *Use of Information and Communication Technologies for improved rural livelihoods in Tanzania* (PhD Thesis). University of Kwazulu Natal.

CIRAD. (2009). *Livestock keeping in urban areas: A review of traditional technologies based on literature and field experience.* http://pigtrop.cirad.fr

CTA. (2009). *The many uses of mobile phones.* CTA, Technical Centre for Agricultural and Rural Cooperation (ACP-EU).

FAO. (1999a), Urban and Peri-urban food production; a new challengefor the Food and Agriculture Organization (FAO) of the United Nations, by A.W.Drescher and B.L. Laquinta. Internal Report. Rome: FAO.

Ferris, S. (2004, June). FOODNET: Information is changing things in the market place. ICT Update.

Gakuru, M., Winters, K., & Stepman, F. (2009). *Inventory of Innovative Farmer Advisory Services using ICTs.* The Forum for Agricultural Research in Africa (FARA).

Gantt, W., & Cantor, E. (2010). Direct data on demand. ICT update: A current awareness bulletin for ACP agriculture, 53, 4.

Guendel, S. (2002). *Peri-urban and urban livestock keeping in East Africa: A coping strategy for the poor?* https://www.eldis.org/static/DOC9069.htm

Hassan, M. S., Yassin, M. D., Shaffril, H. A., Othman, M. S., Samah, B. A., Samah, A. A., & Ramli, S. A. (2011). Receiving the Agriculture Information through Mass Media and Interpersonal Sources among the Rural Community. *American Journal of Agricultural and Biological Sciences, 6*(3), 451-461.

Jacobi, P., Amend, J., & Kiango, S. (2005). *Urban agriculture in Dar Es Salaam: Providing an indispensable part of the diet.* Resource Centres on Urban Agriculture and Food Security (RUAF) Foundation.

Jarvelin, K., & Wilson, T. D. (2003). On conceptual models for information seeking and retrieval research. *Information Research, 9*(1), paper 163.

Jensen, M. (2002). *Information and Communication Technologies (ICTS) in Africa.* A Status Report. http://www.panos.org.uk/files/Why RadioMatters.pdf

Kapange, B. (2002). *ICTs and National Agricultural Research Systems–e-Development for the Grass-roots: The Tanzania Case*. Academic Press.

Karamagi, H., & Nalumansi, L. (2009). No more spilt milk. ICT update: A current awareness bulletin for ACP agriculture, 47, 5.

Kiplagat, R. (2009). Computerizing dairy cooperatives. ICT update: A current awareness bulletin for ACP agriculture, 47, 14.

Kithuka, J., Mutemi, J., & Mohammed, A. H. (2007). *Keeping up with Technology: The use of mobile telephony in delivering community-based decentralized animal health services in Mwingi and Kitui Districts, Kenya*. Farm-Africa working paper.

Maru, A. (2003). *Potential Contributions from Use of New Information and Communication Technologies (ICT) for Livestock Production and Services in India*. https://www.indiaveterinarycommunity.com/profperspective/featuredarticle/feb-04/art-maru.htm

Morton, J., & Matthewman, R. (1996). *Improving livestock production through extension: information needs institutions and opportunities*. Academic Press.

Nazari, M. N., & Abu, A. H. (2010). Radio as an Educational Media Agricultural Development. *The Journal of the South East Asia Research Centre for Communication and Humanities, 2*, 13–20.

Okolla, W. A. (2002). The Kenya Agricultural Commodity Exchange. ICT Update: A current awareness bulletin for ACP agriculture, 9.

Ozowa, V. (1995). Information Needs of Small Scale Farmers in Africa: The Nigerian Example. *Quarterly Bulletin of the International Association of Agricultural Information Specialists, 40*(1).

Reitz, J. M. (2007). *Online Dictionary for Library and Information Science (ODLIS)*. Information. lu.com/odlis/

Schilderman, T. (2002). *Strengthening the knowledge and information systems of the urban poor*. Department for International Development (DFID). https://practicalaction.org/docs/ia3/kis-urban-poor-report-2002.pdf

Souter, D., Scott, N., Garforth, C., Jain, R., & Mascarenhas, O. (2005). *The Economic Impact of Telecommunications on Rural Livelihoods and Poverty Reduction: A Study of rural Communities in India (Gujarat), Mozambique and Tanzania*. https://ideas.repec.org/p/iim/iimawp/2005-11-04.html

URT. (2005). *Livestock sector brief*. Prepared by Food and Agricultural Organization (FAO) and Livestock Information, Sector Analysis and Policy Branch (AGAL).

URT. (2007). *Livestock*. http://www.tanzania.go.tz/livestock.html

Weeks, J. R. (2008). *Population: an introduction to concepts and issues* (10th ed.). Wadsworth Thompson Learning.

Westhuizen, J. V. (2003). Q&A: ICTs and livestock performance. ICT update: A current awareness bulletin for ACP agriculture, 15, 5.

Yahaya, M. K., & Badiru, O. I. (2002). Measuring tha Impact of Agricultural Radio and Television Programmes in Southwest Nigeria. *Journal of Applied Communications*, *86*(3), 2002. doi:10.4148/1051-0834.2171

KEY TERMS AND DEFINITIONS

Information: For the purpose of this study, livestock information is all facts, conclusions, ideas, and creative works related to livestock keeping.

Information and Communication Technologies: In this study, ICT will encompass the definitions of Old ICTs and New ICTs. The term generally refers to electronic and computer-based technologies that are used in communication e.g. mobile phones, radio, television, and the internet.

Information Source: In the context of this study an information source can be defined as any document or person that provide information required by a livestock keeper searching for livestock information, e.g. extension workers, veterinary officers and fellow livestock keepers, customers and potential customers of livestock products and printed materials.

Peri-Urban Areas: In this study, peri-urban is defined as an area immediately surrounding a city or town

Urban Areas: An urban area can be defined differently by different countries depending on population density, human activities and building structures. In the context of this study, an urban area is defined as a geographical location found in a city or town.

Urban Livestock Keeping: An urban livestock keeping can be generally defined as the raising of domesticated animals that is concentrated in and around cities (FAO, 2007). This definition is adopted for this study and the animals involved in this study include cattle, goats, pigs, sheep, and chicken.

Appendix

Table 1. Top 100 Mobile Network Operators in Developing Countries in Africa (4Q 2016, Ranked by Mobile Subscribers)

	Country	Operator
1	Nigeria	MTN
2	Ethiopia	Ethio Telecom
3	Egypt	Vodafone
4	Nigeria	Glo Mobile
5	South Africa	Vodacom
6	Nigeria	Airtel
7	Egypt	Orange
8	South Africa	MTN
9	Kenya	Safaricom
10	Egypt	Etisalat Misr
11	Nigeria	9Mobile
12	Ghana	Scancom (MTN)
13	Morocco	Maroc Telecom
14	South Africa	Cell-C
15	Algeria	Mobilis
16	Algeria	Djezzy
17	Morocco	Méditel
18	Algeria	Ooredoo
19	Sudan	Zain
20	Tanzania	Vodacom
21	Cote d'Ivoire	Orange
22	Tanzania	Tigo
23	Angola	Unitel Angola
24	Mali	Orange
25	Uganda	MTN Uganda
26	Tanzania	Airtel
27	Cameroon	MTN Cameroon
28	DRC	Vodacom
29	Morocco	Inwi
30	Cote d'Ivoire	MTN
31	Mozambique	Movitel
32	Ghana	Vodafone
33	Tunisia	Ooredoo
34	Uganda	Airtel
35	Senegal	Orange
36	Sudan	Sudani
37	Sudan	MTN
38	DRC	Orange
39	Mali	Malitel
40	Burkina Faso	Onatel
41	Kenya	Airtel

continued on following page

Table 1. Continued

	Country	Operator
42	Cote d'Ivoire	Moov
43	DRC	Airtel
44	Zimbabwe	Econet Wireless
45	Libya	Libyana
46	Guinea Republic	Orange
47	DRC	Africell
48	Burkina Faso	Orange
49	Cameroon	Orange
50	Zambia	MTN Zambia
51	Mozambique	mCel
52	Ghana	Millicom
53	Mozambique	Vodacom
54	Tunisia	Tunisie Telecom
55	Zimbabwe	Net.One
56	Zambia	Airtel
57	Ghana	Airtel
58	Niger	Airtel
59	Rwanda	MTN Rwandacell
60	Benin	MTN
61	Senegal	Wari/Tigo
62	Benin	Moov
63	Tunisia	Divona/Orange
64	Madagascar	Orange
65	South Africa	Telkom
66	Sierra Leone	Africell SL
67	Madagascar	Airtel
68	Tanzania	Halotel
69	Malawi	TNM
70	Malawi	Airtel
71	Senegal	Expresso
72	Togo	Togo Telecom
73	Uganda	UTL Telecel
74	Chad	Tigo
75	Cameroon	Nextell
76	Burundi	Econet
77	Rwanda	Tigo
78	Kenya	Telkom Kenya
79	Angola	Movicel
80	Somalia	Hormuud
81	Burkina Faso	Telecel
82	Guinea Republic	MTN
83	Namibia	MTC
84	Chad	Airtel
85	Togo	Moov
86	Congo Brazzaville	MTN Congo
87	Madagascar	Telecom Malagasy
88	Congo Brazzaville	Airtel
89	Mauritania	Mauritel Mobiles
90	Guinea Republic	Cellcom
91	Libya	Almadar
92	Botswana	Mascom
93	Zimbabwe	Telecel
94	Burundi	Lumitel
95	Gabon	Libertis
96	Niger	Orange
97	Rwanda	Airtel
98	Zambia	Zamtel
99	Liberia	Lonestar
100	Sierra Leone	Airtel

Source: Africa and Middle East Telecom Week https://www.africantelecomsnews.com/Operators_Regulators/List_of_101_Top_African_mobile_operators.html

Compilation of References

12th Annual State of Agile Report. (2018, April 8). Retrieved from Collabnet Version One: https://www.stateofagile.com/#ufh-i-423641583-12th-annual-state-of-agile-report/473508

Abdelaziz, A. (2018). *Developing Employability and Job-Related Skills at Mobile Learning Environments: a case study at an industrial training centre* (Doctoral Thesis). Lancaster University, UK, 2018.

Abramovich, S., & Bride, M. M. (2018). Open education resources and perceptions of financial value. *Internet and Higher Education*, *39*, 33–38. doi:10.1016/j.iheduc.2018.06.002

Achora, J. C., & Ngolobe, B. (2009). Digital opportunities for change. ICT update: A current awareness bulletin for ACP agriculture, 50, 20.

Acılar, A. (2011). Exploring the aspects of digital divide in a developing country. *Issues in Informing Science & Information Technology*, *8*, 231–244. doi:10.28945/1415

Adebara, I. (2016). *Using Womb Grammars for Inducing the Grammar of a Subset of Yorùbá Noun Phrases* (Master of Science). Simon Fraser University. Retrieved from http://summit.sfu.ca/item/17390

Adebara, I., & Dahl, V. (2016). Grammar Induction as Automated Transformation between Constraint Solving Models of Language. *KnowProS@IJCAI 2016*, 7.

Adegbola, T. (2017). *Bridging the Last Six Inches of the Digital divide*. Nigeria Computer Society Conference. http://www.ncs.org.ng/wp-content/uploads/2017/08/Bridging-the-Last-Six-Inches-of-the-Digital-Divide-Tunde-Adegbola.pdf

Adegbola, T. (2016). Pattern-based Unsupervised Induction Of Yorùbá Morphology. *Proceedings of the 25th International Conference Companion on World Wide Web - WWW '16 Companion*, 599–604. 10.1145/2872518.2890563

Adegbola, T., & Odilinye, L. U. (2012). Quantifying the effect of corpus size on the quality of automatic diacritization of Yorùbá texts. In *Third Workshop on Spoken Language Technologies for Under-Resourced Languages*, (pp. 48–53). Cape Town, South Africa: International Speech Communication Association.

Adegbola, T., Owolabi, K., & Odejobi, T. (2011). Localising for Yoruba: Experience, Challenges and Future Direction. *Conference on Human Language Technology for Development*, 7-10.

Adejo, P. E., & Haruna, U. (2009). Access of farmers to ICTs for agricultural development in Bauchi local government area, Bauchi state. *Proceedings of the 43rd annual conference of the Agricultural Society of Nigeria*.

Adetunmbi, O. A., Obe, O. O., & Iyanda, J. N. (2016). Development of Standard Yorùbá speech-to-text system using HTK. *International Journal of Speech Technology*, *19*(4), 929–944. doi:10.100710772-016-9380-2

Adewole, L. B., Adetunmbi, A. O., Alese, B. K., & Oluwadare, S. A. (2017). Token Validation in Automatic Corpus Gathering for Yoruba Language. *FUOYE Journal of Engineering and Technology*, *2*(1), 4. doi:10.46792/fuoyejet.v2i1.85

Adeyemo, O. O., & Idowu, A. (2015). Development and integration of Text to Speech Usability Interface for Visually Impaired Users in Yoruba language. *African Journal of Computing and ICT*, *8*(1), 87–94.

Adomi, E. E., & Kpangban, E. (2010). Application of ICTs in Nigerian secondary schools. *Library Philosophy and Practice*. Retrieved April 10, 2020, from https://www.uidaho.edu/~mbolin/lpp2010.htm

Aduwa-Ogiegbean, S. E., & Iyamu, E. O. S. (2005). Using information and communication technology in secondary schools in Nigeria. *Journal of Educational Technology & Society*, *8*(1), 104–112.

Afolabi, A., Omidiora, E., & Arulogun, T. (2013). Development of Text to Speech System for Yoruba Language. *Innovative Systems Design and Engineering*, *4*(9), 1–8.

African Connection, Centre for Strategic Planning. (2002). *The Next Step: a rural ICT programme for Africa, Draft 2*. Prepared by Intelcom Research and Consultancy Ltd.

Agbeyangi, A. O., Eludiora, S. I., & Popoola, O. A. (2016). Web-Based Yorùbá Numeral Translation System. *IAES International Journal of Artificial Intelligence*, *5*(4), 127–134. doi:10.11591/ijai.v5.i4.pp127-134

Agyeman, O. T. (2007). *ICT for education in Nigeria. Survey of ICT and Education in Africa: Nigeria Country Report*. Retrieved November 8, 2019, from www.infodev.org/ict4edu-africa

Aharony. (2010). Twitter Use in libraries: An exploratory analysis. *Journal of Web Librarianship*, *4*(4), 333-350. http://eric.ed.gov/?id=EJ907467

Ajao, J. F., Olawuyi, D. O., & Odejobi, O. O. (2018). Yoruba Handwritten Character Recognition using Freeman Chain Code and K-Nearest Neighbor Classifier. *Jurnal Teknologi Dan Sistem Komputer*, *6*(4), 129–134. doi:10.14710/jtsiskom.6.4.2018.129-134

Ajayi, I. A., & Ekundayo, H. T. (2009). The application of information and communication technology in Nigerian secondary schools. *International NGO Journal*, *4*(5), 281–286. http://citeseerx.ist.psu.edu/viewdoc/download?doi=10.1.1.933.9342&rep=rep1&type=pdf

Ajegbelen, A. J. (2016). Impact of education trust fund (ETF) on tertiary institutions in Nigeria, using college of education as a case study. *Journal of Research & Method in Education*, *6*(3), 18–25. http://www.iosrjournals.org/iosr-jrme/papers/Vol-6%20Issue-3/Version-2/C0603021825.pdf

Ajithkumar, C. (2016). Transforming Indian Higher Education-Role of MOOCs. *International Journal for Innovative Research in Multidisciplinary Field*, *2*(9), 195–201.

Ajoku, L. I. (2014). The place of ICT in teacher preparation and climate change curriculum at the tertiary education level in Nigeria. *Journal of Education and Practice*, *5*(13), 2014185. https://www.iiste.org/Journals/index.php/JEP/article/view/12763/13072

Ajzen, I. (1985). From intentions to actions: a theory of planned behaviour. In J. Kuhl & J. Beckman (Eds.), *Action-Control: From cognition to behaviour* (pp. 11–39). Springer, Verlag. doi:10.1007/978-3-642-69746-3_2

Ajzen, I. (1991). The Theory of Planned Behaviour. *Organizational Behavior and Human Decision Processes*, *50*(2), 179–211. doi:10.1016/0749-5978(91)90020-T

Ajzen, I., & Fishbein, M. (1975). *Belief, attitude, intention and behaviour: An introduction to Theory of Research*. Addison-Wesley.

Àkànbí, L. A., & Odéjobí, O. À. (2011). Automatic recognition of oral vowels in tone language: Experiments with fuzzy logic and neural network models. *Applied Soft Computing*, *11*(1), 1467–1480. doi:10.1016/j.asoc.2010.04.018

Aker, J. C., & Mbiti, I. M. (2010). Mobile phones and economic development in Africa. *The Journal of Economic Perspectives*, *24*(3), 207–232. doi:10.1257/jep.24.3.207

Akinadé, O. O., & Ọdẹ́jọbí, Ọ. A. (2014). Computational modelling of Yorùbá numerals in a number-to-text conversion system. *Journal of Language Modelling*, *2*(1), 167. doi:10.15398/jlm.v2i1.83

Akshay, N., Sreeram, K., Anand, A., Venkataraman, R., & Bhavani, R. (2012). MoVE: Mobile vocational education for rural India. *2012 IEEE International Conference on Technology Enhanced Education (ICTEE)*, 1-5. 10.1109/ICTEE.2012.6208644

Akulich, M., & Kaźmierczyk, J. (2018). The socio-economic approach to the study of modern economic systems. Postcapitalism. Part 2. *Management*, *22*(2), 299–310. doi:10.2478/manment-2018-0038

Al Ahmar, M. A. (2011). A prototype student advising expert system supported with an object-oriented database. *International Journal of Advanced Computer Science and Applications*, *1*(3), 100–105.

Al-Adwan, A., Al-Adwan, A., & Smedley, J. (2013). Exploring students' acceptance of e-learning using technology acceptance model in Jordanian universities. *International Journal of Education and Development Using Information and Communication Technology*, *9*(2), 4–18.

Alajmia, N., Khambarib, M. N. M., Luanc, W. S., & Ahd, N. A. (2019). Mobile Learning in the Workplace: Employee's Perspectives on Readiness, Acceptance, Benefits and Limitations of Training with Mobile Technology in Kuwait. *International Journal of Innovation, Creativity and Change, 10*(9).

Al-Alak, B. A. (2009). Measuring and evaluating business students' satisfaction perceptions at public and private universities in Jordan. *Asian Journal of Marketing*, *3*(2), 33–51. doi:10.3923/ajm.2009.33.51

Alden, B. (n.d.). *Limitations of Agile Methodologies- Agile Methodologies*. Retrieved April 1, 2019, from https://www.umsl.edu/~sauterv/analysis/Fall2013Papers/Buric/limitations-of-agile-methodologies-1.html

Alderfer, C. P. (1969). An empirical test of a new theory of human needs. *Organizational Behavior and Human Performance*, *4*(2), 142–175. doi:10.1016/0030-5073(69)90004-X

Alexander, M. (2018, June 19). *Agile project management: 12 key principles, 4 big hurdles*. Retrieved from CIO United States: https://www.cio.com/article/3156998/agile-project-management-a-beginners-guide.html

Alotaibi, R., Houghton, L., & Sandhu, K. (2017). Factors influencing users' intention to use mobile government applications in Saudi Arabia. *International Journal of Advanced Computer Science and Applications*, *8*(7), 200–211. doi:10.14569/IJACSA.2017.080727

Alumu, S., & Thiagarajan, P. (2016). Massive Open Online Courses and E-learning in Higher Education. *Indian Journal of Science and Technology*, *9*(6), 1–10. doi:10.17485/ijst/2016/v9i6/81170

Alwahaishi, A., & Snasel, V. (2013). Consumers' acceptance and use of information and communications technology: A UTAUT and Flow Based Theoretical Model. *Journal of Technology Management & Innovation*, *89*(2), 61–73. doi:10.4067/S0718-27242013000200005

Alwehaibi, H. O. (2015). The impact of using YouTube in EFL classroom on enhancing EFL students' content learning. *Journal of College Teaching and Learning*, *12*(2), 121–126. doi:10.19030/tlc.v12i2.9182

Ambler, S. W. (2018). *Communication on Agile Software Teams*. Retrieved from Agile Modeling: http://www.agilemodeling.com/essays/communication.htm

Anantatmula, V., & Thomas, M. (2010). *Managing global projects: A structured approach for better performance. Project Management Journal* , 41.

Annan, N. K. (2015). *Information and Communication Technology Convergence*. Retrieved June 14, 2018, from https://www.academia.edu/11195363/Convergence_in_Information_and_Communication_Technology

Anttiroiko, A. V., Valkama, P., & Bailey, S. J. (2013). Smart Cities in the New Service Economy: Building Platforms for Smart Services. *AI & Society, 29*(3), 323–334. doi:10.100700146-013-0464-0

Apagu, V. V., & Wakili, B. A. (2015). Availability and utilization of ICT facilities for teaching and learning of vocational and technical education in Yobe State Technical Colleges. *American Journal of Engineering Research, 4*(2), 113–118.

Appiah, E., & Cronjé, J. (2013). ICT, ideation pedagogy and Innovation Education: setting a new paradigm in graphic design education. In *Proceedings of the 2nd International Conference for Design Education Researchers* (pp. 2-14). Oslo: ABM-media.

Armatas, C., Spratt, C., & Vincent, A. (2014). Putting Connectivist Principles Into Practice: A Case Study of an Online Tertiary Course. *American Journal of Distance Education, 28*(2), 81–91. doi:10.1080/08923647.2014.901782

Artelaris, P., Arvanitidis, P. A., & Petrakos, G. (2011). Convergence patterns in the world economy: Exploring the nonlinearity hypothesis. *Journal of Economic Studies (Glasgow, Scotland), 38*(3), 236–252. doi:10.1108/01443581111152373

Asia Development Bank. (2003). *Toward e-Development in Asia and the Pacific, ADB*. Retrieved October 14, 2007, from https://www.adb.org/documents/policies/ict/ict.pdf

Asiedu, F., Gouro, A. S., Ndlovu, L., Nuru, H., & Lameta, K. (2009), *The role of Science, Technology and Innovation in addressing the challenges to food security and economic empowerment*. www.ypard.org/ypard/.../589_Livestock_Policy_Brief_Final_090529.pdf

Asubiaro, T. (2013). Entropy-Based Generic Stopwords List for Yoruba Texts. *International Journal of Computer and Information Technology, 02*(05), 1065–1068.

Asubiaro, T. (2014). Effects of diacritics on Web search engines' performance for retrieval of Yoruba documents. *Journal of Library and Information Studies., 12*(1), 1–19.

Asubiaro, T. (2017). An Assessment of the Cyber Presence of Academic Libraries in Nigeria. *African Journal of Library Archives and Information Science, 27*(1), 65–76.

Asubiaro, T. (2019). How Collaboration Type, Publication Place, Funding and Author's role affect Citations Received by Publications from Africa? A Bibliometric study of LIS research from 1996 to 2015. *Scientometrics, 120*(3), 1261–1287. Advance online publication. doi:10.100711192-019-03157-1

Asubiaro, T. V. (2015). Statistical Patterns of Diacritized and Undiacritized Yorùbá Texts. *International Journal of Computational Linguistics Research, 6*(3), 77–84.

Asubiaro, T., Adegbola, T., Mercer, R., & Ajiferuke, I. (2018). A word-level language identification strategy for resource-scarce languages: A Word-Level Language Identification Strategy for Resource-Scarce Languages. *Proceedings of the Association for Information Science and Technology, 55*(1), 19–28. doi:10.1002/pra2.2018.14505501004

Atawneh, S., Al-Akhras, M., AlMomani, I., Liswi, A., & Alawairdhi, M. (2020). Collaborative Mobile-Learning Architecture Based on Mobile Agents. *Electronics (Basel), 9*(1), 162. doi:10.3390/electronics9010162

Athanasou, J. A., & Van Esbroeck, R. (Eds.). (2008). *International handbook of career guidance*. Springer Science & Business Media. doi:10.1007/978-1-4020-6230-8

Athukorala, P. (2014). Intra-regional FDI and Economic Integration in South Asia: Trends, Patterns and Prospects. *South Asia Economic Journal, 15*(1), 1–35. doi:10.1177/1391561414525710

Ayittey, G. B. N. (1992). *Africa betrayed.* St. Martin's Press.

Ayittey, G. B. N. (1998). *Africa in chaos.* St. Martin's Press.

Ayittey, G. B. N. (2005). *African unchained: The blueprint for Africa's future.* Macmillan Publishers. doi:10.1007/978-1-137-12278-0

Ayogu, I. I., Adetunmbi, A. O., Ojokoh, B. A., & Oluwadare, S. A. (2017). A comparative study of hidden Markov model and conditional random fields on a Yorùba part-of-speech tagging task. *2017 International Conference on Computing Networking and Informatics (ICCNI)*, 1–6. 10.1109/ICCNI.2017.8123784

Baartman, L. K., & De Bruijn, E. (2011). Integrating knowledge, skills and attitudes: Conceptualising learning processes towards vocational competence. *Educational Research Review, 6*(2), 125–134. doi:10.1016/j.edurev.2011.03.001

Bacca, J., Baldiris, S., Fabregat, R., & Graf, S. (2015). Mobile augmented reality in vocational education and training. *Procedia Computer Science, 75*, 49–58. doi:10.1016/j.procs.2015.12.203

Bakici, T., Almirall, E., & Wareham, J. (2013). A Smart City Initiative: The Case of Barcelona. *Journal of the Knowledge Economy, 4*(2), 135–148. doi:10.100713132-012-0084-9

Bandura, A. (1977). *Self-efficacy: Toward a unifying theory of behavioural change.* Academic Press.

Bandura, A. (1982). Self-Efficacy: Mechanism in human agency. *The American Psychologist, 37*(2), 122–147. doi:10.1037/0003-066X.37.2.122

Bandura, A. (1995). Exercise of personal and collective efficacy in changing societies. In A. Bandura (Ed.), *Self-efficacy in changing societies* (pp. 1–45). Cambridge University Press. doi:10.1017/CBO9780511527692.003

Bannerman, P. (2008, July 16). *Defining Project Success: a multilevel framework.* Retrieved from https://www.pmi.org/learning/library/defining-project-success-multilevel-framework-7096

Baran, E. (2014). A review of research on mobile learning in teacher education. *Journal of Educational Technology & Society, 17*(4), 17–32.

Barolli, L., Nishino, H., & Miwa, H. (2019). *Advances in Intelligent Networking and Collaborative Systems: The 11th International Conference on Intelligent Networking and Collaborative Systems (INCoS-2019).* Springer.

Bashir, M., & Rozaimee, A. B. (2015). A Word Stemming Algorithm for Hausa Language. *IOSR Journal of Computer Engineering, 17*(3), 25–31.

Bashir, M., Rozaimee, A., & Isa, W. M. W. (2017). Automatic Hausa LanguageText Summarization Based on Feature Extraction using Naïve Bayes Model. *World Applied Sciences Journal, 35*(9), 7. doi:10.5829/idosi.wasj.2017.2074.2080

Beachum, L., Bellware, K., Shammas, B., Denham, H., Thebault, R., Copeland, K., Knowles, H., & Sonmez, F. (2020). Live updates: Atlanta mayor tests positive for covid-19; states mandate masks, shut down again. *Washington Post.* Retrieved July 6, 2020, from https://www.washingtonpost.com/nation/2020/07/06/coronavirus-live-updates-us/

Beck, K., Beedle, M., Van Bennekum, A., Cockburn, A., Fowler, M., Grenning, J., . . . Thomas, D. (2001). *Manifesto for Agile Software Development.* Retrieved from http://agilemanifesto.org/

Becta, H. (2004). *Enabling teachers to make successful use of ICT.* Retrieved August 15, 2019, from http://ww.becta.org.uk

Belkin, D. (2019). Colleges mine data on their applicants. *The Street Wall Journal.* Retrieved January 4, 2019, from https://www.wsj.com/articles/the-data-colleges-collect-on-applicants-11548507602

Berendt. (2007). Tags are not metadata but just more content' to some people. International Joint Conferences on Artificial Intelligence. *Proceedings of the International Conference on Weblogs and Social Media (ICWSM).* https://icwsm.org/papers/2--Berendt-Hanser.pdf

Bergstrom, J., Uhr, C., & Frykmer, T. (2016, September). A Complexity Framework for Studying Disaster Response Management. *Journal of Contingencies and Crisis Management, 24*(3), 124–135. doi:10.1111/1468-5973.12113

Bhatiasevi, V. (2015). *An extended UTAUT model to explain the adoption of mobile banking in Thailand. Information Development.* Sage Publications. doi:10.1177/0266666915570764

Bimba, A., Idris, N., Khamis, N., & Noor, N. F. M. (2016). Stemming Hausa text: Using affix-stripping rules and reference look-up. *Language Resources and Evaluation, 50*(3), 687–703. doi:10.100710579-015-9311-x

Binghilams, K. A. (2009). Barriers to the successful integration of ICT in teaching and learning environments: A literature review. Eurasian *Journal of Mathematics, Science & Technology Education, 5*(3), 235–245.

Bishop, A. P., Tidline, T. J., Shoemaker, S., & Salela, P. (1999). Public libraries and networked information services in low-income communities. *Library & Information Science Research, 21*(3), 361–390. doi:10.1016/S0740-8188(99)00017-1

Blackwell, C. K., Lauricella, A. R., Wartella, E., Robb, M., & Schomburg, R. (2013). Adoption and use of technology in early education: The interplay of extrinsic barriers and teacher attitudes. *Computers & Education, 69*, 310–319. doi:10.1016/j.compedu.2013.07.024

Blood, R. (2000). Weblogs: A History and Perspective. *The Weblog Handbooks.* Available at: http://www.rebeccablood.net/essays/weblog_history.html

Blood, R. (2013). Weblogs: A History and Perspective. *Rebecca's Pocket.* Available at: http://www.rebeccablood.net/essays/weblog_history.html

Bolton, M., & Stolcis, G. (2008). Overcoming failure of imagination in crisis management: The Complex Adaptive System. *Public Sector Innovation Journal, 3*(3).

Bordons, M., Zulueta, M. A., Romero, F., & Barrigón, S. (1999). Measuring interdisciplinary collaboration within a university: The effects of the multidisciplinary research programme. *Scientometrics, 46*(3), 383–398. doi:10.1007/BF02459599

Borgman, C. L. (2000). *From Gutenberg to the Global Information Infrastructure: Access to Information in the Networked World.* MIT Press.

Bridgstock, R. (2009). The graduate attributes we've overlooked: Enhancing graduate employability through career management skills. *Higher Education Research & Development, 28*(1), 31–44. doi:10.1080/07294360802444347

Brixiová, Z., Kangoye, T., & Said, M. (2020). Training, human capital, and gender gaps in entrepreneurial performance. *Economic Modelling, 85*, 367–380. doi:10.1016/j.econmod.2019.11.006

Brodnig, G., & Mayer-Schönberger, V. (2000). Bridging the Gap: The role of spatial information technologies in the integration of traditional environmental knowledge and western science. *The Electronic Journal on Information Systems in Developing Countries, 1.* http://www.is.cityu.edu.hk/ejisdc.htm

Brown, T., & Mbati, L. (2015). Mobile Learning: Moving Past the Myths and Embracing the Opportunities. *International Review of Research in Open and Distributed Learning, 16*(2). Advance online publication. doi:10.19173/irrodl.v16i2.2071

Bruneckienė, J., Jucevicius, R., Zykienė, I., Rapsikevičius, J., & Lukauskas, M. (2019). Assessment of investment attractiveness in European countries by artificial neural networks: What competences are needed to make a decision on collective well-being? *Sustainability*, *11*(24), 1–23. doi:10.3390u11246892

Bryson, J. (2017) Disciplinary Perspectives on Skill. In The Oxford Handbook of Skills and Training. Oxford University Press.

Buchanan, T., Sainter, P., & Saunders, G. J. (2013). Factors affecting faculty use of learning technologies: Implications for models of technology adoption. *Journal of Computing in Higher Education*, *25*(1), 1–11. doi:10.100712528-013-9066-6

Buettner, R. (2016). The Weakness of Ties. In *49th Annual Hawaii International Conference on System Sciences*. Kauai, HI: IEEE. DOI: 10.13140/RG.2.1.3249.2241

Buhari Approves N161bn for 2019 TETFund. (2019, January 4). Retrieved from https://punchng.com/buhari-approves-n161bn-for-2019-tetfund-interventions-in-varsities-others/

Burke, M. J., Sarpy, S. A., Smith-Crowe, K., Chan-Serafin, S., Salvador, R. O., & Islam, G. (2006). Relative effectiveness of worker safety and health training methods. *American Journal of Public Health*, *96*(2), 315–324. doi:10.2105/AJPH.2004.059840 PMID:16380566

Bushweller, G. (2017, June 12). Classroom technology: Where schools stand. *Education Week*. Retrieved from https://www.edweek.org/ew/articles/2017/06/14/tracking-20-years-of-change-in-ed-tech.html?intc=EW-TC17-TOC

Bystrom, K., & Jarvelin, K. (1995). Task complexity affects information seeking and use. *Information Processing & Management*, *31*(2), 191–213. doi:10.1016/0306-4573(95)80035-R

Cai, Z., Fan, X., & Du, J. (2017). Gender and attitudes toward technology use: A meta-analysis. *Computers & Education*, *105*, 1–13. doi:10.1016/j.compedu.2016.11.003

Cao, D.-B., & Chow, T. (2008). *A Survey Study of Critical Success Factors in Agile Software Projects*. Academic Press.

Cao, Y., & Zhang, L. (2011). Research about the college students' career counseling expert system based on agent. *Proceedings of the 2nd International Conference on Artificial Intelligence, Management Science and Electronic Commerce (AIMSEC)*, 3208-3211.

Capello, R., & Perucca, G. (2014). Openness to Globalization and Regional Growth Patterns in CEE Countries: From the EU Accession to the Economic Crisis. *Journal of Common Market Studies*, *53*(2), 218–236. doi:10.1111/jcms.12157

Carney, T., & Weber, D. J. (2015). Public Health Intelligence: Learning from the Ebola Crisis. *American Journal of Public Health*, *105*(9), 1740–1744. doi:10.2105/AJPH.2015.302771 PMID:26180978

Carroll, J. M., & Rosson, M. B. (1987). Paradox of the active user. In J. M. Carroll (Ed.), *Interfacing Thought: Cognitive Aspect of Human-Computer Interaction* (pp. 80–111). MIT Press.

Carr, V. H. Jr. (1999). *Technology adoption and diffusion*. The Learning Centre for Interactive Technology.

Caseiro, N., & Coelho, A. (2018). Business intelligence and competitiveness: The mediating role of entrepreneurial orientation. *Competitiveness Review*, *28*(2), 213–226. doi:10.1108/CR-09-2016-0054

Casey, T., & Wilson-Evered, E. (2012). Predicting uptake of technology innovation in online family dispute resolution services: An application and extension of the UTAUT. *Computers in Human Behavior*, *28*(6), 2034–2045. doi:10.1016/j.chb.2012.05.022

Castro Sánchez, J. J., & Alemán, E. C. (2011). Teachers' opinion survey on the use of ICT tools to support attendance-based teaching. *Journal Computers & Education*, *56*(3), 911–915. doi:10.1016/j.compedu.2010.11.005

Cato, J. (2001). *User-Centered Web Design*. Pearson Education.

Cavarec, Y. (2012, October 23). *Revisiting the definition of project success*. Retrieved from https://www.pmi.org/learning/library/revisiting-definition-project-success-6098

Cavus, N., & Uzunboylu, H. (2009). Improving critical thinking skills in mobile learning. *Procedia: Social and Behavioral Sciences*, *1*(1), 434–438. doi:10.1016/j.sbspro.2009.01.078

Centre for International Governance Innovation (CIGI). (2019). *Leveraging the digital transformation for development: A global South strategy for the data-driven economy*. Policy Brief No 148, 2019.

Chao, C. M. (2019). Factors determining the behavioral intention to use mobile learning. An application and extension of the UTAUT model. *Frontiers in Psychology*, *10*, 1–52. doi:10.3389/fpsyg.2019.01652 PMID:31379679

Characteristic of Agile Development Success. (2018, September 28). Retrieved from Collabnet Versionone: https://resources.collab.net/agile-101/agile-development-success

Chatman, E. A. (1996). The Impoverished life-world of outsiders. *Journal of the American Society for Information Science*, *47*(3), 193–206. doi:10.1002/(SICI)1097-4571(199603)47:3<193::AID-ASI3>3.0.CO;2-T

Chatman, E. A. (1999). A Theory of life in the round. *Journal of the American Society for Information Science*, *50*(3), 207–217. doi:10.1002/(SICI)1097-4571(1999)50:3<207::AID-ASI3>3.0.CO;2-8

Chauhan, S., & Jaiswal, M. (2016). Determination of acceptance of ERP software training in business schools: Empirical investigation using UTAUT model. *International Journal of Management Education*, *14*(3), 248–262. doi:10.1016/j.ijme.2016.05.005

Chavez, C., Terceiro, A., Meirelles, P., Jr., & Kon, F. (2011). Free/Libre/Open Source Software Development in Software Engineering Education: Opportunities and Experiences. *Forum de Educacao Em Engenharia de Software (CBSoft'11-SBES-FEES)*, 8.

Chen, M., Zhang, H., Weidong, L., & Zhang, W. (2014). The Global Pattern of Urbanization and Economic Growth: Evidence from the Last Three Decades. *PLoS One*, *9*(8), e103799. doi:10.1371/journal.pone.0103799 PMID:25099392

Chhachhar, A. R., Hassan, M. S., Omar, S. Z., & Soomro, B. (2012). The Role of Television in Dissemination of Agriculture Information among Farmers. *Journal of Applied Environmental and Biological Sciences*, *2*(11), 586-591.

Childers, T., & Post, J. (1975). *The information poor in America*. Scarecrow Press.

Chilimo, W. L. (2009). *Use of Information and Communication Technologies for improved rural livelihoods in Tanzania* (PhD Thesis). University of Kwazulu Natal.

Chua & Goh. (2010). A Study of Web 2.0 applications in library websites. *Library & Information Science Research, 32*, 203-211. Available at http://ejournals.library.ualberta.ca/index.php/EBLIP/article/.../9474/1513

CIA. (2016). *The World Factbook — Central Intelligence Agency*. Retrieved from https://www.cia.gov/library/publications/the-world-factbook/geos/ni.html

Cilliers, P. (1998). *Complexity and Postmodernism: Understanding complex systems*. Routledge.

Cimperman, M., Brenic, M. M., & Trkman, P. (2016). Analyzing older users' home tele-health services acceptance behavior applying an extension of UTAUT model. *International Journal of Medical Informatics*, *90*, 22–31. doi:10.1016/j.ijmedinf.2016.03.002 PMID:27103194

CIRAD. (2009). *Livestock keeping in urban areas: A review of traditional technologies based on literature and field experience*. http://pigtrop.cirad.fr

Click, A., & Petit, J. (2010). Social Networking and Web 2.0 in Information literacy. *The International Information & Library Review, 42*(2), 137–142. doi:10.1080/10572317.2010.10762855

Cockburn, I. M., Henderson, R., & Stern, S. (2018). *The impact of artificial intelligence on innovation* (NBER Working paper No. w24449). Retrieved from National Bureau of Economic Research website: https://www.nber.org/chapters/c14006

Collabnet Version One. (2018). *Characteristics of Agile Development Success*. Retrieved from https://resources.collab.net/agile-101/agile-development-success

Collier, P. (2007). *The Bottom billion: Why the poorest countries are failing and what can be done about it*. Oxford University Press.

Compeau, D. R., & Higgins, C. A. (1995). Computer self-efficacy: Development of a measure and initial test. *Management Information Systems Quarterly, 19*(2), 189–211. doi:10.2307/249688

Connel, B., & Ladd, R. (1990). Aspects of pitch realisation in Yoruba. *Phonology, 7*(1), 1–29. https://doi-org./doi:10.1017/S095267570000110X

Connor, Y. O., & Reilly, P. O. (2018). Examining the infusion of mobile technology by healthcare practitioners in a hospital setting. *Information Systems Frontiers, 20*(6), 1297–1317. doi:10.100710796-016-9728-9

Coombs, A. L. (2013). High tone processes in Ibibio. *Proceedings of Meetings on Acoustics Acoustical Society of America, 19*, 060232–060232. doi:10.1121/1.4800734

Cortese, A. D. (2003). *The critical role of higher education in creating a sustainable future*. Retrieved May 15, 2019, from http://old.syntao.com/Uploads/files/The%20Critical%20Role%20of %20Higher%20Education%20in%20Creating%20a %20Sustainable %20Future.pdf

Covner, B. J. (1963). Engineers in midstream: A study of engineers seeking professional career guidance. *IEEE Transactions on Engineering Management, EM-10*(1), 15–18. doi:10.1109/TEM.1963.6449226

Craven, M., Mysore, M., & Wilson, M. (2020). *COVID-19: Briefing note, May 13, 2020*. Retrieved May 23, 2020, from https://www.mckinsey.com/business-functions/risk/our-insights/covid-19-implications-for-business

Creswell, J. W. (2012). *Educational research: Planning, conducting, and evaluating quantitative and qualitative research* (4th ed.). Pearson.

Crisologo, I. (2013). *The Philippine radar network*. Project NOAH. Retrieved from https://center.noah.up.edu.ph/the-philippine-radar-network/

Cruz-Jesus, F., Oliveira, T., & Bacao, F. (2012). Digital divide across the European Union. *Information & Management, 49*(6), 278–291. doi:10.1016/j.im.2012.09.003

Crysmann, B. (2012). HaG — A Computational Grammar of Hausa. In M. R. Marlo, N. B. Adams, C. R. Green, M. Morrison, & T. M. Purvis (Eds.), *Selected proceedings of the 42nd Annual Conference on African Linguistics (ACAL 42)*, (pp. 321–337). Academic Press.

Crysmann, B. (2015b). Resumption and Extraction in an Implemented HPSG of Hausa. *Proceedings of the Grammar Engineering Across Frameworks (GEAF) 2015 Workshop*, 65–72. 10.18653/v1/W15-3309

Crysmann, B. (2015a). Representing morphological tone in a computational grammar of Hausa. *Journal of Language Modelling, 3*(2), 463. doi:10.15398/jlm.v3i2.126

Crysmann, B. (2017). Reduplication in a computational HPSG of Hausa. *Morphology*, *27*(4), 527–561. doi:10.100711525-017-9306-y

CTA. (2009). *The many uses of mobile phones*. CTA, Technical Centre for Agricultural and Rural Cooperation (ACP-EU).

Cuseo, J. (2003). *Academic advisement and student retention: Empirical connections and systemic interventions*. University of Texas. http://146.85.50.73/retention/media/Academic-advisementv-and-student-retention.pdf

Da Veiga, J. A. L., Ferreira-Lopes, A., & Sequeira, T. N. (2015). Public Debt, Economic Growth and Inflation in African Economies. *The South African Journal of Economics*, *84*(2), 294–322. doi:10.1111aje.12104

Dagba, T. K., Aoga, J. O. R., & Fanou, C. C. (2016). Design of a Yoruba Language Speech Corpus for the Purposes of Text-to-Speech (TTS) Synthesis. In N. T. Nguyen, B. Trawiński, H. Fujita, & T.-P. Hong (Eds.), *ACIIDS 2016: Intelligent Information and Database Systems* (pp. 161–169). doi:10.1007/978-3-662-49381-6_16

Dagger, D., O'Connor, A., Lawless, S., Walsh, E., & Wade, V. P. (2007). Service-oriented e-learning platforms: From monolithic systems to flexible services. *IEEE Internet Computing*, *11*(3), 28–35. doi:10.1109/MIC.2007.70

Daily Digest, D. M. I. (2019). 6 digital strategies to attract international students. *DMI Daily Digest blog*. Retrieved February 16, 2020, from https://digitalmarketinginstitute.com/en-gb/blog/6-digital-strategies-to-attract-international-students

Davies, A. R., & Mullin, S. J. (2011). Greening the economy: Interrogating sustainability innovations beyond the mainstream. *Journal of Economic Geography*, *11*(5), 793–816. doi:10.1093/jeg/lbq050

Davis, J. (2017). *Innovative teaching strategies that improve student engagement. Association for middle level education*. Retrieved November 8, 2019, from https://www.amle.org/BrowsebyTopic/WhatsNew/WNDet/TabId/270/ArtMID/888/ArticleID/876/Innovative-Teaching-Strategies-that-Improve-Student-Engagement.aspx

Davis, F. D. (1989). Perceived usefulness, perceived ease of use, and user acceptance of information technology. *Management Information Systems Quarterly*, *13*(3), 319–340. doi:10.2307/249008

Davis, F. D., Bagozzi, R. P., & Warshaw, P. R. (1989). User acceptance of computer technology: A comparison of two theoretical models. *Management Science*, *35*(8), 982–1004. doi:10.1287/mnsc.35.8.982

Day, J. (2014). Fostering emergent resilience: The complex adaptive supply network of disaster relief. *International Journal of Production Research*, *52*(7), 1970–1988. doi:10.1080/00207543.2013.787496

De Jong, M., Joss, S., Schraven, D., Zhan, C., & Weijnen, M. (2015). Sustainable-smart-resilient-low carbon-eco-knowledge cities; making sense of a multitude of concepts promoting sustainable urbanisation. *Journal of Cleaner Production*, *109*, 25–38. doi:10.1016/j.jclepro.2015.02.004

De Pauw, G., Wagacha, P. W., & De Schryver, G.-M. (2007). Automatic diacritic restoration for resource-scarce languages. *International Conference on Text, Speech and Dialogue*, 170–179. 10.1007/978-3-540-74628-7_24

Dede, C. (1996). The evolution of distance education: Emerging technologies and distributed learning. *American Journal of Distance Education*, *10*(2), 4–36. doi:10.1080/08923649609526919

Dell'Anno, R., & Amendola, A. (2015). Social Exclusion and Economic Growth: An Empirical Investigation in European Economies. *Review of Income and Wealth*, *61*(2), 274–301. doi:10.1111/roiw.12096

Deorah, S., Sridharan, S., & Goel, S. (2010). SAES-expert system for advising academic major. *Proceedings of the 2nd IEEE International Advance Computing Conference (IACC)*, 331-336.

Dogan, M. (1996). The hybridization of social science knowledge. *Library Trends*, *45*(2), 296–314.

Donner, J. (2008). Research approaches to mobile use in developing world: A review of the literature. *The Information Society, 24*(3), 140–159. doi:10.1080/01972240802019970

Dotti, N. F., & Spithoven, A. (2017). Economic drivers and specialization patterns in the spatial distribution of Framework Programme's participation. *Journal of Regional Science, 97*(4), 863–882. doi:10.1111/pirs.12299

Douphrate, D., & Hagevoort, R. (2015). *Using mobile devices to offer safety training to dairy workers.* Retrieved August 18, 2017, from https://www.progressivedairy.com/topics/management/using-mobile-devices-to-offer-safety-training-to-dairy-workers

Duan, Y., Edwards, J. S., & Xu, M. X. (2005). Web-based expert systems: Benefits and challenges. *Information & Management, 42*(6), 799–811. doi:10.1016/j.im.2004.08.005

Dulupçu, M. A., & Okçu, M. (2000). Towards quantum economic development: transcending boundaries. *Ankara Üniversitesi SBF Dergisi.* Retrieved from http://dergiler.ankara.edu.tr/dergiler/42/475/5477.pdf

Dunn, D. S., Saville, B. K., Baker, S. C., & Marek, P. (2013). Evidence-based teaching: Tools and techniques that promote learning in the psychology classroom. *Australian Journal of Psychology, 65*(1), 5–13. doi:10.1111/ajpy.12004

Dyson, L., Litchfield, A., Lawrence, E., Raban, R., & Leijdekkers, P. (2009). Advancing the m-learning research agenda for active, experiential learning: Four case studies. *Australasian Journal of Educational Technology, 25*(2), 250–267. doi:10.14742/ajet.1153

Easterly, W. (2006). *The White Man's Burden: Why the West's efforts to aid the rest have done so much ill and so little good.* Penguin Press.

Eberhard, D., Simons, G., & Fennig, C. (Eds.). (2018). Ethnologue: Languages of the World (twenty-first). Dallas, TX: SIL International.

EduSys. (2019). *What is ICT in education? Advantage & disadvantage* [Blog post]. Retrieved January 5, 2020, from https://www.edusys.co/blog/what-is-ict-in-education

Edwards, R., Raggatt, P., & Small, N. (Eds.). (2014). *The Learning Society: Trends and Issues.* Routledge.

Egelhoff, T. (2014). *How Fast Is Knowledge Doubling?* Retrieved April 2017, From: https://kmmsam.com/how-fast-is-knowledge-doubling/

Ekpenyong, M., & Udoh, E. (2013). Intelligent Prosody Modelling: A Framework for Tone Language Synthesis. Academic Press.

Ekpenyong, M. E., & Inyang, U. G. (2016). Unsupervised mining of under-resourced speech corpora for tone features classification. *2016 International Joint Conference on Neural Networks (IJCNN),* 2374–2381. 10.1109/IJCNN.2016.7727494

Ekpenyong, M. E., Inyang, U. G., & Udoh, E. O. (2016). Adaptive Prosody Modelling for Improved Synthetic Speech Quality. In Z. Vetulani, H. Uszkoreit, & M. Kubis (Eds.), *Human Language Technology* (Vol. 9561, pp. 16–28). Challenges for Computer Science and Linguistics., doi:10.1007/978-3-319-43808-5_2

Ekpenyong, M. E., Inyang, U. G., & Umoren, I. J. (2016). Towards a Hybrid Learning Approach to Efficient Tone Pattern Recognition. In L. Rutkowski, M. Korytkowski, R. Scherer, R. Tadeusiewicz, L. A. Zadeh, & J. M. Zurada (Eds.), *Artificial Intelligence and Soft Computing* (Vol. 9692, pp. 571–583)., doi:10.1007/978-3-319-39378-0_49

Ekpenyong, M. E., & Udoh, E. (2014). Tone modelling in Ibibio speech synthesis. *International Journal of Speech Technology, 17*(2), 145–159. doi:10.100710772-013-9216-2

Ekpenyong, M. E., Urua, E.-A., & Gibbon, D. (2008). Towards an unrestricted domain TTS system for African tone languages. *International Journal of Speech Technology*, *11*(2), 87–96. doi:10.100710772-009-9037-5

Ekpenyong, M., Inyang, U., & Udoh, E. (2018). Unsupervised visualization of Under-resourced speech prosody. *Speech Communication*, *101*, 45–56. doi:10.1016/j.specom.2018.04.011

Ekpenyong, M., Udoinyang, M., & Urua, E.-A. (2009). A Robust Language Processor for African Tone Language Systems. *Georgian Electronic Scientific Journal: Computer Science and Telecommunications*, *6*(23), 1–11.

Ekpenyong, M., Urua, E.-A., Watts, O., King, S., & Yamagishi, J. (2014). Statistical parametric speech synthesis for Ibibio. *Speech Communication*, *56*, 243–251. doi:10.1016/j.specom.2013.02.003

Elijah, O., & Ogunlade, I. (2006). Analysis of the uses of information and communication technology for gender empowment and sustainable poverty alleviation in Nigeria. *International Journal of Education and Development Using Information and Communication Technology*, *2*(3), 45–69.

Eludiora, S. I., & Ayemonisan, O. R. (2018). *Computational Morphological Analysis of Yorùbá Language Words*. Academic Press.

Enemuoh, C., Hepple, M., Onyenwe, I., & Ezeani, I. (2017). Morph-Inflected Word Detection in Igbo via Bitext. *Proceedings of the 55th Annual Meeting of the Association for Computational Linguistics*, 4.

Enguehard, C., & Mangeot, M. (2014). Computerization of African languages-French dictionaries. Collaboration and Computing for Under Resourced Languages in the Linked Open Data Era, 121–128.

Enguehard, C., & Naroua, H. (2009). Evaluation of Virtual Keyboards for West-African Languages. *Language Resources and Evaluation*, 5.

Ertmer, P. A., Ottenbreit-Leftwich, A. T., Sadik, O., Sendurur, E., & Sendurur, P. (2012). Teacher beliefs and technology integration practices: A critical relationship. *Computers & Education*, *59*(2), 423–435. doi:10.1016/j.compedu.2012.02.001

Escosura, L. P. (2005). *Gerschenkron revisited. European patterns of development in historical perspective* (Working Paper 05-79 (10) Dpto de Historia Económica e Instituciones, Economic History and Institutions Series 10, Universidad Carlos III de Madrid, December 2005). Retrieved from https://econpapers.repec.org/paper/ctewhrepe/wh057910.htm

Essuman, J. K. (2001). A review of Educational studies in Guidance and counseling in schools in Ghana. *Ghana Journal of Psychology*, *1*(1), 22–43.

Etim, A. S. (2010). *The adoption and diffusion of information and communication technology in the Base of the Pyramid populations of Sub-Saharan Africa: A study of Nigerian students* (Thesis). University of North Carolina - Dissertations & Theses. doi:10.17615/ngh7-8v35

Etim, A. S., Etim, D. N., & Scott, J. (2020). Mobile health and telemedicine: Awareness, adoption and importance of health study. *International Journal of Healthcare Information Systems and Informatics*. https://www.igi-global.com/journal/international-journal-healthcare-information-systems/1094

Etim, A., Etim, J., Robinson, A., & Smith, P. (2016). Mobile learning apps to support students learning goals. *Int'l Journal of Computing, Communications & Instrumentation Eng.*, *3*(2).

Etim, A. S. (2012). The emerging market of Sub-Saharan Africa and technology adoption: Features users desire in mobile phones. *International Journal of ICT Research and Development in Africa*, *3*(1), 14–26. doi:10.4018/jictrda.2012010102

Etim, A. S. (2020). The ICT convergence and impact on women-owned micro and small business enterprises: An analysis based on information poverty. *International Journal of Gender Studies in Developing Societies, 3*(3), 271–292. doi:10.1504/IJGSDS.2020.104607

Etim, A. S., Huynh, K., Ramaswamy, S., Greer, A., Higdon, T., & Guevara, I. (2016). Educating project managers in the 21st-century economy: A field study on the adoption of social and collaborative tools as low-cost alternatives for project communication. *International Journal of Education Economics and Development, 7*(1/2), 79–94. doi:10.1504/IJEED.2016.079240

Etim, A., & Huynh, K. (2015). The use of social media and collaborative tools for virtual teaming – a global market reach out by Navibank. *International Journal of Management & Information Systems, 19*(1), 1–6. doi:10.19030/ijmis.v19i1.9054

European Centre for the Development of Vocational Training. (2011). *The benefits of vocational education and training.* Publications Office of the European Union.

European University Association. (2007). *Creativity in higher education. Report on the EUA creativity project 2006-2007.* Retrieved December 18, 2019, from https://eua.eu/downloads/publications/creativity%20in%20higher%20education%20%20report%20on%20the %20eua%20creativity%20project%202006-2007.pdf

Ezeani, I., Hepple, M., Onyenwe, I., & Enemuoh, C. (2018b). Multi-task Projected Embedding for Igbo. TSD 2018: Text, Speech, and Dialogue, 285–294.

Ezeani, I., Onyenwe, I., & Hepple, M. (2018). Transferred Embeddings for Igbo Similarity, Analogy, and Diacritic Restoration Tasks. In *Proceedings of SemDeep-3, the 3rd Workshop on Semantic Deep Learning,* (pp. 30–38). Association for Computational Linguistics.

Ezeani, I., Hepple, M., & Onyenwe, I. (2016). Automatic Restoration of Diacritics for Igbo Language. In P. Sojka, A. Horák, I. Kopeček, & K. Pala (Eds.), *Text* (Vol. 9924, pp. 198–205). doi:10.1007/978-3-319-45510-5_23

Ezeani, I., Hepple, M., & Onyenwe, I. (2017). Lexical Disambiguation of Igbo using Diacritic Restoration. *Proceedings of the 1st Workshop on Sense, Concept and Entity Representations and Their Applications,* 53–60. 10.18653/v1/W17-1907

Ezeani, I., Hepple, M., Onyenwe, I., & Enemuoh, C. (2018). Igbo Diacritic Restoration using Embedding Models. *Proceedings of the 2018 Conference of the North American Chapter of the Association for Computational Linguistics.* 10.18653/v1/N18-48008

FAO. (1993). *The potentials of microcomputers in support of agricultural extension, education and training.* Food and Agriculture Organisation of the United Nations.

FAO. (1999a), Urban and Peri-urban food production; a new challenge for the Food and Agriculture Organization (FAO) of the United Nations, by A.W.Drescher and B.L. Laquinta. Internal Report. Rome: FAO.

Federal Ministry of Education. (2019). *National implementation guidelines for ICT in education.* Abuja: Author. Retrieved January 3, 2020, from http://education.gov.ng/ wpcontent/uploads/2019/07/national-implementation-guidelines-for-ict-in-education-2019.pdf

Ferris, S. (2004, June). FOODNET: Information is changing things in the market place. ICT Update.

Fiala, D., & Tutoky, G. (2017). Computer Science Papers in Web of Science: A Bibliometric Analysis. *Publications, 5*(4), 23. doi:10.3390/publications5040023

Finkel, R., & Odejobi, O. A. (2009). A computational approach to Yorùbá morphology. *Proceedings of the First Workshop on Language Technologies for African Languages - AfLaT '09,* 25. 10.3115/1564508.1564514

Fishbein, M., & Ajzen, I. (1975). *Beliefs, attitudes, intention and behaviour: An introduction to Theory and Research.* Addison-Wesley Publishing Company.

Fisher, K. E., Durance, J. C., & Hinton, M. B. (2004). Information grounds and the use of need-based services by immigrants in Queens, New York: A context-based, outcome evaluation approach. *Journal of the American Society for Information Science and Technology, 55*(8), 754–766. doi:10.1002/asi.20019

Flavian, C., Gurrea, R., & Orús, C. (2009). Web design: A key factor for the website success. *Journal of Systems and Information Technology, 11*(2), 168–184. doi:10.1108/13287260910955129

Florant, A., Noel, N., Stewart, S., III, & Wright, J. (2020). *COVID-19: Investing in black lives and livelihoods.* Retrieved May 17, 2020, from https://www.mckinsey.com/industries/public-sector/our-insights/covid-19-investing-in-black-lives-and-livelihoods

Florida, R. (2013). The learning region. In Z. J. Acs (Ed.), *Regional innovation, knowledge, and global change* (2nd ed.). Routledge.

Frese, R. (2003, December 16). *Project Success and Failure: What is Success, What is Failure, and How Can You Improve Your Odds For Success?* Retrieved from http://www.umsl.edu/~sauterv/analysis/6840_f03_papers/frese/

Fuchs, T. & Woessmann, L. (2005). *Computers and Student Learning: Bivariate and Multivariate Evidence on the Availability and Use of Computers at Home and at School.* CES ifo Working Paper No. 8. https://www.ifo.de/DocDL/IfoWorkingPaper-8.pdf

Fu, J. S. (2013). ICT in education: A critical literature review and its implications. *International Journal of Education and Development Using ICT, 9*(1), 112–125. https://www.learntechlib.org/p/111900/

Fu, J. S. (2013). ICT in education: A critical literature review and its implications. *International Journal of Education and Development Using Information and Communication Technology, 9*(1), 112–125.

Gakuru, M., Winters, K., & Stepman, F. (2009). *Inventory of Innovative Farmer Advisory Services using ICTs.* The Forum for Agricultural Research in Africa (FARA).

Galperina, L. P., Girenko, A. T., & Mazurenko, V. P. (2016). The Concept of Smart Economy as the Basis for Sustainable Development of Ukraine. *International Journal of Economics and Financial Issues, 6,* 307–314.

Gan, B., Menkhoff, T., & Smith, R. (2015). Enhancing students' learning process through interactive digital media: New opportunities for collaborative learning. *Computers in Human Behavior, 51,* 652–663. doi:10.1016/j.chb.2014.12.048

Gantt, W., & Cantor, E. (2010). Direct data on demand. ICT update: A current awareness bulletin for ACP agriculture, 53, 4.

Garba, S. A. (2014). Impact of ICT course on preservice teachers' acquisition of ICT literacy skills and competence in Nigeria. *International Journal of Modern Education Research, 1*(2), 37–42. https://www.researchgate.net/profile/Sani_Garba2/publication/273593700_Impact_of_ICT_course_on_pre-service_teachers_acquisition_of_ICT_literacy_skills_and_competence_in_Nigeria/links/5506a9bb0cf24cee3a05c4b8/Impact-of-ICT-course-on-pre-service-teachers-acquisition-of-ICT-literacy-skills-and-competence-in-Nigeria.pdf

Garba, S. A., & Alademerin, C. A. (2014). Exploring the readiness of Nigerian colleges of education toward pre-service teacher preparation for technology integration. *International Journal of Technology & Inclusive Education, 3*(2), 335–342. doi:10.20533/ijtie.2047.0533.2014.0043

Garwood, J. E. (2013). *One-to-one iPads in the elementary classroom: Measuring the impact on student engagement, instructional practices, and teacher perception.* Western Illinois University.

Gassebner, M., Gaston, N., & Lamla, M. J. (2011). The inverse domino effect: Are economic reforms contagious? *International Economic Review*, *52*(1), 183–200. doi:10.1111/j.1468-2354.2010.00624.x

Gati, I., & Gutentag, T. (2015). The stability of aspect-based career preferences and of the recommended list of occupations derived from them. *Journal of Vocational Behavior*, *87*, 11–21. doi:10.1016/j.jvb.2014.11.009

Gati, I., & Ram, G. (2000). Counsellors' judgments of the quality of the pre-screening stage of the career decision-making process. *Journal of Counseling Psychology*, *47*(4), 414–428. doi:10.1037/0022-0167.47.4.414

Gati, I., Saka, N., & Krausz, M. (2001). Should I use a computer-assisted career guidance system? It depends on where your career decision-making difficulties lie. *British Journal of Guidance & Counselling*, *29*(3), 301–321.

Gati, I., & Tal, S. (2008). Decision-making models and career guidance. In *International handbook of career guidance* (pp. 157–185). Springer. doi:10.1007/978-1-4020-6230-8_8

Gauthier, E., Besacier, L., & Voisin, S. (2016). Speed Perturbation and Vowel Duration Modeling for ASR in Hausa and Wolof Languages. *INTERSPEECH*, *3529–3533*, 3529–3533. Advance online publication. doi:10.21437/Interspeech.2016-461

Gauthier, E., Besacier, L., & Voisin, S. (2016a). Automatic Speech Recognition for African Languages with Vowel Length Contrast. *Procedia Computer Science*, *81*, 136–143. doi:10.1016/j.procs.2016.04.041

Gazzola, P., Gonzalez Del Campo, A., & Onyango, V. (2019). Going green vs going smart for sustainable development: Quo vadis? *Journal of Cleaner Production*, *214*, 881–892. doi:10.1016/j.jclepro.2018.12.234

Gbongli, K., Dumar, K., & Mireku, K. K. (2016). MCDM technique to evaluating mobile banking adoption in the Togolese banking industry based on the perceived value; Perceived benefit and perceived sacrifice factors. *International Journal of Data Mining Knowledge Management Process*, *6*(3), 37–56. doi:10.5121/ijdkp.2016.6304

Gbongli, K., Dumor, K., & Mireku, K. K. (2016). MCDM technique to evaluating mobile banking adoption in the Togolese banking industry based on the perceived value: Perceived benefit and perceived sacrifice factors. *International Journal of Data Mining Knowledge Management Process*, *6*, 37–56.

Gefen, D. (2003). TAM or just plain habit: A look at experience online shoppers. *Journal of End User Computing*, *15*(3), 1–13. doi:10.4018/joeuc.2003070101

Gehrke, D., & Turban, E. (1999). Determinants of successful website design: Relative importance and recommendations for effectiveness. *Proceedings of the 32nd Hawaii International Conference on System Sciences*. 10.1109/HICSS.1999.772943

George, D., & Mallery, P. (2016). *IBM SPSS statistics 23 step by step: A simple guide and reference*. Routledge. doi:10.4324/9781315545899

Georgina, D. A., & Hosford, C. C. (2009). Higher education faculty perceptions on technology integration and training. *Teaching and Teacher Education*, *25*(5), 690–696. doi:10.1016/j.tate.2008.11.004

Gibbon, D., Urua, A., & Ekpenyong, M. (2005). Problems and solutions in African tone language Text–To–Speech. *MULTILING 2006 ISCA Tutorial and Research Workshop (ITRW)*, 6.

Gillooly, C. (1998). Disillusionment. *Information Week*, *669*, 46–51.

Ginevicius, R., Gedvilaite, D., Stasiukynas, A., & Sliogeriene, J. (2018). Quantitative Assessment of the Dynamics of the Economic Development of Socioeconomic Systems Based on the MDD Method. *The Engineering Economist*, *29*(3), 264–271. doi:10.5755/j01.ee.29.3.20444

Goleman, D. (2007). *Emotional Intelligence:Why It Can Matter More Than IQ*. Bantam Book.

Goodhue, D., & Thompson, R. L. (1995). Task technology fit and individual performance. *Management Information Systems Quarterly, 19*(2), 213–236. doi:10.2307/249689

Graham, P. (2005). Web 2.0. *Web 2.0 conference.* Available at: http://www.paulgraham.com/web20.html

Grant, A. E., & Meadows, J. H. (2021). *Communication Technology Update and Fundamentals* (17th ed.). Routledge.

Gries, T., Grundmann, R., Palnau, I., & Redlin, M. (2018). Technology diffusion, international integration and participation in developing economies - a review of major concepts and findings. *International Economics and Economic Policy, 15*(1), 215–253. doi:10.100710368-017-0373-7

Griffiths, M. (2012). *PMI-ACP Exam Prep.* RMC Publications Inc.

Guendel, S. (2002). *Peri-urban and urban livestock keeping in East Africa: A coping strategy for the poor?* https://www.eldis.org/static/DOC9069.htm

Gustavsson, T. (2016, August). *Benefits of Agile Project Management in A Non-Software Development Context- A Literature Review.* Retrieved from https://pmworldjournal.net/wp-content/uploads/2016/08/pmwj49-Aug2016-Gustavsson-benefits-of-agile-in-non-software-context-second-edition.pdf

Hair, J. F., Anderson, R. E., Tatham, R. L., & Black, W. C. (1995). *Multivariate data analysis with readings.* Petroleum Publishing.

Hannah, C. (2018). *The 92 hottest EdTech tools according to education experts.* Tutorful. Retrieved January 5, 2020, from https://tutorful.co.uk/blog/the-82-hottest-edtech-tools-of-2017-according-to-education-experts

Harmaakorpi, V. (2006). Regional Development Platform Method (RDPM) as a Tool for Regional Innovation Policy. *European Planning Studies, 14*(8), 1085–1114. doi:10.1080/09654310600852399

Harris-Bowlsbey, J., & Sampson, J. P. Jr. (2005). Use of technology in delivering career services worldwide. *The Career Development Quarterly, 54*(1), 48–56. doi:10.1002/j.2161-0045.2005.tb00140.x

Harrison, D. (Ed.). (2015). *Handbook of Research on Digital Media and Creative Technologies.* IGI Global. doi:10.4018/978-1-4666-8205-4

Hasell, J., Ortiz-Ospina, E., Mathieu, E., Ritchie, H., Beltekian, D., Macdonald, B., & Roser, M. (2020). *Statistics & Research: Coronavirus (COVID-19) testing.* Retrieved May 20, 2020, from https://ourworldindata.org/coronavirus-testing

Hassad, R. A. (2013). Faculty attitude towards technology-assisted Instruction for introductory statistics in the context of educational reform. *Technology Innovations in Statistics Education, 7*(2). Retrieved from https://escholarship.org/dist/wJD5zTgC2vrImRR/dist/prd/content/qt9k19k2f7/qt9k19k2f7.pdf

Hassan, M. S., Yassin, M. D., Shaffril, H. A., Othman, M. S., Samah, B. A., Samah, A. A., & Ramli, S. A. (2011). Receiving the Agriculture Information through Mass Media and Interpersonal Sources among the Rural Community. *American Journal of Agricultural and Biological Sciences, 6*(3), 451-461.

Hassan, S. T., Abolarinwa, J. A., Alenoghena, C. O., Bala, S. A., David, M., & Farzaminia, A. (2017). Intelligent sign language recognition using enhanced fourier descriptor: A case of Hausa sign language. *2017 IEEE 2nd International Conference on Automatic Control and Intelligent Systems (I2CACIS)*, 104–109. 10.1109/I2CACIS.2017.8239041

Haughey, D. (2010, January 2). *A Brief History of Project Management.* Retrieved from Project Smart: https://www.projectsmart.co.uk/brief-history-of-project-management.php

Haven, E., Khrennikov, A., & Robinson, T. (2017). *Quantum Methods in Social Science: A First Course.* World Scientific Publishing Co. Pte. Ltd. Retrieved from: https://EconPapers.repec.org/RePEc:wsi:wsbook:q0080

Hillage, J., & Pollard, E. (1998) *Employability: Developing a Framework for Policy Analysis*. London: DfEE.

Hoeckel, K. (2008). Costs and benefits in vocational education and training. Paris: Organisation for Economic Cooperation and Development.

Hogarty, K. Y., Hines, C. V., Kromrey, J. D., Ferron, J. M., & Mumford, K. R. (2005). The quality of factor solutions in exploratory factor analysis: The influence of sample size, communality, and overdetermination. *Educational and Psychological Measurement*, *65*(2), 202–226. doi:10.1177/0013164404267287

Hoggue, R., & Sorwar, G. (2017). Understanding factors influencing the adoption of m-Health by the elderly: An extension of the UTAUT model. *International Journal of Medical Informatics*, *101*, 75–84. doi:10.1016/j.ijmedinf.2017.02.002 PMID:28347450

Hoque, M. R. (2016). An empirical study of mHealth adoption in a developing country: The moderating effect of gender concern. *BMC Medical Informatics and Decision Making*, *16*(1), 51. doi:10.118612911-016-0289-0 PMID:27142844

Hoque, M. R., Bao, Y., & Sorwar, G. (2016). Investigating factors influencing the adoption of e-Health in developing countries: A patient's perspective. *Informatics for Health & Social Care*, *42*(1), 1–17. doi:10.3109/17538157.2015.10 75541 PMID:26865037

Howley, A., Wood, L., & Hough, B. (2011). Rural elementary school teachers' technology integration. *Journal of Research in Rural Education (Online)*, *26*(9), 1–14. https://jrre.psu.edu/articles/26-9.pdf

Hoy, M. B. (2014). MOOCs 101: An introduction to massive open online courses. *Medical Reference Services Quarterly*, *33*(1), 85–91. doi:10.1080/02763869.2014.866490 PMID:24528267

Hristidis, V., Chen, S. C., Li, T., Luis, S., & Deng, Y. (2010). Survey of data management and analysis in disaster situations. *Journal of Systems and Software*, *83*(10), 1701–1714. doi:10.1016/j.jss.2010.04.065

Huang, L., May, J., Pan, X., & Ji, H. (2016). *Building a Fine-Grained Entity Typing System Overnight for a New X (X = Language, Domain, Genre)*. Retrieved from https://arxiv.org/abs/1603.03112

Huang, L., May, J., Pan, X., Ji, H., Ren, X., Han, J., Zhao, L., & Hendler, J. A. (2017). Liberal Entity Extraction: Rapid Construction of Fine-Grained Entity Typing Systems. *Big Data*, *5*(1), 19–31. doi:10.1089/big.2017.0012 PMID:28328252

Huda, M., Anshari, M., Almunawar, M. N., Shahrill, M., Tan, A., & Jaidin, J. H. … Masari, M. (2016). Innovative teaching in higher education: The big data approach. *The Turkish Online Journal of Educational Technology*. Retrieved December 2, 2019, from https://www.researchgate.net/ profile/Miftachul_Huda4/publication/311576765_Innovative_Teaching_in_Higher_Education_The_Big_Data_Approach/links/584e7f5f08ae4bc8993779eb/Innovative-Teaching-in-Higher-Education-The-Big-Data-Approach.pdf

Hung, D., Tan, S. C., & Chen, D. T. (2005). How the Internet facilitates learning as dialog design considerations for online discussions. *International Journal of Instructional Media*, *32*(1), 37–46.

Hysa, B., & Spalek, S. (2019, April 11). *Opportunities and Threats Presented by Social Media in Project Management*. Retrieved from https://www.ncbi.nlm.nih.gov/pmc/articles/PMC6465589/

Ibrahim, A. (2019). Faculty access, attitudes, and use of instructional and web-based technologies in Nigeria's teacher preparation program: A mixed method study. *Theses and Dissertation (All)*. 1743. Retrieved from https://knowledge.library.iup.edu/etd/1743

Ibrahim, M. E., Yang, Y., Ndzi, D. L., Yang, G., & Al-Maliki, M. (2019). Ontology-based personalized course recommendation framework. *IEEE Access: Practical Innovations, Open Solutions*, *7*, 5180–5199. doi:10.1109/ACCESS.2018.2889635

Idowu, A. I., & Esere, M. (2013). ICT and higher educational system in Nigeria. *Educational Research Review, 8*(21), 2021–2025. doi:10.5897/ERR09.044

Idris, A., Edwards, H., & McDonald, S. (2017). *E-commerce adoption in Developing Countries SMEs: What Do the Prevailing Theoretical Models Offer Us?* International Conference on E-Commerce, Putrajaya, Malaysia.

Ifeanyi-Reuben, N., Ugwu, C., & Adegbola, T. (2017). Analysis and Representation of Igbo Text Document for a Text-Based System. *International Journal of Data Mining Techniques and Applications, 6*(1), 26–32. doi:10.20894/IJDMTA.102.006.001.005

Ifeanyi-Reuben, N., Ugwu, C., & Nwachukwu, E. O. (2017). Comparative Analysis of N-gram Text Representation on Igbo Text Document Similarity. *International Journal of Applied Information Systems, 12*(9), 1–7. doi:10.5120/ijais2017451724

Iheanetu, O., & Adeyeye, M. (2013). Finite state representation of reduplication processes in Igbo. *2013 Africon*, 1–6. doi:10.1109/AFRCON.2013.6757772

Iheanetu, O. U., Nwagwu, W. E., Adegbola, T., & Agarana, M. C. (2017). Corpus-size Quantification for Computational Morphological Analysis of Igbo Language. *Proceedings of the World Congress on Engineering and Computer Science, 6*.

Ikechukwu, E. O., Ebele, G. O., Godwin, E. A., & Ignatius, M. E. (2019). Bootstrapping Method for Developing Part-Of-Speech Tagged Corpus in Low Resource Languages Tagset- A Focus on an African IGBO. *International Journal on Natural Language Computing, 8*(1), 13–27. doi:10.5121/ijnlc.2019.8102

Internet World Stats in Africa. (2019). https://www.internetworldstats.com/africa.htm

Irvin, R. (2007). Information and communication technology (ICT) literacy: Integration and assessment in higher education. *Journal of Systemics, Cybernetics and Informatics, 5*(4), 50–55.

iThink. (2013). *Mobile telephony in developing countries: A global perspective*. The Innovation Knowledge Foundation. Think! Report No 4. Retrieved from www.thinkinnovation.org

IWS. (2019). *Top 20 country in internet users vs. rest of the world*. Internet World Stats. Retrieved January 12, 2020, from https://www.internetworldstats.com/ top20.htm

Jabbar, H. K., & Khan, R. Z. (2016). Survey on development of expert system from 2010 to 2015. *Proceedings of the Second ACM International Conference on Information and Communication Technology for Competitive Strategies*. 10.1145/2905055.2905190

Jacobi, P., Amend, J., & Kiango, S. (2005). *Urban agriculture in Dar Es Salaam: Providing an indispensable part of the diet*. Resource Centres on Urban Agriculture and Food Security (RUAF) Foundation.

Jana, S.K. & Maiti, A. (2020). Innovations in Higher Education in India. In *Theoretical and practical approaches to innovation in higher education*. IGI Global. Doi:10.4018/978-1-7998-1662-1.ch009

Jana, S. K., & Maiti, A. (2019). State-wise Public Expenditure on Higher Education in India: An Empirical Analysis. *Arthashastra Indian Journal of Economics and Research, 8*(2), 7–20. doi:10.17010/aijer/2019/v8i2/145222

Jansen, R., & Sellar, M. (2008). Sustainable Access: An International Perspective. In D. Charbonneau (Ed.), *Global Information Inequalities: Bridging the Information Gap* (pp. 3–18). doi:10.1016/B978-1-84334-361-5.50001-8

Jarvelin, K., & Wilson, T. D. (2003). On conceptual models for information seeking and retrieval research. *Information Research, 9*(1), paper 163.

Jaschik, S., & Lederman, D. (2018) 2018 survey of faculty attitudes on technology: A survey by inside Higher Ed and Gallup. *Inside Higher Ed Report*. Retrieved from https://mediasite.com/wp-content/uploads/2018/11/2018-Faculty-Survey-Mediasite.pdf

Jensen, M. (2002). *Information and Communication Technologies (ICTS) in Africa*. A Status Report. http://www.panos.org.uk/files/Why RadioMatters.pdf

Jia, S. (2019). *Literature review of YouTube in teaching activities*. Paper presented at the Twenty-Third Pacific Asia Conference on Information Systems, China. Retrieved February 1, 2020, from http://www.pacis2019.org/wd/Submissions/ PACIS2019_paper_236.pdf

Johar, G., & Awalluddin, J. (2011). The Role of Technology Acceptance Model in Explaining Effect on E-Commerce Application System. *International Journal of Managing Information Technology, 3*(3), 1–14. doi:10.5121/ijmit.2011.3301

Johnson, A., & Proctor, R. W. (2017). *Skill Acquisition and Training: Achieving Expertise in Simple and Complex Tasks*. Taylor & Francis.

Joshi, N. M. (2015). *Acceptance of MOOCs for Engineering Education in India*. 10th International CALIBER-2015, HP University and IIAS, Shimla, Himachal Pradesh, India. https://nptel.ac.in/NPTEL_Media/pdf/inflibnet.pdf

Jucevicius, R., & Juceviciene, P. (2015). Smart social system. In International practices of smart development (pp. 24-36). Frankfurt am Main: Peter Lang.

Jude, W. I., & Dankaro, J. T. (2012). ICT resource utilization, availability and accessibility by teacher educators for instructional development in College of Education Katsina-Ala. *New Media & Mass Communication, 3*, 1-6. Retrieved from https://www.iiste.org/Journals/index.php/NMMC/article/view/1766/1719

Kaiser, H. F. (1960). The application of electronic computers to factor analysis. *Educational and Psychological Measurement, 20*(1), 141–151. doi:10.1177/001316446002000116

Kanninen, E. (2008). *Learning styles and e-learning*. (Unpublished Master of science thesis). Tempere University of Technology.

Kapange, B. (2002). *ICTs and National Agricultural Research Systems–e-Development for the Grassroots: The Tanzania Case*. Academic Press.

Kaplan, A. M., & Michael, H. (2011). The early bird catches the news: Nine things you should know about micro-blogging. *Business Horizons, 54*(2). Retrieved 26/08/2019. http://michaelhaenlein.net/Publications/Kaplan,%20Andreas%20%20The%20early%20bird%20catches%20the%20...%20news.pdf

Kapoor, K. K., Dwivedi, Y. K., & William, M. D. (2015). Examining the role of three sets of innovation attributes for determining adoption of the interbank mobile payment service. *Information Systems Frontiers, 17*(5), 1039–1056. doi:10.100710796-014-9484-7

Karamagi, H., & Nalumansi, L. (2009). No more spilt milk. ICT update: A current awareness bulletin for ACP agriculture, 47, 5.

Kari, K. H., & Baro, E. E. (2016). Digital Preservation Practices in University Libraries: A Survey of Institutional Repositories in Nigeria. *Preservation. Digital Technology & Culture, 45*(3), 134–144. doi:10.1515/pdtc-2016-0006

Karmakar, A. K., & Jana, S. K. (2015, December). In What Direction is the Wind blowing? Education and Skill Development: The case of BRICS. *The Indian Economic Journal*, (Special Issue), 131–147.

Karnani, A. (2007). Fortune at the bottom of the pyramid: A mirage. *Social Science Research Network*. Retrieved August 12, 2007, from http://ssrn.com/abstract=914518

Kauppila, O.-P., Rajala, R., & Jyrama, A. (2011). Knowledge sharing through virtual teams across borders and boundaries. *Management Learning, 42*(4), 395-418. Retrieved from https://research.aalto.fi/en/publications/knowledge-sharing-through-virtual-teams-across-borders-and-boundaries(c213160d-eca5-448e-a18a-26a2e6bb0abe).html

Keegan, D. J. (1980). On defining distance education. *Distance Education, 1*(1), 13–36. doi:10.1080/0158791800010102

Keen, M. (2009). *Case Study: Web 2.0 SOA Scenario.* Red Paper IBM. Available at: http://www.redbooks.ibm.com/redpapers/pdfs/redp4555.pdf

Kenny, R. F., Park, C., Van Neste-Kenny, J. M., Burton, P. A., & Meiers, J. (2009). Using Mobile Learning to Enhance the Quality of Nursing Practice Education. In M. Ally (Ed.), *Mobile Learning: Transforming the Delivery of Education and Training* (Vol. 1, pp. 25-47). Edmonton, Alberta: AU Press. http://www.aupress.ca/index.php/books/120155

Kesson, A. B. (2013). *Students perception and utilization of counseling in Ghana: A case study of the Accra Metropolis* (Unpublished master's thesis). University of Ghana, Legon.

Kessy, D., Kaemba, M., & Gachoka, M. (2006). The reasons for under use of ICT in education. In the context of Kenya, Tanzania and Zambia. *Proceedings of the Fourth IEEE*.

Kevor, M. O. (2013). E-Counseling for Institutions of Higher Learning in Ghana: What are the Requirements? *International Journal of Research in Computer Application & Management, 3*(5), 131–134.

Khalilzadeh, J., Ozturk, A. B., & Bilgihan, A. (2017). A security-related factors in extended UTAUT model for NFC based mobile payment in the restaurant industry. *Computers in Human Behavior, 70*, 460–474. doi:10.1016/j.chb.2017.01.001

Khandelwal, T., Joshi, G., Singhania, A., & Dutta, A. (2013). Semantic Web-Based E-Counseling System. *International Journal of Computer Science and Electronics Engineering, 1*(1), 2320–4028.

Khanna, S., Kaushik, A., & Barnela, M. (2010). Expert systems advance in education. *Proceedings of the National Conference on Computational Instrumentation*, 109-112.

Kickbusch, I., & Gleicher, D. (2014). Smart Governance for Health. In I. Kickbusch & D. Gleicher (Eds.), *Smart Governance for Health and Well-being: The Evidence*. World Health Organizations.

Kim, H. S. (2014). Patterns of Economic Development in the World. *Journal of Global Economics, 2*(2), 113. doi:10.4172/2375-4389.1000113

Kim, H. S. (2017). Patterns of Economic Development: Correlations Affecting Economic Growth and Quality of Life in 222 Countries. *Politics & Policy, 45*(1), 83–104. doi:10.1111/polp.12190

Kim, S.-J., & Jeong, D. Y. (2006). An analysis of the development and use of theory in library and information science research articles. *Library & Information Science Research, 28*(4), 548–562. doi:10.1016/j.lisr.2006.03.018

King, C. (2015). *3 most common causes of slow internet connection*. Retrieved April 7, 2020, from https://www.linkedin.com/pulse/3-most-common-causes-slow-internet-connection-charlotte-king

King, K., & Palmer, R. (2010). *Planning for technical and vocational skills development*. UNESCO, International Institute for Educational Planning.

Kiplagat, R. (2009). Computerizing dairy cooperatives. ICT update: A current awareness bulletin for ACP agriculture, 47, 14.

Kithuka, J., Mutemi, J., & Mohammed, A. H. (2007). *Keeping up with Technology: The use of mobile telephony in delivering community-based decentralized animal health services in Mwingi and Kitui Districts, Kenya*. Farm-Africa working paper.

Klein, J. T. (1996). Interdisciplinary needs: The current context. *Library Trends, 45*(2), 134–154.

Kling, R., Rosembaum, H., & Sawyer, S. (2005). *Understanding and communicating social informatics: A framework for studying and teaching the human contexts of information and communication technologies*. Information Today.

Ko, J., Sammons, P., & Bakkum, L. (2010). *Effective teaching*. Education Development Trust.

Kolog, E. A., Sutinen, E., Vanhalakka-Ruoho, M., Suhonen, J., & Anohah, E. (2015). Using unified theory of acceptance and use of technology model to predict students' behavioral intention to adopt and use e-counseling in Ghana. *International Journal of Modern Education and Computer Science, 7*(11), 1–11. doi:10.5815/ijmecs.2015.11.01

Kolog, E., Sutinen, E., & Vanhalakka-Ruoho, M. (2014). E-counselling implementation: Students' life stories and counselling technologies in perspective. *International Journal of Education and Development Using ICT, 10*(3), 32–48.

Korez-Vide, R., & Tominc, P. (2016). Competitiveness, Entrepreneurship and Economic Growth. In *Competitiveness of CEE Economies and Businesses*. Springer. doi:10.1007/978-3-319-39654-5_2

Koryuhina, C., & Shamshina, T. (2018). *Challenges of ICT in education. In The 16th international scientific conference information technologies and management*. ISMA University. https://www.isma.lv/FILES/SCIENCE/IT&M2018_THE-SES/03_MDM/15_IT&M2018_Korjuhina_Shamshina.pdf

Kothari, C. R. (2004). Research Methodology: Methods and Techniques. New Age Publishing Limited.

Krishnaveni, R., & Meenakumari, J. (2010). Usage of ICT for Information Administration in Higher education Institutions–A study. *International Journal of Environmental Sciences and Development, 1*(3), 282–286. doi:10.7763/IJESD.2010.V1.55

Kruchten, P., & Gorans, P. (2014). *A Guide to Critical Success Factors in Agile Delivery*. Retrieved from IBM Center for The Business of Goverment: http://www.businessofgovernment.org/sites/default/files/A%20Guide%20to%20Critical%20Success%20Factors%20in%20Agile%20Delivery.pdf

Kulick, S., & Bies, A. (2016). Rapid Development of Morphological Analyzers for Typologically Diverse Languages. *Proceedings of the Tenth International Conference on Language Resources and Evaluation*, 2551–2557.

Kulik, J. A. (1994). Meta-analysis study of findings on computer-based instruction. In E. L. Baker & H. F. O'neil (Eds.), *Technology assessment in education and training*. Lawrence Erlbaum.

Kumar, T. M. (Ed.). (2017). Smart Economy in Smart Cities. International Collaborative Research. doi:10.1007/978-981-10-1610-3

Lai, C. L., & Hwang, G. J. (2014). Effects of mobile learning time on students' conception of collaboration, communication, complex problem–solving, meta–cognitive awareness and creativity. *International Journal of Mobile Learning and Organisation, 8*(3-4), 276–291. doi:10.1504/IJMLO.2014.067029

Lai, P. C. (2014). *Cashless. Cardless, contactless and convenience of MySIM*. GlobalCLAS Technology.

Lai, P. C. (2017). The literature review of technology adoption models and theories for the novelty technology. *Journal of Information Systems and Technology Management, 14*(1), 21–38. doi:10.4301/S1807-17752017000100002

Lai, P. C., & Zainal, A. A. (2015). Perceived Risk as an Extension to TAM Model: Consumers' Intention to Use A Single Platform E-Payment. *Australian Journal of Basic and Applied Sciences, 9*(2), 323–330.

Lamar, M. M. (2012). Using and developing measurement instruments in science education: A Rasch modeling approach. *Science Education, 96*(1), 183–185. doi:10.1002ce.20477

Lampropoulus, G., & Siakas, K. (2018, March). *Communication in Distributed Agile Software Development: Impact of Social Media-Social Networking.* Retrieved from Research Gate: https://www.researchgate.net/publication/327580426_Communication_in_Distributed_Agile_Software_Development_Impact_of_Social_Media_-_Social_Networking

Lassa, J. (2012). *Post disaster governance, complexity and network theory: Evidence from Aceh, Indonesia after the Indian Ocean Tsunami in 2004.* IRGSC working paper. NTT, Indonesia.

Lawal-Adebowale, O. A. (2015). Mobile phone revolution and its dimensional social and economic impacts in Nigeria's context. In P. E. Thomas, M. Srihari, & S. Kaur (Eds.), *Handbook of research on cultural and economic impacts of the information society* (pp. 359–390). IGI Global. doi:10.4018/978-1-4666-8598-7.ch016

Lawal-Adebowale, O. A., & Oyekunle, O. (2014). Agro-students' appraisal of online registration of academic courses in the Federal University of Agriculture Abeokuta, Ogun State Nigeria. *International Journal of Education and Development Using Information and Communication Technology, 10*(4), 139–154.

Lederer, A., Maupin, D., Sena, M., & Zhuang, Y. (2000). The technology acceptance model and the world wide web. *Decision Support Systems, 29*(3), 269–282. doi:10.1016/S0167-9236(00)00076-2

Leimbach, M., Kriegler, E., Roming, N., & Schwanitz, J. (2017). Future growth patterns of world regions – A GDP scenario approach. *Global Environmental Change, 42*, 215–225. doi:10.1016/j.gloenvcha.2015.02.005

Lewis, P. (2016). *Is knowledge doubling - or halving?* Retrieved April 2017, From: http://mobile.wnd.com/2016/05/is-knowledge-doubling-or-halving/

Li, H., He, J., Liu, Q., Fraumeni, B. M., & Zheng, X. (2016). *Regional Distribution and Dynamics of Human Capital in China 1985-2014: Education, Urbanization, and Aging of the Population* (NBER Working Paper No. 22906). Retrieved from https://www.nber.org/papers/w22906

Li, T. (2017). Data-driven Techniques in Disaster Information Management. *ACM Computing Survey, 50*(1). doi:10.1145/3017678

Libby, D. (1999). *RSS 0.91 Spies, revision 3: Netscape communication.* http://scripting.com/netscapeDocs/RSS%200_91%20Spec,%20revision%203.html

Li, D., Fu, Z., & Duan, Y. (2002). Fish-Expert: A web-based expert system for fish disease diagnosis. *Expert Systems with Applications, 23*(3), 311–320. doi:10.1016/S0957-4174(02)00050-7

Lili, L. (2010). Social Networking Websites: An Exploratory Study of Student Peer Socializing in an Online LIS Program. *Journal of Education for Library and Information Science.* Available at: https://works.bepress.com/lili_luo/1/

Lin, J., & Rosenblatt, D. (2012). Shifting patterns of economic growth and rethinking development. *Journal of Economic Policy Reform, 15*(3), 1–24. doi:10.1080/17487870.2012.700565

Linways. (2017). *ICT enabled education: The alchemy of mixing technology and education* [Blog post]. Retrieved November 16, 2019. From https://stories.linways.in/ict-enabled-education-d190bcc91bf0

Litchmore, K. A. (2016, July). *Comparative Study of Agile Methods, People Factors and Process Factors In Relation To Project Success.* Retrieved from http://152.12.30.4:2048/login?url=https://search.proquest.com/abicomplete/docview/1823291748/739BA3AA87BC4BBAPQ/2

Little. (2017). *Digital transformation in developing countries.* Retrieved from www.adl_digital-in_emerging_markets.

Litwin, M. S., & Fink, A. (1995). *How to measure survey reliability and validity.* Sage Publications. doi:10.4135/9781483348957

Liu, X. (2010). *Using and developing measurement instruments in science education: A Rasch modeling approach.* Information Age Publishing (IAP).

Liu, Z. (2015). Study on Accessing to and Sharing of Media Mobile Learning Resources In Higher Vocational Colleges. In *2015 7th International Conference on Information Technology in Medicine and Education (ITME)* (pp. 598-600). IEEE. 10.1109/ITME.2015.171

Liu, Y., Han, S., & Li, H. (2010). Understanding the factors driving m-learning adoption: A literature review. *Campus-Wide Information Systems, 27*(4), 210–226. doi:10.1108/10650741011073761

Lotz, M. (2018, November 21). *Waterfall vs. Agile: Which Methodology is Right for Your Project?* Retrieved from https://www.seguetech.com/waterfall-vs-agile-methodology/

Lucas, B. (2014). *Vocational pedagogy: what it is, why it matters and what we can do about it.* UNESCO-UNEVOC e-Forum. Retrieved June 2017, From: http://hdl.voced.edu.au/10707/321698

Lucas, H. C., & Spitler, V. K. (1999). Technology use and performance: A field study of broker workstation. *Decision Sciences, 30*(2), 291–311. doi:10.1111/j.1540-5915.1999.tb01611.x

Lu, D., Pan, X., Pourdamghani, N., Chang, S.-F., Ji, H., & Knight, K. (2016). A Multi-media Approach to Cross-lingual Entity Knowledge Transfer. *Proceedings of the 54th Annual Meeting of the Association for Computational Linguistics*, 54–65. 10.18653/v1/P16-1006

Luka, M. K., Frank, I. A., & Onwodi, G. (2012). Neural_Network_Based_Hausa_Language_Speech_Recognition. *International Journal of Advanced Research in Artificial Intelligence, 1*(2), 6.

Lule, I., Omwansa, T., & Waema, T. (2012). Application of technology acceptance model in m-banking adoption in Kenya. *International Journal of Computing and ICT Research, 6*(1), 31–43.

Lundell, P. (2014). *The Knowledge Doubling Curve.* Retrieved April 2017, From: https://www.peterlundell.com/the-knowledge-doubling-curve/

Lunenburg, F. (2011). *Self-efficacy in the workplace: Implications for motivation and performance.* Academic Press.

Luo, H., & Lei, J. (2012). Emerging technologies for interactive learning in ICT age. In J. Jia (Ed.), *Educational stages and interactive learning: from kindergarten To workplace training* (pp. 73–91). Information Science Reference. doi:10.4018/978-1-4666-0137-6.ch005

Maassen, M. A., & Dima, A. M. (2018). From Waterfall to Agile Software: Development models in the IT sector, 2006 to 2008. Impacts on company management. *Journal of International Studies.*

Mac Callum, K., & Jeffrey, L., (2013). The influence of students' ICT skills and their adoption of mobile learning. *Australasian Journal of Educational Technology, 29*(3), 303-314.

Mac Callum, K., Jeffrey, L., & Kinshuk. (2014). Comparing the role of ICT literacy and anxiety in the adoption of mobile learning. *Computers in Human Behavior, 39*, 8–19. doi:10.1016/j.chb.2014.05.024

Maitama, J. Z., Haruna, U., Gambo, A. Y., Thomas, A. B., Idris, N. B., Gital, A. Y., & Abubakar, A. (2014). Text Normalization Algorithm for Facebook Chats in Hausa Language. *The 5th International Conference on Information and Communication Technology for The Muslim World (ICT4M).* 10.1109/ICT4M.2014.7020605

Makridakis, S. (2018). Forecasting the Impact of Artificial Intelligence, Part 3 of 4: The Potential Effects of AI on Businesses, Manufacturing, and Commerce. Foresight. *The International Journal of Applied Forecasting, 49*, 18–27.

Malaiya, R. (2012). *Cloud Computing: A case study.* https://cloudcomputingseminar.wordpress.com/

Mango, O. (2015). iPad Use and Student Engagement in the Classroom. *The Turkish Online Journal of Educational Technology, 14*(1), 53–57.

Martin, C., Evans, J., & Karvonen, A. (2018). Smart and sustainable? Five tensions in the visions and practices of the smart-sustainable city in Europe and North America. *Technological Forecasting and Social Change, 133*, 269–278. doi:10.1016/j.techfore.2018.01.005

Martin, C., Evans, J., Karvonenm, A., Paskaleva, K., Yang, D., & Linjordet, D. (2019). Smart-sustainability: A new urban fix? *Sustainable Cities and Society, 45*, 640–648. doi:10.1016/j.scs.2018.11.028

Maru, A. (2003). *Potential Contributions from Use of New Information and Communication Technologies (ICT) for Livestock Production and Services in India.* https://www.indiaveterinarycommunity.com/profperspective/featuredarticle/feb-04/art-maru.htm

Marzilli, C., Delello, J., Marmion, S., McWhorter, R., Roberts, P., & Marzilli, T. S. (2014). Faculty attitudes towards integrating technology and innovation. *International Journal on Integrating Technology in Education, 3*(1), 1–20. doi:10.5121/ijite.2014.3101

Masadeh, M. (2012). Training, education, development and learning: What is the difference? *European Scientific Journal, 8*(10), 62–68.

Maslow, A. H. (1943). A theory of human motivation. *Psychological Review, 50*(40), 370–396. doi:10.1037/h0054346

Matthew, D., Joro, I. D., & Manasseh, H. (2015). The role of information communication technology in Nigeria educational system. *International Journal of Research in Humanities and Social Studies, 2*(2). http://www.ijrhss.org/pdf/v2-i2/8.pdf

McCarroll, T. (1991). What new ages? *Time, 138*, 44–46.

McClea, M., & Yen, D. C. (2005). A framework for the utilization of information technology in higher education admission department. *International Journal of Educational Management, 19*(2/3), 87–101. doi:10.1108/09513540510582390

McCloskey, D. (2004). Evaluating Electronic Commerce Acceptance with The Technology Acceptance Model. *Journal of Computer Information Systems, 44*(2), 49–57.

McLoughlin, C., & Lee, M. J. W. (2008). Mapping the digital terrain: New media and social software as catalysts for pedagogical change. *Hello! Where are you in the landscape of educational technology? Proceedings ascilite Melbourne 2008*, 641-652. http://www.ascilite.org.au/conferences/melbourne08/procs/mcloughlin.html

McNaughton, D., & Light, J. (2013). The iPad and Mobile Technology Revolution: Benefits and Challenges for Individuals who require Augmentative and Alternative Communication. *Augmentative and Alternative Communication, 29*(2), 107–116. doi:10.3109/07434618.2013.784930 PMID:23705813

Mehdi, H. S., & Al-Dera, A. S. (2013). The impact teachers' age, gender, and experience in the use of information and communication technology in EFL teaching. *English Language Teaching, 6*(6), 57–67. doi:10.5539/elt.v6n6p57

Mersino, A. (2018, April 1). *Agile Project Success Rates vs. Waterfall Projects.* Retrieved from Vitality Chicago: https://vitalitychicago.com/blog/agile-projects-are-more-successful-traditional-projects/

MHRD. (2018). *All India Survey of Higher Education 2017-18. Monistry of Human Resource Development.* Govt. of India.

Mingyong, Z. (2015). Investigation into the use of mobile technology in English teaching and learning in institutes of higher vocational education in Hubei province in China. In *Futuristic Trends on Computational Analysis and Knowledge Management (ABLAZE), 2015 International Conference on* (pp. 505-509). IEEE. 10.1109/ABLAZE.2015.7155037

Mir, F. A., & Pinnington, A. (2014). *Exploring the value of project management: Linking Project Management Performance and Project Sucess*. Academic Press.

Mitchell, S. (2008). Easy Wiki Hosting, Scott Hansel man's blog, and Snagging Screens. *MSDN Magazine*. Available at: https://en.wikipedia.org/wiki/Wiki

Mohanty, J. (2001). *Educational Technology*. Rajouri Garden.

Mondal, A., & Mete, J. (2012). ICT in higher education: Opportunities and challenges. *Institutions*, *21*(60), 4.

Moore, G. C., & Benbasat, I. (1991). Development of an instrument to measure the perceptions of adopting an information technology innovation. *Information Systems Research*, *2*(3), 192–222. doi:10.1287/isre.2.3.192

Morgan, C. T., & King, R. A. (1971). *Introduction to psychology* (4th ed.). McGraw-Hill.

Morley, G. (2011). Primary teachers and ICT: Is gender, age or experience important? *Systematics, Cybernetics, &. Informatics (MDPI)*, *9*(7), 5–9. doi:10.1504/ijiome.2010.034636

Morton, J., & Matthewman, R. (1996). *Improving livestock production through extension: information needs institutions and opportunities*. Academic Press.

Muhleisen, M. (2018, June). The long and short of the digital revolution. *Finance & Development*, *55*(2).

Mujumdar, S. (2011). ICT for distance learning symbiosis centre for distance learning, India. In C. Wing (Ed.), *ICT for higher education case studies from Asia and the Pacific*. United Nations Education, Scientific and Cultural Organisation/ Asia and Pacific Regional Bureau for Education.

Muller, R., & Jugdev, K. (2012). *Critical success factors in projects: Pinto, Slevin, and Prescott – the elucidation of project success*. Academic Press.

Mum, Y. Y., & Hwang, Y. (2003). Predicting the use of web-based information systems: Self-efficacy, enjoyment, learning goal orientation, and the technology acceptance model. *International Journal of Human-Computer Studies*, *59*(4), 431–449. doi:10.1016/S1071-5819(03)00114-9

Mutasa, M. (2013). Investigating the significance of disaster information management. *Jàmbá. Journal of Disaster Risk Studies*, *5*(2), e1–e6.

Naidu, S. (2019). The idea of open education. *Distance Education*, *40*(1), 1–4. doi:10.1080/01587919.2018.1564622

Naismith, L., Sharples, M., Vavoula, G., & Lonsdale, P. (2004). *Literature review in mobile technologies and learning*. Retrieved October 22, 2017, from: https://telearn.archives-ouvertes.fr/hal-00190143/document

Nambiar, A. N., & Dutta, A. K. (2010). Expert system for student advising using JESS. *Proceeding of the IEEE International Conference on Educational and Information Technology*, V1-312. 10.1109/ICEIT.2010.5607701

National Commission for Colleges of Education. (2016). *Colleges of education in Nigeria*. Retrieved from http://www.ncceonline.edu.ng

National Universities Commission. (2019). *Universities in Nigeria*. Retrieved from https://nuc.edu.ng/nigerian-univerisities/federal-univeristies/

Nazari, M. N., & Abu, A. H. (2010). Radio as an Educational Media Agricultural Development. *The Journal of the South East Asia Research Centre for Communication and Humanities*, 2, 13–20.

NCC Database. (2019). *Subscriber statistics*. Nigerian Communication Commission. Retrieved January 12, 2020, from https://www.ncc.gov.ng/statistics-reports/ subscriber-data#monthly-subscriber-technology-data

Ndayizigamiye, P. (2012). A Unified Approach Towards E-Commerce Adoption by SMMEs In South Africa. *International Journal of Information Technology and Business Management*, *16*(1), 92–101.

Nezakati, H., Jofreh, M., Liong, G., & Asgari, O. (2012). Assessing E-Commerce Adoption by Small and Medium Enterprises in Malaysia, Singapore and Thailand. *World Applied Sciences Journal*, *19*(10), 1406–1411.

Ng, R. Y. K., Lam, R. Y. S., Ng, K. K., & Lai, I. K. W. (2016, July). A Cross-Institutional Study of Vocational and Professional Education and Training (VPET) Students and Teachers' Needs of Innovative Pedagogical Practices. In *Educational Technology (ISET), 2016 International Symposium on* (pp. 101-105). IEEE.

Ng'ang'a, W. (2010). Towards a Comprehensive, Machine-readable Dialectal Dictionary of Igbo. *Proceedings of the Second Workshop on African Language Technology*.

Nickerson, R. S. (1981). Why interactive computer systems are sometimes not used by people who might benefit from them. *International Journal of Man-Machine Studies*, *15*(4), 469–481. doi:10.1016/S0020-7373(81)80054-5

Ninan, O. D., & Odejobi, O. (2012). Towards a Digital Resource for African Folktales. Istanbul, Turkey: Association for Computational Linguistics.

Ninan, O. D., & Odéjobí, O. A. (2013). Theoretical Issues in the Computational Modelling of Yorùbá Narratives. *Schloss Dagstuhl - Leibniz-Zentrum Fuer Informatik GmbH*. doi:10.4230/oasics.cmn.2013.153

Ninan, O. D., Ajíbádé, G. O., & Odéjobí, O. A. (2016). Appraisal of Computational Model for Yorùbá Folktale Narrative. *Schloss Dagstuhl - Leibniz-Zentrum Fuer Informatik GmbH*. doi:10.4230/oasics.cmn.2016.14

Ninan, O. D. (2017). Computational Analysis of Igbo Numerals in a Number-to-text Conversion System. *Journal of Computer and Education Research*, *5*(10), 241–254. doi:10.18009/jcer.325804

Nistor, N., & Murillo Montes de Oca, A. (2014). Nonsignificant intention–behaviour effects in educational technology acceptance: A case of competing cognitive scripts? *Computers in Human Behavior*, *34*, 333–338. doi:10.1016/j.chb.2014.01.026

NOAH. (2014). *DOST pilots MOSES project*. Retrieved from https://center.noah.up.edu.ph/dost-pilots-moses-project-in-marikina-business-mirror/

Noe, R. A., Clarke, A. D., & Klein, H. J. (2014). Learning in the twenty-first-century workplace. *Annual Review of Organizational Psychology and Organizational Behavior*, *1*(1), 245–275. doi:10.1146/annurev-orgpsych-031413-091321

Noll, M. G., & Meinel, C. (2007). *Web Search Personalization via Social Bookmarking and Tagging: Lecture Note in Computer Science*. Available at: https://link.springer.com/chapter/10.1007%2F978-3-540-76298-0_27

NSSO, Government of India. (2015). Key Indicators of Social Consumption in India: Education. National Sample Survey Office, Ministry of Statistics and Programme Implementation, Government of India.

Nwagwu, W. (2008). Online journals and visibility of science in Africa: A role for African social science citation index. In *Proceedings of the Conference on Electronic Publishing and Dissemination: "Putting African Journals On Line: Opportunities, Implications and Limits"* (pp. 2–14). Dakar, Senegal: Academic Press.

O'Reilly, T. (2005). *What is Web 2.0 Design Patterns and Business Models for the Next Generation of Software*. Available at: http://www.oreilly.com/pub/a/web2/archive/what-is-web-20.html?page=1 Retrieved on 15/02/2019

Ọdẹ'jọbí, Ọ. A., Wong, S. H. S., & Beaumont, A. J. (2007). A fuzzy decision tree-based duration model for Standard Yorùbá text-to-speech synthesis. Computer Speech & Language, 21(2), 325–349. doi:10.1016/j.csl.2006.06.005

Ọdẹ'jọbí, Ọ. A., Wong, S. H. S., & Beaumont, A. J. (2008). A modular holistic approach to prosody modelling for Standard Yorùbá speech synthesis. Computer Speech & Language, 22(1), 39–68. doi:10.1016/j.csl.2007.05.002

Odedra, M., Lawrie, M., Bennett, M., & Goodman, S. (n.d.). *Information Technology in Sub-Saharan Africa*. Retrieved August 2019, from University of Pennsylvania- African Studies Center: http://www.africa.upenn.edu/Comp_Articles/Information_Technology_117.html

Odejobi, O. A. (2008). Recognition of Tones in YorÙbÁ Speech: Experiments With Artificial Neural Networks. In B. Prasad & S. R. M. Prasanna (Eds.), *Speech, Audio, Image and Biomedical Signal Processing using Neural Networks*. Springer. doi:10.1007/978-3-540-75398-8_2

Odéjobí, O. A., Beaumont, A. J., & Wong, S. H. S. (2004). A Computational Model of Intonation for Yorùbá Text-to-Speech Synthesis: Design and Analysis. In P. Sojka, I. Kopeček, & K. Pala (Eds.), *Text* (Vol. 3206, pp. 409–416). Speech and Dialogue. doi:10.1007/978-3-540-30120-2_52

Ọdéjọbí, Ọ. A., Beaumont, A. J., & Wong, S. H. S. (2006). Intonation contour realisation for Standard Yorùbá text-to-speech synthesis: A fuzzy computational approach. *Computer Speech & Language*, *20*(4), 563–588. doi:10.1016/j.csl.2005.08.006

OECD. (2001). *Understanding the Digital Divide. OECD Digital Economy Papers, No. 49*. OECD Publishing. doi:10.1787/236405667766

OECD. (2015). *Students, Computers and Learning: Making the Connection. PISA*. OECD Publishing. doi:10.1787/9789264239555-

OECD. (2016). *Harnessing the digital economy for developing countries*. Working Paper No. 334.

Office of the Auditor General. (2016). *Information and communication technology (ICT) in education*. Report 19. Author. Retrieved May 7, 2020, from https://www.wa.gov.au/reports-and-publications/reports/information-and-communication-technology-ict-in-education/key-findings/internet-speed-bandwidth-agin-devices-impact-use-ict-schools/

Ogwu, E. J., Talib, M., & Odejobi, O. A. (2006). Text-to-speech processing using African language as case study. *Journal of Discrete Mathematical Sciences and Cryptography*, *9*(2), 365–382. doi:10.1080/09720529.2006.10698085

Okebukola, P. (1997). Old, new, and current technology in education. *UNESCO Africa*, *14*(15), 7–18.

Okolla, W. A. (2002). The Kenya Agricultural Commodity Exchange. ICT Update: A current awareness bulletin for ACP agriculture, 9.

Oladayo, O. (2015). Yoruba Language and Numerals' Offline Interpreter Using Morphological and Template Matching. *TELKOMNIKA Indonesian Journal of Electrical Engineering*, *13*(1). Advance online publication. doi:10.11591/telkomnika.v13i1.6782

Oladayo, O. O. (2014). Yoruba Language and Numerals' Offline Interpreter Using Morphological and Template Matching. *IAES International Journal of Artificial Intelligence*, *3*(2), 64–72. doi:10.11591/ijai.v3.i2.pp64-72

Oladiipo Asahiah, F., Ajadi Odejobi, O., & Rotimi Adagunodo, E. (2017). Restoring tone-marks in standard Yorùbá electronic text: Improved model. *Computer Science*, *18*(3), 305. doi:10.7494/csci.2017.18.3.2128

Oladiipo, A. F., Odejobi, O. A., Adagunodo, E. R., & Olubode-Sawe, F. O. (2017). Tone Mark Restoration in Standard Yoruba Texts: A Proposal. *INFOCOMP Journal of Computer Science*, *16*, 8–19.

Olakulehin, F. K. (2007). Information and communication technologies in teacher training and professional development in Nigeria. *Turkish Journal of Distance Education*, *8*(1), 133–142.

Olufunminiyi, E., & Adebayo, S. (2013). Intelligent System for Learning and Understanding of Yoruba Language. *International Journal of Computer and Information Technology*, *2*(5), 5.

Onwuagboke, B. B. C., & Singh, T. K. R. (2016). Faculty attitude and use of ICT in instructional delivery in tertiary institutions in a developing nation. *International Journal of Research Studies in Educational Technology*, *5*(1), 77–88. doi:10.5861/ijrset.2016.1428

Onwuagboke, B. B. C., Singh, T. K. R., & Fook, F. S. (2015). Need for ICT integration for effective instructional delivery in Nigerian colleges of education. *Journal of Education and Practice*, *6*(3), 51–56. https://files.eric.ed.gov/fulltext/EJ1083763.pdf

Onyenwe, I. E., & Hepple, M. (2016). Predicting Morphologically-Complex Unknown Words in Igbo. In P. Sojka, A. Horák, I. Kopeček, & K. Pala (Eds.), *Text* (Vol. 9924, pp. 206–214). doi:10.1007/978-3-319-45510-5_24

Onyenwe, I. E., Hepple, M., Chinedu, U., & Ezeani, I. (2018). A Basic Language Resource Kit Implementation for the Igbo *NLP* Project. *ACM Transactions on Asian and Low-Resource Language Information Processing*, *17*(2), 1–23. doi:10.1145/3146387

Onyenwe, I. E., Hepple, M., Chinedu, U., & Ezeani, I. (2019). Toward an Effective Igbo Part-of-Speech Tagger. *ACM Transactions on Asian and Low-Resource Language Information Processing*, *18*(4), 1–26. doi:10.1145/3314942

Onyenwe, I., Hepple, M., & Uchechukwu, C. (2016). Improving Accuracy of Igbo Corpus Annotation Using Morphological Reconstruction andTransformation-Based Learning. *Actes de La Conférence Conjointe JEP-TALN-RECITAL*, *2016*(11), 1–10.

Onyenwe, I., Hepple, M., Uchechukwu, C., & Ezeani, I. (2015). Use of Transformation-Based Learning in Annotation Pipeline of Igbo, an African Language. *Proceedings of the Recent Advances in Natural Language Processing*.

Onyia, C. R., & Onyia, M. (2011). Faculty perception for technology integration in Nigeria university system: Implication for faculty quality curriculum design. *International Journal of Business and Social Science*, *2*(12), 81–92. http://www.ijbssnet.com/journals/Vol._2_No._12%3B_July_2011/10.pdf

Orife, I. (2018). *Attentive Sequence-to-Sequence Learning for Diacritic Restoration of Yor\`ub\'a Language Text*. Retrieved from https://arxiv.org/abs/1804.00832

Orimaye, S. O., Alhashmi, S. M., & Eu-gene, S. (2012). Sentiment analysis amidst ambiguities in youtube comments on yoruba language (nollywood) movies. *Proceedings of the 21st International Conference Companion on World Wide Web - WWW '12 Companion*, 583. 10.1145/2187980.2188138

Orrel, D. (2018). *Quantum Economics: The New Science of Money*. Icon Books Ltd.

Osborn, D. (2010). *African Languages in a digital age; Challenges and opportunity for indigenous language computing*. Human Sciences Research Council, Cape Town.

Our World in Data. (2020). Daily confirmed COVID-19 cases, rolling 3-day average. *OurWorldinData*. Retrieved July 6, 2020, from https://ourworldindata.org/grapher/daily-covid-cases-3-day-average

Owolabi, T. O., Oyewole, B. K., & Oke, J. O. (2013). Teacher education, information and communication technology: Prospects and challenges of e-teaching profession in Nigeria. *American Journal of Humanities & Social Sciences*, *1*(2), 87–91. doi:10.11634/232907811301314

Oyinloye, O. A., & Odejobi, O. A. (2015). Issues in Computational System for Morphological Analysis of Standard Yorùbá (SY) Verbs. *Proceedings of the World Congress on Engineering 2015.*

Ozdamli, F., & Cavus, N. (2011). Basic Elements and Characteristics of Mobile Learning. *Procedia: Social and Behavioral Sciences*, *28*, 937–942. doi:10.1016/j.sbspro.2011.11.173

Ozowa, V. (1995). Information Needs of Small Scale Farmers in Africa: The Nigerian Example. *Quarterly Bulletin of the International Association of Agricultural Information Specialists, 40*(1).

Ozturk, I. (2001). The role of education in economic development: A theoretical perspective. *Journal of Rural Development and Administration*, *33*(1), 39–47. doi:10.2139srn.1137541

Palen, L. (2008). Research in Brief: Online social media in crisis event. *EDUCAUSE Quarterly*, (3), 2008.

Parasuraman, A. (2000). Technology Readiness Index (TRI): A multiple item scale to measure readiness for embrace of new technologies. *Journal of Service Research*, *2*(4), 307–320. doi:10.1177/109467050024001

Parasuraman, A., & Colby, C. (2001). *Techno ready marketing: how and why your customers adopt technology.* The Free Press.

Parker, C. M. & Castleman, T. (2009). Small firm e-business adoption: a critical analysis of theory. *Journal of Enterprise Information Management*, *22*(1, 2), 167-182.

Pavithran. (2016). *Empirical investigation of mobile banking adoption in developing countries. International J or Enterprise Information Systems, 10(1).*

Peters, K. (2007). m-Learning: Positioning educators for a mobile, connected future. *The International Review of Research in Open and Distributed Learning*, *8*(2). Advance online publication. doi:10.19173/irrodl.v8i2.350

Pett, M. A., Lackey, N. R., & Sullivan, J. J. (2003). Making sense of factor analysis: The use of factor analysis for instrument development in health care research. *Sage (Atlanta, Ga.).*

Pew Research Center. (2018). *Social media use continues to rise in developing countries but plateaus across developing once.* Retrieved from http://assets.pewresearch.org/wp-content/uploads/sites/2/2018/06/15135408/Pew-Research-Center_Global-Tech-Social-Media-Use_2018.06.19.pdf

Pihkala, T., Harmaakorpi, V., & Pekkarinen, A. (2007). The role of Dynamic Capabilities and Social Capital in Breaking Socio – Institutional Inertia in Regional Development. *International Journal of Urban and Regional Research*, *31*(4), 836–852. doi:10.1111/j.1468-2427.2007.00757.x

Pimmer, C., & Pachler, N. (2013). Mobile learning in the workplace. Unlocking the value of mobile technology for work-based education. In M. Ally & A. Tsinakos (Eds.), *Mobile Learning Development for Flexible Learning*. Athabasca University Press.

Pimmer, C., Pachler, N., & Attwell, G. (2010). Towards work-based mobile learning: What we can learn from the fields of work-based learning and mobile learning. *International Journal of Mobile and Blended Learning*, *2*(4), 1–18. doi:10.4018/jmbl.2010100101

Pimmer, C., & Tulenko, K. (2016). The convergence of mobile and social media: Affordances and constraints of mobile networked communication for health workers in low-and middle-income countries. *Mobile Media & Communication, 4*(2), 252–269. doi:10.1177/2050157915622657

Pittman, T., & Gaines, T. (2015). Technology integration in third, fourth and fifth grade classrooms in a Florida school district. *Educational Technology Research and Development, 63*(4), 539–554. doi:10.100711423-015-9391-8

Pokrajac, D., & Rasamny, M. (2006). Interactive virtual expert system for advising (InVEStA). *Proceedings of the IEEE 36th Frontiers in Education Annual Conference*, 18-23. 10.1109/FIE.2006.322295

Poppendieck, M., & Poppendieck, T. (2013). *The Lean Mindset.* Addison Wesley.

Porter, C., & Donthu, N. (2006). Using the technology acceptance model to explain how attitudes determine internet usage: The role of perceived access barriers and demographics. *Journal of Business Research, 59*(9), 999–1007. doi:10.1016/j.jbusres.2006.06.003

Pourdamghani, N., Ghazvininejad, M., & Knight, K. (2018). Using Word Vectors to Improve Word Alignments for Low Resource Machine Translation. *Proceedings of the 2018 Conference of the North American Chapter of the Association for Computational Linguistics: Human Language Technologies*, 524–528. 10.18653/v1/N18-2083

Powell, L. J., & McGrath, S. (2019). *Skills for human development: Transforming vocational education and training.* Routledge. doi:10.4324/9781315657592

Powell-Morse, A. (2016, December 8). *Waterfall Model: What is it and When you should use it?* Retrieved from https://airbrake.io/blog/sdlc/waterfall-model

PRNewswire. (2002, August 13). *Agile Software Launches Industry-First Guaranteed business Results Program.* Retrieved from Proquest: http://152.12.30.4:2048/login?url=https://search.proquest.com/docview/447496132?accountid=15070

Quiang, L., & Ying, C. (2014). Study on Disaster Information Management Systems compatible with VGI and Crowdsourcing. *IEEE Workshop on Advanced Research and Technology in Industry Applications.*

Rahmati, A., & Zhong, L. (2013). Studying smartphone usage: Lessons from a four-month field study. *IEEE Transactions on Mobile Computing, 12*(7), 1417–1427. doi:10.1109/TMC.2012.127

Rao, M. S. (2014). Enhancing employability in engineering and management students through soft skills. *Industrial and Commercial Training, 46*(1), 42–48. doi:10.1108/ICT-04-2013-0023

Rasul, S., Bukhsh, Q., & Batool, S. (2011). A study to analyze the effectiveness of audio visual aids in teaching learning process at university level. *Procedia: Social and Behavioral Sciences, 28*, 78–81. doi:10.1016/j.sbspro.2011.11.016

Razak, T. R., Hashim, M. A., Noor, N. M., Halim, I. H. A., & Shamsul, N. F. F. (2014). Career path recommendation system for UiTM Perlis students using fuzzy logic. *Proceeding of the 5th IEEE International Conference on Intelligent and Advanced Systems (ICIAS)*, 1-5. 10.1109/ICIAS.2014.6869553

Redmond, B. F. (2010). *7 Self-efficacy and Social Cognitive Theories.* Retrieved from http://wikispace.psu.edu/display/PSYCH484/7.Self-EfficacyandSocialCognitiveTheories/

Rehbein, B. (2015). Globalization, Capitalism and Social Inequality. In A. Lenger & F. Schumacher (Eds.), *Understanding the Dynamics of Global Inequality* (pp. 149–157). Springer Berlin Heidelberg. https://link.springer.com/10.1007/978-3-662-44766-6_7

Reiss, S. (1998). Who am I? *The 16 basic desires that motivate our actons and define our personality.* Retrieved February 2, 2017, from http://www.personalityplusinbusiness.com/mbti-and-other-assessments/other-assessments/reiss-profile

Reitz, J. M. (2007). *Online Dictionary for Library and Information Science (ODLIS)*. Information. lu.com/odlis/

Reychav, I., & Wu, D. (2014). Exploring mobile tablet training for road safety: A uses and gratifications perspective. *Computers & Education*, *71*, 43–55. doi:10.1016/j.compedu.2013.09.005

Richardson, W. (2009). Blogs, Wikis, Podcasts, and Other Powerful Web Tools for Classrooms. Corwin Press.

Ricky, Y. K. N., & Rechell, Y. S. L. (2015, December). Using mobile and flexible technologies to enable, engage and enhance learning in Vocational Education and Training (VET). In *Teaching, Assessment, and Learning for Engineering (TALE), 2015 IEEE International Conference on* (pp. 96-101). IEEE.

Ritzhaupt, A. D., Liu, F., Dawson, K., & Barron, A. E. (2013). Differences in Student Information and Communication Technology Literacy Based on Socio-Economic Status, Ethnicity, and Gender: Evidence of a Digital Divide in Florida Schools. *JRTE*, *45*(4), 291–307. doi:10.1080/15391523.2013.10782607

Rodrigues, É., Carreira, M., & Gonçalves, D. (2016). Enhancing typing performance of older adults on tablets. *Universal Access in the Information Society*, *15*(3), 393–418. doi:10.100710209-014-0394-8

Rodzalan, S., & Saat, M. (2012). The Effects of Industrial Training on Students' Generic Skills Development. *Procedia: Social and Behavioral Sciences*, *56*, 357–368. doi:10.1016/j.sbspro.2012.09.664

Roger, E. M., & Shoemaker, F. F. (1971). *Communication of Innovation: A cross cultural approach*. Free Press.

Rogers, E. M. (2003). *Diffusion of innovations* (5th ed.). Free Press.

Roser, M., Ritchie, H., Ortiz-Ospina, E., & Hasell, J. (2020). *Coronavirus Pandemic (COVID-19)*. Retrieved May 20, from https://ourworldindata.org/coronavirus

Rus, R. C., Yasin, R. M., Yunus, F. A. N., Rahim, M. B., & Ismail, I. M. (2015). Skilling for job: A grounded theory of vocational training at industrial training institutes of malaysia. *Procedia: Social and Behavioral Sciences*, *204*, 198–205. doi:10.1016/j.sbspro.2015.08.139

Sachs, J. (2005). *The End of poverty: Economic possibilities for our time*. Penguin Press.

Sachs, J. D. (2000). Globalization and patterns of economic development. *Weltwirtschaftliches Archiv*, *136*(4), 579–600. doi:10.1007/BF02707644

Safiriyu, I. E., Akindeji, O. A:, & Isau, O. A. (2015). Computational modelling of personal pronouns for English to Yorùbá machine translation system. *2015 SAI Intelligent Systems Conference (IntelliSys)*, 733–741. 10.1109/IntelliSys.2015.7361222

Sahin, Y. G., Balta, S., & Ercan, T. (2010). The use of internet resources by university students during their course projects elicitation: A case study. *The Turkish Online Journal of Educational Technology*, *9*(2), 234–244.

Saldana, J. (2016). *The coding manual for qualitative researchers*. Sage.

Saleh, S. (2015). IM Session Identification by Outlier Detection in Cross-correlation Functions. *Conference on Information Sciences and Systems (CISS)*. https://www.researchgate.net/publication/274635819_IM_Session_Identification_by_Outlier_Detection_in_Cross-correlation_Functions

Salifou, L., & Naroua, H. (2014). *Design of A Spell Corrector For Hausa Language*. Academic Press.

Salkind, N. J. (Ed.). (2010). *Encyclopedia of research design* (Vol. 1). Sage. doi:10.4135/9781412961288

Sampson, D. (2006). Exploiting mobile and wireless technologies in vocational training. In *Wireless, Mobile and Ubiquitous Technology in Education, 2006. WMUTE'06. Fourth IEEE International Workshop on* (pp. 63-65). IEEE. 10.1109/WMTE.2006.261347

Sarfaraz, J. (n.d.). Unified theory of acceptance and use of technology (UTAUT) model-mobile banking. *Journal of Internet Banking and Commerce.* Retrieved from icommercecentral.com/open-access/unified-thoery-of-acceptance-and-use-of-technology-utaut=modelmobile-banking.php?aid-865

Sarkar, S. (2012). The role of information and communication technology (ICT) in higher education for the 21st century. *Science, 1*(1), 30–41.

Sarker, S., Ahuja, M., Sarker, S., & Kirkeby, S. (2011). The Role of Communication and Trust in Global Virtual Teams: A Social Network Perspective. *Journal of Management Information Systems, 28*(1), 273–309. doi:10.2753/MIS0742-1222280109

Saunders, P. (2004). *Towards a credible poverty framework: From income poverty to deprivation.* Social Policy Research Centre, University of New South Wales, Sydney, Australia. Retrieved July 7, 2015, from http://www.sprc.unsw.edu.au/dp/DP131.pdf

Saxena, A. (2017). Issues and impediments faced by Canadian teachers while integrating ICT in pedagogical practice. *The Turkish Journal of Educational Technology, 16*(2), 58–70. https://files.eric.ed.gov/fulltext/EJ1137791.pdf

Saylor Academy. (2012). *Chapter 7: Subsaharan Africa.* Retrieved from https://saylordotorg.github.io/text_world-regional-geography-people-places-and-globalization/s10-subsaharan-africa.html

Scannell, K. P. (2011). Statistical unicodification of African languages. *Language Resources and Evaluation, 45*(3), 375–386. doi:10.100710579-011-9150-3

Schilderman, T. (2002). *Strengthening the knowledge and information systems of the urban poor.* Department for International Development (DFID). https://practicalaction.org/docs/ia3/kis-urban-poor-report-2002.pdf

Schlippe, T., Djomgang, E. G. K., Vu, N. T., Ochs, S., & Schultz, T. (2012). Hausa large vocabulary continuos speech recognition. *The 3rd Workshop on Spoken Language Technologies for Under-Resourced Languages (SLTU 2012)*, 11–14. Retrieved from http://www.research-karlsruhe.de/pubs/SLTU2012-Schlippe_Hausa.pdf

Schlippe, T., Ochs, S., Vu, N. T., & Schultz, T. (2012). Automatic Error Recovery for Pronunciation Dictionaries. *13th Annual Conference of the International Speech Communication Association*, 4. Retrieved from https://www.csl.uni-bremen.de/cms/images/documents/publications/Interspeech2012-Schlippe_DictFilter.pdf

Schofield, D., Hollands, R., & Denby, B. (2001). Mine safety in the Twenty-First century: The application of computer graphics and virtual reality. In M. Karmis (Ed.), *Mine Health and Safety Management* (pp. 153–174). Society for Mining, Metallurgy, and Exploration.

Schwaber, K., & Sutherland, J. (2017). *The Definitive Guide to Scrum: The Rules of Game.* Retrieved from https://www.scrumguides.org/docs/scrumguide/v2017/2017-Scrum-Guide-US.pdf

Science and Technology. (2018). How Rwanda is Becoming an African Tech Powerhouse. *Science and Technology.* Retrieved from https://wgi.world/rwandaafrican-tech-powerhouse

Scott, K. S., Sorokti, K. H., & Merrell, J. D. (2016). Learning "beyond the classroom" within an enterprise social network system. *Internet and Higher Education, 29*, 75–90. doi:10.1016/j.iheduc.2015.12.005

Selamat, A., & Akosu, N. (2016). Word-length algorithm for language identification of under-resourced languages. *Journal of King Saud University - Computer and Information Sciences, 28*(4), 457–469. doi:10.1016/j.jksuci.2014.12.004

Seng, K., & Zeki, A. M. (2014). Career Guidance and Employment Management System. *Proceedings of the 3rd IEEE International Conference on Advanced Computer Science Applications and Technologies*, 73-78.

Shah, D. N. (2009). *A complete guide to Internet and web programing.* Dream Take Press. www.scribd.com/document/47763275/A-Complete-Guide-to-Internet-and-Web-Programming

Sharma, R. & Mishra, R. (2014). *A review of theories and models of technology adoption.* Academic Press.

Siddiq, F., & Schererb, R. (2019). Is there a gender gap? A meta-analysis of the gender differences in students' ICT literacy. *Educational Research Review, 27,* 205–217. doi:10.1016/j.edurev.2019.03.007

Simona, C. E. (2015). Developing Presentation Skills in the English Language Courses for the Engineering Students of the 21st Century Knowledge Society: A Methodological Approach. *Procedia: Social and Behavioral Sciences, 203,* 69–74. doi:10.1016/j.sbspro.2015.08.261

Singh, Y. K. (2005). *Instructional technology in education.* Darya Ganj.

Skills Australia, M. (2011). *Skills for prosperity: a roadmap for vocational education and training.* Canberra: Commonwealth of Australia.

Slinger, M. (2011). *Agile Project Management with Scrum.* Paper presented at PMI® Global Congress 2011—North America, Dallas, TX.

Sobey, C. (2012). *A Model of Quantum Economic Development* (MPRA Paper No. 36422). Retrieved from: https://mpra.ub.uni-muenchen.de/36422/

Soejoto, A., Fitrayati, D., Rachmawati, L., & Sholikhah, N. (2016). Typology of regional economic development pattern. *International Journal of Applied Business and Economic Research, 14*(13).

Sonnenburg, S., Braun, M. L., Ong, C. S., Bengio, S., Bottou, L., Holmes, G., & LeCun, Y. (2007). The Need for Open Source Software in Machine Learning. *Journal of Machine Learning Research, 8,* 2443–2466.

Sosimi, A., Adegbola, T., & Fakinlede, O. (2015). A Supervised Phrase Selection Strategy for Phonetically Balanced Standard Yorùbá Corpus. In A. Gelbukh (Ed.), *Computational Linguistics and Intelligent Text Processing* (Vol. 9042, pp. 565–582)., doi:10.1007/978-3-319-18117-2_42

Souter, D., Scott, N., Garforth, C., Jain, R., & Mascarenhas, O. (2005). *The Economic Impact of Telecommunications on Rural Livelihoods and Poverty Reduction: A Study of rural Communities in India (Gujarat), Mozambique and Tanzania.* https://ideas.repec.org/p/iim/iimawp/2005-11-04.html

Spiezia, V. (2012). ICT investments and productivity: Measuring the contribution of ICTS to growth. *OECD Journal: Economic Studies., 2012*(1). Advance online publication. doi:10.1787/eco_studies-2012-5k8xdhj4tv0t

Srivathsan, G., Garg, P., Bharambe, A., Varshney, H., & Bhaskaran, R. (2011). A dialogue system for career counseling. *Proceedings of the ACM International Conference & Workshop on Emerging Trends in Technology,* 630-634. 10.1145/1980022.1980159

Ssewanyana, J. (2007). ICT access and poverty in Uganda. *International Journal of Computing and ICT Research, 1*(2), 10–19.

Stankovic, D., Nikolic, V., Djordjevic, M., & Cao, D.-B. (2013, June 6). A survey study of critical success factors in agile software projects in former Yugoslavia IT companies. *Journal of Systems and Software, 86*(6), 1663–1678. doi:10.1016/j.jss.2013.02.027

Starbird, K., Huang, Y., Orand, M., & Stanek, S. (2015). *Connected through crisis: Emotional proximity and the spread of misinformation online*. ACM.

Stasz, C. (2001). Assessing skills for work: Two perspectives. *Oxford Economic Papers, 53*(3), 385–405. doi:10.1093/oep/53.3.385

Stern, J. (2008). *Introduction to Web 2.0 Technologies*. Available at http://www.wlac.edu/online/documents/Web_2.0%20 v.02.pdf

Stern, J. (2015). *Introduction to web 2.0*. Available at: http://www.ictliteracy.info/rf.pdf/Web2.0_Introduction.pdf

Strayhorn, T. L. (2007). Use of technology among higher education faculty members: Implications for innovative practice. *Student Affairs On-Line, 8*(2). Retrieved from https://www.studentaffairs.com/Customer-Content/www/CMS/files/Journal/Technology-Use-By-Faculty.pdf

Strickland, J. (2007). *How Web 2.0 Works*. Available at: www.computer.howstuffworks.com

Ström, P., & Wahlqvist, E. (2010). Regional and Firm Competitiveness in the Service-Based Economy: Combining Economic Geography and International Business Theory. *Tijdschrift voor Economische en Sociale Geografie, 101*(3), 287–304. doi:10.1111/j.1467-9663.2009.00586.x

Strong, K., & Hutchins, H. (2009). Connectivism: A theory for learning in a world of growing complexity. *Impact: Journal of Applied Research in Workplace E-learning, 1*(1), 53–67.

Subedi, D. (2016). Explanatory sequential mixed method design as the third research community of knowledge claim. *American Journal of Educational Research, 4*(7), 570–577.

Šumak, B., & Šorgo, A. (2016). The acceptance and use of interactive whiteboards among teachers: differences in UTAUT determinants between pre- and post-adopters. *Computer Human Behaviour, 64*, 602–620. doi:.07.037 doi:10.1016/j.chb.2016

Sumak, B., Pusnik, M., Herieko, M., & Sorgo, A. (2017). Differences between prospective, existing, and former users of interactive whiteboards on external factors affecting their adoption, usage and abandonment. *Computers in Human Behavior, 72*, 733–756. doi:10.1016/j.chb.2016.09.006

Sung, Y., Chang, K., & Yang, J. (2015). (2015). How Effective are Mobile Devices for Language Learning? A Meta-Analysis. *Educational Research Review, 16*, 68–84. Advance online publication. doi:10.1016/j.edurev.2015.09.001

Svirina, A., Parfenova, E., & Shurkina, E. (2014). Evaluation of Uncertainty on the Stages of Business Cycle: Implementation of Quantum Principles. *Journal of Systemics, Cybernetics and Informatics, 12*(4), 79–85.

Sweeney, M. (2014, December 2). *Agile vs Waterfall: Which Method is More Successful?* Retrieved from https://clearcode.cc/blog/agile-vs-waterfall-method

Tabachnick, B. G., Fidell, L. S., & Ullman, J. B. (2007). *Using multivariate statistics* (Vol. 5). Pearson.

Tate, D. F., Jackvony, E. H., & Wing, R. R. (2003). Effects of Internet behavioral counseling on weight loss in adults at risk for type 2 diabetes: A randomized trial. *Journal of the American Medical Association, 289*(14), 1833–1836. doi:10.1001/jama.289.14.1833 PMID:12684363

Tenopir, C. (2003). *Use and users of electronic library resources: an overview and analysis of recent research studies*. Washington, DC: Council on Library and Information Resources. Retrieved July 18, 20219, http://webdoc.sub.gwdg.de/ ebook/aw/2004/pub120.pdf

Teo, T. S. H., & Pok, S. H. (2003). Adoption of WAP-enabled mobile phones among internet users. *Omega, 31*(6), 483–498. doi:10.1016/j.omega.2003.08.005

Terry, N., Lewer, J. J., & Macy, A. (2003). *The Efficacy of Alternative Instruction Modes in Economics.* https://www.researchgate.net/publication/228289032_The_Efficacy_of_Alternative_Instruction_Modes_in_Economics

TETFund. (2016). *ICT support intervention.* Retrieved from https://www.tetfund.gov.ng/index.php/component/search/#?Itemid=265

Thaiposri, P., & Wannapiroon, P. (2015). Enhancing students' critical thinking skills through teaching and learning by inquiry-based learning activities using social network and cloud computing. *Procedia: Social and Behavioral Sciences, 174*, 2137–2144. doi:10.1016/j.sbspro.2015.02.013

The Gale Group Inc. (2002). Academic Disciplines. In *Encyclopaedia of Education.* Author.

The Standish Group International, Inc. (2015). *CHAOS Report 2015.* The Standish Group International, Inc.

The Standish Group International. (2013). *Chaos Manifesto 2013: Think Big, Act Small.* Retrieved from https://www.immagic.com/eLibrary/ARCHIVES/GENERAL/GENREF/S130301C.pdf

Thelwall, M. (2000). Computer-based assessment: A versatile educational tool. *Computer Education, 34*(1), 37–39. doi:10.1016/S0360-1315(99)00037-8

Thomas, S. (2016). *Future ready learning: Reimagining the role of technology in education. 2016 National Education Technology Plan.* Office of Educational Technology, US Department of Education. Retrieved from https://tech.ed.gov/files/2017/01/NETP17.pdf

Thomas, T. D., Singh, L., & Gaffar, K. (2013). The utility of the UTAUT model in explaining mobile learning adoption in higher education in Guyana. *International Journal of Education and Development Using Information and Communication Technology, 9*(3), 71–85.

Thompson, R. L., Higgins, C. A., & Howell, J. M. (1991). Personal computing: Toward a conceptual model of utilization. *Management Information Systems Quarterly, 15*(1), 125–143. doi:10.2307/249443

Thomson, A. J., & Willoughby, I. (2004). A web-based expert system for advising on herbicide use in Great Britain. *Computers and Electronics in Agriculture, 42*(1), 43–49. doi:10.1016/S0168-1699(03)00085-1

Trudeau, M. B., Catalano, P. J., Jindrich, D. L., & Dennerlein, J. T. (2013). Tablet Keyboard Configuration Affects Performance, Discomfort and Task Difficulty for Thumb Typing in a Two-Handed Grip. *PLoS One, 8*(6), e67525. doi:10.1371/journal.pone.0067525 PMID:23840730

Tucker, R., & Shalonova, K. (2005). *Supporting the Creation of TTS for Local Language Voice Information Systems. INTERSPEECH-2005*, 453–456.

Turk, D., France, R., & Rumpe, B. (2014, September). *Limitations of Agile Software Processes.* Retrieved from Research Gate: https://www.researchgate.net/profile/Robert_France/publication/266024162_Limitations_of_Agile_Software_Processes/links/00463526ed3341d25b000000/Limitations-of-Agile-Software-Processes.pdf?origin=publication_detail

Turk, D., France, R., & Rumpe, B. (2002, May). Assumptions Underlying Agile Software Development. *Journal of Database Management, 16*(4), 62–87. doi:10.4018/jdm.2005100104

Udu, L. E., & Nkwede, J. O. (2014). Tertiary education trust fund interventions and sustainable development in Nigerian Universities: Evidence from Ebonyi State University, Abakaliki. *Journal of Sustainable Development, 7*(4), 191. doi:10.5539/jsd.v7n4p191

UN-APCICT. (2011). ICT for Disaster Risk Management. Academy of ICT Essentials for Government Leaders. Asian Disaster Preparedness Center.

UNESCO. (2009). *ICTs for higher education.* Paper presented at the 2009 World Conference on Higher Education (WCHE), Paris, France.

UNESCO. (2015). *Digital services for education in Africa.* Retrieved from https://unesdoc.unesco.org/in/documentViewer. xhtml?v=2.1.196&id=p:usmarcdef_0000231867&file=/in/rest/annotationSVC/DownloadWatermarkedAttachment/attach_import_2b9960eb-b645-43cc-8b97-bfb7441a3dc0%3F_%3D231867eng.pdf&updateUrl=updateUrl3227&ark=/ark:/48223/pf0000231867/PDF/231867eng.pdf.multi&fullScreen=true&locale=en#%5B%7B%22num%22%3A83%2C%22gen%22%3A0%7D%2C%7B%22name%22%3A%22XYZ%22%7D%2Cnull%2Cnull%2C0%5D

United Nations. (2015). About the Sustainable Development Goals. *United Nations.* Retrieved March 5, 2020, from https://www.un.org/sustainabledevelopment/sustainable-development-goals/

University Grants Commission. (2017). *National Convention on Digital Initiatives for Higher Education.* https://www.ugc.ac.in/pdfnews/9208605_Brochure-(National-Convention-on-Digital-Initiatives-for-Higher-Education).pdf

URT. (2005). *Livestock sector brief.* Prepared by Food and Agricultural Organization (FAO) and Livestock Information, Sector Analysis and Policy Branch (AGAL).

URT. (2007). *Livestock.* http://www.tanzania.go.tz/livestock.html

Vafeiadis, T., Diamantaras, K. I., Sarigiannidis, G., & Chatzisavvas, K. Ch. (2015). A comparison of machine learning techniques for customer churn prediction. *Simulation Modelling Practice and Theory, 55,* 1–9. doi:10.1016/j.simpat.2015.03.003

Vaidya, C. V. (2020). Mobile Learning. *Our Heritage, 68*(9), 925–930.

van Biljon, J. & Kotze, P. (2007, Oct.). Modeling the factors that influence mobile phone adoption. *South African Institute of Computer Scientist & Information Technologists,* 152-160.

Van der Bijl, J. J., & Shortridge-Baggett, L. M. (2002). The theory and measurement of the self-efficacy construct. In E. A. Lentz & L. M. Shortridge-Baggett (Eds.), Self-efficacy in Nursing. Research and Measurement Perspectives (pp. 9-28). New York: Springer.

Van Gerven, M., & Bohte, S. (2017). Artificial Neural Networks as Models of Neural Information Processing Frontiers Research Topic. *Frontiers in Computational Neuroscience, 11.* Advance online publication. doi:10.3389/fncom.2017.00114 PMID:29311884

van Niekerk, D. R., & Barnard, E. (2013). Generating Fundamental Frequency Contours for Speech Synthesis in Yoruba (F. Bimbot, C. Cerisara, C. Fougeron, G. Gravier, L. Lamel, F. Pellegrino, & P. Perrier, Eds.). Academic Press.

van Niekerk, D. R., & Barnard, E. (2012). Tone realisation in a Yoruba speech recognition corpus. *Workshop on Spoken Language Technologies for Under-Resourced Languages,* 1–7.

Van Niekerk, D. R., & Barnard, E. (2014). Predicting utterance pitch targets in Yorùbá for tone realisation in speech synthesis. *Speech Communication, 56,* 229–242. doi:10.1016/j.specom.2013.01.009

Van Raaji, E. M., & Schepears, I. J. (2008). The acceptance and use of virtual learning environments in China. *Computers & Education, 50*(3), 838–852. doi:10.1016/j.compedu.2006.09.001

Varga, A. (2015). Place-based, Spatially Blind, or Both? Challenges in Estimating the Impacts of Modern Development Policies: The Case of the GMR Policy Impact Modeling Approach. *International Regional Science Review*, *40*(1), 12–37. doi:10.1177/0160017615571587

Vaughan, K. (2017). The role of apprenticeship in the cultivation of soft skills and dispositions. *Journal of Vocational Education and Training*, *69*(4), 540–557. Advance online publication. doi:10.1080/13636820.2017.1326516

Vcwebdesign. (2013, August 5). *What is Agile Methodology? and Why Do We Use It?* Retrieved from Visual Compass: http://vcwebdesign.com/uncategorized/what-agile-methodology-why-do-we-use-it/

Veneziano, V., Rainer, A., & Haider, S. (2014). *When Agile Is Not Good Enough: an initial attempt at understanding how to make ot right*. Retrieved from dblp: https://dblp.uni-trier.de/pers/hd/v/Veneziano:Vito

Venkatesh, V., Brown, S. A., Maruping, L. M., & Bala, H. (2008). Predicting Different Conceptualizations of System Use: The Competing Roles of Behavioural Intention, Facilitating Conditions, And Behavioural Expectation. *Management Information Systems Quarterly*, *32*(3), 483–502. doi:10.2307/25148853

Venkatesh, V., & Davis, F. (2000). A theoretical extension of the technology acceptance model: Four longitudinal field studies. *Management Science*, *46*(2), 186–204. doi:10.1287/mnsc.46.2.186.11926

Venkatesh, V., Morris, Davis, & Davis. (2003). User acceptance of information technology: Towards a unified view. *Management Information Systems Quarterly*, *27*(3), 425–478. doi:10.2307/30036540

Venkatesh, V., Thong, J. Y. L., & Xu, X. (2012). Consumer acceptance and use of information technology: Extending the unified theory of acceptance and use of technology. *Management Information Systems Quarterly*, *36*(1), 157–178. doi:10.2307/41410412

Vu, N. T., & Schultz, T. (2013). Multilingual Multilayer Perceptron For Rapid Language Adaptation Between and Across Language Families. In F. Bimbot, C. Cerisara, C. Fougeron, G. Gravier, L. Lamel, F. Pellegrino, & P. Perrier (Eds.), *INTERSPEECH 2013* (p. 5). Retrieved from https://www.isca-speech.org/archive/interspeech_2013

Waehama, W., McGrath, M., Korthaus, A., & Fong, M. (2014). *ICT Adoption and the UTAUT Model*. Paper presented at the International Conference on Educational Technology with Information Technology, Bangkok, Thailand.

Wang, Q. Y., & Woo, H. L. (2007). Comparing asynchronous online discussions and face-to-face discussions in a classroom setting. *British Journal of Educational Technology*, *38*(2), 272–286. doi:10.1111/j.1467-8535.2006.00621.x

Wang, Z., Chen, H., Xin, R., & Yi, C. (2010). Peer counseling. *Proceedings of the International Conference on Educational and Information Technology*.

Wastiau, P., Blamire, R., Kearney, C., Quittre, V., Van de Gaer, E., & Monseur, C. (2013). The use of ICT in education: A survey of schools in Europe. *European Journal of Education*, *48*(1), 11–27. doi:10.1111/ejed.12020

Weeks, J. R. (2008). *Population: an introduction to concepts and issues* (10th ed.). Wadsworth Thompson Learning.

WEF (World Economic Forum). (2019). *Global Competitiveness Report 2019: How to end a lost decade of productivity growth?* Retrieved from: https://www.weforum.org/reports/how-to-end-a-decade-of-lost-productivity-growth

Wells, N., & Kloppenborg, T. J. (2019). *Project Management Essentials* (2nd ed.). Business Expert Press, LLC.

Wendt, A. (2015). *Quantum Mind and Social Science: Unifying Physical and Social Ontology*. Cambridge University Press. doi:10.1017/CBO9781316005163

Westfall, L. (2010). *The Certified Software Quality Engineer Handbook*. Quality Press.

Westhuizen, J. V. (2003). Q&A: ICTs and livestock performance. ICT update: A current awareness bulletin for ACP agriculture, 15, 5.

WhatIs.Com. (n.d.). *Social Networking.* Available at: https://whatis.techtarget.com/definition/social-networking

Whitehead, F. (2019, November 13). Student recruitment strategy: four universities, five key questions. *The Guardian.* https://www.theguardian.com/higher-education-network/blog/2012/nov/13/student-recruitment-strategy-international-universities

Wieland, K., & Ifenthaler, D. (2009). Evaluating the effectiveness of a simulation-based collaborative learning environment and validating new ways to assess learning outcomes. *Proceedings of 32nd Annual Conference of the Association for Educational Communication and Technology*, 2, 243-250.

Wilke, A., & Magenheim, J. (2017, April). Requirements analysis for the design of workplace-integrated learning scenarios with mobile devices: Mapping the territory for learning in industry 4.0. In *Global Engineering Education Conference (EDUCON)* (pp. 476-485). IEEE. 10.1109/EDUCON.2017.7942890

Wilson, S. M., & Peterson, P. L. (2006). *Theories of learning and teaching: What do they mean for educators?* National Education Association Research.

Wilson, T. D. (1981). On user studies and information needs. *The Journal of Documentation, 37*(1), 3–15. doi:10.1108/eb026702

Wilson, T. D. (1997). Information behavior: An interdisciplinary perspective. *Information Processing & Management, 33*(4), 551–572. doi:10.1016/S0306-4573(97)00028-9

Wondoh, J. (2012). Career choices and national development. *Ghana Web.* https://www.ghanaweb.com/GhanaHomePage/NewsArchive/Career-Choises-and-National-Development-257460

Wong, A. F. L., Quek, C.-L., Divaharan, S., Liu, W.-C., Peer, J., & William, M. D. (2006). Singapore students' and teachers' perception of computer-supported project work classroom learning environment. *Journal of Research on Technology in Education, 38*(4), 449–479. doi:10.1080/15391523.2006.10782469

World Bank. (2012). Information and Communications for Development (2012) Maximizing Mobile. Washington, DC: World Bank.

World Bank. (2018). Decline of global extreme poverty continues but has slowed. *World Bank.* Retrieved June 2, 2020, from https://www.worldbank.org/en/news/press-release/2018/09/19/decline-of-global-extreme-poverty-continues-but-has-slowed-world-bank

World Bank. (2020). Poverty – Overview. *World Bank.* Retrieved May 28, 2020, from https://www.worldbank.org/en/topic/poverty/overview

Yahaya, M. K., & Badiru, O. I. (2002). Measuring tha Impact of Agricultural Radio and Television Programmes in Southwest Nigeria. *Journal of Applied Communications, 86*(3), 2002. doi:10.4148/1051-0834.2171

Yang, C., Huang, Q., Li, Z., Liu, K. L., & Hu, F. (2017). Big Data and Cloud computing: Innovation opportunities and challenges. *International Journal of Digital Earth, 10*(1), 13–53. doi:10.1080/17538947.2016.1239771

Yasvi, M., Yadav, K., & Shubhika. (2017, April 9). *Review On Extreme Programming-XP.* Retrieved. from https://www.researchgate.net/publication/332465869_Review_On_Extreme_Programming-XP/citation/download

Yazici, C., & Cagiltay, K. (2009). Evaluation of a university level computerized language learning architecture through the perceptions of students, instructors and administrators: A case study. *Proceedings of 32nd Annual Conference of the Association for Educational Communication and Technology, 2*, 251-259.

Yebowaah, F.A. (2018). Internet use and its effect on senior high school students in Wa Municipality of Ghana. *Library Philosophy and Practice*, 1817.

Yesilyurt, M. E., Basturk, R., Yesilyurt, F., & Kara, I. (2014). the effect of technological devices on student's academic success: Evidence from Denizli. *Journal of Internet Applications & Management, 5*(1), 39–47. doi:10.5505/iuyd.2014.83007

Yousafzai, A., Chang, V., Gani, A., & Noor, R. M. (2016). Multimedia augmented m-learning: Issues, trends and open challenges. *International Journal of Information Management, 36*(5), 784–792. doi:10.1016/j.ijinfomgt.2016.05.010

Youssef, A. B., & Dahmani, M. (2008). The impact of ICT on student performance in higher education: Direct effects, indirect effects and organisational change. RUSC. *Universities and Knowledge Society Journal, 5*(1), 45–56.

Yuen, A., Fox, B., & Park, J. (2011). The use of ICT for administration and management at the University of Hong Kong. In C. Wing (Ed.), *ICT for higher education case studies from Asia and the Pacific*. United Nations Education, Scientific and Cultural Organisation/Asia and Pacific Regional Bureau for Education.

Yu, J., Liu, C., & Yao, J. (2003). Technology acceptance model for wireless internet. *Internet Research, 13*(3), 206–222. doi:10.1108/10662240310478222

Yu, P. K. (2002). Bridging the Digital Divide: Equality in the Information Age. *Cardozo Arts and Entertainment, 20*(1), 1–52. doi:10.2139srn.309841

Zetian, F., Feng, X., Yun, Z., & Xiaoshuan, Z. (2005). Pig-vet: A web-based expert system for pig disease diagnosis. *Expert Systems with Applications, 29*(1), 93–103. doi:10.1016/j.eswa.2005.01.011

Zheng, L. (2013). Study on Disaster Information Management Systems compatible with VGI and Crowdsourcing. *IEEE Workshop on Advanced Research and Technology in Industry Applications (WARTIA)*.

Zieba, M., Tomczak, S. K., & Tomczak, J. M. (2016). Ensemble boosted trees with synthetic features generation in application to bankruptcy prediction. *Expert Systems with Applications, 58*, 93–101. doi:10.1016/j.eswa.2016.04.001

Zigurs, I., & Buckland, B. K. (1998). A theory of technology fit and group support system effectiveness. *Management Information Systems Quarterly, 22*(3), 313–334. doi:10.2307/249668

Zimmerman, E. (2012). Career couch: Showcasing Your Work. Online Portfolio. *New York Times*. Available at: https://www.nytimes.com/2012/07/01/jobs/an-online-portfolio-can-showcase-your-work-career-couch.html

Zimmermann, H. J. (2012). *Fuzzy sets, decision making, and expert systems* (Vol. 10). Springer Science & Business Media.

About the Contributors

Alice S. Etim is Professor of Management Information Systems at Winston-Salem State University (WSSU), North Carolina, USA. She earned her Ph.D. from the Information School (iSchool) at the University of North Carolina at Chapel Hill, USA. Etim has published many peer-reviewed journal articles and book chapters. Her research areas include Information & Communication Technology (ICT) adoption, diffusion, use and impact on business organizations, project teams and at risk populations including the Base of the Pyramid (BOP) groups in different developing countries. Etim's scholarly works on mobile technology adoption for service delivery - mobile money & payment systems, mobile commerce (mCommerce), mobile health (mHealth) & telemedicine, microfinance, and ICT for sustainable development/poverty reduction are well cited by many scholars. Etim was awarded the Carnegie African Diaspora Fellowship in 2017 & 2020 by the Carnegie Mellon Foundation and International Education. She is also a Research Fellow at the Center for the Study of Economic Mobility (CSEM) at WSSU. She is currently the Editor-in-Chief of the International Journal of ICT Research in Africa and the Middle East (IJICTRAME). She earlier served as Managing Editor and Associate Editor for the same Journal. She has had 12 years of industry work experience as Staff Software Engineer and led projects with IBM Corporation. She holds a Project Management Professional (PMP®) license since 2005. Etim is the recipient of many Bravo and publication awards from IBM Corporation. She also received in 2010 the E. J. Josey Award for her work on the Digital Divide.

* * *

Ahmed Mokhtar Abdelaziz is a head of an English Language Unit at one of Saudi Aramco's Industrial Training Centers in Saudi Arabia. He has a PhD in Educational Research and Technology Enhanced Learning from Lancaster University, UK. He has over 19 years of experience in educational administration and teaching English as a second language.

Amevi Acakpovi received the BSc degree in computer and electrical engineering from the Lokossa Institute of Technology (Republic of Benin), in 2006 and the master's degree in electrical engineering option control of industrial process from the Abomey-Calavi University (Republic of Benin), in 2009 and the PhD in Hybrid Energy Systems from the Accra Institute of Technology/Open University of Malaysia in April 2017. He is currently an associate professor and Dean, Faculty of Engineering, Accra Technical University. He is a scientist and researcher in Renewable Energy Engineering. His research interests include: hybrid energy systems, renewable energy development and management, wireless communication, applied electronics, micro computing, and artificial intelligence. He received the Silver

Award in the 2014 International Research Initiative Conference (IRIC) on Innovation in Engineering. He is a member of IEEE and IET-Ghana.

Eric Amoako holds an HND in Computer Science (2017) from Accra Technical University, Ghana.

Consolata Angello is a Lecturer in the Department of Information and Records Studies at Sokoine University of Agriculture. She specializes in ICTs for Development, Information and Communication Management, Information Literacy, Research Methods for Information Professionals and other related topics in the field.

Nana Yaw Asabere received the BSc degree in computer science from Kwame Nkrumah University of Science and Technology (KNUST), Kumasi, Ghana, in 2005, the MSc degree in ICT from Aalborg University, Aalborg, Denmark, in 2010, and the PhD degree in computer science from the School of Software, Dalian University of Technology, Dalian, China, in Sep. 2014. He is currently a senior lecturer and head of the Department of computer science, Accra Technical University, Ghana and an external senior researcher in the Alpha Lab, School of Software, Dalian University of Technology, China. He has a number of publications in International Journals and Conference Proceedings. His current teaching and research interests include: recommender systems, social computing, and mobile computing. He received the Best Paper Award in the 2013 IEEE International Conference on Ubiquitous Intelligence and Computing (UIC), which constituted part of his PhD re-search and thesis. He has been TPC member of all the Work-shops on Big Scholarly Data since its inception at the 23rd International Conference on World Wide Web (WWW), 2014. He is a member of IEEE.

Toluwase Asubiaro is a Library and Information Science doctoral student at the University of Western Ontario, Canada. He holds a B. Sc. in Mathematics and a master's degree in Information Science. He started his career as a language technology volunteer research assistant at African Languages Technology Initiative (ALT-I), Ibadan, Nigeria. He works as an academic librarian at the University of Ibadan where he is on study leave to pursue a PhD at the University of Western Ontario. He also works in the Language and Technology Research Laboratory (LiT.RL) at the University of Western Ontario as a research assistant on the automatic detection of deception in online environment. He currently holds a Western Graduate Research scholarship (WGRS) as well as the Ontario Government Scholarship (OGS). His major research interests are informetrics, natural language processing (NLP) and information retrieval. He has contributed to the NLP of resource-scarce Nigerian languages. His doctoral thesis proposes methods for weighting direct and indirect citations based on citation context uniqueness.

Jurgita Bruneckiene has extensive scientific, pedagogical and project implementation and leadership experience in research on socio-economic system development and its drivers in the regions. J. Bruneckienė 2008 defended dissertation on the evaluation of the competitiveness of the country's regions by the regional competitiveness index. He has gained experience in modeling the functioning of socio-economic systems and in assessing the impact of an economic phenomenon / factor, and is the creator of the Economic Modeling Program for Regions and Business Development (www.rindex.ktu. lt). J. Bruneckienė has experience in the use of artificial intelligence in the field of economic modeling. Research interests: urban and regional economics and strategic planning, evaluation of regional and urban competitiveness, smart and sustainable economy, net damage caused by cities and regions due to economic shocks, cartels. After the defense of the dissertation, 3 monographs, 10 articles in ISI Web of Science magazines, 40 other articles were prepared and published.

Vivian E. Collins Ortega is working on her MBA degree at Winston Salem State University.

Ernest Etim is a doctoral candidate in the Department of Information Technology, Cape Peninsula University of Technology. His research interests include small and medium-scale enterprises (SMEs), women entrepreneurship development (WED), informal economy and technology in business processes. He has published in a number of peer-review journals.

Abdulsalami Ibrahim earned a Doctor of Education degree in Curriculum and Instruction from Indiana University of Pennsylvania, an M.Ed. in Educational Foundations (Sociology of Education), and a BSc. Science Education (Biology Education) from Usmanu Danfodiyo University Sokoto, Nigeria. Dr. Ibrahim's diverse teaching assignments throughout his decade-long career have given him the ability to work closely with a diverse group of students, families, and administrators. He was a secondary school science teacher and a teacher educator in Nigeria. He served as a teaching associate for two years in the department of professional studies in education at Indiana University of Pennsylvania. Dr. Ibrahim's background in teacher education stirred his research interest in technology integration, multicultural instructional methods, culturally relevant and sustainable strategies, and mixed method research.

Ebelechukwu Gloria Igwe is a doctoral student at the Africa Regional Centre for Information Science, University of Ibadan, Nigeria. She has many publications to her credit on studies relating to Information Science: Knowledge management; Information and Communications Technology (ICT); Information Behaviour. She is also a multidisciplinary fellow with studies on ICT and Agriculture; Cybernetics, Network analysis, Natural Language Processing (NLP), Climate change and Agriculture; Knowledge sharing and Health; Gender studies and Academic productivity; Information sharing and Safety; ICT and Security; ICT and Library Use. She has won full sponsorships to attend the Association of Commonwealth Universities summer school conference in Canada, Early-career African Climate Academics Workshop in Ghana and AfricaLics conference in Algeria. She was a visiting research student at the Faculty of Information and Media Studies (FIMS), Western University, Ontario, Canada in 2018.

Chandra Prakash Jaiswal is working on his MBA degree at Winston Salem State University.

Sebak Kumar Jana is Professor of Economics, Department of Economics, Vidyasagar University, Midnapore, West Bengal, India.

Robertas Jucevicius has many years of scientific and practical experience in strategic management, smart development, national competitiveness, innovation, business cluster development. Managed and participated in creating the short and long-term strategies for Lithuanian industries; He is the author of monographs and studies of industrial and national competitiveness, clusters. The author of more than 30 strategies for innovation policy and industrial competitiveness in Lithuania. He is a member of the Council for National Progress of Lithuania. Research areas: Organizational and Country Strategic Development, Competitiveness, Innovation, Smart Development of Nation, City, Regions, etc.

Emmanuel C. Lallana, PhD, is Chief Executive of ideacorp – an independent, non-profit organization in the Philippines. He works on ICT for development (ICT4D) issues, particularly ICT Policy Development, ICT in Education and e-Governance. He has published on ICT4D issues and trains government officials from developing countries on ICT policy development, eGovernance and Social Media for Development. Dr. Lallana has taught at the University of the Philippines – Diliman, University of Malaya, and De La Salle University – Manila. He has worked with business groups, civil society organizations, national governments (Philippines and Bhutan) and international organizations (United Nations and the World Bank). He served the Philippine government as Deputy Director General, Foreign Service Institute, Department of Foreign Affairs and Commissioner, Commission on Information and Communication Technology.

Okanlade Lawal-Adebowale holds a PhD in Agricultural Communication and lecturers in the Department of Agricultural Extension and Rural Development, Federal University of Agriculture Abeokuta, Nigeria. His research focus is on ICT in agriculture, education and rural social reconfiguration. He is a member of leanered associations in Nigeria, which are Rural Sociological Association of Nigeria (RuSAN), Agricultural Society of Nigeria (ASN), Agricultural Extension Society of Nigeria (AESON) and Farm Management Association (FAMAN). He has about 50publications to his credit in local and internal journals, conference proceedings, and chapters in books.

Mantas Lukauskas (Ph.D.) graduated from the Faculty of Mathematics and Natural Sciences, Kaunas university of Technology with a Master's degree with honors in Big Data Analysis. He is currently a PhD student in Computer Science. He has done a Master's thesis "Evaluation of investment attractiveness of European countries by artificial neural networks", which uses artificial intelligence to solve economic problems. An active student and researcher.

Crystal Machado holds a doctoral degree in Educational Leadership; two master's degrees, one in School Administration and the other in Primary Education; and two bachelor's degrees, one in Business and the other in Education. Prior to joining Indiana University of Pennsylvania (IUP) where she currently teaches, Crystal worked as a K-12 teacher, an administrator, and middle/ high school assistant principal in Pakistan. She is currently a professor in the Department of Professional Studies in Education at Indiana University of Pennsylvania (IUP), where she works with pre-service and in-service teachers and administrators. She also coordinated the Master's in Education program for several years Crystal demonstrates her commitment to promoting equitable practices in higher education through her teaching, research, and service. She is committed to creating technology-rich and multicultural learning environments that promote high levels of student engagement, critical thinking, cross-cultural competence, and reflective practice. She has presented on these topics at international, national, and regional conferences. She served as technology leadership SIG chair for the Society for Information Technology and Teacher Education for two years. She reviews papers for several journals.

Adwaita Maiti is Assistant Professor, Department of Economics, Prabhat Kumar College, Contai, Purba Medinipur, West Bengal, India and a Ph.D. Scholar, Department of Economics, Vidyasagar University, Midnapore, West Bengal, India.

Sherwin E. Ona is an associate professor of Political Science at De La Salle University (DLSU). His current engagements and interests are in the areas of Open Government, Cybersecurity policies and Disaster informatics. He is also the current chairperson of the political science department. Dr. Ona also served as consultant to various government agencies such as the Department of Science and Technology (2012), the Commission on Higher Education (2016) and the Department of Information and Communications Technology for the National Government Portal-Government Interoperability Initiative (2018). In 2019, Dr. Ona assisted the UN-Asia Pacific Center for ICT for Development (APCICT) in developing a case related to interoperability initiatives in the Philippines.

Olalekan Oyekunle holds a PhD in Agricultural Communication and specializes in media and ICT usage in agriculture and rural development. He is an advisory service providers for rural economic and social development. He is a member of a number of learned societies and has up to 40 publications to his credit both in international and local journals and conference proceedings.

Jonas Rapsikevičius (PhD) is conducting research and preparing a dissertation on the impact of structural reforms on economic resilience to negative shocks and activity. One of the strands of structural reforms is to reduce regional divergence, so it is related to the project theme. An active young scientist and researcher who has published his research results in peer-reviewed scientific publications and international conferences. Expected dissertation defense - 2022. He has completed a PhD module in equivalent courses on the application of dynamic stochastic equilibrium models at the Barcelona BSE School of Economics. Has excellent knowledge and expertise in financial analytics and economic market analysis.

Marsheilla Subroto is working on her MBA degree at Winston Salem State University.

Wisdom Kwawu Torgby holds an MSc in IT and is currently a Senior Lecturer in the Department of Computer Science in Accra Technical University, Ghana.

Ezer Yeboah-Boateng is currently the Dean of the Faculty of Computing and Information Systems (FoCIS), at the Ghana Technology University College (GTUC). He holds a Ph.D. in Cyber-Security from Aalborg University, Copenhagen in Denmark, an M.S. in Telecommunications from the Stratford University, Falls Church, VA in USA, and a B.Sc. (Honors) in Electrical & Electronic Engineering, from University of Science & Technology (UST), Kumasi, Ghana. Ezer is a professional Telecoms Engineer and ICT Specialist with a strong background in telecommunications switching systems, cyber-security, digital forensics, business development, digital transformation, project management, change management, knowledge management, strategic IT-enabled business value creation and capabilities to develop market-oriented strategies aimed at promoting growth and market share. An Executive with over 25 years of domestic and global experience conceptualizing ideas, seizing opportunities, building operations, leading highly successful new business development initiatives and ventures. A Consultant with emphasis on Telecommunications infrastructure, Cyber-security, Cloud Computing, digital forensics, Internet, and network integration technologies, with additional experience related to dealing with refurbished and overstock telecommunications equipment, and manufacturing. Strong presentation, negotiation, and team building skills. A professional researcher and passionate teacher with over 10 years of higher education professional practice in telecoms and computer engineering, plus over 6 years high-school, teaching, mentorship and instruction; including over 20 peer-reviewed publications.

Ineta Zykienė defended his doctoral dissertation on "Attractiveness of Business Areas for Business Development in the Context of Smart Development" in 2018. She actively participates in scientific and pedagogical activities, scientific conferences, publishes scientific articles in international publications. Research interests: attractiveness of local areas for business development and its evaluation in the context of smart development, evaluation of impact of economic viability of communities on sustainable urban development.

Index

Ensure Quality Research is Introduced to the Academic Community

Become an IGI Global Reviewer for Authored Book Projects

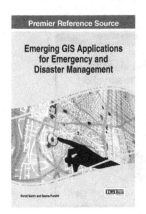

Premier Reference Source

Emerging GIS Applications for Emergency and Disaster Management

Premier Reference Source

Managerial Strategies and Green Solutions for Project Sustainability

Premier Reference Source

Comparative Approaches to Using R and Python for Statistical Data Analysis

Premier Reference Source

Solutions for High-Touch Communications in a High-Tech World

The overall success of an authored book project is dependent on quality and timely reviews.

In this competitive age of scholarly publishing, constructive and timely feedback significantly expedites the turnaround time of manuscripts from submission to acceptance, allowing the publication and discovery of forward-thinking research at a much more expeditious rate. Several IGI Global authored book projects are currently seeking highly-qualified experts in the field to fill vacancies on their respective editorial review boards:

Applications and Inquiries may be sent to:
development@igi-global.com

Applicants must have a doctorate (or an equivalent degree) as well as publishing and reviewing experience. Reviewers are asked to complete the open-ended evaluation questions with as much detail as possible in a timely, collegial, and constructive manner. All reviewers' tenures run for one-year terms on the editorial review boards and are expected to complete at least three reviews per term. Upon successful completion of this term, reviewers can be considered for an additional term.

If you have a colleague that may be interested in this opportunity, we encourage you to share this information with them.